Apr 2014

THE STORY OF
MANKIND

||||||||||||||||||||||||||||||||||||||||||||||||||||||||||||||||||||

Eternity

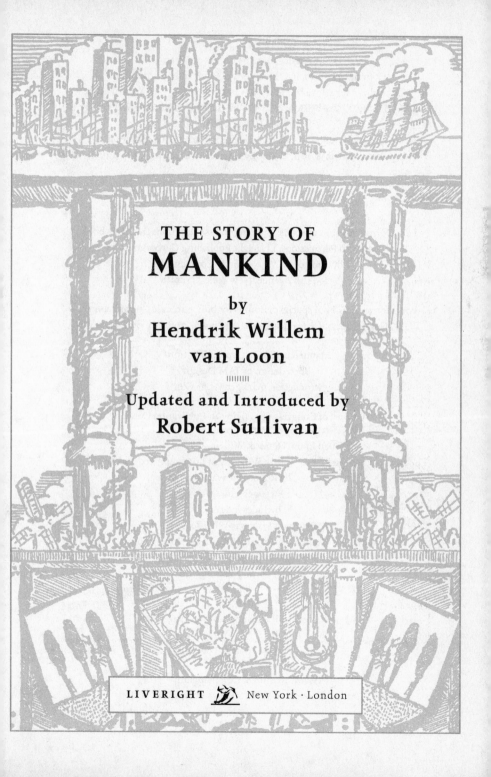

THE STORY OF
MANKIND

by
Hendrik Willem
van Loon

|||||||

Updated and Introduced by
Robert Sullivan

LIVERIGHT New York · London

For information about permission to reproduce selections from this book,
write to Permissions, Liveright Publishing Corporation,
a division of W. W. Norton & Company, Inc.,
500 Fifth Avenue, New York, NY 10110

For information about special discounts for bulk purchases, please contact
W. W. Norton Special Sales at specialsales@wwnorton.com or 800-233-4830

Manufacturing by Courier Westford
Book design by JAM Design
Production manager: Anna Oler

Library of Congress Cataloging-in-Publication Data

Van Loon, Hendrik Willem, 1882–1944.
The story of mankind / by Hendrik Willem van Loon; updated and introduced
by Robert Sullivan.
pages cm
Includes index.
ISBN 978-0-87140-715-3 (hardcover)
1. World history—Juvenile literature. I. Sullivan, Robert, 1963– II. Title
D21.V3 2013
909—dc23
2013038457

Liveright Publishing Corporation
500 Fifth Avenue, New York, N.Y. 10110
www.wwnorton.com

W. W. Norton & Company Ltd.
Castle House, 75/76 Wells Street, London W1T 3QT

1 2 3 4 5 6 7 8 9 0

Publisher's Note Concerning the Updated Edition

IN 1972 THE publishers updated the book with the assistance of Dr. Edward C. Prehn, Professor Paul Sears of Yale University, and Professor Edwin C. Broome of New York University. In 1984 and 1999 Professor John Merriman of Yale University updated the text, and illustrations were added by Adam Simon. For the present update, Robert Sullivan has added new chapters and an introduction.

TO

JIMMIE

"What is the use of a book without pictures?" said Alice.

Contents

IIIIIIIIIIIIIIIIIIIIIIIIIIIIIIIIIIIIII

List of Illustrations

||||||||||||||||||||||||||||||||||||||||||||||||||||||||||||||||||||||||||||||

New Introduction

‖‖

HENDRIK WILLEM VAN LOON was a big man with a small dog and an idea that the story of the world was much too large for just a few people to consider. When you read his books you get the idea that by writing them he considered himself to be akin to an engineer on an old train. Stories and facts from the past were to be fed into minds, in order that the engine of progress might speed on. An acute awareness of the constant pulse of history was our only way forward, or so he seemed to think. I am going to guess that his feelings in this regard had something to do with his being born when he was, in 1882, a time when people began to specialize.

Of course, there has always been specialization of one kind or another. If you lived in Denmark during the Iron Age and you were good at melting metal and forging it into tools or weapons, then you might not have had as much to do with taking care of the livestock. In the 1880s, however, a new science called management came rushing into the factories of the world. With management running the show, work wasn't just work anymore; it was something that could be broken down into pieces and parts, like species of birds or types of diseases. Thus, it was during this time that the assembly line was born, much to the dismay of workers, and then specialization crept into all areas of life, including academics and (most important as far as the book you have in your hands goes) history. Van Loon's work was in complete opposition to that specialization. He was at war with what he saw as the narrow minds of experts who could not see beyond their file cabinets. He was sometimes called a "popularizer." The historian Arthur Schlesinger Jr. praised van Loon for the very act of popularizing, writing that "in an age when knowledge grows increasingly specialized, the capacity to write about serious subjects in a lucid and arresting way becomes a necessity of civilized society." Van Loon, Schlesinger added, was a man filled with "gusto."

Not that van Loon did not partake in some of that specialization. He studied history after all, as opposed to chemistry or the geology of Antarctica. He got his Ph.D. at the University of Munich, and he lectured in European history at Cornell University and Antioch College. In addition to *The Story of Mankind*, he wrote dozens of other books, including *The Rise of the Dutch Kingdom, R. v. R.: The Life and Times of Rembrandt van Rijn* and, in 1939 (with Grace Castagnetta), *The Last of the Troubadours: The Life and Music of Carl Michael Bellman 1740–1795*. As Cornelis A. van Minnen notes in his 2005 biography of van Loon, *The Story of Mankind* was written almost on a whim, when the publisher, Horace Liveright, decided to try a children's version of a kind of book that was popular among adults, the so-called "outline." There was Charles and Mary Beard's *Rise of American Civilization* (1927), Lewis Mumford's *Story of Utopias* (1922), and Will Durant's *Story of Philosophy* (1926). These books were written clearly with the idea that the layperson was capable of understanding the work of experts and specialists, if it was written with sentences that were crafted for humans, that were anti–inside baseball. Will Durant was the most popular author of outline histories for adults, and Durant noted that van Loon's book would be as satisfying for the parents as it would be for the children they bought it for. "The world was becoming scandalously informed about history," Durant said.

How do we read *The Story of Mankind* today, in a time when we are both more specialized and more generalized, when the fact about anything can be a few clicks away? (Even when, on this date, about one-third of the world has no access to the Internet, a fact that people who are connected are—despite their connections—not likely to know?) Van Loon's masterwork has its mistakes, as well as misunderstandings, and there are gaps, to be sure. And when we look back at his life, we will not have too much trouble seeing that he suffered from some of the biases that many people living in the United States had during van Loon's time, with an aversion to some immigrant groups, for example. Overall, though, the book embraces a spirit of self-improvement—with hope for himself, for the reader, and for the future of mankind. This matched how he seems to have felt about the world in the 1940s, when he talked about "a common consciousness of 'belonging together,'" and he referred to President Franklin Roosevelt's New Deal not so much as a lot of laws and regulations but as "a new attitude of mind." When he presented a radio program in New York, and later on NBC, he did so, he said, "for the benefit of humanity." He really thought we were on an upswing, even when the Nazis were attacking his European homeland—van Loon was born in Rotterdam. We could get past it. That's what he thought was so good about the world.

He died in 1944, a year before World War II ended, but by that point Hitler was about to fall and most people could see the end of the fighting coming. Van Loon seems to have an idea that the United States would be the nation to lead the world into a better future, which has not always been how things have gone. As usual, the story of mankind has been a mixed bag.

The Story of Mankind, on the other hand, has continued to do well. Several authors have attempted to update it, no one attempting to update van Loon's spirit, of course, which appears not to have diminished. The book now comes across as something like a note passed on for generations, with some cobwebs and some bindings weak from wear, but also with adornments being added as it passes through hands. It requires work on the part of the reader, though no more work than has ever been required, in 1920, or 1820, or at the dawn of human time. The past, after all, is most alive when it is being considered, or better yet reconsidered. Look for truths. Study them. Study them deeply. Observe them from different angles. Don't mistake anything as indisputable, as very few things are, and don't be afraid to look closely at that which has not previously been looked at. Henry David Thoreau taught school in Massachusetts in 1837. He liked to say that the Dark Ages were only dark because we are in the dark about them.

IF YOU HAD visited van Loon when he was in the midst of writing *The Story of Mankind*, then you would have been on Barrow Street in the Greenwich Village neighborhood of Manhattan, in 1920, and you would have climbed four flights of stairs to see him typing out the manuscripts and drawing all the pictures, probably with a certain amount of childish delight. When I use the phrase "childish delight," by the way, I mean it to say that he was drawing it without hiding how happy he was at the moment. It seems to me that adults tend to think they are more mature than children when what they really are is more practiced at hiding exactly how happy or perhaps unhappy they are.

Van Loon was well known for illustrating his own happiness. When he died, an obituary called him a "laughing philosopher," and if you know only one thing about the movie version of *The Story of Mankind*, it should be this: the long list of film stars from the past that appeared in Warner's Brothers' 1957 version—Vincent Price, Ronald Colman, Hedy Lamarr, Dennis Hopper, Agnes Moorehead, and Virginia Mayo—also included Groucho, Harpo, and Chico Marx, aka the Marx Brothers. Groucho Marx was born in 1890, in New York City, and like van Loon was also a laughing philosopher—his film *Duck Soup*, in 1933, is an argument against war. It was Groucho who said, "Outside of a dog, a book is man's best friend. Inside of a dog it's too dark to read."

And if you were back at van Loon's apartment in 1920, you might have noticed that his dog sometimes sat on his desk, perhaps to monitor his progress through the history of the world. And when *The Story of Mankind* was done—written in just two months—you would have seen the author happily send off the book, and then move to Ohio to teach at Antioch College for a while, until eventually he decided to move on from that job. On that day, he left a note in the classroom, which the students read when they arrived. "I do not believe in long good byes when good friends part," he said. "We have, I hope, each learned a good deal from the other during the time we have spent together. And now it is time for me to say farewell."

ROBERT SULLIVAN
Brooklyn, New York
2013

Foreword

||||||||||||||||||||||||||||||||||||||||||||

For Hansje and Willem:

When I was twelve or thirteen years old, an uncle of mine who gave me my love for books and pictures promised to take me upon a memorable expedition. I was to go with him to the top of the tower of Old St. Lawrence in Rotterdam.

And so, one fine day, a sexton with a key as large as that of St. Peter opened a mysterious door. "Ring the bell," he said, "when you come back and want to get out," and with a great grinding of rusty old hinges he separated us from the noise of the busy street and locked us into a world of new and strange experiences.

For the first time in my life I was confronted by the phenomenon of audible silence. When we had climbed the first flight of stairs, I added another discovery to my limited knowledge of natural phenomena—that of tangible darkness. A match showed us where the upward road continued. We went to the next floor and then to the next and the next until I had lost count and then there came still another floor, and suddenly we had plenty of light. This floor was on an even height with the roof of the church, and it was used as a storeroom. Covered with many inches of dust, there lay the abandoned symbols of a venerable faith which had been discarded by the good people of the city many years ago. That which had meant life and death to our ancestors was here reduced to junk and rubbish. The industrious rat had built his nest among the carved images and the ever watchful spider had opened up shop between the outspread arms of a kindly saint.

The next floor showed us from where we had derived our light. Enormous open windows with heavy iron bars made the high and barren room the roosting place of hundreds of pigeons. The wind blew through the iron bars and the air was filled with a weird and pleasing music. It was the noise of the town below us, but a noise which had been purified and cleansed by the distance. The rumbling of heavy carts and the clinking of horses' hoofs, the winding of cranes and pulleys, the hissing sound of the patient steam which had been set to do the work of man in a thousand different ways—they had all been blended into a softly rustling whisper which provided a beautiful background for the trembling cooing of the pigeons.

Here the stairs came to an end and the ladders began. And after the first ladder (a slippery old thing which made one feel his way with a cautious foot) there was a new and even greater wonder, the town-clock. I saw the heart of time. I could hear the heavy pulsebeats of the rapid seconds—one—two—three—up to sixty. Then a sudden quivering noise when all the wheels seemed to stop and another minute had been chopped off eternity. Without pause it began again—one—two—three—until at last after a warning rumble and the scraping of many wheels a thunderous voice, high above us, told the world that it was the hour of noon.

On the next floor were the bells. The nice little bells and their terrible sisters. In the centre the big bell, which made me turn stiff with fright when I heard it in the middle of the night telling a story of fire or flood. In solitary grandeur it seemed to reflect upon those six hundred years during which it had shared the joys and the sorrows of the good people of Rotterdam. Around it, neatly arranged like the blue jars in an old-fashioned apothecary shop, hung the little fellows, who twice each week played a merry tune for the benefit of the country-folk who had come to market to buy and sell and hear what the big world had been doing. But in a corner—all alone and shunned by the others—a big black bell, silent and stern, the bell of death.

Then darkness once more and other ladders, steeper and even more dangerous than those we had climbed before, and suddenly the fresh air of the wide heavens. We had reached the highest gallery. Above us the sky. Below us the city—a little toy-town, where busy ants were hastily crawling hither and thither, each one intent upon his or her particular business, and beyond the jumble of stones, the wide greenness of the open country.

It was my first glimpse of the big world.

Since then, whenever I have had the opportunity, I have gone to the top of the tower and enjoyed myself. It was hard work, but it repaid in full the mere physical exertion of climbing a few stairs.

Besides, I knew what my reward would be. I would see the land and the sky, and I would listen to the stories of my kind friend the watchman, who lived in a small shack, built in a sheltered corner of the gallery. He looked after the clock and was a father to the bells, and he warned of fires, but he enjoyed many free hours and then he smoked a pipe and thought his own peaceful thoughts. He had gone to school almost fifty years before and he had rarely read a book, but he had lived on the top of his tower for so many years that he had absorbed the wisdom of that wide world which surrounded him on all sides.

History he knew well, for it was a living thing with him. "There," he would say, pointing to a bend of the river, "there, my boy, do you see those trees? That is where the Prince of Orange cut the dikes to drown the land and save Leyden." Or he would tell me the tale of the old Meuse, until the broad river ceased to be a convenient harbour and became a wonderful highroad, carrying the ships of De Ruyter and Tromp upon that famous last voyage, when they gave their lives that the sea might be free to all.

Then there were the little villages, clustering around the protecting church which once, many years ago, had been the home of their patron saints. In the distance we could see the leaning tower of Delft. Within sight of its high arches, William the Silent had been murdered and there Grotius had learned to construe his first Latin sentences. And still further away, the long low body of the church of Gouda, the early home of the man whose wit had proved mightier than the armies of many an emperor, the charity-boy whom the world came to know as Erasmus.

Finally the silver line of the endless sea and as a contrast, immediately below us, the patchwork of roofs and chimneys and houses and gardens and hospitals and schools and railways, which we called our home. But the tower showed us the old home in a new light. The confused commotion of the streets and the market-place, of the factories and the workshop, became the well-ordered expression of human energy and purpose. Best of all, the wide view of the glorious past, which surrounded us on all sides, gave us new courage to face the problems of the future when we had gone back to our daily tasks.

History is the mighty tower of experience, which time has built amidst the endless fields of bygone ages. It is no easy task to reach the top of this ancient structure and get the benefit of the full view. There is no elevator, but young feet are strong and it can be done.

Here I give you the key that will open the door.

When you return, you too will understand the reason for my enthusiasm.

HENDRIK WILLEM VAN LOON.

THE STORY OF
MANKIND

〡〡〡

High up in the north in the land called Svithjod, there stands a rock. It is a hundred miles high and a hundred miles wide. Once every thousand years a little bird comes to this rock to sharpen its beak.

When the rock has thus been worn away, then a single day of eternity will have gone by.

1

The Setting of the Stage

We live under the shadow of a gigantic question mark.

Who are we?

Where do we come from?

Whither are we bound?

Slowly, but with persistent courage, we have been pushing this question mark further and further towards that distant line, beyond the horizon, where we hope to find our answer.

We have not gone very far.

We still know very little but we have reached the point where (with a fair degree of accuracy) we can guess at many things.

In this chapter I shall tell you how (according to our best belief) the stage was set for the first appearance of man.

If we represent the time during which it has been possible for animal life to exist upon our planet by a line of this length, then the tiny line just below indicates the age

during which man (or a creature more or less resembling man) has lived upon this earth.

Man was the last to come but the first to use his brain for

the purpose of conquering the forces of nature. That is the reason why we are going to study him, rather than cats or dogs or horses or any of the other animals, who, all in their own way, have a very interesting historical development behind them.

In the beginning, the planet upon which we live was (as far as we now know) a large ball of flaming matter, a tiny cloud of smoke in the endless ocean of space. Gradually, in the course of millions of years, the surface burned itself out, and was covered with a thin layer of rocks. Upon these life-less rocks the rain descended in endless torrents, wearing out the hard granite and carrying the dust to the valleys that lay hidden between the high cliffs of the steaming earth.

It Rained Incessantly

Finally the hour came when the sun broke through the clouds and saw how this little planet was covered with a few small puddles which were to develop into the mighty oceans of the eastern and western hemispheres.

Then one day the great wonder happened. What had been dead gave birth to life.

The first living cell floated upon the waters of the sea.

For millions of years it drifted aimlessly with the currents. But during all that time it was developing certain habits that it might survive more easily upon the inhospitable earth.

Some of these cells were happiest in the dark depths of the lakes and the pools. They took root in the slimy sediments which had been carried down from the tops of the hills and they became plants. Others preferred to move about and they grew strange jointed legs, like scorpions, and began to crawl along the bottom of the sea amidst the plants and the pale green things that looked like jelly-fishes. Still others (covered with scales) depended upon a swimming motion to go from place to place in their search for food, and gradually they populated the ocean with myriads of fishes.

Meanwhile the plants had increased in number and they had to search for new dwelling places. There was no more room for them at the bottom of the sea. Reluctantly they left the water and made a new home in the marshes and on the mudbanks that lay at the foot of the mountains. Twice a day the tides of the ocean covered them with their brine. For the rest of the time, the plants made the best of their uncomfortable situation and tried to survive in the thin air which surrounded the surface of the planet. After centuries of training, they learned how to live as comfortably in the air as they had done in the water. They increased in size and became shrubs and trees and at last they learned how to grow lovely flowers which attracted the attention of the busy big bumble-bees and the birds who carried the seeds far and wide until the whole earth had become covered with green pastures, or lay dark under the shadow of the big trees.

But some of the fishes too had begun to leave the sea, and they had learned how to breathe with lungs as well as with gills. We call such creatures amphibious, which means that they are able to live with equal ease on the land and in the water. The first frog who crosses your path can tell you all about the pleasures of the double existence of the amphibian.

Once outside of the water, these animals gradually adapted themselves more and more to life on land. Some became rep-

The Ascent of Man

tiles (creatures who crawl like lizards) and they shared the
silence of the forests with the insects. That they might move
faster through the soft soil, they improved upon their legs
and their size increased until the world was populated with
gigantic forms (which the hand-books of biology list under
the names of Ichthyosaurus and Megalosaurus and Bronto-
saurus) who grew to be thirty to forty feet long and who
could have played with elephants as a full grown cat plays
with her kittens.

Some of the members of this reptilian family began to
live in the tops of the trees, which were then often more
than a hundred feet high. They no longer needed their legs
for the purpose of walking, but it was necessary for them to
move quickly from branch to branch. And so they changed
a part of their skin into a sort of parachute, which stretched
between the sides of their bodies and the small toes of their

fore-feet, and gradually they covered this skinny parachute with feathers and made their tails into a steering gear and flew from tree to tree and developed into true birds.

The Plants Leave the Sea

Then a strange thing happened. All the gigantic reptiles died within a short time. We do not know the reason. Perhaps it was due to a sudden change in climate. Perhaps they had grown so large that they could neither swim nor walk nor crawl, and they starved to death within sight but not within reach of the big ferns and trees. Whatever the cause, the million-year-old world-empire of the big reptiles was over.

The world now began to be occupied by very different creatures. They were the descendants of the reptiles but they were quite unlike these because they fed their young from the "mammæ" or the breasts of the mother. Wherefore modern science calls these animals "mammals." They had shed the scales of the fish. They did not adopt the feathers of the bird, but they covered their bodies with hair. The mammals, however, developed other habits which gave their race a great advantage over the other animals. The female of the species carried the eggs of the young inside her body until they were hatched and while all other living beings, up to that time, had left their children exposed to the dangers of cold and heat, and the attacks of wild beasts, the mammals kept their young with them for long time and sheltered them while they were still too weak to fight their enemies. In this way the young mammals were given a much better chance to survive, because they learned many things from their mothers, as you will know if you have ever watched a cat teaching her kittens to take care of themselves and how to wash their faces and how to catch mice.

But of these mammals I need not tell you much for you know them well. They surround you on all sides. They are your daily companions in the streets and in your home, and you can see your less familiar cousins behind the bars of the zoological garden.

And now we come to the parting of the ways when man suddenly leaves the endless procession of dumbly living and dying creatures and begins to use his reason to shape the destiny of his race.

One mammal in particular seemed to surpass all others in its ability to find food and shelter. It had learned to use its forefeet for the purpose of holding its prey, and by dint of practice it had developed a hand-like claw. After innumerable attempts it had learned how to balance the whole of the body upon the hind legs. (This is a difficult act, which every child has to learn anew although the human race has been doing it for over a million years.)

This creature, half ape and half monkey but superior to both, became the most successful hunter and could make a living in every clime. For greater safety, it usually moved about in groups. It learned how to make strange grunts to warn its young of approaching danger and after many hundreds of thousands of years it began to use these throaty noises for the purpose of talking.

This creature, though you may hardly believe it, was your first "man-like" ancestor.

2

Our Earliest Ancestors

We know very little about the first "true" men. We have never seen their pictures. In the deepest layer of clay of an ancient soil we have sometimes found pieces of their bones. These lay buried amidst the broken skeletons of other animals that have long since disappeared from the face of the earth. Anthropologists (learned scientists who devote their lives to the study of man as a member of the animal kingdom) have taken these bones and they have been able to reconstruct our earliest ancestors with a fair degree of accuracy.

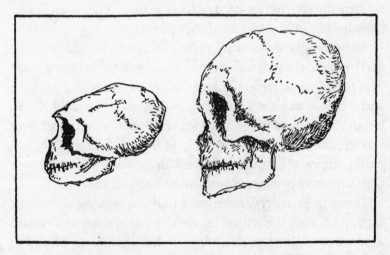

The Growth of the Human Skull

The great-great-grandfather of the human race was a very
ugly and unattractive mammal. He was quite small, much
smaller than the people of today. The heat of the sun and
the biting wind of the cold winter had coloured his skin a
dark brown. His head and most of his body, his arms and legs
too, were covered with long, coarse hair. He had very thin
but strong fingers which made his hands look like those of a
monkey. His forehead was low and his jaw was like the jaw
of a wild animal which uses its teeth both as fork and knife.
He wore no clothes. He had seen no fire except the flames
of the rumbling volcanoes which filled the earth with their
smoke and their lava.

He lived in the damp blackness of vast forests, as the pyg-
mies of Africa do to this very day. When he felt the pangs of
hunger he ate raw leaves and the roots of plants or he took
the eggs away from an angry bird and fed them to his own
young. Once in a while, after a long and patient chase, he
would catch a sparrow or a small wild dog or perhaps a rab-
bit. These he would eat raw for he had never discovered that
food tasted better when it was cooked.

During the hours of day, this primitive human being
prowled about looking for things to eat.

When night descended upon the earth, he hid his wife
and his children in a hollow tree or behind some heavy boul-
ders for he was surrounded on all sides by ferocious animals
and when it was dark these animals began to prowl about,
looking for something to eat for their mates and their own
young, and they liked the taste of human beings. It was a
world where you must either eat or be eaten, and life was
very unhappy because it was full of fear and misery.

In summer, man was exposed to the scorching rays of the
sun, and during the winter his children would freeze to death
in his arms. When such a creature hurt itself, (and hunting
animals are forever breaking their bones or spraining their

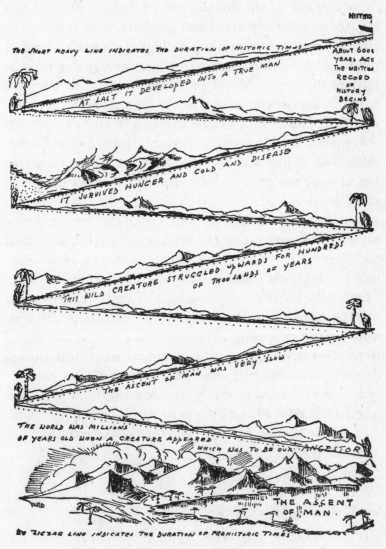

THE SHORT HEAVY LINE INDICATES THE DURATION OF HISTORIC TIMES

HISTORY

ABOUT 6000 YEARS AGO THE WRITTEN RECORD OR HISTORY BEGINS

AT LAST IT DEVELOPED INTO A TRUE MAN

IT SURVIVED HUNGER AND COLD AND DISEASE

THIS WILD CREATURE STRUGGLED UPWARDS FOR HUNDREDS OF THOUSANDS OF YEARS

THE ASCENT OF MAN WAS VERY SLOW

THE WORLD WAS MILLIONS OF YEARS OLD WHEN A CREATURE APPEARED WHICH WAS TO BE OUR ANCESTOR

THE ASCENT OF MAN.

THE ZIGZAG LINE INDICATES THE DURATION OF PREHISTORIC TIMES

Prehistory and History

ankles) he had no one to take care of him and he must die a horrible death.

Like many of the animals who fill the zoo with their strange noises, early man liked to jabber. That is to say, he endlessly repeated the same unintelligible gibberish because it pleased him to hear the sound of his voice. In due time he learned that he could use this guttural noise to warn his fellow beings whenever danger threatened and he gave certain little shrieks which came to mean "there is a tiger!" or "here come five elephants." Then the others grunted something back at him and their growl meant, "I see them," or "let us run away and hide." And this was probably the origin of all language.

But, as I have said before, of these beginnings we know so very little. Early man had no tools and he built himself no houses. He lived and died and left no trace of his existence except a few collar-bones and a few pieces of his skull. These tell us that many thousands of years ago the world was inhabited by certain mammals who were quite different from all the other animals—who had probably developed from another unknown ape-like animal which had learned to walk on its hind legs and use its fore-paws as hands— and who were most probably connected with the creatures who happened to be our own immediate ancestors.

It is little enough we know and the rest is darkness.

3

Prehistoric Man

Prehistoric Man Begins to Make
Things for Himself

Early man did not know what time meant. He kept no records of birthdays or wedding anniversaries or the hour of death. He had no idea of days or weeks or even year. But in a general way he kept track of the seasons for he had noticed that the cold winter was invariably followed by the mild spring—that spring grew into the hot summer when fruits ripened and the wild ears of corn were ready to be eaten and that summer ended when sudden gusts of wind swept the leaves from the trees and a number of animals were getting ready for the long hibernal sleep.

But now, something unusual and rather frightening had happened. Something was the matter with the weather. The warm days of summer had come very late. The fruits had not ripened. The tops of the mountains which used to be covered with grass now lay deeply hidden underneath a heavy burden of snow.

Then, one morning, a number of wild people, different from the other creatures who lived in that neighbourhood, came wandering down from the region of the high peaks. They looked lean and appeared to be starving. They uttered sounds which no one could understand. They seemed to say that they were hungry. There was not food enough for both the old inhabitants and the newcomers. When they tried to stay more than a few days there was a terrible battle with claw-like hands and feet and whole families were killed. The others fled back to their mountain slopes and died in the next blizzard.

But the people in the forest were greatly frightened. All the time the days grew shorter and the nights grew colder than they ought to have been.

Finally, in a gap between two high hills, there appeared a tiny speck of greenish ice. Rapidly it increased in size. A gigantic glacier came sliding downhill. Huge stones were being pushed into the valley. With the noise of a dozen thunderstorms torrents of ice and mud and blocks of granite suddenly tumbled among the people of the forest and killed them while they slept. Century-old trees were crushed into kindling wood. And then it began to snow.

It snowed for months and months. All the plants died and the animals fled in search of the southern sun. Man hoisted his young upon his back and followed them. But he could not travel as fast as the wilder creatures and he was forced to choose between quick thinking or quick dying. He seems to have preferred the former for he has managed to survive the terrible glacial periods which upon four different occasions threatened to kill every human being on the face of the earth.

In the first place it was necessary that man clothe himself lest he freeze to death. He learned how to dig holes and cover them with branches and leaves and in these traps he caught bears and hyenas, which he then killed with heavy stones and whose skins he used as coats for himself and his family.

Next came the housing problem. This was simple. Many animals were in the habit of sleeping in dark caves. Man now

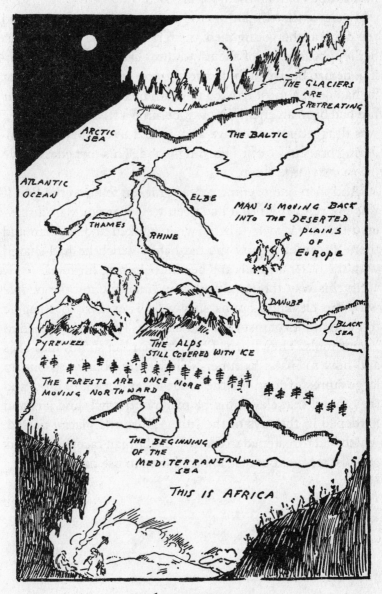

Prehistoric Europe

followed their example, drove the animals out of their warm homes and claimed them for his own.

Even so, the climate was too severe for most people and the old and the young died at a terrible rate. Then a genius bethought himself of the use of fire. Once, while out hunting, he had been caught in a forest-fire. He remembered that he had been almost roasted to death by the flames. Thus far fire had been an enemy. Now it became a friend. A dead tree was dragged into the cave and lighted by means of smouldering branches from a burning wood. This turned the cave into a cozy little room.

And then one evening a dead chicken fell into the fire. It was not rescued until it had been well roasted. Man discovered that meat tasted better when cooked and he then and there discarded one of the old habits which he had shared with the other animals and began to prepare his food.

In this way thousands of years passed. Only the people with the cleverest brains survived. They had to struggle day and night against cold and hunger. They were forced to invent tools. They learned how to sharpen stones into axes and how to make hammers. They were obliged to put up large stores of food for the endless days of the winter and they found that clay could be made into bowls and jars and hardened in the rays of the sun. And so the glacial period, which had threatened to destroy the human race, became its greatest teacher because it forced man to use his brain.

4

Hieroglyphics

The Egyptians Invent the Art of Writing and the
Record of History Begins

These earliest ancestors of ours who lived in the great
European wilderness were rapidly learning many new
things. It is safe to say that in due course of time they would
have given up the ways of savages and would have developed a civilisation of their own. But suddenly there came an
end to their isolation. They were discovered.

A traveler from an unknown southland who had dared
to cross the sea and the high mountain passes had found his
way to the wild people of the European continent. He came
from Africa. His home was in Egypt.

The valley of the Nile had developed a high stage of civilisation thousands of years before the people of the west had
dreamed of the possibilities of a fork or a wheel or a house.
And we shall therefore leave our great-great-grandfathers in
their caves, while we visit the southern and eastern shores
of the Mediterranean, where stood the earliest school of the
human race.

The Egyptians have taught us many things. They were
excellent farmers. They knew all about irrigation. They
built temples which were afterwards copied by the Greeks

and which served as the earliest models for the churches in which we worship nowadays. They had invented a calendar which proved such a useful instrument for the purpose of measuring time that it has survived with a few changes until today. But most important of all, the Egyptians had learned how to preserve speech for the benefit of future generations. They had invented the art of writing.

We are so accustomed to newspapers and books and magazines that we take it for granted that the world has always been able to read and write. As a matter of fact, writing, the most important of all inventions, is quite new. Without written documents we should be like cats and dogs, who can only teach their kittens and their puppies a few simple things and who, because they cannot write, possess no way in which they can make use of the experience of those generations of cats and dogs that have gone before.

In the first century before our era, when the Romans came to Egypt, they found the valley full of strange little pictures which seemed to have something to do with the history of the country. But the Romans were not interested in "anything foreign" and did not inquire into the origin of these queer figures which covered the walls of the temples and the walls of the palaces and endless reams of flat sheets made out of the papyrus reed. The last of the Egyptian priests who had understood the holy art of making such pictures had died several years before. Egypt deprived of its independence had become a store-house filled with important historical documents which no one could decipher and which were of no earthly use to either man or beast.

Seventeen centuries went by and Egypt remained a land of mystery. But in the year 1798 a French general by the name of Bonaparte happened to visit eastern Africa to prepare for an attack upon the British Indian colonies. He did not get beyond the Nile, and his campaign was a failure. But, quite

accidentally, the famous French expedition solved the problem of the ancient Egyptian picture-language.

One day a young French officer, much bored by the dreary
life of his little fortress on the Rosetta River (a mouth of the
Nile), decided to spend a few idle hours rummaging among
the ruins of the Nile Delta. And behold! he found a stone
which greatly puzzled him. Like everything else in Egypt
it was covered with little figures. But this particular slab of
black basalt was different from anything that had ever been
discovered. It carried three inscriptions. One of these was in
Greek. The Greek language was known. "All that is necessary," so he reasoned, "is to compare the Greek text with the
Egyptian figures, and they will at once tell their secrets."

The plan sounded simple enough but it took more than
twenty years to solve the riddle. In the year 1802 a French
professor by the name of Champollion began to compare the
Greek and the Egyptian texts of the famous Rosetta stone.
In the year 1823 he announced that he had discovered the
meaning of fourteen little figures. A short time later he died
from overwork, but the main principles of Egyptian writing
had become known. Today the story of the valley of the Nile
is better known to us than the story of the Mississippi River.
We possess a written record which covers four thousand
years of chronicled history.

As the ancient Egyptian hieroglyphics (the word means
"sacred writing") have played such a very great rôle in history, (a few of them in modified form have even found their
way into our own alphabet,) you ought to know something
about the ingenious system which was used fifty centuries
ago to preserve the spoken word for the benefit of the coming generations.

Of course, you know what a sign language is. Every
Indian story of our western plains has a chapter devoted to
strange messages written in the form of little pictures which

tell how many buffaloes were killed and how many hunters there were in a certain party. As a rule it is not difficult to understand the meaning of such messages.

Ancient Egyptian, however, was not a sign-language. The clever people of the Nile had passed beyond that stage long before. Their pictures meant a great deal more than the object which they represented, as I shall try to explain to you now.

Suppose that you were Champollion, and that you were examining a stack of papyrus sheets, all covered with hiero-glyphics. Suddenly you came across a picture of a man with a saw. "Very well," you would say, "that means of course that a farmer went out to cut down a tree." Then you take another papyrus. It tells the story of a queen who had died at the age of eighty-two. In the midst of a sentence appears the picture of the man with the saw. Queens of eighty-two do not han-dle saws. The picture therefore must mean something else. But what?

This is the riddle which the Frenchman finally solved. He discovered that the Egyptians were the first to use what we now call "phonetic writing"—a system of characters which reproduce the "sound" (or phone) of the spoken word and which make it possible for us to translate all our spoken words into a written form, with the help of only a few dots and dashes and pothooks.

Let us return for a moment to the little fellow with the saw. The word "saw" either means a certain tool which you will find in a carpenter's shop, or it means the past tense of the verb "to see."

This is what had happened to the word during the course of centuries. First of all it had meant only the particular tool which it represented. Then that meaning had been lost and it had become the past participle of a verb. After several hun-dred years, the Egyptians lost sight of both these meanings and the picture came to stand for a single letter, the

letter S. A short sentence will show you what I mean. Here is a modern English sentence as it would have been written in hieroglyphics.

The either means one of these two round objects

in your head which allow you to see or it means "I," the person who is talking.

A is either an insect which gathers honey, or it

represents the verb "to be" which means "to exist." Again, it may be the first part of a verb like "be-come" or "be-have." In

this particular instance it is followed by which means

a "leaf" or "leave" or "lieve" (the sound of all three words is the same).

The "eye" you know all about.

Finally you get the picture of a It is a giraffe. It is

part of the old sign-language out of which the hieroglyphics developed.

You can now read that sentence without much difficulty.

"I believe I saw a giraffe."

Having invented this system, the Egyptians developed it

during thousands of years until they could write anything they wanted, and they used these "canned words" to send messages to friends, to keep business accounts and to keep a record of the history of their country, that future generations might benefit by the mistakes of the past.

5

The Nile Valley

The Beginning of Civilisation in the
Valley of the Nile

The history of man is the record of a hungry creature in search of food. Wherever food was plentiful, thither man has travelled to make his home.

The fame of the valley of the Nile must have spread at an early date. From the interior of Africa and from the desert of Arabia and from the western part of Asia people had flocked to Egypt to claim their share of the rich farms. Together these invaders had formed a new race which called itself "Remi" or "the Men" just as we sometimes call America "God's own country." They had good reason to be grateful to a fate which had carried them to this narrow strip of land. In the summer of each year the Nile turned the valley into a shallow lake and when the waters receded all the grain-fields and the pastures were covered with several inches of the most fertile clay.

In Egypt a kindly river did the work of a million men and made it possible to feed the teeming population of the first large cities of which we have any record. It is true that all the arable land was not in the valley. But a complicated system of small canals and well-sweeps carried water from the

The Valley of Egypt

river-level to the top of the highest banks and an even more intricate system of irrigation trenches spread it throughout the land.

While man of the prehistoric age had been obliged to spend sixteen hours out of every twenty-four gathering food for himself and the members of his tribe, the Egyptian peasant or the inhabitant of the Egyptian city found himself possessed of a certain leisure. He used this spare time to make himself many things that were merely ornamental and not the least bit useful.

More than that. One day he discovered that his brain was capable of thinking all kinds of thoughts which had nothing to do with the problems of eating and sleeping and finding a home for the children. The Egyptian began to speculate upon many strange problems that confronted him. Where did the stars come from? Who made the noise of the thunder which frightened him so terribly? Who made the River Nile rise with such regularity that it was possible to base the calender upon the appearance and the disappearance of the annual floods? Who was he, himself, a strange little creature surrounded on all sides by death and sickness and yet happy and full of laughter?

He asked these many questions and certain people obligingly stepped forward to answer these inquiries to the best of their ability. The Egyptians called them "priests" and they became the guardians of his thoughts and gained great respect in the community. They were highly learned men who were entrusted with the sacred task of keeping the written records. They understood that it is not good for man to think only of his immediate advantage in this world and they drew his attention to the days of the future when his soul would dwell beyond the mountains of the west and must give an account of his deeds to Osiris, the mighty god who was the ruler of the living and the dead and who judged the acts of men according to their merits. Indeed, the priests made so much of that future day in the realm of Isis and Osiris that the Egyptians began to regard life merely as a short preparation for the hereafter and turned the teeming valley of the Nile into a land devoted to the dead.

In a strange way, the Egyptians had come to believe that no soul could enter the realm of Osiris without the possession of the body which had been its place of residence in this world. Therefore as soon as a man was dead his relatives took his corpse and had it embalmed. For weeks it was soaked in a solution of natron and then it was filled with pitch. The Persian word for pitch was "mumiai" and the embalmed body was called a "mummy." It was wrapped in yards and yards of specially prepared linen and it was placed in a specially prepared coffin ready to be removed to its final home. But an Egyptian grave was a real home where the body was surrounded by pieces of furniture and musical instruments (to while away the dreary hours of waiting) and by little statues of cooks and bakers and barbers (that the occupant of this dark home might be decently provided with food and need not go about unshaven).

Originally these graves had been dug into the rocks of the western mountains but as the Egyptians moved north-

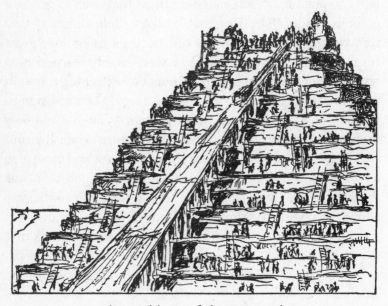

The Building of the Pyramids

ward they were obliged to build their cemeteries in the desert. The desert, however, is full of wild animals and equally wild robbers and they broke into the graves and disturbed the mummy or stole the jewelry that had been buried with the body. To prevent such unholy desecration the Egyptians used to build small mounds of stones on top of the graves. These little mounds gradually grew in size, because the rich people built higher mounds than the poor and there was a good deal of competition to see who could make the highest hill of stones. The record was made by King Khufu, whom the Greeks called Cheops and who lived thirty centuries before our era. His mound, which the Greeks called a pyramid (because the Egyptian word for high was "pir-em-us") was over five hundred feet high.

It covered more than thirteen acres of desert which is three times as much space as that occupied by the church of St. Peter, the largest edifice of the Christian world.

During twenty years, over a hundred thousand men were busy carrying the necessary stones from the other side of the river—ferrying them across the Nile (how they ever managed to do this, we do not understand), dragging them in many instances a long distance across the desert and finally hoisting them into their correct position. But so well did the king's architects and engineers perform their task that the narrow passage-way which leads to the royal tomb in the heart of the stone monster has never yet been pushed out of shape by the weight of those thousands of tons of stone which press upon it from all sides.

6

The Story of Egypt

The Rise and Fall of Egypt

The River Nile was a kind friend but occasionally it was a hard taskmaster. It taught the people who lived along its banks the noble art of "team-work." They depended upon each other to build their irrigation trenches and keep their dikes in repair. In this way they learned how to get along with their neighbours and their mutual-benefit association quite easily developed into an organised state.

Then one man grew more powerful than most of his neighbours and he became the leader of the community and their commander-in-chief when the envious neighbours of western Asia invaded the prosperous valley. In due course of time he became their king and ruled all the land from the Mediterranean to the mountains of the west.

But these political adventures of the old pharaohs (the word meant "the man who lived in the big house") rarely interested the patient and toiling peasant of the grainfields. Provided he was not obliged to pay more taxes to his king than he thought just, he accepted the rule of pharaoh as he accepted the rule of mighty Osiris.

It was different, however, when a foreign invader came and robbed him of his possessions. After twenty centuries of independent life, a savage Arab tribe of shepherds, called the Hyksos, attacked Egypt and for five hundred years they were the masters of the valley of the Nile. They were highly unpopular and great hate was also felt for the Hebrews who came to the land of Goshen to find a shelter after their long wandering through the desert and who helped the foreign usurper by acting as his tax-gatherers and his civil servants.

But shortly after the year 1700 B.C. the people of Thebes began a revolution and after a long struggle the Hyksos were driven out of the country and Egypt was free once more.

A thousand years later, when Assyria conquered all of western Asia, Egypt became part of the empire of Sardana-palus. In the seventh century B.C. it became once more an independent state which obeyed the rule of a king who lived in the city of Saïs at the delta of the Nile. But in the year 525 B.C., Cambyses, the king of the Persians, took possession of Egypt and in the fourth century B.C. when Persia was con-quered by Alexander the Great, Egypt too became a Mace-donian province. It regained a semblance of independence when one of Alexander's generals set himself up as king of a new Egyptian state and founded the dynasty of the Ptole-mies, who resided in the newly built city of Alexandria.

Finally, in the year 39 B.C., the Romans came. The last Egyptian queen, Cleopatra, tried her best to save the country. Her beauty and charm were more dangerous to the Roman generals than half a dozen Egyptian army corps. Twice she was successful in her attacks upon the hearts of her Roman conquerors. But in the year 30 B.C., Augustus, the nephew and heir of Cæsar, landed in Alexandria. He did not share his late uncle's admiration for the lovely princess. He destroyed her armies, but spared her life that he might make her march in his triumph as part of the spoils of war. When Cleopatra heard of this plan, she killed herself by taking poison. And Egypt became a Roman province.

7

Mesopotamia

Mesopotamia—The Second Centre of
Eastern Civilisation

I am going to take you to the top of the highest pyramid and I am going to ask that you imagine yourself possessed of the eyes of a hawk. Way, way off, in the distance, far beyond the yellow sands of the desert, you will see something green and shimmering. It is a valley situated between two rivers. It is the Paradise of the Old Testament. It is the land of mystery and wonder which the Greeks called Mesopotamia—the "country between the rivers."

The names of the two rivers are the Euphrates (which the Babylonians called the Purattu) and the Tigris (which was known as the Diklat). They begin their course amidst the snows of the mountains of Armenia where Noah's Ark found a resting place and slowly they flow through the southern plain until they reach the muddy banks of the Persian Gulf. They perform a very useful service. They turn the arid regions of western Asia into a fertile garden.

The valley of the Nile had attracted people because it had offered them food upon fairly easy terms. The "land between the rivers" was popular for the same reason. It was a country full of promise and both the inhabitants of the northern

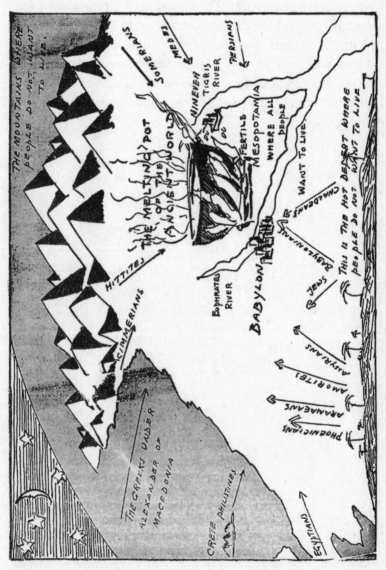

Mesopotamia, the Melting Pot of the Ancient World

mountains and the tribes which roamed through the southern deserts tried to claim this territory as their own and
most exclusive possession. The constant rivalry between the
mountaineers and the desert-nomads led to endless warfare.
Only the strongest and the bravest could hope to survive
and that will explain why Mesopotamia became the home
of a very strong race of men who were capable of creating a
civilisation which was in every respect as important as that
of Egypt.

8

The Sumerians

The Sumerian Nail Writers, Whose Clay Tablets
Tell Us the Story of Assyria and Babylonia, the
Great Semitic Melting Pot

The fifteenth century was an age of great discoveries. Columbus tried to find a way to the island of Cathay and stumbled upon a new and unsuspected continent. An Austrian bishop equipped an expedition which was to travel eastward and find the home of the grand duke of Muscovy, a voyage which led to complete failure, for Moscow was not visited by western men until a generation later. Meanwhile a certain Venetian by the name of Barbero had explored the ruins of western Asia and had brought back reports of a most curious language which he had found carved in the rocks of the temples of Shiraz and engraved upon endless pieces of baked clay.

But Europe was busy with many other things and it was not until the end of the eighteenth century that the first "cuneiform inscriptions" (so-called because the letters were wedge-shaped and wedge is called "cuneus" in Latin) were brought to Europe by a Danish surveyor, named Niebuhr. Then it took thirty years before a patient German schoolmaster by the name of Grotefend had deciphered the first

four letters, the D, the A, the R and the SH, the name of
the Persian king Darius. And another twenty years had to go
by until a British officer, Henry Rawlinson, who found the
famous inscription of Behistun, gave us a workable key to
the nail-writing of western Asia.

Compared to the problem of deciphering these nail-writ-
ings, the job of Champollion had been an easy one. The
Egyptians used pictures. But the Sumerians, the earliest
inhabitants of Mesopotamia, who had hit upon the idea of
scratching their words in tablets of clay, had discarded pictures entirely and had evolved a system of V-shaped figures
which showed little connection with the pictures out of
which they had been developed. A few examples will show
you what I mean. In the beginning a star, when drawn with

a nail into a brick, looked as follows: This sign, how-

ever, was too cumbersome and after a short while when the
meaning of "heaven" was added to that of star the picture

was simplified in this way which made it even more

of a puzzle. In the same way an ox changed from into

 and a fish changed from into The sun

was originally a plain circle and became If

we were using the Sumerian script today we would make an

 look like . This system of writing down our

ideas looks rather complicated but for more than thirty centuries it was used by the Sumerians and the Babylonians and the Assyrians and the Persians and all the different races which forced their way into the fertile valley.

The story of Mesopotamia is one of endless warfare and conquest. First the Sumerians came from the north. They were a white people who had lived in the mountains. They

A Tower of Babel

had been accustomed to worship their gods on the tops of hills. After they had entered the plain they constructed artificial little hills on top of which they built their altars. They did not know how to build stairs and they therefore surrounded their towers with sloping galleries. Our engineers have borrowed this idea, as you may see in our big railroad stations where ascending galleries lead from one floor to another. We may have borrowed other ideas from the Sumerians but we do not know it. The Sumerians were entirely absorbed by those races that entered the fertile valley at a later date. Their towers, however, still stand amidst the ruins of Mesopotamia. The Jews saw them when they went into exile in the land of Babylon and they called them towers of Bab-Illi, or towers of Babel.

In the fortieth century before our era, the Sumerians had entered Mesopotamia. They were soon afterwards overpowered by the Akkadians, one of the many tribes from the desert

Nineveh

of Arabia who speak a common dialect and who are known as the "Semites," because in the olden days people believed them to be the direct descendants of Shem, one of the three sons of Noah. A thousand years later, the Akkadians were forced to submit to the rule of the Amorites, another Semitic desert tribe whose great king Hammurabi built himself a magnificent palace in the holy city of Babylon and who gave his people a set of laws which made the Babylonian state the best administered empire of the ancient world. Next the Hittites, whom you will also meet in the Old Testament, overran the fertile valley and destroyed whatever they could not carry away. They in turn were vanquished by the followers of the great desert god, Ashur, who called themselves Assyrians and who made the city of Nineveh the center of a vast and terrible empire which conquered all of western Asia and Egypt and gathered taxes from countless subject races until

The Holy City of Babylon

the end of the seventh century before the birth of Christ when the Chaldeans, also a Semitic tribe, re-established Babylon and made that city the most important capital of that day. Nebuchadnezzar, the best known of their kings, encouraged the study of science, and our modern knowledge of astronomy and mathematics is all based upon certain first principles which were discovered by the Chaldeans. In the year

538 B.C. a crude tribe of Persian shepherds invaded this old land and overthrew the empire of the Chaldeans. Two hundred years later, they in turn were overthrown by Alexander the Great, who turned the fertile valley, the old melting pot of so many Semitic races, into a Greek province. Next came the Romans and after the Romans, the Turks, and Mesopotamia, the second centre of the world's civilisation, became a vast wilderness where huge mounds of earth told a story of ancient glory.

9

Moses

|||||||||||||||||||||||||||||||||||||||||||||||||||||||||||||||||||||||||||||||||||||||||||||||||||||||||||||||||||||||||||||||||||

The Story of Moses, the Leader of
the Jewish People

Some time during the twentieth century before our era, a small and unimportant tribe of Semitic shepherds had left its old home, which was situated in the land of Ur on the mouth of the Euphrates, and had tried to find new pastures within the domain of the kings of Babylonia. They had been driven away by the royal soldiers and they had moved westward looking for a little piece of unoccupied territory where they might set up their tents.

This tribe of shepherds was known as the Hebrews or, as we call them, the Jews. They had wandered far and wide, and after many years of dreary peregrinations they had been given shelter in Egypt. For more than five centuries they had dwelt among the Egyptians and when their adopted country had been overrun by the Hyksos marauders (as I told you in the story of Egypt) they had managed to make themselves useful to the foreign invader and had been left in the undisturbed possession of their grazing fields. But after a long war of independence the Egyptians had driven the Hyksos out of the valley of the Nile and then the Jews had come upon evil times for they had been degraded to the rank of common slaves and they had been forced to work on the royal roads

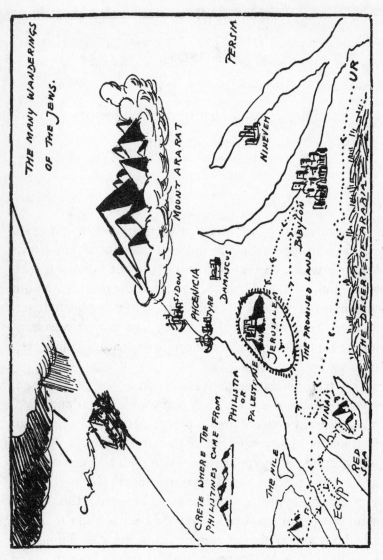

The Wanderings of the Jews

and on the Pyramids. And as the frontiers were guarded by the Egyptian soldiers it had been impossible for the Jews to escape.

After many years of suffering they were saved from their miserable fate by a young Jew, called Moses, who for a long time had dwelt in the desert and there had learned to appreciate the simple virtues of his earliest ancestors, who had kept away from cities and city-life and had refused to let themselves be corrupted by the ease and the luxury of a foreign civilisation.

Moses decided to bring his people back to a love of the ways of the patriarchs. He succeeded in evading the Egyptian troops that were sent after him and led his fellow tribesmen into the heart of the plain at the foot of Mount Sinai. During his long and lonely life in the desert, he had learned to revere the strength of the great God of the Thunder and the Storm, who ruled the high Heavens and upon whom the shepherds depended for life and light and breath. This God, one of the many divinities who were widely worshipped in western Asia, was called Jehovah, and through the teaching of Moses, he became the sole master of the Hebrew race.

One day, Moses disappeared from the camp of the Jews. It was whispered that he had gone away carrying two tablets of rough-hewn stone. That afternoon, the top of the mountain was lost to sight. The darkness of a terrible storm hid it from the eye of man. But when Moses returned, behold! there stood engraved upon the tablets the words which Jehovah had spoken unto the people of Israel amidst the crash of his thunder and the blinding flashes of his lightning. And from that moment, Jehovah was recognised by all the Jews as the highest master of their fate, the only true God, who had taught them how to live holy lives when he bade them to follow the wise lessons of his Ten Commandments.

They followed Moses when he bade them continue their journey through the desert. They obeyed him when he told them what to eat and drink and what to avoid that they might keep well in the hot climate. And finally after many years of wandering they came to a land which seemed pleasant and prosperous. It was called Palestine, which means the country of the "Pilistu," the Philistines, a small tribe of Cretans who had settled along the coast after they had been driven away from their own island. Unfortunately, the mainland, Palestine, was already inhabited by another Semitic race, called the Canaanites. But the Jews forced their way into the valleys and built themselves cities and constructed a mighty temple in a town which they named Jerusalem, the home of peace.

Moses Sees the Holy Land

As for Moses, he was no longer the leader of his people. He had been allowed to see the mountain ridges of Palestine from afar. Then he had closed his tired eyes for all time. He had worked faithfully and hard to please Jehovah. Not only had he guided his brethren out of foreign slavery into the free and independent life of a new home but he had also made the Jews the first of all nations to worship a single God.

10

The Phœnicians

The Phœnicians, Who Gave Us Our Alphabet

The Phœnicians, who were the neighbours of the Jews, were a Semitic tribe which at a very early age had settled along the shores of the Mediterranean. They had built themselves two well-fortified towns, Tyre and Sidon, and within a short time they had gained a monopoly of the trade of the western seas. Their ships went regularly to Greece and Italy and Spain and they even ventured beyond the Strait of Gibraltar to visit the Scilly Islands where they could buy tin. Wherever they went, they built themselves small trading stations, which they called colonies. Many of these were the origin of modern cities, such as Cadiz and Marseilles.

They bought and sold whatever promised to bring them a good profit. They were not troubled by a conscience. If we are to believe all their neighbours they did not know what the words "honesty" or "integrity" meant. They regarded a well-filled treasure chest the highest ideal of all good citizens. Indeed they were very unpleasant people and did not have a single friend. Nevertheless they have rendered all coming generations one service of the greatest possible value. They gave us our alphabet.

The Phœnicians had been familiar with the art of writing, invented by the Sumerians. But they regarded these pothooks as a clumsy waste of time. They were practical business men and could not spend hours engraving two or three letters. They set to work and invented a new system of writing which was greatly superior to the old one. They borrowed a few pictures from the Egyptians and they simplified a number of the wedge-shaped figures of the Sumerians. They sacrificed the pretty looks of the older system for the advantage of speed and they reduced the thousands of different images to a short and handy alphabet of twenty-two letters.

The Phœnician Trader

In due course of time, this alphabet travelled across the Ægean Sea and entered Greece. The Greeks added a few letters of their own and carried the improved system to Italy. The Romans modified the figures somewhat and in turn taught them to the wild barbarians of western Europe. Those wild barbarians were our own ancestors, and that is the reason why this book is written in characters that are of Phœnician origin and not in the hieroglyphics of the Egyptians or in the nail-script of the Sumerians.

11

The Indo-Europeans

The Indo-European Persians Conquer the
Semitic and the Egyptian World

The world of Egypt and Babylon and Assyria and Phœnicia
had existed almost thirty centuries and the venerable races
of the fertile valley were getting old and tired. Their doom
was sealed when a new and more energetic race appeared
upon the horizon. We call this race the Indo-European
race, because it conquered not only Europe but also made
itself the ruling class in the country which is now known as
British India.

These Indo-Europeans were white men like the Semites
but they spoke a different language which is regarded as the
common ancestor of all European tongues with the exception of Hungarian and Finnish and the Basque dialects of
northern Spain.

When we first hear of them, they had been living along
the shores of the Caspian Sea for many centuries. But one
day they had packed their tents and they had wandered forth
in search of a new home. Some of them had moved into the
mountains of central Asia and for many centuries they had
lived among the peaks which surround the plateau of Iran
and that is why we call them Aryans. Others had followed

the setting sun and they had taken possession of the plains of Europe as I shall tell you when I give you the story of Greece and Rome.

For the moment we must follow the Aryans. Under the leadership of Zarathustra (or Zoroaster) who was their great teacher many of them had left their mountain homes to follow the swiftly flowing Indus River on its way to the sea.

Others had preferred to stay among the hills of western Asia and there they had founded the half-independent communities of the Medes and the Persians, two peoples whose names we have copied from the old Greek history-books. In the seventh century before the birth of Christ, the Medes

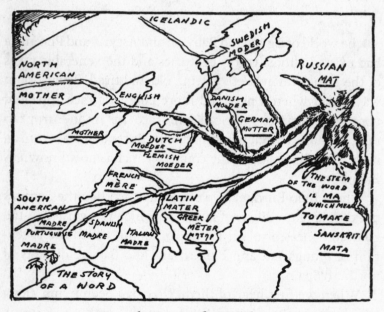

The Story of a Word

had established a kingdom of their own called Media, but this perished when Cyrus, the chief of a clan known as the Anshan, made himself king of all the Persian tribes and started upon a career of conquest which soon made him and

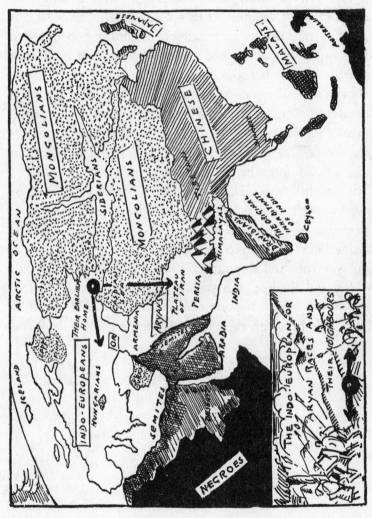

The Indo-Europeans and Their Neighbours

his children the undisputed masters of the whole of western Asia and of Egypt.

Indeed, with such energy did these Indo-European Persians push their triumphant campaigns in the west that they soon found themselves in serious difficulties with certain other Indo-European tribes which centuries before had moved into Europe and had taken possession of the Greek peninsula and the islands of the Ægean Sea.

These difficulties led to the three famous wars between Greece and Persia during which King Darius and King Xerxes of Persia invaded the northern part of the peninsula. They ravaged the lands of the Greeks and tried very hard to get a foothold upon the European continent.

But in this they did not succeed. The navy of Athens proved unconquerable. By cutting off the lines of supplies of the Persian armies, the Greek sailors invariably forced the Asiatic rulers to return to their base.

It was the first encounter between Asia, the ancient teacher, and Europe, the young and eager pupil. A great many of the other chapters of this book will tell you how the struggle between east and west has continued until this very day.

12
The Ægean Sea

The People of the Ægean Sea
Carried the Civilisation of Old Asia
into the Wilderness of Europe

When Heinrich Schliemann was a little boy his father told him the story of Troy. He liked that story better than anything else he had ever heard and he made up his mind, that as soon as he was big enough to leave home, he would travel to Greece and "find Troy." That he was the son of a poor country parson in a Mecklenburg village did not bother him. He knew that he would need money but he decided to gather a fortune first and do the digging afterwards. As a matter of fact, he managed to get a large fortune within

The Trojan Horse

a very short time, and as soon as he had enough money to equip an expedition, he went to the northwest corner of Asia Minor, where he supposed that Troy had been situated.

In that particular nook of old Asia Minor stood a high mound covered with grainfields. According to tradition it had been the home of Priamus, the king of Troy. Schliemann, whose enthusiasm was somewhat greater than his knowledge, wasted no time in preliminary explorations. At once he began to dig. And he dug with such zeal and such speed that his trench went straight through the heart of the city for which he was looking and carried him to the ruins of another buried town which was at least a thousand years older than the Troy of which Homer had written. Then something very interesting occurred. If Schliemann had found a few polished stone hammers and perhaps a few pieces of crude pottery,

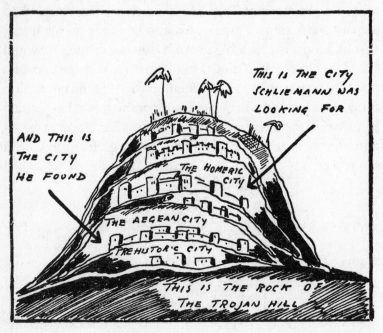

Schliemann Digs for Troy

no one would have been surprised. Instead of discovering
such objects, which people had generally associated with
the prehistoric men who had lived in these regions before
the coming of the Greeks, Schliemann found beautiful stat-
uettes and very costly jewelry and ornamented vases of a
pattern that was unknown to the Greeks. He ventured the
suggestion that fully ten centuries before the great Trojan
War, the coast of the Ægean had been inhabited by a mys-

Mycenæ in Argolis

terious race of men who in many ways had been the superiors of the wild Greek tribes who had invaded their country
and had destroyed their civilisation or absorbed it until it had
lost all trace of originality. And this proved to be the case. In
the late seventies of the last century, Schliemann visited the
ruins of Mycenæ, ruins which were so old that Roman guide-
books marvelled at their antiquity. There again, beneath the

flat slabs of stone of a small round enclosure, Schliemann stumbled upon a wonderful treasure-trove, which had been left behind by those mysterious people who had covered the Greek coast with their cities and who had built walls, so big and so heavy and so strong, that the Greeks called them the work of the Titans, those god-like giants who in very olden days had used to play ball with mountain peaks.

A very careful study of these many relics has done away with some of the romantic features of the story. The makers of these early works of art and the builders of these strong fortresses were no sorcerers, but simple sailors and traders. They had lived in Crete, and on the many small islands of the Ægean Sea. They had been hardy mariners and they had turned the Ægean into a centre of commerce for the exchange of goods between the highly civilised east and the slowly developing wilderness of the European mainland.

For more than a thousand years they had maintained an island empire which had developed a very high form of art.

The Ægean Sea

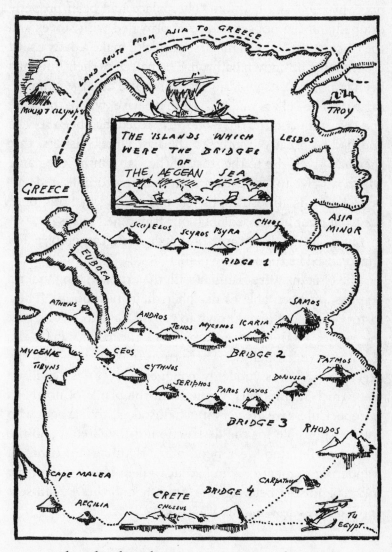

The Island Bridges Between Asia and Europe

Indeed their most important city, Cnossus, on the northern coast of Crete, had been entirely modern in its insistence upon hygiene and comfort. The palace had been properly drained and the houses had been provided with stoves and the Cnossians had been the first people to make a daily use of the hitherto unknown bathtub. The palace of their king had been famous for its winding staircases and its large banqueting hall. The cellars underneath this palace, where the wine and the grain and the olive-oil were stored, had been so vast and had so greatly impressed the first Greek visitors, that they had given rise to the story of the "labyrinth," the name which we give to a structure with so many complicated passages that it is almost impossible to find our way out, once the front door has closed upon our frightened selves.

But what finally became of this great Ægean empire and what caused its sudden downfall, that I can not tell.

The Cretans were familiar with the art of writing, but no one has yet been able to decipher their inscriptions. Their history therefore is unknown to us. We have to reconstruct the record of their adventures from the ruins which the Ægeans have left behind. These ruins make it clear that the Ægean world was suddenly conquered by a less civilised race which had recently come from the plains of northern Europe. Unless we are very much mistaken, the savages who were responsible for the destruction of the Cretan and the Ægean civilisation were none other than certain tribes of wandering shepherds who had just taken possession of the rocky peninsula between the Adriatic and the Ægean seas and who are known to us as Greeks.

13

The Greeks

Meanwhile the Indo-European Tribe of
the Hellenes Was Taking Possession of Greece

The Pyramids were a thousand years old and were beginning to show the first signs of decay, and Hammurabi, the wise king of Babylon, had been dead and buried several centuries, when a small tribe of shepherds left their homes along the banks of the River Danube and wandered southward in

An Ægean City on the Greek Mainland

The Achæans Take an Ægean City

search of fresh pastures. They called themselves Hellenes, after Hellen, the son of Deucalion and Pyrrha. According to the old myths these were the only two human beings who had escaped the great flood, which countless years before had destroyed all the people of the world, when they had grown so wicked that they disgusted Zeus, the mighty god, who lived on Mount Olympus.

Of these early Hellenes we know nothing. Thucydides, the historian of the fall of Athens, describing his earliest ancestors, said that they "did not amount to very much," and this was probably true. They were very ill-mannered. They lived like pigs and threw the bodies of their enemies to the wild dogs who guarded their sheep. They had very little respect for other people's rights, and they killed the natives of the Greek peninsula (who were called the Pelasgians) and stole their farms and took their cattle and made their wives and daughters slaves and wrote endless songs praising the courage of the clan of the Achæans, who had led the Hellenic advance-guard into the mountains of Thessaly and the Peloponnesus.

But here and there, on the tops of high rocks, they saw the castles of the Ægeans and those they did not attack for they feared the metal swords and the spears of the Ægean soldiers and knew that they could not hope to defeat them with their clumsy stone axes.

For many centuries they continued to wander from valley to valley and from mountain side to mountain side. Then the whole of the land had been occupied and the migration had come to an end.

That moment was the beginning of Greek civilisation. The Greek farmer, living within sight of the Ægean colonies, was finally driven by curiosity to visit his haughty neighbours. He discovered that he could learn many useful things from the men who dwelt behind the high stone walls of Mycenæ and Tiryns.

He was a clever pupil. Within a short time he mastered the art of handling those strange iron weapons which the Ægeans had brought from Babylon and from Thebes. He came to understand the mysteries of navigation. He began to build little boats for his own use.

And when he had learned everything the Ægeans could

The Fall of Cnossus

teach him he turned upon his teachers and drove them back
to their islands. Soon afterwards he ventured forth upon the
sea and conquered all the cities of the Ægean. Finally in
the fifteenth century before our era he plundered and ravaged Cnossus and ten centuries after their first appearance
upon the scene the Hellenes were the undisputed rulers
of Greece, of the Ægean and of the coastal regions of Asia
Minor. Troy, the last great commercial stronghold of the
older civilisation, was destroyed in the eleventh century B.C.
European history was to begin in all seriousness.

14

The Greek Cities

The Greek Cities That Were Really States

Ｗe modern people love the sound of the word "big." We
pride ourselves upon the fact that we belong to the "biggest"
country in the world and possess the "biggest" navy and
grow the "biggest" oranges and potatoes, and we love to live
in cities of "millions" of inhabitants and when we are dead
we are buried in the "biggest cemetery of the whole state."

A citizen of ancient Greece, could he have heard us talk,
would not have known what we meant. "Moderation in all
things" was the ideal of his life and mere bulk did not impress
him at all. And this love of moderation was not merely a hollow phrase used upon special occasions: it influenced the life
of the Greeks from the day of their birth to the hour of their
death. It was part of their literature and it made them build
small but perfect temples. It found expression in the clothes
which the men wore and in the rings and the bracelets of
their wives. It followed the crowds that went to the theatre
and made them hoot down any playwright who dared to sin
against the iron law of good taste or good sense.

The Greeks even insisted upon this quality in their politicians and in their most popular athletes. When a powerful runner came to Sparta and boasted that he could stand
longer on one foot than any other man in Hellas the people

drove him from the city because he prided himself upon an accomplishment at which he could be beaten by any common goose.

"That is all very well," you will say, "and no doubt it is a great virtue to care so much for moderation and perfection, but why should the Greeks have been the only people to develop this quality in olden times?" For an answer I shall point to the way in which the Greeks lived.

The people of Egypt or Mesopotamia had been the "subjects" of a mysterious supreme ruler who lived miles and miles away in a dark palace and who was rarely seen by the masses of the population. The Greeks, on the other hand, were "free citizens" of a hundred independent little "cities"

Mount Olympus, Where the Gods Lived

the largest of which counted fewer inhabitants than a large modern village. When a peasant who lived in Ur said that he was a Babylonian he meant that he was one of millions of other people who paid tribute to the king who at that particular moment happened to be master of western Asia. But

when a Greek said proudly that he was an Athenian or a The-
ban he spoke of a small town, which was both his home and
his country and which recognised no master but the will of
the people in the market-place.

To the Greek, his fatherland was the place where he was
born; where he had spent his earliest years playing hide and
seek amidst the forbidden rocks of the Acropolis; where he
had grown into manhood with a thousand other boys and
girls, whose nicknames were as familiar to him as those
of your own schoolmates. His fatherland was the holy soil
where his father and mother lay buried. It was the small
house within the high city-walls where his wife and children
lived in safety. It was a complete world which covered no
more than four or five acres of rocky land. Don't you see how
these surroundings must have influenced a man in everything he did and said and thought? The people of Babylon
and Assyria and Egypt had been part of a vast mob. They had
been lost in the multitude. The Greek, on the other hand,
had never lost touch with his immediate surroundings. He
never ceased to be part of a little town where everybody
knew every one else. He felt that his intelligent neighbours
were watching him. Whatever he did, whether he wrote
plays or made statues out of marble or composed songs, he
remembered that his efforts were going to be judged by all
the free-born citizens of his home-town who knew about
such things. This knowledge forced him to strive after perfection, and perfection, as he had been taught from childhood, was not possible without moderation.

In this hard school, the Greeks learned to excel in many
things. They created new forms of government and new
forms of literature and new ideals in art which we have never
been able to surpass. They performed these miracles in little
villages that covered less ground than four or five modern
city blocks.

And look, what finally happened!

In the fourth century before our era, Alexander of Macedonia conquered the world. As soon as he had done with fighting, Alexander decided that he must bestow the benefits of the true Greek genius upon all mankind. He took it away from the little cities and the little villages and tried to make it blossom and bear fruit amidst the vast royal residences of his newly acquired empire. But the Greeks, removed from the familiar sight of their own temples, removed from the well-known sounds and smells of their own crooked streets, at once lost the cheerful joy and the marvellous sense of moderation which had inspired the work of their hands and brains while they laboured for the glory of their old city-states. They became cheap artisans, content with second-rate work. The day the little city-states of old Hellas lost their independence and were forced to become part of a big nation, the old Greek spirit died. And it has been dead ever since.

15

Greek Self-Government

The Greeks Were the First People to Try
the Difficult Experiment of Self-Government

In the beginning, all the Greeks had been equally rich
and equally poor. Every man had owned a certain number
of cows and sheep. His mud-hut had been his castle. He had
been free to come and go as he wished. Whenever it was
necessary to discuss matters of public importance, all the citizens had gathered in the market-place. One of the older men
of the village was elected chairman and it was his duty to
see that everybody had a chance to express his views. In case
of war, a particularly energetic and self-confident villager
was chosen commander-in-chief, but the same people who
had voluntarily given this man the right to be their leader
claimed an equal right to deprive him of his job, once the
danger had been averted.

But gradually the village had grown into a city. Some people had worked hard and others had been lazy. A few had
been unlucky and still others had been just plain dishonest
in dealing with their neighbours and had gathered wealth.
As a result, the city no longer consisted of a number of men
who were equally well-off. On the contrary it was inhabited
by a small class of very rich people and a large class of very
poor ones.

The Temple

There had been another change. The old commander-in-chief, who had been willingly recognised as "headman" or "king" because he knew how to lead his men to victory, had disappeared from the scene. His place had been taken by the nobles—a class of rich people who during the course of time had got hold of an undue share of the farms and estates.

These nobles enjoyed many advantages over the common crowd of freemen. They were able to buy the best weapons which were to be found on the market of the eastern Mediterranean. They had much spare time in which they could practise the art of fighting. They lived in strongly built houses and they could hire soldiers to fight for them. They were constantly quarrelling among each other to decide who should rule the city. The victorious nobleman then assumed a sort

A Greek City-State

of kingship over all his neighbours and governed the town until he in turn was killed or driven away by still another ambitious nobleman.

Such a king, by the grace of his soldiers, was called a "tyrant" and during the seventh and sixth centuries before our era every Greek city was for a time ruled by such tyrants, many of whom, by the way, happened to be exceedingly capable men. But in the long run, this state of affairs became unbearable. Then attempts were made to bring about reforms and out of these reforms grew the first democratic government of which the world has a record.

It was early in the seventh century that the people of Athens decided to do some housecleaning and give the large number of freemen once more a voice in the government as they were supposed to have had in the days of their Achæan ancestors. They asked a man by the name of Draco to provide them with a set of laws that would protect the poor against the aggressions of the rich. Draco set to work. Unfortunately he was a professional lawyer and very much out of touch with ordinary life. In his eyes a crime was a crime and when he had finished his code, the people of Athens discovered that these Draconian laws were so severe that they could not possibly be put into effect. There would not have been rope enough to hang all the criminals under their new system of jurisprudence which made the stealing of an apple a capital offence.

The Athenians looked about for a more humane reformer. At last they found some one who could do that sort of thing better than anybody else. His name was Solon. He belonged to a noble family and he had travelled all over the world and had studied the forms of government of many other countries. After a careful study of the subject, Solon gave Athens a set of laws which bore testimony to that wonderful principle of moderation which was part of the Greek character. He tried to improve the condition of the peasant without, however, destroying the prosperity of the nobles who were (or rather who could be) of such great service to the state as soldiers. To protect the poorer classes against abuse on the part of the judges (who were always elected from the class of the nobles because they received no salary) Solon made a provision whereby a citizen with a grievance had the right to state his case before a jury of thirty of his fellow Athenians.

Most important of all, Solon forced the average freeman to take a direct and personal interest in the affairs of the city. No longer could he stay at home and say "oh, I am too busy today" or "it is raining and I had better stay indoors." He was expected to do his share; to be at the meeting of the town council; and carry part of the responsibility for the safety and the prosperity of the state.

This government by the "demos," the people, was often far from successful. There was too much idle talk. There were too many hateful and spiteful scenes between rivals for official honor. But it taught the Greek people to be independent and to rely upon themselves for their salvation and that was a very good thing.

16

Greek Life

How the Greeks Lived

But how, you will ask, did the ancient Greeks have time to look after their families and their business if they were forever running to the market-place to discuss affairs of state? In this chapter I shall tell you.

In all matters of government, the Greek democracy recognised only one class of citizens—the freemen. Every Greek city was composed of a small number of free-born citizens, a large number of slaves and a sprinkling of foreigners.

At rare intervals (usually during a war, when men were needed for the army) the Greeks showed themselves willing to confer the rights of citizenship upon the "barbarians" as they called the foreigners. But this was an exception. Citizenship was a matter of birth. You were an Athenian because your father and your grandfather had been Athenians before you. But however great your merits as a trader or a soldier, if you were born of non-Athenian parents, you remained a "foreigner" until the end of time.

The Greek city, therefore, whenever it was not ruled by a king or a tyrant, was run by and for the freemen, and this would not have been possible without a large army of slaves who outnumbered the free citizens at the rate of six or five to one and who performed those tasks to which we modern people must devote most of our time and energy if we wish to provide for our families and pay the rent of our apartments.

The slaves did all the cooking and baking and candlestick making of the entire city. They were the tailors and the carpenters and the jewellers and the school-teachers and the bookkeepers and they tended the store and looked after the factory while the master went to the public meeting to discuss questions of war and peace or visited the theatre to see

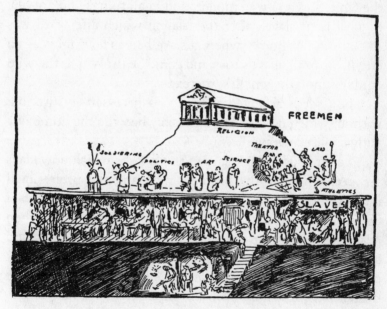

Greek Society

the latest play of Æschylus or hear a discussion of the revolutionary ideas of Euripides, who had dared to express certain doubts upon the omnipotence of the great god Zeus.

Indeed, ancient Athens resembled a modern club. All the free-born citizens were hereditary members and all the slaves were hereditary servants, and waited upon the needs of their masters, and it was very pleasant to be a member of the organisation.

But when we talk about slaves, we do not mean the sort of people about whom you have read in the pages of "Uncle Tom's Cabin." It is true that the position of those slaves who tilled the fields was a very unpleasant one, but the average freeman who had come down in the world and who had been obliged to hire himself out as a farm hand led just as miserable a life. In the cities, furthermore, many of the slaves were more prosperous than the poorer classes of the freemen. For the Greeks, who loved moderation in all things, did not like to treat their slaves after the fashion which afterward was so common in Rome, where a slave had as few rights as an engine in a modern factory and could be thrown to the wild animals upon the smallest pretext.

The Greeks accepted slavery as a necessary institution, without which no city could possibly become the home of a truly civilised people.

The slaves also took care of those tasks which nowadays are performed by the business men and the professional men. As for those household duties which take up so much of the time of your mother and which worry your father when he comes home from his office, the Greeks, who understood the value of leisure, had reduced such duties to the smallest possible minimum by living amidst surroundings of extreme simplicity.

To begin with, their homes were very plain. Even the rich nobles spent their lives in a sort of adobe barn, which lacked all the comforts which a modern workman expects as his natural right. A Greek home consisted of four walls and a roof. There was a door which led into the street but there were no windows. The kitchen, the living rooms and the sleeping quarters were built around an open courtyard in which there was a small fountain, or a statue and a few plants to make it look bright. Within this courtyard the family lived when it did not rain or when it was not too cold. In one corner of the yard the cook (who was a slave) prepared the meal and in another corner, the teacher (who was also a slave) taught the children the alpha beta gamma and the tables of multiplication and in still another corner the lady of the house, who rarely left her domain (since it was not considered good form for a married woman to be seen on the street too often), was repairing her husband's coat with her seamstresses (who were slaves,) and in the little office, right off the door, the master was inspecting the accounts which the overseer of his farm (who was a slave) had just brought to him.

When dinner was ready the family came together but the meal was a very simple one and did not take much time. The Greeks seem to have regarded eating as an unavoidable evil and not a pastime, which kills many dreary hours and eventually kills many dreary people. They lived on bread and on wine, with a little meat and some green vegetables. They drank water only when nothing else was available because they did not think it very healthy. They loved to call on each other for dinner, but our idea of a festive meal, where everybody is supposed to eat much more than is good for him, would have disgusted them. They came together at the table for the purpose of a good talk and a good glass of wine and water, but as they were moderate people they despised those who drank too much.

The same simplicity which prevailed in the dining room also dominated their choice of clothes. They liked to be clean and well groomed, to have their hair and beards neatly cut, to feel their bodies strong with the exercise and the swimming of the gymnasium, but they never followed the Asiatic fashion which prescribed loud colours and strange patterns. They wore a long white coat and they managed to look as smart as a modern Italian officer in his long blue cape.

They loved to see their wives wear ornaments but they

thought it very vulgar to display their wealth (or their wives) in public and whenever the women left their home they were as inconspicuous as possible.

In short, the story of Greek life is a story not only of moderation but also of simplicity. "Things," chairs and tables and books and houses and carriages, are apt to take up a great deal of their owner's time. In the end they invariably make him their slave and his hours are spent looking after their wants, keeping them polished and brushed and painted. The Greeks, before everything else, wanted to be "free," both in mind and in body. That they might maintain their liberty, and be truly free in spirit, they reduced their daily needs to the lowest possible point.

17

The Greek Theatre

The Origins of the Theatre, the First
Form of Public Amusement

At a very early stage of their history the Greeks had begun to collect the poems which had been written in honour of their brave ancestors who had driven the Pelasgians out of Hellas and had destroyed the power of Troy. These poems were recited in public and everybody came to listen to them. But the theatre, the form of entertainment which has become almost a necessary part of our own lives, did not grow out of these recited heroic tales. It had such a curious origin that I must tell you something about it in a separate chapter.

The Greeks had always been fond of parades. Every year they held solemn processions in honor of Dionysos, the god of the wine. As everybody in Greece drank wine (the Greeks thought water only useful for the purpose of swimming and sailing) this particular divinity was as popular as a god of the soda-fountain would be in our own land.

And because the wine-god was supposed to live in the vineyards, amidst a merry mob of satyrs (strange creatures who were half man and half goat), the crowd that joined the procession used to wear goat-skins and to hee-haw like real billygoats. The Greek word for goat is "tragos" and the Greek word for singer is "oidos." The singer who meh-mehed like a goat therefore was called a "tragos-oidos" or goat singer, and it is this strange name which developed into the modern word "tragedy," which means in the theatrical sense a piece with an unhappy ending, just as comedy (which really means the singing of something "comos" or gay) is the name given to a play which ends happily.

But how, you will ask, did this noisy chorus of masqueraders, stamping around like wild goats, ever develop into the noble tragedies which have filled the theatres of the world for almost two thousand years?

The connecting link between the goat-singer and Hamlet is really very simple as I shall show you in a moment.

The singing chorus was very amusing in the beginning and attracted large crowds of spectators who stood along the side of the road and laughed. But soon this business of hee-hawing grew tiresome and the Greeks thought dullness an evil only comparable to ugliness or sickness. They asked for something more entertaining. Then an inventive young poet from the village of Icaria in Attica hit upon a new idea which proved a tremendous success. He made one of the members of the goat-chorus step forward and engage in conversation with the leader of the musicians who marched at the head of the parade playing upon their pipes of Pan. This individual was allowed to step out of line. He waved his arms and gesticulated while he spoke (that is to say he "acted" while the others merely stood by and sang) and he asked a lot of questions, which the bandmaster answered according to the roll of papyrus upon which the poet had written down these answers before the show began.

This rough and ready conversation—the dialogue— which told the story of Dionysos or one of the other gods, became at once popular with the crowd. Henceforth every Dionysian procession had an "acted scene" and very soon the "acting" was considered more important than the procession and the meh-mehing.

Æschylus, the most successful of all "tragedians," who wrote no less than eighty plays during his long life (from 526 to 455), made a bold step forward when he introduced two "actors" instead of one. A generation later Sophocles increased the number of actors to three. When Euripides began to write his terrible tragedies in the middle of the fifth century B.C., he was allowed as many actors as he liked and when Aristophanes wrote those famous comedies in which he poked fun at everybody and everything, including the gods of Mount Olympus, the chorus had been reduced to the rôle of mere bystanders who were lined up behind the principal performers and who sang "this is a terrible world" while the hero in the foreground committed a crime against the will of the gods.

This new form of dramatic entertainment demanded a proper setting, and soon every Greek city owned a theatre, cut out of the rock of a nearby hill. The spectators sat upon wooden benches and faced a wide circle (our present orchestra where you pay three dollars and thirty cents for a seat). Upon this half-circle, which was the stage, the actors and the chorus took their stand. Behind them there was a tent where they made up with large clay masks which hid their faces and which showed the spectators whether the actors were supposed to be happy and smiling or unhappy and weeping. The Greek word for tent is "skene" and that is the reason why we talk of the "scenery" of the stage.

When once the tragedy had become part of Greek life, the people took it very seriously and never went to the theatre to give their minds a vacation. A new play became as important an event as an election and a successful playwright was received with greater honours than those bestowed upon a general who had just returned from a famous victory.

18

The Persian Wars

How the Greeks Defended Europe Against
an Asiatic Invasion and Drove the Persians
Back Across the Ægean Sea

The Greeks had learned the art of trading from the
Ægeans who had been the pupils of the Phœnicians. They
had founded colonies after the Phœnician pattern. They had
even improved upon the Phœnician methods by a more general use of money in dealing with foreign customers. In the
sixth century before our era they had established themselves
firmly along the coast of Asia Minor and they were taking away trade from the Phœnicians at a fast rate. This the
Phœnicians of course did not like but they were not strong
enough to risk a war with their Greek competitors. They sat
and waited nor did they wait in vain.

In a former chapter, I have told you how a humble tribe of
Persian shepherds had suddenly gone upon the warpath and
had conquered the greater part of western Asia. The Persians
were too civilised to plunder their new subjects. They contented themselves with a yearly tribute. When they reached
the coast of Asia Minor they insisted that the Greek colonies
of Lydia recognize the Persian kings as their over-lords and
pay them a stipulated tax. The Greek colonies objected. The

Persians insisted. Then the Greek colonies appealed to the home-country and the stage was set for a quarrel.

For if the truth be told, the Persian kings regarded the Greek city-states as very dangerous political institutions and bad examples for all other people who were supposed to be the patient slaves of the mighty Persian kings.

Of course, the Greeks enjoyed a certain degree of safety because their country lay hidden beyond the deep waters of the Ægean. But here their old enemies, the Phœnicians, stepped forward with offers of help and advice to the Persians. If the Persian king would provide the soldiers, the Phœnicians would guarantee to deliver the necessary ships to carry them to Europe. It was the year 492 before the birth of Christ, and Asia made ready to destroy the rising power of Europe.

The Persian Fleet Is Destroyed Near Mount Athos

As a final warning the king of Persia sent messengers to the Greeks asking for "earth and water" as a token of their submission. The Greeks promptly threw the messengers into the nearest well where they would find both "earth and water" in large abundance and thereafter of course peace was impossible.

But the gods of high Olympus watched over their children and when the Phœnician fleet carrying the Persian troops was near Mount Athos, the storm-god blew his cheeks until he almost burst the veins of his brow, and the fleet was destroyed by a terrible hurricane and the Persians were all drowned.

Two years later more Persians came. This time they sailed across the Ægean Sea and landed near the village of Marathon. As soon as the Athenians heard this they sent their army of ten thousand men to guard the hills that surrounded the Marathonian plain. At the same time they despatched a fast runner to Sparta to ask for help. But Sparta was envious

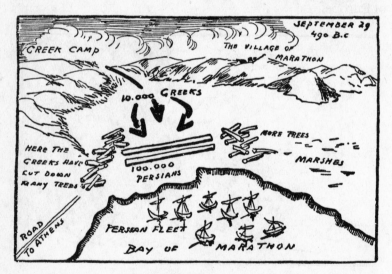

The Battle of Marathon

of the fame of Athens and refused to come to her assistance. The other Greek cities followed her example with the exception of tiny Platæa, which sent a thousand men. On September 12 of the year 490, Miltiades, the Athenian commander,

Thermopylæ

threw this little army against the hordes of the Persians. The Greeks broke through the Persian barrage of arrows and their spears caused terrible havoc among the disorganised Asiatic troops who had never been called upon to resist such an enemy.

That night the people of Athens watched the sky grow red with the flames of burning ships. Anxiously they waited for news. At last a little cloud of dust appeared upon the road that led to the north. It was Pheidippides, the runner. He stumbled and gasped for his end was near. Only a few days before had he returned from his errand to Sparta. He had hastened to join Miltiades. That morning he had taken part in the attack and later he had volunteered to carry the news of victory to his beloved city. The people saw him fall and they rushed forward to support him. "We have won," he whispered and then he died, a glorious death which made him envied of all men.

As for the Persians, they tried, after this defeat, to land near Athens but they found the coast guarded and disappeared, and once more the land of Hellas was at peace.

Eight years they waited and during this time the Greeks were not idle. They knew that a final attack was to be expected but they did not agree upon the best way to avert the danger. Some people wanted to increase the army. Others said that a strong fleet was necessary for success. The two parties led by Aristides (for the army) and Themistocles (the leader of the bigger-navy men) fought each other bitterly and nothing was done until Aristides was exiled. Then Themistocles had his chance and he built all the ships he could and turned the Piræus into a strong naval base.

In the year 481 B.C. a tremendous Persian army appeared in Thessaly, a province of northern Greece. In this hour of danger, Sparta, the great military city of Greece, was elected commander-in-chief. But the Spartans cared little what happened to northern Greece provided their own country was not invaded. They neglected to fortify the passes that led into Greece.

A small detachment of Spartans under Leonidas had been told to guard the narrow road between the high mountains and the sea which connected Thessaly with the southern provinces. Leonidas obeyed his orders. He fought and held the pass with unequalled bravery. But a traitor by the name of Ephialtes who knew the little byways of Malis guided a regiment of Persians through the hills and made it possible for

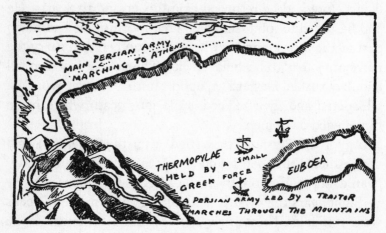

The Battle of Thermopylæ

The Persians Burn Athens

them to attack Leonidas in the rear. Near the Warm Wells—
the Thermopylæ—a terrible battle was fought. When night
came Leonidas and his faithful soldiers lay dead under the
corpses of their enemies.

But the pass had been lost and the greater part of Greece
fell into the hands of the Persians. They marched upon Athens, threw the garrison from the rocks of the Acropolis and
burned the city. The people fled to the island of Salamis. All
seemed lost. But on September 20 of the year 480 Themistocles forced the Persian fleet to give battle within the narrow
straits which separated the island of Salamis from the mainland and within a few hours he destroyed three-quarters of
the Persian ships.

In this way the victory of Thermopylæ came to naught.
Xerxes was forced to retire. The next year, so he decreed,
would bring a final decision. He took his troops to Thessaly
and there he waited for spring.

Greece

But this time the Spartans understood the seriousness of the hour. They left the safe shelter of the wall which they had built across the isthmus of Corinth and under the leadership of Pausanias they marched against Mardonius, the Persian general. The united Greeks (some one hundred thousand men from a dozen different cities) attacked the three hundred thousand men of the enemy near Platæa. Once more the heavy Greek infantry broke through the Persian barrage of arrows. The Persians were defeated, as they had been at Marathon, and this time they left for good. By a strange coincidence, the same day that the Greek armies won their victory near Platæa, the Athenian ships destroyed the enemy's fleet near Cape Mycale in Asia Minor.

Thus did the first encounter between Asia and Europe end. Athens had covered herself with glory and Sparta had fought bravely and well. If these two cities had been able to come to an agreement, if they had been willing to forget their little jealousies, they might have become the leaders of a strong and united Hellas.

But alas, they allowed the hour of victory and enthusiasm to slip by, and the same opportunity never returned.

19

Athens vs. Sparta

|||||||||||||||||||||||||||||||||||||||||||||||||||||||||||||||||||||||||||||||||||||||||||||||||||||||||||||||||||||||||||||||||||||||||

How Athens and Sparta Fought a Long and
Disastrous War for the Leadership of Greece

Athens and Sparta were both Greek cities and their people spoke a common language. In every other respect they
were different. Athens rose high from the plain. It was a city
exposed to the fresh breezes from the sea, willing to look at
the world with the eyes of a happy child. Sparta, on the other
hand, was built at the bottom of a deep valley, and used the
surrounding mountains as a barrier against foreign thought.
Athens was a city of busy trade. Sparta was an armed camp
where people were soldiers for the sake of being soldiers. The
people of Athens loved to sit in the sun and discuss poetry or
listen to the wise words of a philosopher. The Spartans, on
the other hand, never wrote a single line that was considered
literature, but they knew how to fight, they liked to fight and
they sacrificed all human emotions to their ideal of military
preparedness.

No wonder that these sombre Spartans viewed the success of Athens with malicious hate. The energy which the
defence of the common home had developed in Athens was
now used for purposes of a more peaceful nature. The Acrop-

olis was rebuilt and was made into a marble shrine to the goddess Athena. Pericles, the leader of the Athenian democracy, sent far and wide to find famous sculptors and painters and scientists to make the city more beautiful and the young Athenians more worthy of their home. At the same time he kept a watchful eye on Sparta and built high walls which connected Athens with the sea and made her the strongest fortress of that day.

An insignificant quarrel between two little Greek cities led to the final conflict. For thirty years the war between Athens and Sparta continued. It ended in a terrible disaster for Athens.

During the third year of the war the plague had entered the city. More than half of the people and Pericles, the great leader, had been killed. The plague was followed by a period of bad and untrustworthy leadership. A brilliant young fellow by the name of Alcibiades had gained the favor of the popular assembly. He suggested a raid upon the Spartan colony of Syracuse in Sicily. An expedition was equipped and everything was ready. But Alcibiades got mixed up in a street brawl and was forced to flee. The general who succeeded him was a bungler. First he lost his ships and then he lost his army, and the few surviving Athenians were thrown into the stone-quarries of Syracuse, where they died from hunger and thirst.

The expedition had killed all the young men of Athens. The city was doomed. After a long siege the town surrendered in April of the year 404. The high walls were demolished. The navy was taken away by the Spartans. Athens ceased to exist as the centre of the great colonial empire which it had conquered during the days of its prosperity. But that wonderful desire to learn and to know and to investigate which had distinguished her free citizens during the days of greatness and prosperity did not perish with the walls and the ships. It continued to live. It became even more brilliant.

Athens no longer shaped the destinies of the land of Greece. But now, as the home of the first great university, the city began to influence the minds of intelligent people far beyond the narrow frontiers of Hellas.

20

Alexander the Great

Alexander the Macedonian Establishes
a Greek World Empire, and
What Became of This High Ambition

When the Achæans had left their homes along the banks
of the Danube to look for pastures new, they had spent some
time among the mountains of Macedonia. Ever since, the
Greeks had maintained certain more or less formal relations
with the people of this northern country. The Macedonians
from their side had kept themselves well informed about
conditions in Greece.

Now it happened, just when Sparta and Athens had finished their disastrous war for the leadership of Hellas, that
Macedonia was ruled by an extraordinarily clever man by
the name of Philip. He admired the Greek spirit in letters and
art but he despised the Greek lack of self-control in political
affairs. It irritated him to see a perfectly good people waste
its men and money upon fruitless quarrels. So he settled the
difficulty by making himself the master of all Greece and
then he asked his new subjects to join him on a voyage which
he meant to pay to Persia in return for the visit which Xerxes
had paid the Greeks 150 years before.

Unfortunately Philip was murdered before he could start

upon this well-prepared expedition. The task of avenging the destruction of Athens was left to Philip's son Alexander, the beloved pupil of Aristotle, wisest of all Greek teachers.

Alexander bade farewell to Europe in the spring of the year 334 B.C. Seven years later he reached India. In the meantime he had destroyed Phœnicia, the old rival of the Greek merchants. He had conquered Egypt and had been worshipped by the people of the Nile Valley as the son and heir of the pharaohs. He had defeated the last Persian king—he had over-thrown the Persian Empire—he had given orders to rebuild Babylon—he had led his troops into the heart of the Himalayan Mountains and had made the entire world a Macedonian province and dependency. Then he stopped and announced even more ambitious plans.

The newly formed empire must be brought under the influence of the Greek mind. The people must be taught the Greek language—they must live in cities built after a Greek model. The Alexandrian soldier now turned school-master. The military camps of yesterday became the peaceful centres of the newly imported Greek civilisation. Higher and higher did the flood of Greek manners and Greek customs rise, when suddenly Alexander was stricken with a fever and died in the old palace of King Hammurabi of Babylon in the year 323.

Then the waters receded. But they left behind the fertile clay of a higher civilisation and Alexander, with all his childish ambitions and his silly vanities, had performed a most valuable service. His empire did not long survive him. A number of ambitious generals divided the territory among themselves. But they too remained faithful to the dream of a great world brotherhood of Greek and Asiatic ideas and knowledge.

They maintained their independence until the Romans added western Asia and Egypt to their other domains. The strange inheritance of this Hellenistic civilisation (part Greek, part Persian, part Egyptian and Babylonian) fell to the Roman conquerors. During the following centuries, it got such a firm hold upon the Roman world that we feel its influence in our own lives this very day.

21

A Summary

A Short Summary of Chapters 1 to 20

Thus far, from the top of our high tower we have been looking eastward. But from this time on, the history of Egypt and Mesopotamia is going to grow less interesting and I must take you to study the western landscape.

Before we do this, let us stop a moment and make clear to ourselves what we have seen.

First of all I showed you prehistoric man—a creature very simple in his habits and very unattractive in his manners. I told you how he was the most defenceless of the many animals that roamed through the early wilderness of the five continents, but being possessed of a larger and better brain, he managed to hold his own.

Then came the glaciers and the many centuries of cold weather, and life on this planet became so difficult that man was obliged to think three times as hard as ever before if he wished to survive. Since, however, that "wish to survive" was (and is) the mainspring which keeps every living being going full tilt to the last gasp of its breath, the brain of glacial man was set to work in all earnestness. Not only did these hardy people manage to exist through the long cold spells which killed many ferocious animals, but when the earth became warm and comfortable once more, prehistoric man had learned a number of things which gave him such great advantages over his less intelligent neighbours that the danger of extinction (a very serious one during the first half million years of man's residence upon this planet) became a very remote one.

I told you how these earliest ancestors of ours were slowly plodding along when suddenly (and for reasons that are not well understood) the people who lived in the valley of the Nile rushed ahead and almost overnight created the first centre of civilisation.

Then I showed you Mesopotamia, "the land between the rivers," which was the second great school of the human race. And I made you a map of the little island bridges of the Ægean Sea, which carried the knowledge and the science of the old east to the young west, where lived the Greeks.

Next I told you of an Indo-European tribe, called the Hellenes, who thousands of years before had left the heart of Asia and who had in the eleventh century before our era pushed their way into the rocky peninsula of Greece and who, since then, have been known to us as the Greeks. And I told you the story of the little Greek cities that were really states, where the civilisation of old Egypt and Asia was transfigured (that is a big word, but you can "figure out" what it means) into something quite new, something that was much nobler and finer than anything that had gone before.

When you look at the map you will see how by this time civilisation has described a semi-circle. It begins in Egypt, and by way of Mesopotamia and the Ægean Islands it moves westward until it reaches the European continent. The first four thousand years, Egyptians and Babylonians and Phœnicians and a large number of Semitic tribes (please remember that the Jews were but one of a large number of Semitic peoples) have carried the torch that was to illuminate the world. They now hand it over to the Indo-European Greeks, who become the teachers of another Indo-European tribe, called the Romans. But meanwhile the Semites have pushed westward along the northern coast of Africa and have made themselves the rulers of the western half of the Mediterranean just when the eastern half has become a Greek (or Indo-European) possession.

This, as you shall see in a moment, leads to a terrible conflict between the two rival races, and out of their struggle arises the victorious Roman Empire, which is to take this Egyptian-Mesopotamian–Greek civilisation to the furthermost corners of the European continent, where it serves as the foundation upon which our modern society is based.

I know all this sounds very complicated, but if you get hold of these few principles, the rest of our history will become a great deal simpler. The maps will make clear what the words fail to tell. And after this short intermission, we go back to our story and give you an account of the famous war between Carthage and Rome.

22
Rome and Carthage

The Semitic Colony of Carthage on the Northern Coast of Africa and the Indo–European City of Rome on the West Coast of Italy Fought Each Other for the Possession of the Western Mediterranean and Carthage Was Destroyed

The little Phœnician trading post of Kart-hadshat stood on a low hill which overlooked the African Sea, a stretch of water ninety miles wide which separates Africa from Europe. It was an ideal spot for a commercial centre. Almost too ideal. It grew too fast and became too rich. When in the sixth century before our era, Nebuchadnezzar of Babylon destroyed Tyre, Carthage broke off all further relations with the mother country and became an independent state—the great western advance-post of the Semitic races.

Unfortunately the city had inherited many of the traits which for a thousand years had been characteristic of the Phœnicians. It was a vast business-house, protected by a strong navy, indifferent to most of the finer aspects of life. The city and the surrounding country and the distant colonies were all ruled by a small but exceedingly powerful group of rich men. The Greek word for rich is "ploutos" and the Greeks called such a government by "rich men" a "plutocracy." Carthage was a plutocracy and the real power of the state lay in the hands of a dozen big ship-owners and mine-owners and merchants who met in the back room of an office and regarded their common fatherland as a business enterprise which ought to yield them a decent profit. They were, however, wide awake and full of energy and worked very hard.

As the years went by the influence of Carthage upon her neighbours increased until the greater part of the African

Carthage

coast, Spain and certain regions of France were Carthaginian possessions, and paid tribute, taxes and dividends to the mighty city on the African Sea.

Of course, such a "plutocracy" was forever at the mercy of the crowd. As long as there was plenty of work and wages were high, the majority of the citizens were quite contented, allowed their "betters" to rule them and asked no embarrassing questions. But when no ships left the harbor, when no ore was brought to the smelting-ovens, when dockworkers and stevedores were thrown out of employment, then there were grumblings and there was a demand that the popular assembly be called together as in the olden days when Carthage had been a self-governing republic.

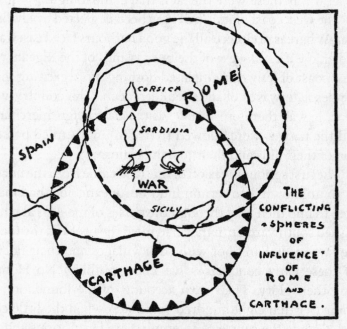

Spheres of Influence

To prevent such an occurrence the plutocracy was obliged to keep the business of the town going at full speed. They had managed to do this very successfully for almost five hundred years when they were greatly disturbed by certain rumours which reached them from the western coast of Italy. It was said that a little village on the banks of the Tiber had suddenly risen to great power and was making itself the acknowledged leader of all the Latin tribes who inhabited central Italy. It was also said that this village, which, by the way, was called Rome, intended to build ships and go after the commerce of Sicily and the southern coast of France.

Carthage could not possibly tolerate such competition. The young rival must be destroyed lest the Carthaginian rulers lose their prestige as the absolute rulers of the western Mediterranean. The rumors were duly investigated and in a general way these were the facts that came to light.

The west coast of Italy had long been neglected by civilisation. Whereas in Greece all the good harbours faced eastward and enjoyed a full view of the busy islands of the Ægean, the west coast of Italy contemplated nothing more exciting than the desolate waves of the Mediterranean. The country was poor. It was therefore rarely visited by foreign merchants and the natives were allowed to live in undisturbed possession of their hills and their marshy plains.

The first serious invasion of this land came from the north. At an unknown date certain Indo-European tribes had managed to find their way through the passes of the Alps and had pushed southward until they had filled the heel and the toe of the famous Italian boot with their villages and their flocks. Of these early conquerors we know nothing. No Homer sang their glory. Their own accounts of the foundation of Rome (written eight hundred years later when the little city had become the centre of an empire) are fairy stories and do not belong in a history. Romulus and Remus jumping across each other's walls (I always forget who jumped across whose wall) make entertaining reading, but the foundation of the city of Rome was a much more prosaic affair. Rome began as a thousand American cities have done, by being a convenient place for barter and horse-trading. It lay in the heart of the plains of central Italy. The Tiber provided direct access to the sea. The land-road from north to south found here a convenient ford which could be used all the year around.

How the City of Rome Happened

And seven little hills along the banks of the river offered the inhabitants a safe shelter against their enemies who lived in the mountains and those who lived beyond the horizon of the nearby sea.

The mountaineers were called the Sabines. They were a rough crowd with an unholy desire for easy plunder. But they were very backward. They used stone axes and wooden shields and were no match for the Romans with their steel swords. The sea-people on the other hand were dangerous foes. They were called the Etruscans and they were (and still are) one of the great mysteries of history. Nobody knew (or knows) whence they came; who they were; what had driven them away from their original homes. We have found the remains of their cities and their cemeteries and their waterworks all along the Italian coast. We are familiar with their inscriptions. But as no one has ever been able to decipher the Etruscan alphabet, these written messages are, so far, merely annoying and not at all useful.

Our best guess is that the Etruscans came originally from Asia Minor and that a great war or a pestilence in that country had forced them to go away and seek a new home elsewhere. Whatever the reason for their coming, the Etruscans played a great rôle in history. They carried the pollen of the ancient civilisation from the east to the west and they taught the Romans, who, as we know, came from the north, the first principles of architecture and street-building and fighting and art and cookery and medicine and astronomy.

But just as the Greeks had not loved their Ægean teachers, in this same way did the Romans hate their Etruscan masters. They got rid of them as soon as they could and the opportunity offered itself when Greek merchants discovered the commercial possibilities of Italy and when the first Greek vessels reached Rome. The Greeks came to trade, but they stayed to instruct. They found the tribes who inhabited the Roman country-side (and who were called the Latins) quite willing to learn such things as might be of practical use. At once they understood the great benefit that could be derived from a written alphabet and they copied that of the Greeks. They also understood the commercial advantages of a well-regulated system of coins and measures and weights. Eventually the Romans swallowed Greek civilisation hook, line and sinker.

They even welcomed the gods of the Greeks to their country. Zeus was taken to Rome where he became known as Jupiter and the other divinities followed him. The Roman gods, however, never were quite like their cheerful cousins who had accompanied the Greeks on their road through life and through history. The Roman gods were state function-aries. Each one managed his own department with great prudence and a deep sense of justice, but in turn he was exact in demanding the obedience of his worshippers. This obedience the Romans rendered with scrupulous care. But they never established the cordial personal relations and that charming friendship which had existed between the old Hel-lenes and the mighty residents of the high Olympian peak.

The Romans did not imitate the Greek form of govern-ment, but being of the same Indo-European stock as the people of Hellas, the early history of Rome resembles that of Athens and the other Greek cities. They did not find it diffi-cult to get rid of their kings, the descendants of the ancient tribal chieftains. But once the kings had been driven from the city, the Romans were forced to bridle the power of the nobles, and it took many centuries before they managed to establish a system which gave every free citizen of Rome a chance to take a personal interest in the affairs of his town.

Thereafter the Romans enjoyed one great advantage over the Greeks. They managed the affairs of their country with-out making too many speeches. They were less imaginative than the Greeks and they preferred an ounce of action to a pound of words. They understood the tendency of the multitude (the "plebs," as the assemblage of free citizens was called) only too well to waste valuable time upon mere talk. They therefore placed the actual business of running the city into the hands of two "consuls" who were assisted by a council of elders, called the Senate (because the word "senex" means an old man). As a matter of custom and practical advantage the senators were elected from the nobility. But their power had been strictly defined.

Rome at one time had passed through the same sort of struggle between the poor and the rich which had forced Athens to adopt the laws of Draco and Solon. In Rome this conflict had occurred in the fifth century B.C. As a result the freemen had obtained a written code of laws which protected them against the despotism of the aristocratic judges by the institution of the "tribune." These tribunes were city-magistrates, elected by the freemen. They had the right to protect any citizen against those actions of the government officials which were thought to be unjust. A consul had the right to condemn a man to death, but if the case had not been absolutely proved the tribune could interfere and save the poor fellow's life.

But when I use the word "Rome," I seem to refer to a little city of a few thousand inhabitants. And the real strength of Rome lay in the country districts outside her walls. And it was in the government of these outlying provinces that Rome at an early age showed her wonderful gift as a colonising power.

In very early times Rome had been the only strongly fortified city in central Italy, but it had always offered a hospitable refuge to other Latin tribes who happened to be in danger of attack. The Latin neighbours had recognised the advantages of a close union with such a powerful friend and they had tried to find a basis for some sort of defensive and offensive alliance. Other nations, Egyptians, Babylonians, Phœnicians, even Greeks, would have insisted upon a treaty of submission on the part of the "barbarians." The Romans did nothing of the sort. They gave the "outsider" a chance to become partners in a common "res publica"—or common-wealth.

"You want to join us," they said. "Very well, go ahead and join. We shall treat you as if you were full-fledged citizens of Rome. In return for this privilege we expect you to fight for our city, the mother of us all, whenever it shall be necessary."

The "outsider" appreciated this generosity and he showed his gratitude by his unswerving loyalty.

Whenever a Greek city had been attacked, the foreign residents had moved out as quickly as they could. Why defend something which meant nothing to them but a temporary boarding house in which they were tolerated as long as they paid their bills? But when the enemy was before the gates of Rome, all the Latins rushed to her defence. It was their mother who was in danger. It was their true "home" even if they lived a hundred miles away and had never seen the walls of the sacred hills.

No defeat and no disaster could change this sentiment. In the beginning of the fourth century B.C. the wild Gauls forced their way into Italy. They had defeated the Roman army near the River Allia and had marched upon the city. They had taken Rome and then they expected that the people would come and sue for peace. They waited, but nothing happened. After a short time the Gauls found themselves surrounded by a hostile population which made it impossible for them to obtain supplies. After seven months, hunger forced them to withdraw. The policy of Rome to treat the "foreigner" on equal terms had proved a great success and Rome stood stronger than ever before.

This short account of the early history of Rome shows

you the enormous difference between the Roman ideal of a healthy state, and that of the ancient world which was embodied in the town of Carthage. The Romans counted upon the cheerful and hearty co-operation between a number of "equal citizens." The Carthaginians, following the example of Egypt and western Asia, insisted upon the unreasoning (and therefore unwilling) obedience of "subjects" and when these failed they hired professional soldiers to do their fighting for them.

You will now understand why Carthage was bound to fear such a clever and powerful enemy and why the plutocracy of Carthage was only too willing to pick a quarrel that they might destroy the dangerous rival before it was too late.

But the Carthaginians, being good business men, knew that it never pays to rush matters. They proposed to the Romans that their respective cities draw two circles on the map and that each town claim one of these circles as her own "sphere of influence" and promise to keep out of the other fellow's circle. The agreement was promptly made and was broken just as promptly when both sides thought it wise to send their armies to Sicily where a rich soil and a bad government invited foreign interference.

The war which followed (the so-called First Punic War) lasted twenty-four years. It was fought out on the high seas and in the beginning it seemed that the experienced Carthaginian navy would defeat the newly created Roman fleet. Following their ancient tactics, the Carthaginian ships would either ram the enemy vessels or by a bold attack from the side they would break their oars and would then kill the sailors of the helpless vessel with their arrows and with fire balls. But Roman engineers invented a new craft which carried a boarding bridge across which the Roman infantrymen stormed the hostile ship. Then there was a sudden end to Carthaginian victories. At the battle of Mylæ their fleet was

A Fast Roman Warship

badly defeated. Carthage was obliged to sue for peace, and Sicily became part of the Roman domains.

Twenty-three years later new trouble arose. Rome (in quest of copper) had taken the island of Sardinia. Carthage (in quest of silver) thereupon occupied all of southern Spain. This made Carthage a direct neighbour of the Romans. The latter did not like this at all and they ordered their troops to cross the Pyrenees and watch the Carthaginian army of occupation.

The stage was set for the second outbreak between the two rivals. Once more a Greek colony was the pretext for a war. The Carthaginians were besieging Saguntum on the east coast of Spain. The Saguntians appealed to Rome and Rome, as usual, was willing to help. The Senate promised the help of the Latin armies, but the preparation for this expedition took some time, and meanwhile Saguntum had been taken and had been destroyed. This had been done in direct opposition to the will of Rome. The Senate decided upon war. One Roman army was to cross the African sea and make a landing on Carthaginian soil. A second division was to keep the Carthaginian armies occupied in Spain to prevent them from rushing to the aid of the home town. It was an excellent plan and everybody expected a great victory. But the Gods had decided otherwise.

It was the fall of the year 218 before the birth of Christ and the Roman army which was to attack the Carthaginians in Spain had left Italy. People were eagerly waiting for news of an easy and complete victory when a terrible rumour began to spread through the plain of the Po. Wild mountaineers, their lips trembling with fear, told of hundreds of thousands of brown men accompanied by strange beasts "each one as big as a house," who had suddenly emerged from the clouds of snow which surrounded the old Grain pass through which Hercules, thousands of years before, had driven the oxen of Geryon on his way from Spain to Greece. Soon an endless stream of bedraggled refugees appeared before the gates of Rome, with more complete details. Hannibal, the son of Hamilcar, with fifty thousand soldiers, nine thousand horsemen and thirty-seven fighting elephants, had crossed the Pyrenees. He had defeated the Roman army of Scipio on the banks of the Rhone and he had guided his army safely across the mountain passes of the Alps although it was October and the roads were thickly covered with snow and ice. Then he had joined forces with the Gauls and together they had defeated a second Roman army just before they crossed the Trebia and laid siege to Placentia, the northern terminus of the road which connected Rome with the province of the Alpine districts.

The Senate, surprised but calm and energetic as usual, hushed up the news of these many defeats and sent two fresh armies to stop the invader. Hannibal managed to surprise these troops on a narrow road along the shores of the Trasimene Lake and there he killed all the Roman officers and most of their men. This time there was a panic among the people of Rome, but the Senate kept its nerve. A third army was organised and the command was given to Quintus Fabius Maximus with full power to act "as was necessary to save the state."

Fabius knew that he must be very careful lest all be lost. His raw and untrained men, the last available soldiers, were no match for Hannibal's veterans. He refused to accept battle but forever he followed Hannibal, destroyed everything eatable, destroyed the roads, attacked small detachments and generally weakened the morale of the Carthaginian troops by a most distressing and annoying form of guerilla warfare.

Such methods, however, did not satisfy the fearsome crowds who had found safety behind the walls of Rome. They wanted "action." Something must be done and must be done quickly. A popular hero by the name of Varro, the sort of man who went about the city telling everybody how much better he could do things than slow old Fabius, the "Delayer," was made commander-in-chief by popular acclamation. At the battle of Cannæ (216) he suffered the most terrible defeat of Roman history. More than seventy thousand men were killed. Hannibal was master of all Italy.

He marched from one end of the peninsula to the other, proclaiming himself the "deliverer from the yoke of Rome" and asking the different provinces to join him in warfare upon the mother city. Then once more the wisdom of Rome bore noble fruit. With the exceptions of Capua and Syracuse, all Roman cities remained loyal. Hannibal, the deliverer, found himself opposed by the people whose friend he pretended to be. He was far away from home and did not like the situation. He sent messengers to Carthage to ask for fresh supplies and new men. Alas, Carthage could not send him either.

The Romans with their boarding-bridges were the masters of the sea. Hannibal must help himself as best he could.

Hannibal Crosses the Alps

He continued to defeat the Roman armies that were sent out against him, but his own numbers were decreasing rapidly and the Italian peasants held aloof from this self-appointed "deliverer."

After many years of uninterrupted victories, Hannibal found himself besieged in the country which he had just conquered. For a moment, the luck seemed to turn. Hasdrubal, his brother, had defeated the Roman armies in Spain. He had crossed the Alps to come to Hannibal's assistance. He sent messengers to the south to tell of his arrival and ask the other army to meet him in the plain of the Tiber. Unfortunately the messengers fell into the hands of the Romans and Hannibal waited in vain for further news until his brother's head, neatly packed in a basket, came rolling into his camp and told him of the fate of the last of the Carthaginian troops.

With Hasdrubal out of the way, young Publius Scipio easily reconquered Spain and four years later the Romans were ready for a final attack upon Carthage. Hannibal was called back. He crossed the African Sea and tried to organise the defences of his home-city. In the year 202 at the battle of Zama, the Carthaginians were defeated. Hannibal fled to Tyre. From there he went to Asia Minor to stir up the Syrians and the Macedonians against Rome. He accomplished very little but his activities among these Asiatic powers gave the Romans an excuse to carry their warfare into the territory of the east and annex the greater part of the Ægean world.

Driven from one city to another, a fugitive without a home, Hannibal at last knew that the end of his ambitious dream had come. His beloved city of Carthage had been ruined by the war. She had been forced to sign a terrible peace. Her navy had been sunk. She had been forbidden to make war without Roman permission. She had been condemned to pay the Romans millions of dollars for endless

Hannibal's Travels

The Death of Hannibal

years to come. Life offered no hope of a better future. In the year 190 B.C. Hannibal took poison and killed himself.

Forty years later, the Romans forced their last war upon Carthage. Three long years the inhabitants of the old Phœnician colony held out against the power of the new republic. Hunger forced them to surrender. The few men and women who had survived the siege were sold as slaves. The city was set on fire. For two whole weeks the store-houses and the palaces and the great arsenal burned. Then a terrible curse was pronounced upon the blackened ruins and the Roman legions returned to Italy to enjoy their victory.

For the next thousand years, the Mediterranean remained a European sea. But as soon as the Roman Empire had been destroyed, Asia made another attempt to dominate this great inland sea, as you will learn when I tell you about Mohammed.

23

The Rise of Rome

How Rome Happened

The Roman Empire was an accident. No one planned it. It "happened." No famous general or statesman or cutthroat ever got up and said "Friends, Romans, Citizens, we must found an empire. Follow me and together we shall conquer all the land from the Gates of Hercules to Mount Taurus."

Rome produced famous generals and equally distinguished statesmen and cutthroats, and Roman armies fought all over the world. But the Roman empire-making was done without a preconceived plan. The average Roman was a very matter-of-fact citizen. He disliked theories about govern-

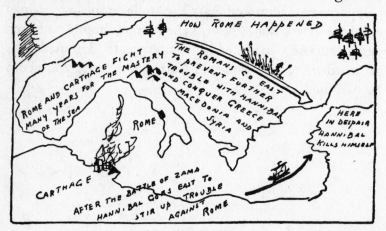

How Rome Happened

ment. When someone began to recite "eastward the course of Roman Empire, etc., etc.," he hastily left the Forum. He just continued to take more and more land because circumstances forced him to do so. He was not driven by ambition or by greed. Both by nature and inclination he was a farmer and wanted to stay at home. But when he was attacked he was obliged to defend himself and when the enemy happened to cross the sea to ask for aid in a distant country then the patient Roman marched many dreary miles to defeat this dangerous foe and when this had been accomplished, he stayed behind to administer his newly conquered provinces lest they fall into the hands of wandering barbarians and become themselves a menace to Roman safety. It sounds rather complicated and yet to the contemporaries it was so very simple, as you shall see in a moment.

In the year 203 B.C. Scipio had crossed the African Sea and had carried the war into Africa. Carthage had called Hannibal back. Badly supported by his mercenaries, Hannibal had been defeated near Zama. The Romans had asked for his surrender and Hannibal had fled to get aid from the kings of Macedonia and Syria, as I told you in my last chapter.

The rulers of these two countries (remnants of the empire of Alexander the Great) just then were contemplating an expedition against Egypt. They hoped to divide the rich Nile Valley between themselves. The king of Egypt had heard of this and he had asked Rome to come to his support. The stage was set for a number of highly interesting plots and counter-plots. But the Romans, with their lack of imagination, rang the curtain down before the play had been fairly started. Their legions completely defeated the heavy Greek phalanx which was still used by the Macedonians as their battle formation. That happened in the year 197 B.C. at the battle in the plains of Cynoscephalæ or "Dogs' Heads," in central Thessaly.

The Romans then marched southward to Attica and

informed the Greeks that they had come to "deliver the Hellenes from the Macedonian yoke." The Greeks, having learned nothing in their years of semi-slavery, used their new freedom in a most unfortunate way. All the little city-states once more began to quarrel with each other as they had done in the good old days. The Romans, who had little understanding and less love for these silly bickerings of a race which they rather despised, showed great forbearance. But tiring of

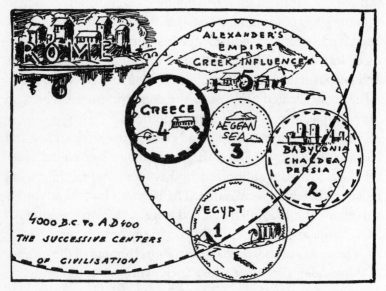

Civilisation Goes Westward

these endless dissensions, they lost patience, invaded Greece, burned down Corinth (to "encourage the other Greeks") and sent a Roman governor to Athens to rule this turbulent province. In this way, Macedonia and Greece became buffer states which protected Rome's eastern frontier.

Meanwhile right across the Hellespont lay the kingdom of Syria, and Antiochus III, who ruled that vast land, had shown great eagerness when his distinguished guest, General Hannibal, explained to him how easy it would be to invade Italy and sack the city of Rome.

Lucius Scipio, a brother of Scipio, the African fighter who had defeated Hannibal and his Carthaginians at Zama, was sent to Asia Minor. He destroyed the armies of the Syrian king near Magnesia (in the year 190 B.C.). Shortly afterwards, Antiochus was lynched by his own people. Asia Minor became a Roman protectorate and the small city-republic of Rome was mistress of most of the lands which bordered upon the Mediterranean.

24

The Roman Empire

How the Republic of Rome, After Centuries of
Unrest and Revolution, Became an Empire

When the Roman armies returned from these many victorious campaigns, they were received with great jubilation.
Alas and alack! this sudden glory did not make the country
any happier. On the contrary. The endless campaigns had
ruined the farmers who had been obliged to do the hard
work of empire-making. It had placed too much power in the
hands of the successful generals (and their private friends)
who had used the war as an excuse for wholesale robbery.

The old Roman Republic had been proud of the simplicity which had characterised the lives of her famous men.
The new republic felt ashamed of the shabby coats and the
high principles which had been fashionable in the days of its
grandfathers. It became a land of rich people ruled by rich
people for the benefit of rich people. As such it was doomed
to disastrous failure, as I shall now tell you.

Within less than a century and a half, Rome had become
the mistress of practically all the land around the Mediterranean. In those early days of history a prisoner of war lost
his freedom and became a slave. The Roman regarded war
as a very serious business and he showed no mercy to a

conquered foe. After the fall of Carthage, the Carthaginian women and children were sold into bondage together with their own slaves. And a like fate awaited the obstinate inhabitants of Greece and Macedonia and Spain and Syria when they dared to revolt against the Roman power.

Two thousand years ago a slave was merely a piece of machinery. Nowadays a rich man invests his money in factories. The rich people of Rome (senators, generals and war-profiteers) invested theirs in land and in slaves. The land they bought or took in the newly acquired provinces. The slaves they bought in open market wherever they happened to be cheapest. During most of the third and second centuries before Christ there was a plentiful supply, and as a result the landowners worked their slaves until they dropped dead in their tracks, when they bought new ones at the nearest bargain-counter of Corinthian or Carthaginian captives.

And now behold the fate of the free-born farmer!

He had done his duty toward Rome and he had fought her battles without complaint. But when he came home after ten, fifteen or twenty years, his lands were covered with weeds and his family had been ruined. But he was a strong man and willing to begin life anew. He sowed and planted and waited for the harvest. He carried his grain to the market together with his cattle and his poultry, to find that the large landowners who worked their estates with slaves could underbid him all along the line. For a couple of years he tried to hold his own. Then he gave up in despair. He left the country and he went to the nearest city. In the city he was as hungry as he had been before on the land. But he shared his misery with thousands of other disinherited beings. They crouched together in filthy hovels in the suburbs of the large cities. They were apt to get sick and die from terrible epidemics. They were all profoundly discontented. They had fought for their country and this was their reward. They

Rome

were always willing to listen to those plausible spell-binders who gather around a public grievance like so many hungry vultures, and soon they became a grave menace to the safety of the state.

But the class of the newly rich shrugged its shoulders. "We have our army and our policemen," they argued, "they will keep the mob in order." And they hid themselves behind the high walls of their pleasant villas and cultivated their gardens and read the poems of a certain Homer which a Greek slave had just translated into very pleasing Latin hexameters.

In a few families, however, the old tradition of unselfish service to the common-wealth continued. Cornelia, the daughter of Scipio Africanus, had been married to a Roman by the name of Gracchus. She had two sons, Tiberius and Gaius. When the boys grew up they entered politics and tried to bring about certain much-needed reforms. A census had shown that most of the land of the Italian peninsula was owned by two thousand noble families. Tiberius Gracchus, having been elected a tribune, tried to help the freemen. He revived two ancient laws which restricted the number of acres which a single owner might possess. In this way he hoped to revive the valuable old class of small and independent freeholders. The newly rich called him a robber and an enemy of the state. There were street riots. A party of thugs was hired to kill the popular tribune. Tiberius Gracchus was attacked when he entered the assembly and was beaten to death. Ten years later his brother Gaius tried the experiment of reforming a nation against the expressed wishes of a strong privileged class. He passed a "poor law" which was meant to help the destitute farmers. Eventually it made the greater part of the Roman citizens into professional beggars.

He established colonies of destitute people in distant parts of the empire, but these settlements failed to attract the right sort of people. Before Gaius Gracchus could do more harm he too was murdered and his followers were either killed or exiled. The first two reformers had been gentlemen. The two who came after were of a very different stamp. They were professional soldiers. One was called Marius. The name of the other was Sulla. Both enjoyed a large personal following.

Sulla was the leader of the landowners. Marius, the victor in a great battle at the foot of the Alps when the Teutons and the Cimbri had been annihilated, was the popular hero of the disinherited freemen.

Now it happened in the year 88 B.C. that the Senate of Rome was greatly disturbed by rumours that came from Asia. Mithridates, king of a country along the shores of the Black Sea, and a Greek on his mother's side, had seen the possibility of establishing a second Alexandrian Empire. He began his campaign for world-domination with the murder of all Roman citizens who happened to be in Asia Minor, men, women and children. Such an act, of course, meant war. The Senate equipped an army to march against the king of Pontus and punish him for his crime. But who was to be commander-in-chief? "Sulla," said the Senate, "because he is consul." "Marius," said the mob, "because he has been consul five times and because he is the champion of our rights."

Possession is nine points of the law. Sulla happened to be in actual command of the army. He went east to defeat Mithridates and Marius fled to Africa. There he waited until he heard that Sulla had crossed into Asia. He then returned to Italy, gathered a motley crew of malcontents, marched on Rome and entered the city with his professional highway-men, spent five days and five nights slaughtering his enemies in the senatorial party, got himself elected consul and promptly died from the excitement of the last fortnight.

There followed four years of disorder. Then Sulla, having defeated Mithridates, announced that he was ready to return to Rome and settle a few old scores of his own. He was as good as his word. For weeks his soldiers were busy executing those of their fellow-citizens who were suspected of democratic sympathies. One day they got hold of a young fellow who had been often seen in the company of Marius. They were going to hang him when some one interfered. "The boy is too young," he said, and they let him go. His name was Julius Cæsar. You shall meet him again on the next page.

As for Sulla, he became "dictator," which meant sole and supreme ruler of all the Roman possessions. He ruled Rome for four years, and he died quietly in his bed, having spent the last year of his life tenderly raising his cabbages, as was the custom of so many Romans who had spent a lifetime killing their fellow-men.

But conditions did not grow better. On the contrary, they grew worse. Another general, Gnæus Pompeius, or Pompey, a close friend of Sulla, went east to renew the war against the ever troublesome Mithridates. He drove that energetic potentate into the mountains were Mithridates took poison and killed himself, well knowing what fate awaited him as a Roman captive. Next he re-established the authority of Rome over Syria, destroyed Jerusalem, roamed through western Asia, trying to revive the myth of Alexander the Great, and at last (in the year 62) returned to Rome with a dozen ship-loads of defeated kings and princes and generals, all of whom were forced to march in the triumphal procession of this enormously popular Roman who presented his city with the sum of forty million dollars in plunder.

It was necessary that the government of Rome be placed in the hands of a strong man. Only a few months before, the town had almost fallen into the hands of a good-for-nothing young aristocrat by the name of Catiline, who had gambled away his money and hoped to reimburse himself for his losses by a little plundering. Cicero, a public-spirited lawyer, had discovered the plot, had warned the Senate and had forced Catiline to flee. But there were other young men with similar ambitions and it was no time for idle talk.

Pompey organised a triumvirate which was to take charge of affairs. He became the leader of this vigilante committee. Gaius Julius Cæsar, who had made a reputation for himself as governor of Spain, was the second in command. The third was an indifferent sort of person by the name of Crassus. He had been elected because he was incredibly rich, having been a successful contractor of war supplies. He soon went upon an expedition against the Parthians and was killed.

As for Cæsar, who was by far the ablest of the three, he decided that he needed a little more military glory to become a popular hero. He crossed the Alps and conquered that part of the world which is now called France. Then he hammered a solid wooden bridge across the Rhine and invaded the land of the wild Teutons. Finally he took ship and visited England. Heaven knows where he might have ended if he had not

Cæsar Goes West

been forced to return to Italy. Pompey, so he was informed, had been appointed dictator for life. This of course meant that Cæsar was to be placed on the list of the "retired officers," and the idea did not appeal to him. He remembered that he had begun life as a follower of Marius. He decided to teach the senators and their "dictator" another lesson. He crossed the Rubicon River which separated the province of Cis-alpine Gaul from Italy. Everywhere he was received as the "friend of the people." Without difficulty Cæsar entered Rome and Pompey fled to Greece. Cæsar followed him and defeated his followers near Pharsalus. Pompey sailed across the Mediterranean and escaped to Egypt. When he landed he was murdered by order of young King Ptolemy. A few days later Cæsar arrived. He found himself caught in a trap. Both the Egyptians and the Roman garrison, which had remained faithful to Pompey, attacked his camp.

Fortune was with Cæsar. He succeeded in setting fire to the Egyptian fleet. Incidentally the sparks of the burning vessels fell on the roof of the famous library of Alexandria (which was just off the water front) and destroyed it. Next he attacked the Egyptian army, drove the soldiers into the Nile, drowned Ptolemy and established a new government under Cleopatra, the sister of the late king. Just then word reached him that Pharnaces, the son and heir of Mithridates, had gone on the warpath. Cæsar marched northward, defeated Pharnaces in a war which lasted five days, sent word of his victory to Rome in the famous sentence "veni, vidi, vici," which is Latin for "I came, I saw, I conquered," and returned to Egypt where he fell desperately in love with Cleopatra, who followed him to Rome when he returned to take charge of the government, in the year 46. He marched at the head of not less than four different victory-parades, having won four different campaigns.

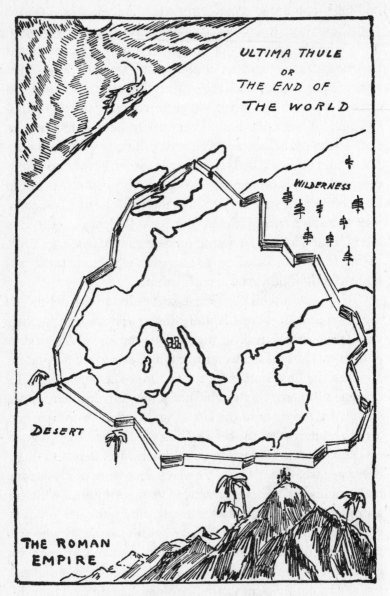

The Great Roman Empire

Then Cæsar appeared in the Senate to report upon his adventures, and the grateful Senate made him "dictator" for ten years. It was a fatal step.

The new dictator made serious attempts to reform the Roman state. He made it possible for freemen to become members of the Senate. He conferred the rights of citizenship upon distant communities as had been done in the early days of Roman history. He permitted "foreigners" to exercise influence upon the government. He reformed the administration of the distant provinces which certain aristocratic families had come to regard as their private possessions. In short he did many things for the good of the majority of the people but which made him thoroughly unpopular with the most powerful men in the state. Half a hundred young aristocrats formed a plot "to save the republic." On the Ides of March (March 15, according to that new calendar with Cæsar had brought with him from Egypt) Cæsar was murdered when he entered the Senate. Once more Rome was without a master.

There were two men who tried to continue the tradition of Cæsar's glory. One was Antony, his former secretary. The other was Octavian, Cæsar's grandnephew and heir to his estate. Octavian remained in Rome, but Antony went to Egypt to be near Cleopatra with whom he too had fallen in love, as seems to have been the habit of Roman generals.

A war broke out between the two. In the battle of Actium, Octavian defeated Antony. Antony killed himself and Cleopatra was left alone to face the enemy. She tried very hard to make Octavian her third Roman conquest. When she saw that she could make no impression upon this very proud aristocrat, she killed herself, and Egypt became a Roman province.

As for Octavian, he was a very wise young man and he did not repeat the mistake of his famous uncle. He knew how people will shy at words. He was very modest in his demands when he returned to Rome. He did not want to be a "dictator." He would be entirely satisfied with the title of "the Honourable." But when the Senate, a few years later, addressed him as Augustus—the illustrious—he did not object and a few years later the man in the street called him Cæsar, or kaiser, while the soldiers, accustomed to regard Octavian as their commander-in-chief, referred to him as the chief, the imperator or emperor. The republic had become an empire, but the average Roman was hardly aware of the fact.

In 14 A.D. his position as the absolute ruler of the Roman people had become so well established that he was made an object of that divine worship which hitherto had been reserved for the Gods. And his successors were true "emperors"—the absolute rulers of the greatest empire the world had ever seen.

If the truth be told, the average citizen was sick and tired of anarchy and disorder. He did not care who ruled him provided the new master gave him a chance to live quietly and without the noise of eternal street riots. Octavian assured his subjects forty years of peace. He had no desire to extend the frontiers of his domains. In the year 9 A.D. he had contemplated an invasion of the northwestern wilderness which was inhabited by the Teutons. But Varus, his general, had been killed with all his men in the Teutoburg Woods, and after that the Romans made no further attempts to civilise these wild people.

They concentrated their efforts upon the gigantic problem of internal reform. But it was too late to do much good. Two centuries of revolution and foreign war had repeatedly killed the best men among the younger generations. It had ruined the class of the free farmers. It had introduced slave labor, against which no freeman could hope to compete. It had turned the cities into beehives inhabited by pauperized and

unhealthy mobs of runaway peasants. It had created a large
bureaucracy—petty officials who were underpaid and who
were forced to take graft in order to buy bread and clothing
for their families. Worst of all, it had accustomed people to
violence, to blood shed, to a barbarous pleasure in the pain
and suffering of others.

Outwardly, the Roman state during the first century of
our era was a magnificent political structure, so large that
Alexander's empire became one of its minor provinces.
Underneath this glory there lived millions upon millions of
poor and tired human beings, toiling like ants who have built
a nest underneath a heavy stone. They worked for the benefit
of some one else. They shared their food with the animals of
the fields. They lived in stables. They died without hope.

It was the 753rd year since the founding of Rome. Gaius
Julius Cæsar Octavianus Augustus was living in the palace
of the Palatine Hill, busily engaged upon the task of ruling
his empire.

In a little village of distant Syria, Mary, the wife of Joseph
the carpenter, was tending her little boy, born in a stable of
Bethlehem.

This is a strange world.

Before long, the palace and the stable were to meet in
open combat.

And the stable was to emerge victorious.

25

Joshua of Nazareth

|||||||||||||||||||||||||||||||||||||||||||||||||||||||||||||||||||||||||||||||||||||||||||||||||||||||||||||||||||||||||||||||||||||||||||||

The Story of Joshua of Nazareth, Whom
the Greeks Called Jesus

In the autumn of the year of the city 815 (which would be
62 A.D., in our way of counting time) Æsculapius Cultellus,
a Roman physician, wrote to his nephew who was with the
army in Syria as follows:

My dear Nephew,
A few days ago I was called in to prescribe for a sick
man named Paul. He appeared to be a Roman citizen
of Jewish parentage, well educated and of agreeable
manners. I had been told that he was here in connection with a law-suit, an appeal from one of our provin-
cial courts, Cæsarea or some such place in the eastern
Mediterranean. He had been described to me as a "wild
and violent" fellow who had been making speeches
against the people and against the law. I found him
very intelligent and of great honesty.

A friend of mine who used to be with the army in
Asia Minor tells me that he heard something about him
in Ephesus where he was preaching sermons about a
strange new god. I asked my patient if this were true

and whether he had told the people to rebel against the will of our beloved emperor. Paul answered me that the kingdom of which he had spoken was not of this world and he added many strange utterances which I did not understand, but which were probably due to his fever.

His personality made a great impression upon me and I was sorry to hear that he was killed on the Ostian Road a few days ago. Therefore I am writing this letter to you. When next you visit Jerusalem, I want you to find out something about my friend Paul and the strange Jewish prophet, who seems to have been his teacher. Our slaves are getting much excited about this so-called Messiah, and a few of them, who openly talked of the new kingdom (whatever that means) have been crucified. I would like to know the truth about all these rumours and I am

Your devoted Uncle,
ÆSCULPAIUS CULTELLUS.

Six weeks later, Gladius Ensa, the nephew, a captain of the VII Gallic Infantry, answered as follows:

My dear Uncle,

I received your letter and I have obeyed your instructions.

Two weeks ago our brigade was sent to Jerusalem. There have been several revolutions during the last century and there is not much left of the old city. We have been here now for a month and to-morrow we shall continue our march to Petra, where there has been trouble with some of the Arab tribes. I shall use this evening to answer your questions, but pray do not expect a detailed report.

I have talked with most of the older men in this city but few have been able to give me any definite information. A few days ago a pedlar came to the camp. I bought some of his olives and I asked him whether he had ever heard of the famous Messiah who was killed when he was young. He said that he remembered it very clearly, because his father had taken him to Golgotha (a hill just outside the city) to see the execution, and to show him what became of the enemies of the laws of the people of Judæa. He gave me the address of one Joseph, who had been a personal friend of the

The Holy Land

Messiah and told me that I had better go and see him if I wanted to know more.

This morning I went to call on Joseph. He was quite an old man. He had been a fisherman on one of the fresh-water lakes. His memory was clear, and from him at last I got a fairly definite account of what had happened during the troublesome days before I was born.

Tiberius, our great and glorious emperor, was on the throne, and an officer of the name of Pontius Pilatus was governor of Judæa and Samaria. Joseph knew little about this Pilatus. He seemed to have been an honest enough official who left a decent reputation as procurator of the province. In the year 783 or 784 (Joseph had forgotten when) Pilatus was called to Jerusalem on account of a riot. A certain young man (the son of a carpenter of Nazareth) was said to be planning a revolution against the Roman government. Strangely enough our own intelligence officers, who are usually well informed, appear to have heard nothing about it, and when they investigated the matter they reported that the carpenter was an excellent citizen and that there was no reason to proceed against him. But the old-fashioned leaders of the Jewish faith, according to Joseph, were much upset. They greatly disliked his popularity with the masses of the poorer Hebrews. The "Nazarene" (so they told Pilatus) had publicly claimed that a Greek or a Roman or even a Philistine, who tried to live a decent and honourable life, was quite as good as a Jew who spent his days studying the ancient laws of Moses. Pilatus does not seem to have been impressed by this argument, but when the crowds around the temple threatened to lynch Jesus, and kill all his followers, he decided to take the carpenter into custody to save his life.

He does not appear to have understood the real nature of the quarrel. Whenever he asked the Jewish priests to explain their grievances, they shouted "heresy" and "treason" and got terribly excited. Finally, so Joseph told me, Pilatus sent for Joshua (that was the name of the Nazarene, but the Greeks who live in this part of the world always refer to him as Jesus) to examine him personally. He talked to him for several hours. He asked him about the "dangerous doctrines" which he was said to have preached on the shores of the sea of Galilee. But Jesus answered that he never referred to politics. He was not so much interested in the bodies of men as in man's soul. He wanted all people to regard their neighbours as their brothers and to love one single god, who was the father of all living beings.

Pilatus, who seems to have been well versed in the doctrines of the Stoics and the other Greek philosophers, does not appear to have discovered anything seditious in the talk of Jesus. According to my informant he made another attempt to save the life of the kindly prophet. He kept putting the execution off. Meanwhile the Jewish people, lashed into fury by their priests, got frantic with rage. There had been many riots in Jerusalem before this and there were only a few Roman soldiers within calling distance. Reports were being sent to the Roman authorities in Cæsarea that Pilatus had "fallen a victim to the teachings of the Nazarene." Petitions were being circulated all through the city to have Pilatus recalled, because he was an enemy of the emperor. You know that our governors have strict instructions to avoid an open break with their foreign subjects. To save the country from civil war, Pilatus finally sacrificed his prisoner, Joshua, who behaved with great dignity and who forgave all those who hated him. He was crucified amidst the howls and the laughter of the Jerusalem mob.

That is what Joseph told me, with tears running

down his old cheeks. I gave him a gold piece when I left him, but he refused it and asked me to hand it to one poorer than himself. I also asked him a few questions about your friend Paul. He had known him slightly. He seems to have been a tent maker who gave up his profession that he might preach the words of a loving and forgiving god, who was so very different from that Jehovah of whom the Jewish priests are telling us all the time. Afterwards, Paul appears to have travelled much in Asia Minor and in Greece, telling the slaves that they were all children of one loving father and that happiness awaits all, both rich and poor, who have tried to live honest lives and have done good to those who were suffering and miserable.

I hope that I have answered your questions to your satisfaction. The whole story seems very harmless to me as far as the safety of the state is concerned. But then, we Romans never have been able to understand the people of this province. I am sorry that they have killed your friend Paul. I wish that I were at home again, and I am, as ever,

Your dutiful nephew,
GLADIUS ENSA.

26

The Fall of Rome

The Twilight of Rome

The text-books of ancient history give the date 476 as the year in which Rome fell, because in that year the last emperor was driven off his throne. But Rome, which was not built in a day, took a long time falling. The process was so slow and so gradual that most Romans did not realise how their old world was coming to an end. They complained about the unrest of the times—they grumbled about the high prices of food and about the low wages of the workmen—they cursed the profiteers who had a monopoly of the grain and the wool and the gold coin. Occasionally they rebelled against an unusually rapacious governor. But the majority of the people during the first four centuries of our era ate and drank (whatever their purse allowed them to buy) and hated or loved (according to their nature) and went to the theatre (whenever there was a free show of fighting gladiators) or starved in the slums of the big cities, utterly ignorant of the fact that their empire had outlived its usefulness and was doomed to perish.

How could they realise the threatened danger? Rome made a fine showing of outward glory. Well-paved roads connected the different provinces, the imperial police were active and showed little tenderness for highwaymen. The frontier was closely guarded against the savage tribes who seemed to be occupying the waste lands of northern Europe. The whole world was paying tribute to the mighty city of Rome, and a score of able men were working day and night to undo the mistakes of the past and bring about a return to the happier conditions of the early republic.

But the underlying causes of the decay of the state, of which I have told you in a former chapter, had not been removed and reform therefore was impossible.

Rome was, first and last and all the time, a city-state as Athens and Corinth had been city-states in ancient Hellas. It had been able to dominate the Italian peninsula. But Rome as the ruler of the entire civilised world was a political impossibility and could not endure. Her young men were killed in her endless wars. Her farmers were ruined by long military service and by taxation. They either became professional beggars or hired themselves out to rich landowners who gave them board and lodging in exchange for their services and made them "serfs," those unfortunate human beings who are neither slaves nor freemen, but who have become part of the soil upon which they work, like so many cows, and the trees.

The empire, the state, had become everything. The common citizen had dwindled down to less than nothing. As for the slaves, they had heard the words that were spoken by Paul. They had accepted the message of the humble carpenter of Nazareth. They did not rebel against their masters. On the contrary, they had been taught to be meek and they obeyed their superiors. But they had lost all interest in the affairs of this world which had proved such a miserable place of abode. They were willing to fight the good fight that they might enter into the Kingdom of Heaven. But they were not willing to engage in warfare for the benefit of an ambitious emperor who aspired to glory by way of a foreign campaign in the land of the Parthians or the Numidians or the Scots.

And so conditions grew worse as the centuries went by. The first emperors had continued the tradition of "leadership" which had given the old tribal chieftains such a hold upon their subjects. But the emperors of the second and third centuries were barrack-emperors, professional soldiers, who existed by the grace of their body-guards, the so-called Prætorians. They succeeded each other with terrifying rapidity, murdering their way into the palace and being murdered out of it as soon as their successors had become rich enough to bribe the guards into a new rebellion.

Meanwhile the barbarians were hammering at the gates of the northern frontier. As there were no longer any native Roman armies to stop their progress, foreign mercenaries had to be hired to fight the invader. As the foreign soldier happened to be of the same blood as his supposed enemy, he was apt to be quite lenient when he engaged in battle.

When the Barbarians Got Through with a Roman City

Finally, by way of experiment, a few tribes were allowed to settle within the confines of the empire. Others followed. Soon these tribes complained bitterly of the greedy Roman tax-gatherers, who took away their last penny. When they got no redress they marched to Rome and loudly demanded that they be heard.

This made Rome very uncomfortable as an imperial residence. Constantine (who ruled from 323 to 337) looked for a new capital. He chose Byzantium, the gateway for the commerce between Europe and Asia. The city was renamed Constantinople, and the court moved eastward. When Constantine died, his two sons, for the sake of a more efficient administration, divided the empire between them. The elder lived in Rome and ruled in the west. The younger stayed in Constantinople and was master of the east.

Then came the fourth century and the terrible visitation of the Huns, those mysterious Asiatic horsemen who for more than two centuries maintained themselves in northern Europe and continued their career of bloodshed until they were defeated near Chalons-sur-Marne in France in the year 451. As soon as the Huns had reached the Danube they had begun to press hard upon the Goths. The Goths, in order to save themselves, were thereupon obliged to invade Rome. The emperor Valens tried to stop them, but was killed near Adrianople in the year 378. Twenty-two years later, under their king, Alaric, these same West Goths marched westward and attacked Rome. They did not plunder, and destroyed only a few palaces. Next came the Vandals, and showed less respect for the venerable traditions of the city. Then the Burgundians. Then the East Goths. Then the Alemanni. Then the Franks. There was no end to the invasions. Rome at last was at the mercy of every ambitious highway robber who could gather a few followers.

In the year 402 the emperor fled to Ravenna, which was a sea-port and strongly fortified, and there, in the year 475, Odoacer, commander of a regiment of the German mercenaries, who wanted the farms of Italy to be divided among themselves, gently but effectively pushed Romulus Augustulus, the last of the emperors who ruled the western division, from his throne, and proclaimed himself patrician or ruler of Rome. The eastern emperor, who was very busy with his own affairs, recognised him, and for ten years Odoacer ruled what was left of the western provinces.

A few years later, Theodoric, king of the East Goths, invaded the newly formed patriciate, took Ravenna, murdered Odoacer at his own dinner table and established a Gothic kingdom amidst the ruins of the western part of the empire. This patriciate state did not last long. In the sixth century a motley crowd of Longobards and Saxons and Slavs and Avars invaded Italy, destroyed the Gothic kingdom, and established a new state of which Pavia became the capital.

Then at last the imperial city sank into a state of utter neglect and despair. The ancient palaces had been plundered time and again. The schools had been burned down. The teachers had been starved to death. The rich people had been thrown out of their villas which were now inhabited by evil-smelling and hairy barbarians. The roads had fallen into decay. The old bridges were gone and commerce had come to a standstill. Civilisation, the product of thousands of years of patient labour on the part of Egyptians and Babylonians and Greeks and Romans, which had lifted man high above the most daring dreams of his earliest ancestors, threatened to perish from the western continent.

It is true that in the far east, Constantinople continued to be the centre of an empire for another thousand years. But it hardly counted as a part of the European continent. Its interests lay in the east. It began to forget its western origin. Gradually the Roman language was given up for the Greek. The Roman alphabet was discarded and Roman law was written in Greek characters and explained by Greek judges. The emperor became an Asiatic despot, worshipped as the god-like kings of Thebes had been worshipped in the valley

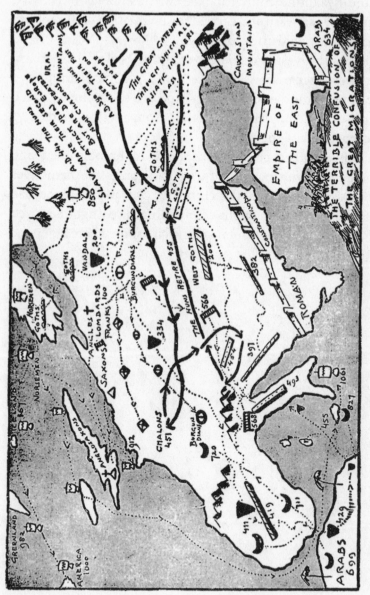

The Invasions of the Barbarians

of the Nile, three thousand years before. When missionaries of the Byzantine church looked for fresh fields of activity, they went eastward and carried the civilisation of Byzantium into the vast wilderness of Russia.

As for the west, it was left to the mercies of the barbarians. For twelve generations, murder, war, arson, plundering were the order of the day. One thing—and one thing alone—saved Europe from complete destruction, from a return to the days of cave-men and the hyena.

This was the church—the flock of humble men and women who for many centuries had confessed themselves the followers of Jesus, the carpenter of Nazareth, who had been killed that the mighty Roman Empire might be saved the trouble of a street-riot in a little city somewhere along the Syrian frontier.

27

Rise of the Church

How Rome Became the Centre of the
Christian World

The average intelligent Roman who lived under the empire had taken very little interest in the gods of his fathers. A few times a year he went to the temple, but merely as a matter of custom. He looked on patiently when the people celebrated a religious festival with a solemn procession. But he regarded the worship of Jupiter and Minerva and Neptune as something rather childish, a survival from the crude days of the early republic and not a fit subject of study for a man who had mastered the works of the Stoics and the Epicureans and the other great philosophers of Athens.

This attitude made the Roman a very tolerant man. The government insisted that all people, Romans, foreigners, Greeks, Babylonians, Jews, should pay a certain outward respect to the image of the emperor which was supposed to stand in every temple, just as a picture of the president of the United States is apt to hang in an American post office. But this was a formality without any deeper meaning. Generally speaking everybody could honour, revere and adore whatever gods he pleased, and as a result, Rome was filled with all sorts of queer little temples and synagogues, dedicated to the worship of Egyptian and African and Asiatic divinities.

When the first disciples of Jesus reached Rome and began to preach their new doctrine of a universal brotherhood of man, nobody objected. The man in the street stopped and listened. Rome, the capital of the world, had always been full of wandering preachers, each proclaiming his own "mystery." Most of the self-appointed priests appealed to the senses— promised golden rewards and endless pleasure to the followers of their own particular god. Soon the crowd in the street noticed that the so-called Christians (the followers of the Christ or "anointed") spoke a very different language. They did not appear to be impressed by great riches or a noble position. They extolled the beauties of poverty and humility and meekness. These were not exactly the virtues which had made Rome the mistress of the world. It was rather interesting to listen to a "mystery" which told people in the hey-day of their glory that their worldly success could not possibly bring them lasting happiness.

Besides, the preachers of the Christian mystery told dreadful stories of the fate that awaited those who refused to listen to the words of the true God. It was never wise to take chances. Of course the old Roman gods still existed, but were they strong enough to protect their friends against the powers of this new deity who had been brought to Europe from distant Asia? People began to have doubts. They returned to listen to further explanations of the new creed. After a while they began to meet the men and women who preached the words of Jesus. They found them very different from the average Roman priests. They were all dreadfully poor. They were kind to slaves and to animals. They did not try to gain riches, but gave away whatever they had. The example of their unselfish lives forced many Romans to forsake the old religion. They joined the small communities of Christians who met in the back rooms of private houses or somewhere in an open field, and the temples were deserted.

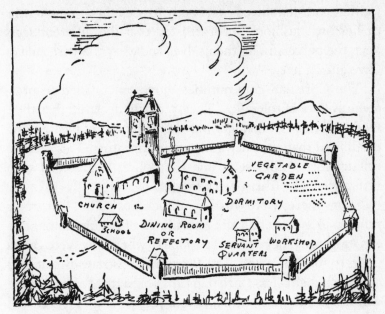

A Cloister

This went on year after year and the number of Christians continued to increase. Presbyters or priests (the original Greek meant "elder") were elected to guard the interests of the small churches. A bishop was made the head of all the communities within a single province. Peter, who had followed Paul to Rome, was the first bishop of Rome. In due time his successors (who were addressed as Father or Papa) came to be known as Popes.

The church became a powerful institution within the empire. The Christian doctrines appealed to those who despaired of this world. They also attracted many strong men who found it impossible to make a career under the imperial government, but who could exercise their gifts of leadership among the humble followers of the Nazarene teacher. At last the state was obliged to take notice. The Roman Empire (I have said this before) was tolerant through indifference. It allowed everybody to seek salvation after his or her own fashion. But it insisted that the different sects keep the peace among themselves and obey the wise rule of "live and let live."

The Christian communities, however, refused to prac- tise any sort of tolerance. They publicly declared that their God, and their God alone, was the true ruler of Heaven and earth, and that all other gods were impostors. This seemed unfair to the other sects and the police discouraged such utterances. The Christians persisted.

Soon there were further difficulties. The Christians refused to go through the formalities of paying homage to the emperor. They refused to appear when they were called upon to join the army. The Roman magistrates threatened to punish them. The Christians answered that this miserable world was only the ante-room to a very pleasant Heaven and that they were more than willing to suffer death for their principles. The Romans, puzzled by such conduct, sometimes killed the offenders, but more often they did not. There was a certain amount of lynching during the earliest years of the

The Goths Are Coming!

church, but this was the work of that part of the mob which accused their meek Christian neighbours of every conceivable crime (such as slaughtering and eating babies, bringing about sickness and pestilence, betraying the country in times of danger) because it was a harmless sport and devoid of danger, as the Christians refused to fight back.

Meanwhile Rome continued to be invaded by the barbarians and when her armies failed, Christian missionaries went forth to preach their gospel of peace to the wild Teutons. They were strong men without fear of death. They spoke a language which left no doubt as to the future of unrepentant sinners. The Teutons were deeply impressed. They still had a deep respect for the wisdom of the ancient city of Rome. Those men were Romans. They probably spoke the truth. Soon the Christian missionary became a power in the savage regions of the Teutons and the Franks. Half a dozen missionaries were as valuable as a whole regiment of soldiers. The emperors began to understand that the Christian might be of great use to them. In some of the provinces they were given equal rights with those who remained faithful to the old gods. The great change, however, came during the last half of the fourth century.

Constantine, sometimes (Heaven knows why) called Constantine the Great, was emperor. He was a terrible ruffian, but people of tender qualities could hardly hope to survive in that hard-fighting age. During a long and checkered career, Constantine had experienced many ups and downs. Once, when almost defeated by his enemies, he thought that he would try the power of this new Asiatic deity of whom everybody was talking. He promised that he too would become a Christian if he were successful in the coming battle. He won the victory and thereafter he was convinced of the power of the Christian God and allowed himself to be baptised.

From that moment on, the Christian church was officially

recognised and this greatly strengthened the position of the new faith.

But the Christians still formed a very small minority of all the people (not more than five or six percent) and in order to win, they were forced to refuse all compromise. The old gods must be destroyed. For a short spell the emperor Julian, a lover of Greek wisdom, managed to save the pagan gods from further destruction. But Julian died of his wounds during a campaign in Persia and his successor Jovian re-established the church in all its glory. One after the other the doors of the ancient temples were then closed. Then came the emperor Justinian (who built the church of St. Sophia in Constantinople), who discontinued the school of philosophy at Athens which had been founded by Plato.

That was the end of the old Greek world, in which man had been allowed to think his own thoughts and dream his own dreams according to his desires. The somewhat vague rules of conduct of the philosophers had proved a poor compass by which to steer the ship of life after a deluge of savagery and ignorance had swept away the established order of things. There was need of something more positive and more definite. This the church provided.

During an age when nothing was certain, the church stood like a rock and never receded from those principles which it held to be true and sacred. This steadfast courage gained the admiration of the multitudes and carried the church of Rome safely through the difficulties which destroyed the Roman state.

There was, however, a certain element of luck in the final success of the Christian faith. After the disappearance of Theodoric's Roman-Gothic kingdom, in the fifth century, Italy was comparatively free from foreign invasion. The Lombards and Saxons and Slavs who succeeded the Goths were weak and backward tribes. Under those circumstances it was possible for the bishops of Rome to maintain the independence of their city. Soon the remnants of the empire, scattered throughout the peninsula, recognised the dukes of Rome (or bishops) as their political and spiritual rulers.

The stage was set for the appearance of a strong man. He came in the year 590 and his name was Gregory. He belonged to the ruling classes of ancient Rome, and he had been "prefect" or mayor of the city. Then he had become a monk and a bishop and finally, and much against his will, (for he wanted to be a missionary and preach Christianity to the heathen of England), he had been dragged to the church of St. Peter to be made Pope. He ruled only fourteen years but when he died the Christian world of western Europe had officially recognised the bishops of Rome, the Popes, as the head of the entire church.

This power, however, did not extend to the east. In Constantinople the emperors continued the old custom which had recognised the successors of Augustus and Tiberius both as head of the government and as high priest of the established religion. In the year 1453 the eastern Roman Empire was conquered by the Turks. Constantinople was taken, and Constantine Paleologue, the last Roman emperor, was killed on the steps of the church of the Holy Sophia.

A few years before, Zoë, the daughter of his brother Thomas, had married Ivan III of Russia. In this way did the grand dukes of Moscow fall heir to the traditions of Constantinople. The double eagle of old Byzantium (reminiscent of the days when Rome had been divided into an eastern and a western part) became the coat of arms of modern Russia. The tsar, who had been merely the first of the Russian nobles, assumed the aloofness and the dignity of a Roman emperor before whom all subjects, both high and low, were inconsiderable slaves.

The court was refashioned after the oriental pattern

which the eastern emperors had imported from Asia and
from Egypt and which (so they flattered themselves) resembled the court of Alexander the Great. This strange inheritance which the dying Byzantine Empire bequeathed to an
unsuspecting world continued to live with great vigour for
six more centuries, amidst the vast plains of Russia. The last
man to wear the crown with the double eagle of Constantinople, Tsar Nicholas, was murdered only the other day,
so to speak. His body was thrown into a well. His son and
his daughters were all killed. All his ancient rights and prerogatives were abolished, and the church was reduced to
the position which it had held in Rome before the days of
Constantine.

The western church, however, fared very differently, as
we shall see in the next chapter when the whole Christian
world is going to be threatened with destruction by the rival
creed of an Arab camel-driver.

28

Mohammed

Ahmed, the Camel-Driver, Who Became
the Prophet of the Arabian Desert, and Whose
Followers Almost Conquered the Entire
Known World for the Greater Glory of Allah,
the Only True God

Since the days of Carthage and Hannibal we have said nothing of the Semitic people. You will remember how they filled all the chapters devoted to the story of the ancient world. The Babylonians, the Assyrians, the Phœnicians, the Jews, the Arameans, the Chaldeans, all of them Semites, had been the rulers of western Asia for thirty or forty centuries. They had been conquered by the Indo-European Persians who had come from the east and by the Indo-European Greeks who had come from the west. A hundred years after the death of Alexander the Great, Carthage, a colony of Semitic Phœnicians, had fought the Indo-European Romans for the mastery of the Mediterranean. Carthage had been defeated and destroyed and for eight hundred years the Romans had been masters of the world. In the seventh century, however, another Semitic tribe appeared upon the scene and challenged the power of the west. They were the

Arabs, peaceful shepherds who had roamed through the desert since the beginning of time without showing any signs of imperial ambitions.

Then they listened to Mohammed, mounted their horses and in less than a century they had pushed to the heart of Europe and proclaimed the glories of Allah, "the only God," and Mohammed, "the prophet of the only God," to the frightened peasants of France.

The story of Ahmed, the son of Abdallah and Aminah (usually known as Mohammed, or "he who will be praised"), reads like a chapter in the "Thousand and One Nights." He was a camel-driver, born in Mecca. He seems to have been an epileptic and he suffered from spells of unconsciousness when he dreamed strange dreams and heard the voice of the angel Gabriel, whose words were afterwards written down in a book called the Koran. His work as a caravan leader carried him all over Arabia and he was constantly falling in with Jewish merchants and with Christian traders, and he came to see that the worship of a single god was a very excellent thing. His own people, the Arabs, still revered queer stones and trunks of trees as their ancestors had done, tens of thousands of years before. In Mecca, their holy city, stood a little square building, the Kaaba, full of idols and strange odds and ends of hoo-doo worship.

Mohammed decided to be the Moses of the Arab people. He could not well be a prophet and a camel-driver at the same time. So he made himself independent by marrying his employer, the rich widow Chadija. Then he told his neighbours in Mecca that he was the long-expected prophet sent by Allah to save the world. The neighbours laughed most heartily and when Mohammed continued to annoy them with his speeches they decided to kill him. They regarded him as a lunatic and a public bore who deserved no mercy. Mohammed heard of the plot and in the dark of night he fled

The Flight of Mohammed

to Medina together with Abu Bekr, his trusted pupil. This happened in the year 622. It is the most important date in Mohammedan history and is known as the Hegira—the year of the great flight.

In Medina, Mohammed, who was a stranger, found it easier to proclaim himself a prophet than in his home city, where every one had known him as a simple camel-driver. Soon he was surrounded by an increasing number of followers, or Moslems, who accepted the Islam, "the submission to the will of God," which Mohammed praised as the highest of all virtues. For seven years he preached to the people of Medina. Then he believed himself strong enough to begin a campaign against his former neighbours who had dared to sneer at him and his holy mission in his old camel-driving days. At the head of an army of Medinese he marched across the desert. His followers took Mecca without great difficulty, finding it easy to convince the others that Mohammed was really a great prophet.

From that time on until the year of his death, Mohammed was fortunate in everything he undertook.

There are two reasons for the success of Islam. In the first place, the creed which Mohammed taught to his followers was very simple. The disciples were told that they must love

Allah, the Ruler of the World, the Merciful and Compassion-
ate. They must honour and obey their parents. They were
warned against dishonesty in dealing with their neighbours
and were admonished to be humble and charitable, to the
poor and to the sick. Finally they were ordered to abstain
from strong drink and to be very frugal in what they ate.
That was all. There were no priests, who acted as shepherds
of their flocks and asked that they be supported at the common expense. The Mohammedan churches or mosques
were merely large stone halls without benches or pictures,
where the faithful could gather (if they felt so inclined) to
read and discuss chapters from the Koran, the Holy Book.
But the average Mohammedan carried his religion with him
and never felt himself hemmed in by the restrictions and regulations of an established church. Five times a day he turned
his face towards Mecca, the Holy City, and said a simple
prayer. For the rest of the time he let Allah rule the world
as he saw fit and accepted whatever fate brought him with
patient resignation.

Such an attitude toward life gave every Mohammedan a
certain amount of contentment. It bade him be at peace with
himself and with the world in which he lived and that was a
very good thing.

The second reason which explains the success of the Moslems in their warfare upon the Christians had to do with the
conduct of those Mohammedan soldiers who went forth to
do battle for the true faith. The prophet promised that those
who fell, facing the enemy, would go directly to Heaven.
This made sudden death in the field preferable to a long but
dreary existence upon this earth. It gave the Mohammedans an enormous advantage over the Crusaders who were in
constant dread of a dark hereafter, and who stuck to the good
things of this world as long as they possibly could. Incidentally it explains why even to-day Moslem soldiers will charge

into the fire of European machine guns quite indifferent to the fate that awaits them and why they are such dangerous and persistent enemies.

Having put his religious house in order, Mohammed now began to enjoy his power as the undisputed ruler of a large number of Arab tribes. But success has been the undoing of a large number of men who were great in the days of adversity. He tried to gain the good will of the rich people by a number of regulations which could appeal to those of wealth. He allowed the faithful to have four wives. As one wife was a costly investment in those olden days when brides were bought directly from the parents, four wives became a positive luxury except to those who possessed camels and dromedaries and date orchards beyond the dreams of avarice. A religion which at first had been meant for the hardy hunters of the high-skied desert was gradually transformed to suit the needs of the merchants who lived in the bazaars of the cities. It was a regrettable change from the original program and it did very little good to the cause of Mohammedanism. As for the prophet himself, he went on preaching the truth of Allah and proclaiming new rules of conduct until he died, quite suddenly, of a fever on June 7 of the year 632.

His successor as caliph (or leader) of the Moslems was his father-in-law, Abu Bekr, who had shared the early dangers of the prophet's life. Two years later, Abu Bekr died and Omar ibn Al-Khattab followed him. In less than ten years he conquered Egypt, Persia, Phœnicia, Syria and Palestine and made Damascus the capital of the first Mohammedan world empire.

Omar was succeeded by Ali, the husband of Mohammed's daughter, Fatima, but a quarrel broke out upon a point of Moslem doctrine and Ali was murdered. After his death, the caliphate was made hereditary and the leaders of the faithful who had begun their career as the spiritual head of a religious sect became the rulers of a vast empire. They built a new city on the shores of the Euphrates, near the ruins of Babylon and called it Bagdad, and organising the Arab horsemen into regiments of cavalry, they set forth to bring the happiness of their Moslem faith to all unbelievers. In the year 700 A.D. a Mohammedan general by the name of Tarik crossed the old Gates of Hercules and reached the high rock on the European side which he called the Gibel-al-tarik, the Hill of Tarik or Gibraltar.

Eleven years later in the battle of Xeres de la Frontera, he defeated the king of the Visigoths and then the Moslem army moved northward and following the route of Hannibal, they crossed the passes of the Pyrenees. They defeated the duke of Aquitania, who tried to halt them near Bordeaux, and marched upon Paris. But in the year 732 (one hundred years after the death of the prophet) they were beaten

The Struggle Between the Cross and the Crescent

in a battle between Tours and Poitiers. On that day, Charles Martel (Charles the Hammer), the Frankish chieftain, saved Europe from a Mohammedan conquest. He drove the Moslems out of France, but they maintained themselves in Spain where Abd-ar-Rahman founded the caliphate of Cordova, which became the greatest centre of science and art of mediæval Europe.

This Moorish kingdom, so-called because the people came from Mauretania in Morocco, lasted seven centuries. It was only after the capture of Granada, the last Moslem stronghold, in the year 1492, that Columbus received the royal grant which allowed him to go upon a voyage of discovery. The Mohammedans soon regained their strength in the new conquests which they made in Asia and Africa and to-day there are as many followers of Mohammed as there are of Christ.

29

Charlemagne

How Charlemagne, the King of the Franks,
Came to Bear the Title of Emperor and
Tried to Revive the Old Ideal of World Empire

The battle of Poitiers had saved Europe from the Mohammedans. But the enemy within—the hopeless disorder which
had followed the disappearance of the Roman police officer—
that enemy remained. It is true that the new converts of the
Christian faith in Northern Europe felt a deep respect for
the mighty bishop of Rome. But that poor bishop did not
feel any too safe when he looked toward the distant mountains. Heaven knew what fresh hordes of barbarians were
ready to cross the Alps and begin a new attack on Rome.
It was necessary—very necessary—for the spiritual head of
the world to find an ally with a strong sword and a powerful
fist who was willing to defend His Holiness in case of danger.

And so the Popes, who were not only very holy but also
very practical, cast about for a friend, and presently they
made overtures to the most promising of the Germanic
tribes who had occupied north-western Europe after the fall
of Rome. They were called the Franks. One of their earliest kings, called Merovech, had helped the Romans in the
battle of the Catalaunian fields in the year 451 when they

defeated the Huns. His descendants, the Merovingians, had
continued to take little bits of imperial territory until the
year 486 when King Clovis (the old French word for "Louis")
felt himself strong enough to beat the Romans in the open.
But his descendants were weak men who left the affairs of
state to their prime minister, the "major domus" or master
of the palace.

Pepin the Short, the son of the famous Charles Martel,
who succeeded his father as master of the palace, hardly
knew how to handle the situation. His royal master was a
devout theologian, without any interest in politics. Pepin
asked the Pope for advice. The Pope who was a practical person answered that the "power in the state belonged to him
who was actually possessed of it." Pepin took the hint. He
persuaded Childeric, the last of the Merovingians to become
a monk and then made himself king with the approval of
the other Germanic chieftains. But this did not satisfy the
shrewd Pepin. He wanted to be something more than a barbarian chieftain. He staged an elaborate ceremony at which
Boniface, the great missionary of the European north-west,
anointed him and made him a "king by the grace of God." It
was easy to slip those words, "Dei gratia," into the coronation service. It took almost fifteen hundred years to get them
out again.

Pepin was sincerely grateful for this kindness on the part
of the church. He made two expeditions to Italy to defend
the Pope against his enemies. He took Ravenna and several
other cities away from the Longobards and presented them
to His Holiness, who incorporated these new domains into
the so-called Papal State, which remained an independent
country until half a century ago.

After Pepin's death, the relations between Rome and Aix-
la-Chapelle or Nymwegen or Ingelheim (the Frankish kings
did not have one official residence, but traveled from place

to place with all their ministers and court officers) became more and more cordial. Finally the Pope and the king took a step which was to influence the history of Europe in a most profound way.

Charles, commonly known as Carolus Magnus or Charlemagne, succeeded Pepin in the year 768. He had conquered the land of the Saxons in eastern Germany and had built towns and monasteries all over the greater part of northern Europe. At the request of certain enemies of Abd-ar-Rahman, he had invaded Spain to fight the Moors. But in the Pyrenees he had been attacked by the wild Basques and had been forced to retire. It was upon this occasion that Roland, the great margrave of Brittany, showed what a Frankish chieftain of those early days meant when he promised to be faithful to his king, and gave his life and that of his trusted followers to safeguard the retreat of the royal army.

During the last ten years of the eighth century, however, Charles was obliged to devote himself exclusively to affairs of the south. The Pope, Leo III, had been attacked by a band of Roman rowdies and had been left for dead in the street. Some kind people had bandaged his wounds and had helped him to escape to the camp of Charles, where he asked for help. An army of Franks soon restored quiet and carried Leo back to the Lateran Palace which ever since the days of Constantine had been the home of the Pope. That was in December of the year 799. On Christmas day of the next year, Charlemagne, who was staying in Rome, attended the service in the ancient church of St. Peter. When he arose from prayer, the Pope placed a crown upon his head, called him emperor of the Romans and hailed him once more with the title of "Augustus" which had not been heard for hundreds of years.

Once more northern Europe was part of a Roman Empire, but the dignity was held by a German chieftain who could read just a little and never learned to write. But he could

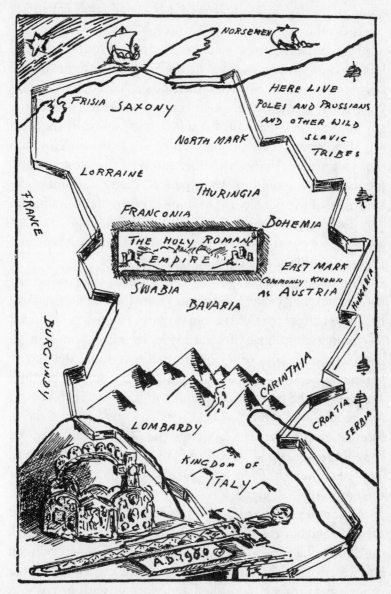

The Holy Roman Empire of German Nationality

fight and for a short while there was order and even the rival emperor in Constantinople sent a letter of approval to his "dear Brother."

Unfortunately this splendid old man died in the year 814. His sons and his grandsons at once began to fight for the largest share of the imperial inheritance. Twice the Carolingian lands were divided, by the treaties of Verdun in the year 843 and by the treaty of Mersen-on-the-Meuse in the year 870. The latter treaty divided the entire Frankish kingdom into two parts. Charles the Bold received the western half. It contained the old Roman province called Gaul where the language of the people had become thoroughly Romanized. The Franks soon learned to speak this language and this accounts for the strange fact that a purely Germanic land like France should speak a Latin tongue.

The other grandson got the eastern part, the land which the Romans had called Germania. Those inhospitable regions had never been part of the old empire. Augustus had tried to conquer this "far east," but his legions had been annihilated in the Teutoburg Woods in the year 9 and the people had never been influenced by the higher Roman civilisation. They spoke the popular Germanic tongue. The Teuton word for people was "thiot." The Christian missionaries therefore called the German language the "lingua theotisca" or the "lingua teutisca," the "popular dialect," and this word "teutisca" was changed into "Deutsch" which accounts for the name "Deutschland."

As for the famous imperial crown, it very soon slipped off the heads of the Carolingian successors and rolled back onto the Italian plain, where it became a sort of plaything of a number of little potentates who stole the crown from each other amidst much bloodshed and wore it (with or without the permission of the Pope) until it was the turn of some more ambitious neighbour. The Pope, once more sorely beset by

The Mountain Pass

his enemies, sent north for help. He did not appeal to the ruler of the west Frankish kingdom this time. His messengers crossed the Alps and addressed themselves to Otto, a Saxon prince who was recognised as the greatest chieftain of the different Germanic tribes.

Otto, who shared his people's affection for the blue skies and the gay and beautiful people of the Italian peninsula, hastened to the rescue. In return for his services, the Pope, Leo VIII, made Otto "emperor," and the eastern half of Charles' old kingdom was henceforth known as the "Holy Roman Empire of the German Nation."

This strange political creation managed to live to the ripe old age of 839 years. In the year 1801 (during the presidency of Thomas Jefferson) it was most unceremoniously relegated to the historical scrapheap. The brutal fellow who destroyed the old Germanic Empire was the son of a Corsican notary-public who had made a brilliant career in the service of the French Republic. He was ruler of Europe by the grace of his famous Guard Regiments, but he desired to be something more. He sent to Rome for the Pope and the Pope came and stood by while General Napoleon placed the imperial crown upon his own head and proclaimed himself heir to the tradition of Charlemagne. For history is like life. The more things change, the more they remain the same.

30

The Norsemen

Why the People of the Tenth Century
Prayed the Lord to Protect Them
from the Fury of the Norsemen

In the third and fourth centuries, the Germanic tribes of central Europe had broken through the defences of the empire that they might plunder Rome and live on the fat of the land. In the eighth century it became the turn of the Germans to be the "plundered-ones." They did not like this at all, even if their enemies were their first cousins, the Norsemen, who lived in Denmark and Sweden and Norway.

What forced these hardy sailors to turn pirate we do not know, but once they had discovered the advantages and pleasures of a buccaneering career there was no one who could stop them. They would suddenly descend upon a peaceful Frankish or Frisian village, situated on the mouth of a river. They would kill all the men and steal all the women. Then they would sail away in their fast-sailing ships and when the soldiers of the king or emperor arrived upon the scene, the robbers were gone and nothing remained but a few smouldering ruins.

During the days of disorder which followed the death of Charlemagne, the Northmen developed great activity. Their

The Norsemen Are Coming

fleets made raids upon every country and their sailors established small independent kingdoms along the coast of Holland and France and England and Germany, and they even
found their way into Italy. The Northmen were very intelligent. They soon learned to speak the language of their subjects and gave up the uncivilised ways of the early Vikings
(or sea-kings) who had been very picturesque but also very
unwashed and terribly cruel.

The Home of Norsemen

Early in the tenth century a Viking by the name of Rollo
had repeatedly attacked the coast of France. The king of
France, too weak to resist these northern robbers, tried to
bribe them into "being good." He offered them the province of Normandy, if they would promise to stop bothering the rest of his domains. Rollo accepted this bargain and
became "duke of Normandy."

The Norsemen Go to Russia

But the passion of conquest was strong in the blood of his children. Across the Channel, only a few hours away from the European mainland, they could see the white cliffs and the green fields of England. Poor England had passed through difficult days. For two hundred years it had been a Roman colony. After the Romans left, it had been conquered by the Angles and the Saxons, two German tribes from Schleswig. Next the Danes had taken the greater part of the country and had established the kingdom of Cnut. The Danes had been driven away and now (it was early in the eleventh century) another Saxon king, Edward the Confessor, was on the throne. But Edward was not expected to live long and he had no children. The circumstances favoured the ambitious dukes of Normandy.

In 1066 Edward died. Immediately William of Normandy crossed the Channel, defeated and killed Harold of Wessex (who had taken the crown) at the battle of Hastings, and proclaimed himself king of England.

In another chapter I have told you how in the year 800 a

The World of the Norsemen

The Normans Look Across the Channel

German chieftain had become a Roman emperor. Now in the year 1066 the grandson of a Norse pirate was recognised as king of England.

Why should we ever read fairy stories, when the truth of history is so much more interesting and entertaining?

31

Feudalism

How Central Europe, Attacked from
Three Sides, Became an Armed Camp and
Why Europe Would Have Perished Without
Those Professional Soldiers and Administrators
Who Were Part of the Feudal System

The following, then, is the state of Europe in the year 1000, when most people were so unhappy that they welcomed the prophecy foretelling the approaching end of the world and rushed to the monasteries, that the Day of Judgement might find them engaged upon devout duties.

At an unknown date, the Germanic tribes had left their old home in Asia and had moved westward into Europe. By sheer pressure of numbers they had forced their way into the Roman Empire. They had destroyed the great western empire, but the eastern part, being off the main route of the great migrations, had managed to survive and feebly continued the traditions of Rome's ancient glory.

During the days of disorder which had followed (the true "Dark Ages" of history, the sixth and seventh centuries of our era) the German tribes had been persuaded to accept the Christian religion and had recognised the bishop of Rome as the Pope or spiritual head of the world. In the ninth century, the organising genius of Charlemagne had revived the Roman Empire and had united the greater part of western Europe into a single state. During the tenth century this empire had gone to pieces. The western part had become a separate kingdom, France. The eastern half was known as the Holy Roman Empire of the German nation, and the rulers of this federation of states then pretended that they were the direct heirs of Cæsar and Augustus.

Unfortunately the power of the kings of France did not stretch beyond the moat of their royal residence, while the Holy Roman emperor was openly defied by his powerful subjects whenever it suited their fancy or their profit.

To increase the misery of the masses of the people, the triangle of western Europe (look at page 137, please) was forever exposed to attacks from three sides. On the south lived the ever dangerous Mohammedans. The western coast was ravaged by the Northmen. The eastern frontier (defenceless except for the short stretch of the Carpathian Mountains) was at the mercy of hordes of Huns, Hungarians, Slavs and Tartars.

The peace of Rome was a thing of the remote past, a dream of the "good old days" that were gone forever. It was a question of "fight or die," and quite naturally people preferred to fight. Forced by circumstances, Europe became an armed camp and there was a demand for strong leadership. Both king and emperor were far away. The frontiersmen (and most of Europe in the year 1000 was "frontier") must help themselves. They willingly submitted to the representatives of the king who were sent to administer the outlying districts, *provided they could protect them against their enemies.*

Soon central Europe was dotted with small principalities, each one ruled by a duke or a county or a baron or a bishop, as the case might be, and organised as a fighting unit.

These dukes and counts and barons had sworn to be faithful to the king who had given them their "feudum" (hence our word "feudal") in return for their loyal services and a certain amount of taxes. But travel in those days was slow and the means of communication were exceedingly poor. The royal or imperial administrators therefore enjoyed great independence, and within the boundaries of their own province they assumed most of the rights which in truth belonged to the king.

But you would make a mistake if you supposed that the people of the eleventh century objected to this form of government. They supported feudalism because it was a very practical and necessary institution. Their lord and master usually lived in a big stone house erected on the top of a steep rock or built between deep moats, but within sight of his subjects. In case of danger the subjects found shelter behind the walls of the baronial stronghold. That is why they tried to live as near the castle as possible and it accounts for the many European cities which began their career around a feudal fortress.

But the knight of the early Middle Ages was much more than a professional soldier. He was the civil servant of that day. He was the judge of his community and he was the chief of police. He caught the highwaymen and protected the wandering pedlars who were the merchants of the eleventh century. He looked after the dikes so that the countryside should not be flooded (just as the first noblemen had done in the valley of the Nile four thousand years before). He encouraged the troubadours who wandered from place to place telling the stories of the ancient heroes who had fought in the great wars of the migrations. Besides, he protected the churches and the monasteries within his territory, and although he could neither read nor write (it was considered unmanly to know such things), he employed a number of priests who kept his accounts and who registered the marriages and the births and the deaths which occurred within the baronial or ducal domains.

In the fifteenth century the kings once more became strong enough to exercise those powers which belonged to them because they were "anointed of God." Then the feudal knights lost their former independence. Reduced to the rank of country squires, they no longer filled a need and soon they became a nuisance. But Europe would have perished without the "feudal system" of the Dark Ages. There were many bad knights as there are many bad people to-day. But generally speaking, the rough-fisted barons of the twelfth and thirteenth centuries were hard-working administrators who rendered a most useful service to the cause of progress. During that era the noble torch of learning and art which had illuminated the world of the Egyptians and the Greeks and the Romans was burning very low. Without the knights and their good friends, the monks, civilisation would have been extinguished entirely, and the human race would have been forced to begin once more where the cave-man had left off.

32

Chivalry

It was quite natural that the professional fighting-men of the Middle Ages should try to establish some sort of organisation for their mutual benefit and protection. Out of this need for close organisation, knighthood or chivalry was born.

We know very little about the origins of knighthood. But as the system developed, it gave the world something which it needed very badly—a definite rule of conduct which softened the barbarous customs of that day and made life more livable than it had been during the five hundred years of the Dark Ages. It was not an easy task to civilise the rough frontiersmen who had spent most of their time fighting Mohammedans and Huns and Norsemen. Often they were guilty of backsliding, and having vowed all sorts of oaths about mercy and charity in the morning, they would murder all their prisoners before evening. But progress is ever the result of slow and ceaseless labour, and finally the most unscrupulous of knights was forced to obey the rules of his "class" or suffer the consequences.

These rules were different in the various parts of Europe, but they all made much of "service" and "loyalty to duty." The Middle Ages regarded service as something very noble and beautiful. It was no disgrace to be a servant, provided you were a good servant and did not slacken on the job. As for loyalty, at a time when life depended upon the faithful performance of many unpleasant duties, it was the chief virtue of the fightingman.

A young knight therefore was asked to swear that he would be faithful as a servant to God and as a servant to his king. Furthermore, he promised to be generous to those whose need was greater than his own. He pledged his word that he would be humble in his personal behaviour and would never boast of his own accomplishments and that he would be a friend of all those who suffered (with the exception of the Mohammedans, whom he was expected to kill on sight).

Around these vows, which were merely the Ten Commandments expressed in terms which the people of the Middle Ages could understand, there developed a complicated system of manners and outward behaviour. The knights tried to model their own lives after the example of those heroes of Arthur's Round Table and Charlemagne's court of whom the troubadours had told them. They hoped that they might prove as brave as Lancelot and as faithful as Roland. They carried themselves with dignity and they spoke careful and gracious words that they might be known as true knights, however humble the cut of their coat or the size of their purse.

In this way the order of knighthood became a school of those good manners which are the oil of the social machinery. Chivalry came to mean courtesy and the feudal castle showed the rest of the world what clothes to wear, how to eat, how to ask a lady for a dance and the thousand and one little things of every-day behaviour which help to make life interesting and agreeable.

Like all human institutions, knighthood was doomed to perish as soon as it had outlived its usefulness.

The Crusades, about which one of the next chapters tells,

were followed by a great revival of trade. Cities grew over-night. The townspeople became rich, hired good school-teachers and soon were the equals of the knights. The invention of gunpowder deprived the heavily armed "che-valier" of his former advantage and the use of mercenaries made it impossible to conduct a battle with the delicate nice-ties of a chess tournament. The knight became superfluous. Soon he became a ridiculous figure, with his devotion to ideals that had no longer any practical value. It was said that the noble Don Quixote de la Mancha had been the last of the true knights. After his death, his trusted sword and his armour were sold to pay his debts.

But somehow or other that sword seems to have fallen into the hands of a number of men. Washington carried it during the hopeless days of Valley Forge. It was the only defence of Gordon, when he had refused to desert the people who had been entrusted to his care, and stayed to meet his death in the besieged fortress of Khartoum.

And I am not quite sure but that it proved of invaluable strength in winning the Great War.

33

Pope vs. Emperor

The Strange Double Loyalty of the People of the
Middle Ages and How It Led to Endless Quarrels
Between the Popes and the Holy Roman Emperors

It is very difficult to understand the people of by-gone ages.
Your own grandfather, whom you see every day, is a mysterious being who lives in a different world of ideas and clothes
and manners. I am now telling you the story of some of your
grandfathers who are twenty-five generations removed, and
I do not expect you to catch the meaning of what I write
without re-reading this chapter a number of times.

The average man of the Middle Ages lived a very simple and uneventful life. Even if he was a free citizen, able
to come and go at will, he rarely left his own neighbourhood. There were no printed books and only a few manuscripts. Here and there, a small band of industrious monks
taught reading and writing and some arithmetic. But science
and history and geography lay buried beneath the ruins of
Greece and Rome.

Whatever people knew about the past they had learned
by listening to stories and legends. Such information, which
goes from father to son, is often slightly incorrect in details,
but it will preserve the main facts of history with astonishing

accuracy. After more than two thousand years, the mothers of India still frighten their naughty children by telling them that "Iskander will get them," and Iskander is none other than Alexander the Great, who visited India in the year 330 before the birth of Christ, but whose story has lived through all these ages.

The people of the early Middle Ages never saw a text-book of Roman history. They were ignorant of many things which every school-boy to-day knows before he has entered the third grade. But the Roman Empire, which is merely a name to you, was to them something very much alive. They felt it. They willingly recognised the Pope as their spiritual leader because he lived in Rome and represented the idea of the Roman superpower. And they were profoundly grateful when Charlemagne, and afterwards Otto the Great, revived the idea of a world empire and created the Holy Roman Empire, that the world might again be as it always had been.

But the fact that there were two different heirs to the Roman tradition placed the faithful burghers of the Middle Ages in a difficult position. The theory behind the mediæval political system was both sound and simple. While the worldly master (the emperor) looked after the the physical well-being of his subjects, the spiritual master (the Pope) guarded their souls.

In practice, however, the system worked very badly. The emperor invariably tried to interfere with the affairs of the church and the Pope retaliated and told the emperor how he should rule his domains. Then they told each other to mind their own business in very unceremonious language and the inevitable end was war.

Under those circumstances, what were the people to do? A good Christian obeyed both the Pope and his king. But the Pope and the emperor were enemies. Which side should a dutiful subject and an equally dutiful Christian take?

It was never easy to give the correct answer. When the emperor happened to be a man of energy and was sufficiently well provided with money to organise an army, he was very apt to cross the Alps and march on Rome, besiege the Pope in his own palace if need be and force His Holiness to obey the imperial instructions or suffer the consequences.

But more frequently the Pope was the stronger. Then the emperor or the king together with all his subjects was excommunicated. This meant that all churches were closed, that no one could be baptised, that no dying man could be given absolution—in short, that half of the functions of mediæval government came to an end.

More than that, the people were absolved from their oath of loyalty to their sovereign and were urged to rebel against their master. But if they followed this advice of the distant Pope and were caught, they were hanged by their near-by liege lord and that too was very unpleasant.

Indeed, the poor fellows were in a difficult position and none fared worse than those who lived during the latter half of the eleventh century, when the emperor Henry IV of Germany and Pope Gregory VII fought a two-round battle which decided nothing and upset the peace of Europe for almost fifty years.

In the middle of the eleventh century there had been a strong movement for reform in the church. The election of the Popes, thus far, had been a most irregular affair. It was to the advantage of the Holy Roman emperors to have a well-disposed priest elected to the Holy See. They frequently came to Rome at the time of election and used their influence for the benefit of one of their friends.

In the year 1059 this had been changed. By a decree of Pope Nicholas II the principal priests and deacons of the churches in and around Rome were organised into the so-called College of Cardinals, and this gathering of prominent churchmen (the word "cardinal" meant "principal") was given the exclusive power of electing the future Popes.

In the year 1073 the College of Cardinals elected a priest by the name of Hildebrand, the son of very simple parents in Tuscany, as Pope, and he took the name of Gregory VII. His energy was unbounded. His belief in the supreme powers of his holy office was built upon a granite rock of conviction and courage. In the mind of Gregory, the Pope was not only the absolute head of the Christian church, but also the highest court of appeal in all worldly matters. The Pope who had elevated simple German princes to the dignity of emperor could depose them at will. He could veto any law passed by duke or king or emperor, but whosoever should question a Papal decree, let him beware, for the punishment would be swift and merciless.

Gregory sent ambassadors to all the European courts to inform the potentates of Europe of his new laws and asked them to take due notice of their contents. William the Conqueror promised to be good, but Henry IV, who since the age of six had been fighting with his subjects, had no intention of submitting to the Papal will. He called together a college of German bishops, accused Gregory of every crime under the sun and then had him deposed by the Council of Worms.

The Pope answered with excommunication and a demand that the German princes rid themselves of their unworthy ruler. The German princes, only too happy to be rid of Henry, asked the Pope to come to Augsburg and help them elect a new emperor.

Gregory left Rome and travelled northward. Henry, who was no fool, appreciated the danger of his position. At all costs he must make peace with the Pope, and he must do it at once. In the midst of winter he crossed the Alps and hastened to Canossa where the Pope had stopped for a short rest. Three long days, from January 25 to 28 of the year 1077,

Henry IV at Canossa

Henry, dressed as a penitent pilgrim (but with a warm sweater underneath his monkish garb), waited outside the gates of the castle of Canossa. Then he was allowed to enter and was pardoned for his sins. But the repentance did not last long. As soon as Henry had returned to Germany, he behaved exactly as before. Again he was excommunicated. For the second time a council of German bishops deposed Gregory, but this time, when Henry crossed the Alps, he was at the head of a large army, besieged Rome and forced Gregory to retire to Salerno, where he died in exile. This first violent outbreak decided nothing. As soon as Henry was back in Germany, the struggle between Pope and emperor was continued.

The Hohenstaufen family which got hold of the imperial German throne shortly afterwards, were even more independent than their predecessors. Gregory had claimed that the Popes were superior to all kings because they (the Popes) at the Day of Judgement would be responsible for the behaviour of all the sheep of their flock, and in the eyes of God, a king was one of that faithful herd.

Frederick of Hohenstaufen, commonly known as Barbarossa or Red Beard, set up the counter-claim that the empire had been bestowed upon his predecessor "by God

The Castle

himself" and as the empire included Italy and Rome, he began a campaign which was to add these "lost provinces" to the northern country. Barbarossa was accidentally drowned in Asia Minor during the Second Crusade, but his son Frederick II, a brilliant young man who in his youth had been exposed to the civilisation of the Mohammedans of Sicily, continued the war. The Popes accused him of heresy. It is true that Frederick seems to have felt a deep and serious contempt for the rough Christian world of the north, for the boorish German knights and the intriguing Italian priests. But he held his tongue, went on a Crusade and took Jerusalem from the infidel and was duly crowned as king of the Holy City. Even this act did not placate the Popes. They deposed Frederick and gave his Italian possessions to Charles of Anjou, the brother of that King Louis of France who became famous as St. Louis. This led to more warfare. Conrad V, the son of Conrad IV, and the last of the Hohenstaufens, tried to regain the kingdom, and was defeated and decapitated at Naples. But twenty years later, the French who had made themselves thoroughly unpopular in Sicily were all murdered during the so-called Sicilian Vespers, and so it went.

The quarrel between the Popes and the emperors was never settled, but after a while the two enemies learned to leave each other alone.

In the year 1273, Rudolph of Hapsburg was elected emperor. He did not take the trouble to go to Rome to be crowned. The Popes did not object and in turn they kept away from Germany. This meant peace but two entire centuries which might have been used for the purpose of internal organisation had been wasted in useless warfare.

It is an ill wind, however, that bloweth no good to some one. The little cities of Italy, by a process of careful balancing, had managed to increase their power and their independence at the expense of both emperors and Popes. When the rush for the Holy Land began, they were able to handle the transportation problem of the thousands of eager pilgrims who were clamoring for passage, and at the end of the Crusades they had built themselves such strong defences of brick and of gold that they could defy Pope and emperor with equal indifference.

Church and state fought each other and a third party—the mediæval city—ran away with the spoils.

34

The Crusades

But All These Different Quarrels Were Forgotten
When the Turks Took the Holy Land, Desecrated
the Holy Places and Interfered Seriously with the
Trade from East to West. Europe Went Crusading

During three centuries there had been peace between
Christians and Moslems except in Spain and in the eastern
Roman Empire, the two states defending the gateways of
Europe. The Mohammedans having conquered Syria in the
seventh century were in possession of the Holy Land. But
they regarded Jesus as a great prophet (though not quite as
great as Mohammed), and they did not interfere with the
pilgrims who wished to pray in the church which St. Helena, the mother of the emperor Constantine, had built on
the spot of the Holy Grave. But early in the eleventh century,
a Tartar tribe from the wilds of Asia, called the Seljuks or
Turks, became masters of the Mohammedan state in western
Asia and then the period of tolerance came to an end. The
Turks took all of Asia Minor away from the eastern Roman
emperors and they made an end to the trade between east
and west.

Alexis, the emperor, who rarely saw anything of his Christian neighbours of the west, appealed for help and pointed to

the danger which threatened Europe should the Turks take Constantinople.

The Italian cities which had established colonies along the coast of Asia Minor and Palestine, in fear for their possessions, reported terrible stories of Turkish atrocities and Christian suffering. All Europe got excited.

Pope Urban II, a Frenchman from Reims, who had been educated at the same famous cloister of Cluny which had trained Gregory VII, thought that the time had come for action. The general state of Europe was far from satisfactory. The primitive agricultural methods of that day (unchanged since Roman times) caused a constant scarcity of food. There was unemployment and hunger and these are apt to lead to discontent and riots. Western Asia in older days had fed millions. It was an excellent field for the purpose of immigration.

Therefore at the Council of Clermont in France in the year 1095 the Pope arose, described the terrible horrors which the infidels had inflicted upon the Holy Land, gave a glowing description of this country which ever since the days of Moses had been overflowing with milk and honey and exhorted the knights of France and the people of Europe in general to leave wife and child and deliver Palestine from the Turks.

A wave of religious hysteria swept across the continent. All reason stopped. Men would drop their hammer and saw, walk out of their shop and take the nearest road to the east to go and kill Turks. Children would leave their homes to "go to Palestine" and bring the terrible Turks to their knees by the mere appeal of their youthful zeal and Christian piety. Fully ninety percent of those enthusiasts never got within sight of the Holy Land. They had no money. They were forced to beg or steal to keep alive. They became a danger to the safety of the highroads and they were killed by the angry country people.

The First Crusade, a wild mob of honest Christians,

defaulting bankrupts, penniless noblemen and fugitives from justice, following the lead of half-crazy Peter the Hermit and Walter-without-a-Cent, began their campaign against the infidels by murdering all the Jews whom they met by the way. They got as far as Hungary and then they were all killed.

This experience taught the church a lesson. Enthusiasm alone would not set the Holy Land free. Organisation was as necessary as good will and courage. A year was spent in training and equipping an army of two hundred thousand men. They were placed under command of Godfrey of Bouillon, Robert, duke of Normandy, Robert, count of Flanders, and a number of other noblemen, all experienced in the art of war.

In the year 1096 this Second Crusade started upon its long voyage. At Constantinople the knights did homage to the

The First Crusade

Emperor. (For as I have told you, traditions die hard, and a Roman emperor, however poor and powerless, was still held in great respect.) Then they crossed into Asia, killed all the Moslems who fell into their hands, stormed Jerusalem,

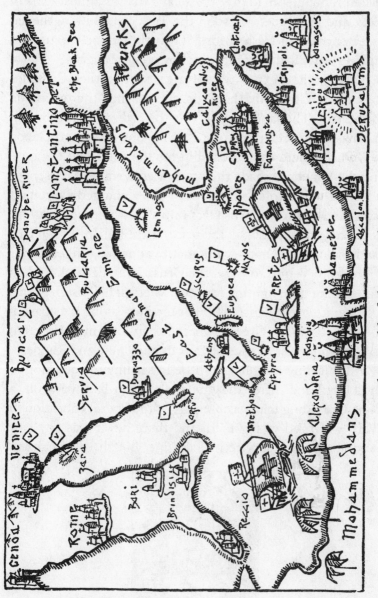

The World of the Crusaders

massacred the Mohammedan population and marched to the Holy Sepulchre to give praise and thanks amidst tears of piety and gratitude. But soon the Turks were strengthened by the arrival of fresh troops. Then they retook Jerusalem and in turn killed the faithful followers of the cross.

During the next two centuries, seven other Crusades took place. Gradually the Crusaders learned the technique of the trip. The land voyage was too tedious and too dangerous. They preferred to cross the Alps and go to Genoa or Venice where they took ship for the east. The Genoese and the Venetians made this trans-Mediterranean passenger service a very profitable business. They charged exorbitant rates, and when the Crusaders (most of whom had very little money) could not pay the price, these Italian "profiteers" kindly allowed them to "work their way across." In return for a fare from Venice to Acre, the Crusader undertook to do a stated amount of fighting for the owners of his vessel. In this way Venice greatly increased her territory along the coast of the Adriatic and in Greece, where Athens became a Venetian colony, and in the islands of Cyprus and Crete and Rhodes.

All this, however, helped little in settling the question of the Holy Land. After the first enthusiasm had worn off, a short Crusading trip became part of the liberal education of every well-bred young man, and there never was any lack of candidates for service in Palestine. But the old zeal was

The Crusaders Take Jerusalem

The Crusader's Grave

gone. The Crusaders, who had begun their warfare with deep hatred for the Mohammedans and great love for the Christian people of the eastern Roman Empire and Armenia, suffered a complete change of heart. They came to despise the Greeks of Byzantium, who cheated them and frequently betrayed the cause of the cross, and the Armenians and all the other Levantine races, and they began to appreciate the virtues of their enemies who proved to be generous and fair opponents.

Of course, it would never do to say this openly. But when the Crusader returned home, he was likely to imitate the manners which he had learned from his heathenish foe, compared to whom the average western knight was still a good deal of a country bumpkin. He also brought with him several new food-stuffs, such as peaches and spinach which he planted in his garden and grew for his own benefit. He gave up the barbarous custom of wearing a load of heavy armour and appeared in the flowing robes of silk or cotton which were the traditional habit of the followers of the prophet and were originally worn by the Turks. Indeed the Crusades, which had begun as a punitive expedition against the heathen, became a course of general instruction in civilisation for millions of young Europeans.

From a military and political point of view the Crusades

were a failure. Jerusalem and a number of cities were taken and lost. A dozen little kingdoms were established in Syria and Palestine and Asia Minor, but they were re-conquered by the Turks and after the year 1244 (when Jerusalem became definitely Turkish) the status of the Holy Land was the same as it had been before 1095.

But Europe had undergone a great change. The people of the west had been allowed a glimpse of the light and the sunshine and the beauty of the east. Their dreary castles no longer satisfied them. They wanted a broader life. Neither church nor state could give this to them.

They found it in the cities.

35

The Mediæval City

Why the People of the Middle Ages Said That
"City Air Is Free Air"

The early part of the Middle Ages had been an era of pioneering and of settlement. A new people, who thus far had lived outside the wild range of forest, mountains and marshes which protected the north-eastern frontier of the Roman Empire, had forced its way into the plains of western Europe and had taken possession of most of the land. They were restless, as all pioneers have been since the beginning of time. They liked to be "on the go." They cut down the forests and they cut each other's throats with equal energy. Few of them wanted to live in cities. They insisted upon being "free," they loved to feel the fresh air of the hillsides fill their lungs while they drove their herds across the wind-swept pastures. When they no longer liked their old homes, they pulled up stakes and went away in search of fresh adventures.

The weaker ones died. The hardy fighters and the courageous women who had followed their men into the wilderness survived. In this way they developed a strong race of men. They cared little for the graces of life. They were too busy to play the fiddle or write pieces of poetry. They had little love for discussions. The priest, "the learned man" of the village (and before the middle of the thirteenth century, a layman who could read and write was regarded as a "sissy"), was supposed to settle all questions which had no direct practical value. Meanwhile the German chieftain, the Frankish baron, the Northman duke (or whatever their names and titles) occupied their share of the territory which once had been part of the great Roman Empire and among the ruins of past glory, they built a world of their own which pleased them mightily and which they considered quite perfect.

They managed the affairs of their castle and the surrounding country to the best of their ability. They were as faithful to the commandments of the church as any weak mortal could hope to be. They were sufficiently loyal to their king or emperor to keep on good terms with those distant but always dangerous potentates. In short, they tried to do right and to be fair to their neighbours without being exactly unfair to their own interests.

It was not an ideal world in which they found themselves. The greater part of the people were serfs of "villeins," farm hands who were as much a part of the soil upon which they lived as the cows and sheep whose stables they shared. Their fate was not particularly happy nor was it particularly unhappy. But what was one to do? The good Lord who ruled the world of the Middle Ages had undoubtedly ordered everything for the best. If He, in His wisdom, had decided that there must be both knights and serfs, it was not the duty of these faithful sons of the church to question the arrangement. The serfs therefore did not complain but when they were too hard driven, they would die off like cattle which are not fed and stabled in the right way, and then something would be hastily done to better their condition. But if the progress of the world had been left to the serf and his feudal master, we would still be living after the fashion of the twelfth century, saying "abracadabra" when we tried to stop a tooth-ache, and feeling a deep contempt and hatred for the dentist who offered to help us with his "science," which most likely was of Mohammedan or heathenish origin and therefore both wicked and useless.

When you grow up you will discover that many people do not believe in "progress" and they will prove to you by the terrible deeds of some of our own contemporaries that "the world does not change." But I hope that you will not pay much attention to such talk. You see, it took our ancestors almost a million years to learn how to walk on their hind legs. Other centuries had to go by before their animal-like grunts developed into an understandable language. Writing—the art of preserving our ideas for the benefit of future generations, without which no progress is possible—was invented only four thousand years ago. The idea of turning the forces of nature into the obedient servants of man was quite new in the days of your own grandfather. It seems to me, therefore, that we are making progress at an unheard-of rate of speed. Perhaps we have paid a little too much attention to the mere physical comforts of life. That will change in due course of time and we shall then attack the problems which are not related to health and to wages and plumbing and machinery in general.

But please do not be too sentimental about the "good old days." Many people who only see the beautiful churches and the great works of art which the Middle Ages have left behind grow quite eloquent when they compare our own ugly civilisation with its hurry and its noise and the evil smells of backfiring motor trucks with the cities of a thousand years ago. But these mediæval churches were invariably surrounded by miserable hovels compared to which a modern tenement house stands forth as a luxurious palace. It is true that the noble Lancelot and the equally noble Parsifal, the pure young hero who went in search of the Holy Grail, were not bothered by the odor of gasoline. But there were other smells of the barnyard variety—odors of decaying refuse which had been thrown into the street—of pig-sties surrounding the bishop's palace—of unwashed people who had inherited their coats and hats from their grandfathers and who had never learned the blessing of soap. I do not want to paint too unpleasant a picture. But when you read in the ancient chronicles that the king of France, looking out of the windows of his palace, fainted at the stench caused by the pigs rooting in the streets of Paris, when an ancient manuscript recounts a few details of an epidemic of the plague or of small-pox, then you begin to understand that "progress" is something more than a catchword used by modern advertising men.

No, the progress of the last six hundred years would not have been possible without the existence of cities. I shall, therefore, have to make this chapter a little longer than many of the others. It is too important to be reduced to three or four pages, devoted to mere political events.

The ancient world of Egypt and Babylonia and Assyria had been a world of cities. Greece had been a country of city-states. The history of Phœnicia was the history of two cities called Sidon and Tyre. The Roman Empire was the "hinterland" of a single town. Writing, art, science, astronomy, architecture, literature, the theatre—the list is endless—have all been products of the city.

For almost four thousand years the wooden bee-hive which we call a town had been the workshop of the world. Then came the great migrations. The Roman Empire was destroyed. The cities were burned down and Europe once more became a land of pastures and little agricultural villages. During the Dark Ages the fields of civilisation had lain fallow.

The Crusades had prepared the soil for a new crop. It was

time for the harvest, but the fruit was plucked by the burghers of the free cities.

I have told you the story of the castles and the monasteries, with their heavy stone enclosures—the homes of the knights and the monks, who guarded men's bodies and their souls. You have seen how a few artisans (butchers and bakers and an occasional candlestick maker) came to live near the castle to tend to the wants of their masters and to find protection in case of danger. Sometimes the feudal lord allowed these people to surround their houses with a stockade. But they were dependent for their living upon the good will of the mighty seigneur of the castle. When he went about they knelt before him and kissed his hand.

Then came the Crusades and many things changed. The migrations had driven people from the north-east to the west. The Crusades made millions of people travel from the west to the highly civilised regions of the south-east. They discovered that the world was not bounded by the four walls of their little settlement. They came to appreciate better clothes, more comfortable houses, new dishes, products of the mysterious Orient. After their return to their old homes, they insisted that they be supplied with those articles. The pedlar with his pack upon his back—the only merchant of the Dark Ages—added these goods to his old merchandise, bought a cart, hired a few ex-Crusaders to protect him against the crime wave which followed this great international war and went forth to do business upon a more modern and larger scale. His career was not an easy one. Every time he entered the domains of another lord he had to pay tolls and taxes. But the business was profitable all the same and the pedlar continued to make his rounds.

Soon certain energetic merchants discovered that the goods which they had always imported from afar could be made at home. They turned part of their homes into a work shop. They ceased to be merchants and became manufacturers. They sold their products not only to the lord of the castle and to the abbot in his monastery, but they exported them to nearby towns. The lord and the abbot paid them with products of their farms, eggs and wines, and with honey, which in those early days was used as sugar. But the citizens of distant towns were obliged to pay in cash and the manufacturer and the merchant began to own little pieces of gold, which entirely changed their position in the society of the early Middle Ages.

It is difficult for you to imagine a world without money. In a modern city one cannot possibly live without money. All day long you carry a pocket full of small discs of metal to "pay your way." You need a nickel for the street-car, a dollar for a dinner, three cents for an evening paper. But many people of the early Middle Ages never saw a piece of coined money from the time they were born to the day of their death. The gold and silver of Greece and Rome lay buried beneath the ruins of their cities. The world of the migrations, which had succeeded the empire, was an agricultural world. Every farmer raised enough grain and enough sheep and enough cows for his own use.

The mediæval knight was a country squire and was rarely forced to pay for materials in money. His estates produced everything that he and his family ate and drank and wore on their backs. The bricks for his house were made along the banks of the nearest river. Wood for the rafters of the hall was cut from the baronial forest. The few articles that had to come from abroad were paid for in goods—in honey—in eggs—in fagots.

But the Crusades upset the routine of the old agricultural life in a very drastic fashion. Suppose that the duke of Hildesheim was going to the Holy Land. He must travel thousands of miles and he must pay his passage and his hotel-

The Castle and the City

bills. At home he could pay with products of his farm. But he could not well take a hundred dozen eggs and a cart-load of hams with him to satisfy the greed of the shipping agent of Venice or the innkeeper of the Brenner Pass. These gentlemen insisted upon cash. His Lordship therefore was obliged to take a small quantity of gold with him upon his voyage. Where could he find this gold? He could borrow it from the Lombards, the descendants of the old Longobards, who had turned professional money-lenders, who seated behind their exchange-table (commonly known as "banco" or bank) were glad to let His Grace have a few hundred gold pieces in exchange for a mortgage upon his estates, that they might be repaid in case His Lordship should die at the hands of the Turks.

That was dangerous business for the borrower. In the end,

the Lombards invariably owned the estates and the knight became a bankrupt, who hired himself out as a fighting-man to a more powerful and more careful neighbour.

His Grace could also go to that part of the town where the Jews were forced to live. There he could borrow money at a rate of fifty or sixty percent interest. That, too, was bad business. But was there a way out? Some of the people of the little city which surrounded the castle were said to have money. They had known the young lord all his life. His father and their fathers had been good friends. They would not be unreasonable in their demands. Very well. His Lordship's clerk, a monk who could write and keep accounts, sent a note to the best known merchants and asked for a small loan. The townspeople met in the work-room of the jeweller who made chalices for the nearby churches and discussed this demand. They could not well refuse. It would serve no purpose to ask for "interest." In the first place, it was against the religious principles of most people to take interest and in the second place, it would never be paid except in agricultural products and of these the people had enough and to spare.

"But," suggested the tailor who spent his days quietly sitting upon his table and who was somewhat of a philosopher, "suppose that we ask some favour in return for our money. We are all fond of fishing. But His Lordship won't let us fish in his brook. Suppose that we let him have a hundred ducats and that he give us in return a written guarantee allowing us to fish all we want in all of his rivers. Then he gets the hundred which he needs, but we get the fish and it will be good business all around."

The day His Lordship accepted this proposition (it seemed such an easy way of getting a hundred gold pieces) he signed the death-warrant of his own power. His clerk drew up the agreement. His Lordship made his mark (for he could not sign his name) and departed for the east. Two years later he came back, dead broke. The townspeople were fishing in the castle pond. The sight of this silent row of anglers annoyed His Lordship. He told his equerry to go and chase the crowd away. They went, but that night a delegation of merchants visited the castle. They were very polite. They congratulated His Lordship upon his safe return. They were sorry His Lordship had been annoyed by the fishermen, but as His Lordship might perhaps remember he had given them permission to do so himself, and the tailor produced the charter which had been kept in the safe of the jeweller ever since the master had gone to the Holy Land.

His Lordship was much annoyed. But once more he was in dire need of some money. In Italy he had signed his name to certain documents which were now in the possession of Salvestro dei Medici, the well-known banker. These documents were "promissory notes" and they were due two months from date. Their total amount came to 340 pounds, Flemish gold. Under these circumstances, the noble knight could not well show the rage which filled his heart and his proud soul. Instead, he suggested another little loan. The merchants retired to discuss the matter.

After three days they came back and said "yes." They were only too happy to be able to help their master in his difficulties, but in return for the 345 golden pounds would he give them another written promise (another charter) that they, the townspeople, might establish a council of their own to be elected by all the merchants and free citizens of the city, said council to manage civic affairs without interference from the side of the castle?

His Lordship was confoundedly angry. But again, he needed the money. He said yes, and signed the charter. Next week, he repented. He called his soldiers and went to the house of the jeweller and asked for the documents which his

The Belfry

crafty subjects had cajoled out of him under the pressure of
circumstances. He took them away and burned them. The
townspeople stood by and said nothing. But when next His
Lordship needed money to pay for the dowry of his daughter, he was unable to get a single penny. After that little affair
at the jeweller's his credit was not considered good. He was
forced to eat humble-pie and offer to make certain reparations. Before His Lordship got the first installment of the
stipulated sum, the townspeople were once more in possession of all their old charters and a brand new one which permitted them to build a "city-hall" and a strong tower where
all the charters might be kept protected against fire and theft,
which really meant protected against future violence on the
part of the lord and his armed followers.

This, in a very general way, is what happened during the
centuries which followed the Crusades. It was a slow process, this gradual shifting of power from the castle to the city.
There was some fighting. A few tailors and jewellers were
killed and a few castles went up in smoke. But such occurrences were not common. Almost imperceptibly the towns
grew richer and the feudal lords grew poorer. To maintain
themselves they were forever forced to exchange charters of
civic liberty in return for ready cash. The cities grew. They
offered an asylum to runaway serfs who gained their liberty

The Mediæval Town

after they had lived a number of years behind the city walls. They came to be the home of the more energetic elements of the surrounding country districts. They were proud of their new importance and expressed their power in the churches and public buildings which they erected around the old market-place, where centuries before the barter of eggs and sheep and honey and salt had taken place. They wanted their children to have a better chance in life than they had enjoyed themselves. They hired monks to come to their city and be school-teachers. When they heard of a man who could paint pictures upon boards of wood, they offered him a pension if he would come and cover the walls of their chapels and their town hall with scenes from the Holy Scriptures.

Meanwhile His Lordship, in the dreary and draughty halls of his castle, saw all this up-start splendour and regretted the day when first he had signed away a single one of his sovereign rights and prerogatives. But he was helpless. The townspeople with their well-filled strong-boxes snapped their fingers at him. They were freemen, fully prepared to hold what they had gained by the sweat of their brow and after a struggle which had lasted for more than ten generations.

Gunpowder

36

Mediæval Self-Government

How the People of the Cities
Asserted Their Right to Be Heard
in the Royal Councils of Their Country

As long as people were "nomads," wandering tribes of shepherds, all men had been equal and had been responsible for the welfare and safety of the entire community.

But after they had settled down and some had become rich and others had grown poor, the government was apt to fall into the hands of those who were not obliged to work for their living and who could devote themselves to politics.

I have told you how this had happened in Egypt and in Mesopotamia and in Greece and in Rome. It occurred among the Germanic population of western Europe as soon as order had been restored. The western European world was ruled in the first place by an emperor who was elected by the seven or eight most important kings of the vast Roman Empire of the German nation and who enjoyed a great deal of imaginary and very little actual power. It was ruled by a number of kings who sat upon shaky thrones. The every-day government was in the hands of thousands of feudal princelets. Their subjects were peasants or serfs. There were few cities. There was hardly any middle class. But during the thir-

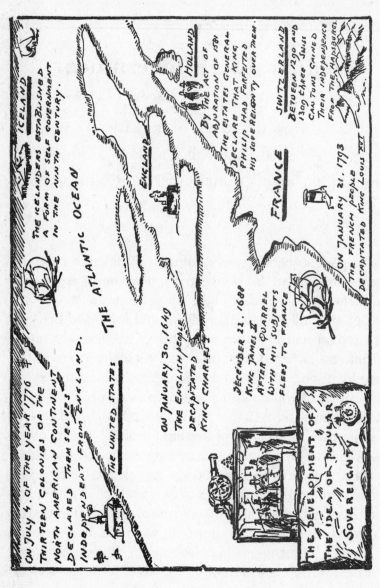

The Spreading of the Idea of Popular Sovereignty

teenth century (after an absence of almost a thousand years) the middle class—the merchant class—once more appeared upon the historical stage and its rise in power, as we saw in the last chapter, had meant a decrease in the influence of the castle folk.

Thus far, the king, in ruling his domains, had only paid attention to the wishes of his noblemen and his bishops. But the new world of trade and commerce which grew out of the Crusades forced him to recognise the middle class or suffer from an ever increasing emptiness of his exchequer. Their Majesties (if they had followed their hidden wishes) would have as lief consulted their cows and their pigs as the good burghers of their cities. But they could not help themselves. They swallowed the bitter pill because it was gilded, but not without a struggle.

In England, during the absence of Richard the Lion Hearted (who had gone to the Holy Land, but who was spending the greater part of his Crusading voyage in an Austrian jail), the government of the country had been placed in the hands of John, a brother of Richard, who was his inferior in the art of war, but his equal as a bad administrator. John had begun his career as a regent by losing Normandy and the greater part of the French possessions. Next, he had managed to get into a quarrel with Pope Innocent III, the famous enemy of the Hohenstaufens. The Pope had excommunicated John (as Gregory VII had excommunicated the emperor Henry IV two centuries before). In the year 1213 John had been obliged to make an ignominious peace just as Henry IV had been obliged to do in the year 1077.

Undismayed by his lack of success, John continued to abuse his royal power until his disgruntled vassals made a prisoner of their anointed ruler and forced him to promise that he would be good and would never again interfere with the ancient rights of his subjects. All this happened on a little

island in the Thames, near the village of Runnymede, on
June 15 of the year 1215. The document to which John signed
his name was called the Big Charter—the Magna Carta. It
contained very little that was new. It re-stated in short and
direct sentences the ancient duties of the king and enumerated the privileges of his vassals. It paid little attention to the
rights (if any) of the vast majority of the people, the peasants, but it offered certain securities to the rising class of the
merchants. It was a charter of great importance because it
defined the powers of the king with more precision than
had ever been done before. But it was still a purely mediæval
document. It did not refer to common human beings, unless
they happened to be the property of the vassal, which must
be safe-guarded against royal tyranny just as the baronial
woods and cows were protected against an excess of zeal on
the part of the royal foresters.

A few years later, however, we begin to hear a very different note in the councils of His Majesty.

John, who was bad, both by birth and inclination, solemnly had promised to obey the Great Charter and then
had broken every one of its many stipulations. Fortunately,
he soon died and was succeeded by his son Henry III, who
was forced to recognise the charter anew. Meanwhile, Uncle
Richard, the Crusader, had cost the country a great deal of
money and the king was obliged to ask for a few loans that he
might pay his obligations to the Jewish money-lenders. The
large land owners and the bishops who acted as councillors
to the king could not provide him with the necessary gold
and silver. The king then gave orders that a few representatives of the cities be called upon to attend the sessions of his
Great Council. They made their first appearance in the year
1265. They were supposed to act only as financial experts
who were not supposed to take a part in the general discussion of matters of state, but to give advice exclusively upon
the question of taxation.

Gradually, however, these representatives of the "commons" were consulted upon many of the problems and the meeting of noblemen, bishops and city delegates developed into a regular Parliament, a place "où l'on parlait," which means in English where people talked, before important affairs of state were decided upon.

But the institution of such a general advisory board with certain executive powers was not an English invention, as seems to be the general belief, and government by a "king and his Parliament" was by no means restricted to the British Isles. You will find it in every part of Europe. In some countries, like France, the rapid increase of the royal power after the Middle Ages reduced the influence of the "Parliament" to nothing. In the year 1302 representatives of the cities had been admitted to the meeting of the French Parlia-

The Home of Swiss Liberty

ment, but five centuries had to pass before this "Parliament" was strong enough to assert the rights of the middle class, the so-called Third Estate, and break the power of the king. Then they made up for lost time and during the French Revolution, abolished the king, the clergy and the nobles, and

made the representatives of the common people the rulers
of the land. In Spain the "Cortes" (the king's council) had
been opened to the commoners as early as the first half of the
twelfth century. In the German Empire, a number of important cities had obtained the rank of "imperial cities" whose
representatives must be heard in the imperial Diet.

In Sweden, representatives of the people attended the sessions of the Riksdag at the first meeting of the year 1359. In
Denmark the Daneholf, the ancient national assembly, was
reestablished in 1314, and, although the nobles often regained
control of the country at the expense of the king and the people, the representatives of the cities were never completely
deprived of their power.

In the Scandinavian country, the story of representative
government is particularly interesting. In Iceland, the "Alth-
ing," the assembly of all free landowners, who managed the
affairs of the island, began to hold regular meetings in the
ninth century and continued to do so for more than a thousand years.

In Switzerland, the freemen of the different cantons
defended their assemblies against the attempts of a number
of feudal neighbours with great success.

The Abjuration of Philip II

Finally, in the Low Countries, in Holland, the councils of the different duchies and counties were attended by representatives of the Third Estate as early as the thirteenth century.

In the sixteenth century a number of these small provinces rebelled against their king, abjured His Majesty in a solemn meeting of the "Estates General," removed the clergy from the discussions, broke the power of the nobles and assumed full executive authority over the newly established republic of the United Seven Netherlands. For two centuries, the representatives of the town councils ruled the country without a king, without bishops and without noblemen. The city had become supreme and the good burghers had become the rulers of the land.

37

The Mediæval World

What the People of the Middle Ages Thought of
the World in Which They Happened to Live

Dates are a very useful invention. We could not do without them but unless we are very careful, they will play tricks with us. They are apt to make history too precise. For example, when I talk of the point-of-view of mediæval man, I do not mean that on December 31 of the year 476, suddenly all the people of Europe said, "Ah, now the Roman Empire has come to an end and we are living in the Middle Ages. How interesting!"

You could have found men at the Frankish court of Charlemagne who were Romans in their habits, in their manners, in their out-look upon life. On the other hand, when you grow up you will discover that some of the people in this world have never passed beyond the stage of the cave-man. All times and all ages overlap, and the ideas of succeeding generations play tag with each other. But it is possible to study the minds of a good many true representatives of the Middle Ages and then give you an idea of the average man's attitude toward life and the many difficult problems of living.

First of all, remember that the people of the Middle Ages

The Mediæval World

never thought of themselves as free-born citizens, who could come and go at will and shape their fate according to their ability or energy or luck. On the contrary, they all considered themselves part of the general scheme of things, which included emperors and serfs, Popes and heretics, heroes and swashbucklers, rich men, poor men, beggar men and thieves. They accepted this divine ordinance and asked no questions. In this, of course, they differed radically from modern people who accept nothing and who are forever trying to improve their own financial and political situation.

To the man and woman of the thirteenth century, the world hereafter—a Heaven of wonderful delights and a Hell of brimstone and suffering—meant something more than empty words or vague theological phrases. It was an actual fact and the mediæval burghers and knights spent the greater part of their time preparing for it. We modern people regard a noble death after a well-spent life with the quiet calm of the ancient Greeks and Romans. After three-score years of work and effort, we go to sleep with the feeling that all will be well.

But during the Middle Ages, the King of Terrors with his grinning skull and his rattling bones was man's steady companion. He woke his victims up with terrible tunes on his scratchy fiddle—he sat down with them at dinner—he smiled at them from behind trees and shrubs when they took a girl out for a walk. If you had heard nothing but hair-raising yarns about cemeteries and coffins and fearful diseases when you were very young, instead of listening to the fairy stories of Andersen and Grimm, you, too, would have lived all your days in a dread of the final hour and the gruesome Day of Judgement. That is exactly what happened to the children of the Middle Ages. They moved in a world of devils and spooks and only a few occasional angels. Sometimes, their fear of the future filled their souls with humility and piety, but often it influenced them the other way and made them cruel and sentimental. They would first of all murder all the women and children of a captured city and then they would devoutly march to a holy spot and with their hands gory with the blood of innocent victims, they would pray that a merciful Heaven forgive them their sins. Yea, they would do more than pray, they would weep bitter tears and would confess themselves the most wicked of sinners. But the next day, they would once more butcher a camp of Saracen enemies without a spark of mercy in their hearts.

Of course, the Crusaders were knights and obeyed a somewhat different code of manners from the common men. But in such respects the common man was just the same as his master. He, too, resembled a shy horse, easily frightened by a shadow or a silly piece of paper, capable of excellent and faithful service but liable to run away and do terrible damage when his feverish imagination saw a ghost.

In judging these good people, however, it is wise to remember the terrible disadvantages under which they lived. They were really barbarians who posed as civilised people. Charlemagne and Otto the Great were called "Roman emperors," but they were savages who lived amidst glorious ruins but who did not share the benefits of the civilisation which their fathers and grandfathers had destroyed. They knew nothing. They were ignorant of almost every fact which a boy of twelve knows to-day. They were obliged to go to one single book for all their information. That was the Bible. But those parts of the Bible which have influenced the history of the human race for the better are those chapters of the New Testament which teach us the great moral lessons of love, charity and forgiveness. As a handbook of astronomy, zoölogy, botany, geometry and all the other sciences, the venerable book is not entirely reliable. In the twelfth century, a second book was added to the mediæval library,

the great encyclopædia of useful knowledge, compiled by
Aristotle, the Greek philosopher of the fourth century before
Christ. Why the Christian church should have been willing
to accord such high honors to the teacher of Alexander the
Great, whereas they condemned all other Greek philosophers on account of their heathenish doctrines, I really do
not know. But next to the Bible, Aristotle was recognized as
the only reliable teacher whose works could be safely placed
into the hands of true Christians.

His works had reached Europe in a somewhat round-
about way. They had gone from Greece to Alexandria. They
had then been translated from the Greek into the Arabic language by the Mohammedans who conquered Egypt in the
seventh century. They had followed the Moslem armies into
Spain and the philosophy of the great Stagirite (Aristotle was
a native of Stagira in Macedonia) was taught in the Moorish
universities of Cordova. The Arabic text was then translated
into Latin by the Christian students who had crossed the
Pyrenees to get a liberal education and this much-travelled
version of the famous books was at last taught at the different
schools of northwestern Europe. It was not very clear, but
that made it all the more interesting.

With the help of the Bible and Aristotle, the most brilliant
men of the Middle Ages now set to work to explain all things
between Heaven and earth in their relation to the expressed
will of God. These brilliant men, the so-called Scholiasts
or Schoolmen, were really very intelligent, but they had
obtained their information exclusively from books, and never
from actual observation. If they wanted to lecture on the
sturgeon or on caterpillars, they read the Old and New Testaments and Aristotle, and told their students everything these
good books had to say upon the subject of caterpillars and
sturgeons. They did not go out to the nearest river to catch a
sturgeon. They did not leave their libraries and repair to the

backyard to catch a few caterpillars and look at these animals and study them in their native haunts. Even such famous scholars as Albertus Magnus and Thomas Aquinas did not inquire whether the sturgeons in the land of Palestine and the caterpillars of Macedonia might not have been different from the sturgeons and the caterpillars of western Europe.

When occasionally an exceptionally curious person like Roger Bacon appeared in the council of the learned and began to experiment with magnifying glasses and funny little telescopes and actually dragged the sturgeon and the caterpillar into the lecturing room and proved that they were different from the creatures described by the Old Testament and by Aristotle, the Schoolmen shook their dignified heads. Bacon was going too far. When he dared to suggest that an hour of actual observation was worth more than ten years with Aristotle and that the works of that famous Greek might as well have remained untranslated for all the good they had ever done, the Scholiasts went to the police and said, "This man is a danger to the safety of the state. He wants us to study Greek that we may read Aristotle in the original. Why should he not be contented with our Latin-Arabic translation which has satisfied our faithful people for so many hundred years? Why is he so curious about the insides of fishes and the insides of insects? He is probably a wicked magician trying to upset the established order of things by his black magic." And so well did they plead their cause that the frightened guardians of the peace forbade Bacon to write a single word for more than ten years. When he resumed his studies he had learned a lesson. He wrote his books in a queer cipher which made it impossible for his contemporaries to read them, a trick which became common as the church became more desperate in its attempts to prevent people from asking questions which would lead to doubts and infidelity.

This, however, was not done out of any wicked desire to

keep people ignorant. The feeling which prompted the heretic hunters of that day was really a very kindly one. They firmly believed—nay, they knew—that this life was but the preparation for our real existence in the next world. They felt convinced that too much knowledge made people uncomfortable, filled their minds with dangerous opinions and led to doubt and hence to perdition. A mediæval Schoolman who saw one of his pupils stray away from the revealed authority of the Bible and Aristotle, that he might study things for himself, felt as uncomfortable as a loving mother who sees her young child approach a hot stove. She knows that he will burn his little fingers if he is allowed to touch it and she tries to keep him back, if necessary she will use force. But she really loves the child and if he will only obey her, she will be as good to him as she possibly can be. In the same way the mediæval guardians of people's souls, while they were strict in all matters pertaining to the faith, slaved day and night to render the greatest possible service to the members of their flock. They held out a helping hand whenever they could and the society of that day shows the influence of thousands of good men and pious women who tried to make the fate of the average mortal as bearable as possible.

A serf was a serf and his position would never change. But the good Lord of the Middle Ages who allowed the serf to remain a slave all his life had bestowed an immortal soul upon this humble creature and therefore he must be protected in his rights, that he might live and die as a good Christian. When he grew too old or too weak to work he must be taken care of by the feudal master for whom he had worked. The serf, therefore, who led a monotonous and dreary life, was never haunted by fear of to-morrow. He knew that he was "safe"—that he could not be thrown out of employment, that he would always have a roof over his head (a leaky roof, perhaps, but a roof all the same) and that he would always have something to eat.

This feeling of "stability" and of "safety" was found in all classes of society. In the towns the merchants and the artisans established guilds which assured every member of a steady income. It did not encourage the ambitious to do better than their neighbours. Too often the guilds gave protection to the "slacker" who managed to "get by." But they established a general feeling of content and assurance among the labouring classes which no longer exists in our day of general competition. The Middle Ages were familiar with the dangers of what we modern people call "corners," when a single rich man gets hold of all the available grain or soap or pickled herring, and then forces the world to buy from him at his own price. The authorities, therefore, discouraged wholesale trading and regulated the price at which merchants were allowed to sell their goods.

The Middle Ages disliked competition. Why compete and fill the world with hurry and rivalry and a multitude of pushing men, when the Day of Judgement was near at hand, when riches would count for nothing and when the good serf would enter the golden gates of Heaven while the bad knight was sent to do penance in the deepest pit of Inferno?

In short, the people of the Middle Ages were asked to surrender part of their liberty of thought and action, that they might enjoy greater safety from poverty of the body and poverty of the soul.

And with a very few exceptions, they did not object. They firmly believed that they were mere visitors upon this planet—that they were here to be prepared for a greater and more important life. Deliberately they turned their backs upon a world which was filled with suffering and wickedness and injustice. They pulled down the blinds that the rays of the sun might not distract their attention from that chapter in the Apocalypse which told them of that heavenly light which was to illumine their happiness in all eternity. They tried to close their eyes to most of the joys of the world in which they lived that they might enjoy those which awaited them in the near future. They accepted life as a necessary evil and welcomed death as the beginning of a glorious day.

The Greeks and the Romans had never bothered about the future but had tried to establish their Paradise right here upon this earth. They had succeeded in making life extremely pleasant for those of their fellow-men who did not happen to be slaves. Then came the other extreme of the Middle Ages, when man built himself a Paradise beyond the highest clouds and turned this world into a vale of tears for high and low, for rich and poor, for the intelligent and the dumb. It was time for the pendulum to swing back in the other direction, as I shall tell you in my next chapter.

38

Mediæval Trade

How the Crusades Once More Made the
Mediterranean a Busy Centre of Trade and
How the Cities of the Italian Peninsula
Became the Great Distributing Centre for the
Commerce with Asia and Africa

There were three good reasons why the Italian cities should have been the first to regain a position of great importance during the late Middle Ages. The Italian peninsula had been settled by Rome at a very early date. There had been more roads and more towns and more schools than anywhere else in Europe.

The barbarians had burned as lustily in Italy as elsewhere, but there had been so much to destroy that more had been able to survive. In the second place, the Pope lived in Italy and as the head of a vast political machine, which owned land and serfs and buildings and forests and rivers and conducted courts of law, he was in constant receipt of a great deal of money. The Papal authorities had to be paid in gold and silver as did the merchants and ship-owners of Venice and Genoa. The cows and the eggs and the horses and all the other agricultural products of the north and the west must

Mediaeval Trade

be changed into actual cash before the debt could be paid in
the distant city of Rome. This made Italy the one country
where there was a comparative abundance of gold and silver.
Finally, during the Crusades, the Italian cities had become
the point of embarkation for the Crusaders and had profi-
teered to an almost unbelievable extent.

And after the Crusades had come to an end, these same
Italian cities remained the distributing centres for those Oriental goods upon which the people of Europe had come to
depend during the time they had spent in the near east.

Of these towns, few were as famous as Venice. Venice was
a republic built upon a mud bank. Thither people from the
mainland had fled during the invasions of the barbarians in
the fourth century. Surrounded on all sides by the sea, they
had engaged in the business of salt-making. Salt had been very
scarce during the Middle Ages, and the price had been high.
For hundreds of years Venice had enjoyed a monopoly of this
indispensable table commodity (I say indispensable, because
people, like sheep, fall ill unless they get a certain amount
of salt in their food). The people had used this monopoly to
increase the power of their city. At times they had even dared
to defy the power of the Popes. The town had grown rich
and had begun to build ships, which engaged in trade with
the Orient. During the Crusades, these ships were used to
carry passengers to the Holy Land, and when the passengers
could not pay for their tickets in cash, they were obliged to
help the Venetians who were forever increasing their colonies in the Ægean Sea, in Asia Minor and in Egypt.

By the end of the fourteenth century, the population had
grown to two hundred thousand, which made Venice the
biggest city of the Middle Ages. The people were without
influence upon the government which was the private affair
of a small number of rich merchant families. They elected
a Senate and a doge (or duke), but the actual rulers of the

city were the members of the famous Council of Ten—who maintained themselves with the help of a highly organised system of secret-service men and professional murderers, who kept watch upon all citizens and quietly removed those who might be dangerous to the safety of their high-handed and unscrupulous Committee of Public Safety.

The other extreme of government, a democracy of very turbulent habits, was to be found in Florence. This city controlled the main road from northern Europe to Rome and used the money which it had derived from this fortunate economic position to engage in manufacturing. The Florentines tried to follow the example of Athens. Noblemen, priests and members of the guilds all took part in the discussions of civic affairs. This led to great civic upheaval. People were forever being divided into political parties and these parties fought each other with intense bitterness and exiled their enemies and confiscated their possessions as soon as they had gained a victory in the council. After several centuries of this rule by organised mobs, the inevitable happened. A powerful family made itself master of the city and governed the town and the surrounding country after the fashion of the old Greek "tyrants." They were called the Medici. The earliest Medici had been physicians ("medicus" is Latin for "physician," hence their name), but later they had turned banker. Their banks and their pawnshops were to be found in all the more important centres of trade. Even to-day our American pawnshops display the three golden balls which were part of the coat of arms of the mighty house of the Medici, who became rulers of Florence and married their daughters to the kings of France and were buried in graves worthy of a Roman Cæsar.

Then there was Genoa, the great rival of Venice, where the merchants specialised in trade with Tunis in Africa and the grain depots of the Black Sea. Then there were more than two hundred other cities, some large and some small, each a perfect commercial unit, all of them fighting their neighbours and rivals with the undying hatred of neighbours who are depriving each other of their profits.

Once the products of the Orient and Africa had been brought to these distributing centres, they must be prepared for the voyage to the west and the north.

Genoa carried her goods by water to Marseilles, from where they were reshipped to the cities along the Rhone, which in turn served as the market-places of northern and western France.

Venice used the land route to northern Europe. This ancient road led across the Brenner Pass, the old gateway for the barbarians who had invaded Italy. Past Innsbrück, the merchandise was carried to Basel. From there it drifted down the Rhine to the North Sea and England, or it was taken to Augsburg where the Fugger family (who were both bankers and manufacturers and who prospered greatly by "shaving" the coins with which they paid their workmen), looked after the further distribution to Nuremberg and Leipzig and the cities of the Baltic and to Wisby (on the island of Gotland) which looked after the needs of the northern Baltic and dealt

Great Novgorod

directly with the republic of Novgorod, the old commercial centre of Russia which was destroyed by Ivan the Terrible in the middle of the sixteenth century.

The little cities on the coast of north-western Europe had an interesting story of their own. The mediæval world ate a great deal of fish. There were many fast days and then people were not permitted to eat meat. For those who lived away from the coast and from the rivers, this meant a diet of eggs or nothing at all. But early in the thirteenth century a Dutch fisherman had discovered a way of curing herring, so that it could be transported to distant points. The herring fisheries of the North Sea then became of great importance. But some time during the thirteenth century, this useful little fish (for reasons of its own) moved from the North Sea to the Baltic and the cities of that inland sea began to make money. All the world now sailed to the Baltic to catch herring and as that fish could only be caught during a few months each year (the rest of the time it spends in deep water, raising large families of little herrings) the ships would have been idle during the rest of the time unless they had found another occupation. They were then used to carry the wheat of northern and central Russia to southern and western Europe. On the return voyage they brought spices and silks and carpets and oriental rugs from Venice and Genoa to Bruges and Hamburg and Bremen.

Out of such simple beginnings there developed an important system of international trade which reached from the manufacturing cities of Bruges and Ghent (where the almighty guilds fought pitched battles with the kings of France and England and established a labour tyranny which completely ruined both the employers and the workmen) to the republic of Novgorod in northern Russia, which was a mighty city until Tsar Ivan, who distrusted all merchants, took the town and killed sixty thousand people in less than a month's time and reduced the survivors to beggary.

That they might protect themselves against pirates and excessive tolls and annoying legislation, the merchants of the north founded a protective league which was called the "Hansa." The Hansa, which had its headquarters in Lübeck, was a voluntary association of more than one hundred cities. The association maintained a navy of its own which patrolled the seas and fought and defeated the kings of England and Denmark when they dared to interfere with the rights and the privileges of the mighty Hanseatic merchants.

I wish that I had more space to tell you some of the wonderful stories of this strange commerce which was carried on across the high mountains and across the deep seas amidst such dangers that every voyage became a glorious adventure. But it would take several volumes and it cannot be done here.

The Middle Ages, as I have tried to show you, had been a

The Hansa Ship

period of very slow progress. The people who were in power believed that "progress" was a very undesirable invention of the Evil One and ought to be discouraged, and as they happened to occupy the seats of the mighty, it was easy to enforce their will upon the patient serfs and the illiterate knights. Here and there a few brave souls sometimes ventured forth into the forbidden region of science, but they fared badly and were considered lucky when they escaped with their lives and a jail sentence of twenty years.

In the twelfth and thirteenth centuries the flood of international commerce swept over western Europe as the Nile had swept across the valley of ancient Egypt. It left behind a fertile sediment of prosperity. Prosperity meant leisure hours and these leisure hours gave both men and women a chance to buy manuscripts and take an interest in literature and art and music.

Then once more was the world filled with that divine curiosity which has elevated man from the ranks of those other mammals who are his distant cousins but who have remained dumb, and the cities, of whose growth and development I have told you in my last chapter, offered a safe shelter to these brave pioneers who dared to leave the very narrow domain of the established order of things.

They set to work. They opened the windows of their cloistered and studious cells. A flood of sunlight entered the dusty rooms and showed them the cobwebs which had gathered during the long period of semi-darkness.

They began to clean house. Next they cleaned their gardens.

Then they went out into the open fields, outside the crumbling town walls, and said, "This is a good world. We are glad that we live in it."

At that moment, the Middle Ages came to an end and a new world began.

39

The Renaissance

People Once More Dared to Be Happy Just Because
They Were Alive. They Tried to Save the Remains
of the Older and More Agreeable Civilisation of
Rome and Greece and They Were So Proud of Their
Achievements That They Spoke of a "Renaissance"
or Re-birth of Civilisation

The Renaissance was not a political or religious movement. It was a state of mind.

The men of the Renaissance continued to be the obedient
sons of the mother church. They were subjects of kings and
emperors and dukes and murmured not.

But their outlook upon life was changed. They began to
wear different clothes—to speak a different language—to
live different lives in different houses.

They no longer concentrated all their thoughts and their
efforts upon the blessed existence that awaited them in
Heaven. They tried to establish their Paradise upon this
planet, and, truth to tell, they succeeded in a remarkable
degree.

I have quite often warned you against the danger that lies
in historical dates. People take them too literally. They think

of the Middle Ages as a period of darkness and ignorance. "Click," says the clock, and the Renaissance begins and cities and palaces are flooded with the bright sunlight of an eager intellectual curiosity.

As a matter of fact, it is quite impossible to draw such sharp lines. The thirteenth century belonged most decidedly to the Middle Ages. All historians agree upon that. But was it a time of darkness and stagnation merely? By no means. People were tremendously alive. Great states were being founded. Large centres of commerce were being developed. High above the turretted towers of the castle and the peaked roof of the town-hall rose the slender spire of the newly built Gothic cathedral. Everywhere the world was in motion. The high and mighty gentlemen of the city-hall, who had just become conscious of their own strength (by way of their recently acquired riches) were struggling for more power with their feudal masters. The members of the guilds who had just become aware of the important fact that "numbers count" were fighting the high and mighty gentlemen of the city-hall. The king and his shrewd advisers went fishing in these troubled waters and caught many a shining bass of profit which they proceeded to cook and eat before the noses of the surprised and disappointed councillors and guild brethren.

To enliven the scenery during the long hours of evening when the badly lighted streets did not invite further political and economic dispute, the troubadours and minnesingers told their stories and sang their songs of romance and adventure and heroism and loyalty to all fair women. Meanwhile youth, impatient of the slowness of progress, flocked to the universities, and thereby hangs a story.

The Middle Ages were "internationally minded." That sounds difficult, but wait until I explain it to you. We modern people are "nationally minded." We are Americans or

Englishmen or Frenchmen or Italians and speak English or French or Italian and go to English and French and Italian universities, unless we want to specialise in some particular branch of learning which is only taught elsewhere, and then we learn another language and go to Munich or Madrid or Moscow. But the people of the thirteenth or fourteenth century rarely talked of themselves as Englishmen or Frenchmen or Italians. They said, "I am a citizen of Sheffield or Bordeaux or Genoa." Because they all belonged to one and the same church they felt a certain bond of brotherhood. And as all educated men could speak Latin, they possessed an international language which removed the stupid language barriers which have grown up in modern Europe and which place the small nations at such an enormous disadvantage. Just as an example, take the case of Erasmus, the great preacher of tolerance and laughter, who wrote his books in the sixteenth century. He was the native of a small Dutch village. He wrote in Latin and all the world was his audience. If he were alive to-day, he would write in Dutch. Then only five or six million people would be able to read him. To be understood by the rest of Europe and America, his publishers would be obliged to translate his books into twenty different languages. That would cost a lot of money and most likely the publishers would never take the trouble or the risk.

Six hundred years ago that could not happen. The greater part of the people were still very ignorant and could not read or write at all. But those who had mastered the difficult art of handling the goose quill belonged to an international republic of letters which spread across the entire continent and which knew of no boundaries and respected no limitations of language or nationality. The universities were the strongholds of this republic. Unlike modern fortifications, they did not follow the frontier. They were to be found wherever a teacher and a few pupils happened to find themselves together. There again the Middle Ages and the Renaissance differed from our own time. Nowadays, when a new university is built, the process (almost invariably) is as follows: Some rich man wants to do something for the community in which he lives or a particular religious sect wants to build a school to keep its faithful children under decent supervision, or a state needs doctors and lawyers and teachers. The university begins as a large sum of money which is deposited in a bank. This money is then used to construct buildings and laboratories and dormitories. Finally professional teachers are hired, entrance examinations are held and the university is on the way.

But in the Middle Ages things were done differently. A wise man said to himself, "I have discovered a great truth. I must impart my knowledge to others." And he began to preach his wisdom wherever and whenever he could get a few people to listen to him, like a modern soap-box orator. If he was an interesting speaker, the crowd came and stayed. If he was dull, they shrugged their shoulders and continued their way. By and by certain young men began to come regularly to hear the words of wisdom of this great teacher. They brought copy-books with them and a little bottle of ink and a goose quill and wrote down what seemed to be important. One day it rained. The teacher and his pupils retired to an

The Mediæval Laboratory

empty basement or the room of the "professor." The learned man sat in his chair and the boys sat on the floor. That was the beginning of the university, the "universitas," a corporation of professors and students during the Middle Ages, when the "teacher" counted for everything and the building in which he taught counted for very little.

As an example, let me tell you of something that happened in the ninth century. In the town of Salerno near Naples there were a number of excellent physicians. They attracted people desirous of learning the medical profession and for almost a thousand years (until 1817) there was a University of Salerno which taught the wisdom of Hippocrates, the great Greek doctor who had practised his art in ancient Hellas in the fifth century before the birth of Christ.

Then there was Abelard, the young priest from Brittany, who early in the twelfth century began to lecture on theology and logic in Paris. Thousands of eager young men flocked to the French city to hear him. Other priests who disagreed with him stepped forward to explain their point of view. Paris was soon filled with a clamouring multitude of Englishmen and Germans and Italians and students from Sweden and Hungary and around the old cathedral which stood on a little island in the Seine there grew the famous University of Paris.

In Bologna in Italy, a monk by the name of Gratian had compiled a text-book for those whose business it was to know the laws of the church. Young priests and many laymen then came from all over Europe to hear Gratian explain his ideas. To protect themselves against the landlords and the inn-keepers and the boarding house ladies of the city, they formed a corporation (or university) and behold the beginning of the University of Bologna.

Next there was a quarrel in the University of Paris. We do not know what caused it, but a number of disgruntled teachers together with their pupils crossed the Channel and found a hospitable home in a little village on the Thames called Oxford, and in this way the famous University of Oxford came into being. In the same way, in the year 1222, there had been a split in the University of Bologna. The discontented teachers (again followed by their pupils) had moved to Padua and their proud city thenceforward boasted of a university of its own. And so it went from Valladolid in Spain to Cracow in distant Poland and from Poitiers in France to Rostock in Germany.

It is quite true that much of the teaching done by these early professors would sound absurd to our ears, trained to listen to logarithms and geometrical theorems. The point, however, which I want to make is this—the Middle Ages and especially the thirteenth century were not a time when the world stood entirely still. Among the younger generation,

The Renaissance

there was life, there was enthusiasm and there was a restless if somewhat bashful asking of questions. And out of this turmoil grew the Renaissance.

But just before the curtain went down upon the last scene of the mediæval world, a solitary figure crossed the stage, of whom you ought to know more than his mere name. This man was called Dante. He was the son of a Florentine lawyer who belonged to the Alighieri family and he saw the light of day in the year 1265. He grew up in the city of his ancestors while Giotto was painting his stories of the life of St. Francis of Assisi upon the walls of the church of the Holy Cross, but often when he went to school, his frightened eyes would see the puddles of blood which told of the terrible and endless warfare that raged forever between the Guelphs and the Ghibellines, the followers of the Pope and the adherents of the emperors.

When he grew up, he became a Guelph, because his father had been one before him, just as an American boy might become a Democrat or a Republican, simply because his father had happened to be a Democrat or a Republican. But after a few years, Dante saw that Italy, unless united under a single head, threatened to perish as a victim of the disordered jealousies of a thousand little cities. Then he became a Ghibelline.

He looked for help beyond the Alps. He hoped that a mighty emperor might come and re-establish unity and order. Alas! he hoped in vain. The Ghibellines were driven out of Florence in the year 1302. From that time on until the day of his death amidst the dreary ruins of Ravenna, in the year 1321, Dante was a homeless wanderer, eating the bread of charity at the table of rich patrons whose names would have sunk into the deepest pit of oblivion but for this single fact, that they had been kind to a poet in his misery. During the many years of exile, Dante felt compelled to justify himself and his actions when he had been a political leader in his home-town, and when he had spent his days walking along the banks of the Arno that he might catch a glimpse of the lovely Beatrice Portinari, who died the wife of another man, a dozen years before the Ghibelline disaster.

He had failed in the ambitions of his career. He had faithfully served the town of his birth and before a corrupt

Dante

court he had been accused of stealing the public funds and had been condemned to be burned alive should he venture back within the realm of the city of Florence. To clear himself before his own conscience and before his contemporaries, Dante then created an imaginary world and with great detail he described the circumstances which had led to his defeat and depicted the hopeless condition of greed and lust and hatred which had turned his fair and beloved Italy into a battlefield for the pitiless mercenaries of wicked and selfish tyrants.

He tells us how on the Thursday before Easter of the year 1300 he had lost his way in a dense forest and how he found his path barred by a leopard and a lion and a wolf. He gave himself up for lost when a white figure appeared amidst the trees. It was Virgil, the Roman poet and philosopher, sent upon his errand of mercy by the Blessed Virgin and by Beatrice, who from high Heaven watched over the fate of her true lover. Virgil then takes Dante through Purgatory and through Hell. Deeper and deeper the path leads them until they reach the lowest pit where Lucifer himself stands frozen into the eternal ice surrounded by the most terrible of sinners, traitors and liars and those who have achieved fame and success by lies and by deceit. But before the two wanderers have reached this terrible spot, Dante has met all those who in some way or other have played a rôle in the history of his beloved city. Emperors and Popes, dashing knights and whining usurers, they are all there, doomed to eternal punishment or awaiting the day of deliverance, when they shall leave Purgatory for Heaven.

It is a curious story. It is a handbook of everything the people of the thirteenth century did and felt and feared and prayed for. Through it all moves the figure of the lonely Florentine exile, forever followed by the shadow of his own despair.

And behold! When the gates of death were closing upon the sad poet of the Middle Ages, the portals of life swung open to the child who was to be the first of the men of the Renaissance. That was Francesco Petrarca, the son of the notary public of the little town of Arezzo.

Francesco's father had belonged to the same political party as Dante. He too had been exiled and thus it happened that Petrarca (or Petrarch, as we call him) was born away from Florence. At the age of fifteen he was sent to Montpellier in France that he might become a lawyer like his father. But the boy did not want to be a jurist. He hated the law. He wanted to be a scholar and a poet—and because he wanted to be a scholar and a poet beyond everything else, he became one, as people of a strong will are apt to do. He made long voyages, copying manuscripts in Flanders and in the cloisters along the Rhine and in Paris and Liège and finally in Rome. Then he went to live in a lonely valley of the wild mountains of Vaucluse, and there he studied and wrote and soon he had become so famous for his verse and for his learning that both the University of Paris and the king of Naples invited him to come and teach their students and subjects. On the way to his new job, he was obliged to pass through Rome. The people had heard of his fame as an editor of half-forgotten

Roman authors. They decided to honour him and in the ancient Forum of the Imperial City, Petrarch was crowned with the laurel wreath of the poet.

From that moment on, his life was an endless career of honour and appreciation. He wrote the things which people wanted most to hear. They were tired of theological disputations. Poor Dante could wander through Hell as much as he wanted. But Petrarch wrote of love and of nature and the sun and never mentioned those gloomy things which seemed to have been the stock in trade of the last generation. And when Petrarch came to a city, all the people flocked out to meet him and he was received like a conquering hero. If he happened to bring his young friend Boccaccio, the story teller, with him, so much the better. They were both men of their time, full of curiosity, willing to read everything once, digging in forgotten and musty libraries that they might find still another manuscript of Virgil or Ovid or Lucretius or any of the other old Latin poets. They were good Christians. Of course they were! Everyone was. But no need of going around with a long face and wearing a dirty coat just because some day or other you were going to die. Life was good. People were meant to be happy. You desired proof of this? Very well. Take a spade and dig into the soil. What did you find? Beautiful old statues. Beautiful old vases. Ruins of ancient buildings. All these things were made by the people of the greatest empire that ever existed. They ruled all the world for a thousand years. They were strong and rich and handsome (just look at that bust of the emperor Augustus!). Of course, they were not Christians and they would never be able to enter Heaven. At best they would spend their days in Purgatory, where Dante had just paid them a visit.

But who cared? To have lived in a world like that of ancient Rome was Heaven enough for any mortal being. And anyway, we live but once. Let us be happy and cheerful for the mere joy of existence.

Such, in short, was the spirit that had begun to fill the narrow and crooked streets of the many little Italian cities.

You know what we mean by the "bicycle craze" or the "automobile craze." Some one invents a bicycle. People who for hundreds of thousands of years have moved slowly and painfully from one place to another go "crazy" over the prospect of rolling rapidly and easily over hill and dale. Then a clever mechanic makes the first automobile. No longer is it necessary to pedal and pedal and pedal. You just sit and let little drops of gasoline do the work for you. Then everybody wants an automobile. Everybody talks about Rolls-Royces and flivvers and carburetors and mileage and oil. Explorers penetrate into the hearts of unknown countries that they may find new supplies of gas. Forests arise in Sumatra and in the Congo to supply us with rubber. Rubber and oil become so valuable that people fight wars for their possession. The whole world is "automobile mad" and little children can say "car" before they learn to whisper "papa" and "mamma."

In the fourteenth century, the Italian people went crazy about the newly discovered beauties of the buried world of Rome. Soon their enthusiasm was shared by all the people of western Europe. The finding of an unknown manuscript became the excuse for a civic holiday. The man who wrote a grammar became as popular as the fellow who nowadays invents a new spark-plug. The humanist, the scholar who devoted his time and his energies to a study of "homo" or mankind (instead of wasting his hours upon fruitless theological investigations), that man was regarded with greater honour and a deeper respect than was ever bestowed upon a hero who had just conquered all the Cannibal Islands.

In the midst of this intellectual upheaval, an event occurred which greatly favoured the study of the ancient philosophers and authors. The Turks were renewing their attacks upon Europe. Constantinople, capital of the last remnant of the original Roman Empire, was hard pressed. In the

year 1393 the emperor, Manuel Paleologue, sent Emmanuel
Chrysoloras to western Europe to explain the desperate
state of old Byzantium and to ask for aid. This aid never
came. The Roman Catholic world was more than willing
to see the Greek Catholic world go to the punishment that
awaited such wicked heretics. But however indifferent western Europe might be to the fate of the Byzantines, they were
greatly interested in the ancient Greeks whose colonists had
founded the city on the Bosphorus five centuries after the
Trojan War. They wanted to learn Greek that they might
read Aristotle and Homer and Plato. They wanted to learn
it very badly, but they had no books and no grammars and
no teachers. The magistrates of Florence heard of the visit
of Chrysoloras. The people of their city were "crazy to learn
Greek." Would he please come and teach them? He would,
and behold! the first professor of Greek teaching alpha, beta,
gamma to hundreds of eager young men, begging their
way to the city of the Arno, living in stables and in dingy
attics that they might learn how to decline the verb παιδενω
παιδενει' παιδενει and enter into the companionship of Sophocles and Homer.

Meanwhile in the universities, the old Schoolmen, teaching their ancient theology and their antiquated logic; explaining the hidden mysteries of the Old Testament and discussing
the strange science of their Greek-Arabic-Spanish-Latin edition of Aristotle, looked on in dismay and horror. Next, they
turned angry. This thing was going too far. The young men
were deserting the lecture halls of the established universities to go and listen to some wild-eyed "humanist" with his
new-fangled notions about a "re-born civilization."

They went to the authorities. They complained. But one
cannot force an unwilling horse to drink and one cannot
make unwilling ears listen to something which does not
really interest them. The Schoolmen were losing ground rap-

idly. Here and there they scored a short victory. They combined forces with those fanatics who hated to see other people enjoy a happiness which was foreign to their own souls. In Florence, the centre of the Great Re-birth, a terrible fight was fought between the old order and the new. A Dominican monk, sour of face and bitter in his hatred of beauty, was the leader of the mediæval rear-guard. He fought a valiant battle. Day after day he thundered his warnings of God's holy wrath through the wide halls of Santa Maria del Fiore. "Repent," he cried, "repent of your godlessness, of your joy in things that are not holy!" He began to hear voices and to see flaming swords that flashed through the sky. He preached to the little children that they might not fall into the errors of these ways which were leading their fathers to perdition. He organised companies of boyscouts, devoted to the service of the great God whose prophet he claimed to be. In a sudden moment of frenzy, the frightened people promised to do penance for their wicked love of beauty and pleasure. They carried their books and their statues and their paintings to the market-place and celebrated a wild "carnival of the vanities" with holy singing and most unholy dancing, while Savonarola applied his torch to the accumulated treasures.

But when the ashes cooled down, the people began to realise what they had lost. This terrible fanatic had made them destroy that which they had come to love above all things. They turned against him. Savonarola was thrown into jail. He was tortured. But he refused to repent for anything he had done. He was an honest man. He had tried to live a holy life. He had willingly destroyed those who deliberately refused to share his own point of view. It had been his duty to eradicate evil wherever he found it. A love of heathenish books and heathenish beauty in the eyes of this faithful son of the church had been an evil. But he stood alone. He had fought the battle of a time that was dead and gone. The Pope in Rome never moved a finger to save him. On the contrary, he approved of his "faithful Florentines" when they dragged Savonarola to the gallows, hanged him and burned his body amidst the cheerful howling and yelling of the mob.

It was a sad ending, but quite inevitable. Savonarola would have been a great man in the eleventh century. In the fifteenth century he was merely the leader of a lost cause. For better or worse, the Middle Ages had come to an end when the Pope had turned humanist and when the Vatican became the most important museum of Roman and Greek antiquities.

40

The Age of Expression

The People Began to Feel the Need of
Giving Expression to Their Newly Discovered
Joy of Living. They Expressed Their Happiness in
Poetry and in Sculpture and in Architecture and
in Painting and in the Books They Printed

In the year 1471 there died a pious old man who had spent seventy-two of his ninety-one years behind the sheltering walls of the cloister of Mount St. Agnes near the good town of Zwolle, the old Dutch Hanseatic city on the River Ysel. He was known as Brother Thomas and because he had been born in the village of Kempen, he was called Thomas à Kempis. At the age of twelve he had been sent to Deventer, where Gerhard Groot, a brilliant graduate of the universities of Paris, Cologne and Prague, and famous as a wandering preacher, had founded the Society of the Brothers of the Common Life. The good brothers were humble laymen who tried to live the simple life of the early apostles of Christ while working at their regular jobs as carpenters and housepainters and stone masons. They maintained an excellent school, that deserving boys of poor parents might be taught the wisdom of the fathers of the church. At this school, little

Thomas had learned how to conjugate Latin verbs and how to copy manuscripts. Then he had taken his vows, had put his little bundle of books upon his back, had wandered to Zwolle and with a sigh of relief he had closed the door upon a turbulent world which did not attract him.

Thomas lived in an age of turmoil, pestilence and sudden death. In central Europe, in Bohemia, the devoted disciples of Johannes [John] Huss, the friend and follower of John Wycliffe, the English reformer, were avenging with a terrible warfare the death of their beloved leader who had been burned at the stake by order of that same Council of Constance which had promised him a safe-conduct if he would come to Switzerland and explain his doctrines to the Pope, the emperor, 23 cardinals, 33 archbishops and bishops, 150 abbots and more than 100 princes and dukes who had gathered together to reform their church.

In the west, France had been fighting for a hundred years that she might drive the English from her territories and just then was saved from utter defeat by the fortunate appearance of Joan of Arc. And no sooner had this struggle come to an end than France and Burgundy were at each other's throats, engaged upon a struggle of life and death for the supremacy of western Europe.

In the south, a Pope at Rome was calling the curses of

John Huss

Heaven down upon a second Pope who resided at Avignon, in southern France, and who retaliated in kind. In the far east the Turks were destroying the last remnants of the Roman Empire and the Russians had started upon a final crusade to crush the power of their Tartar masters.

But of all this, Brother Thomas in his quiet cell never heard. He had his manuscripts and his own thoughts and he was contented. He poured his love of God into a little volume. He called it the "Imitation of Christ." It has since been translated into more languages than any other book save the Bible. It has been read by quite as many people as ever studied the Holy Scriptures. It has influenced the lives of countless millions. And it was the work of a man whose highest ideal of existence was expressed in the simple wish that "he might quietly spend his days sitting in a little corner with a little book."

Good Brother Thomas represented the purest ideals of the Middle Ages. Surrounded on all sides by the forces of the victorious Renaissance, with the humanists loudly proclaiming the coming of modern times, the Middle Ages gathered strength for a last sally. Monasteries were reformed. Monks gave up the habits of riches and vice. Simple, straightforward and honest men, by the example of their blameless and devout lives, tried to bring the people back to the ways of righteousness and humble resignation to the will of God. But all to no avail. The new world rushed past these good people. The days of quiet meditation were gone. The great era of "expression" had begun.

Here and now let me say that I am sorry that I must use so many "big words." I wish that I could write this history in words of one syllable. But it cannot be done. You cannot write a text-book of geometry without reference to a hypotenuse and triangles and a rectangular parallelopiped. You simply have to learn what those words mean or do without mathematics. In history (and in all life) you will eventually be obliged to learn the meaning of many strange words of Latin and Greek origin. Why not do it now?

When I say that the Renaissance was an era of expression, I mean this: People were no longer contented to be the audience and sit still while the emperor and the Pope told them what to do and what to think. They wanted to be actors upon the stage of life. They insisted upon giving "expression" to their own individual ideas. If a man happened to be interested in statesmanship like the Florentine historian Niccolò Machiavelli, then he "expressed" himself in his books which revealed his own idea of a successful state and an efficient ruler. If, on the other hand, he had a liking for painting, he "expressed" his love for beautiful lines and lovely colours in the pictures which have made the names of Giotto, Fra Angelico, Rafael and a thousand others household words wherever people have learned to care for those things which express a true and lasting beauty.

The Manuscript and the Printed Book

The Cathedral

If this love for colour and line happened to be combined with an interest in mechanics and hydraulics, the result was a Leonardo da Vinci, who painted his pictures, experimented with his balloons and flying machines, drained the marshes of the Lombardian plains and "expressed" his joy and interest in all things between Heaven and earth in prose, in painting, in sculpture and in curiously conceived engines. When a man of gigantic strength, like Michelangelo, found the brush and the palette too soft for his strong hands, he turned to sculpture and to architecture, and hacked the most terrific creatures out of heavy blocks of marble and drew the plans for the church of St. Peter, the most concrete "expression" of the glories of the triumphant church. And so it went.

All Italy (and very soon all of Europe) was filled with men and women who lived that they might add their mite to the sum total of our accumulated treasures of knowledge and beauty and wisdom. In Germany, in the city of Mainz, Johann zum Gänsefleisch, commonly known as Johann Gutenberg, had just invented a new method of copying books. He had studied the old woodcuts and had perfected a system by which individual letters of soft lead could be placed in such a way that they formed words and whole pages. It is true, he soon lost all his money in a law-suit which had to do with the original invention of the press. He died in poverty, but the "expression" of his particular inventive genius lived after him.

Soon Aldus in Venice and Etienne in Paris and Plantin in Antwerp and Froben in Basel were flooding the world with carefully edited editions of the classics printed in the Gothic letters of the Gutenberg Bible, or printed in the Italian type, or printed in Greek letters or in Hebrew.

Then the whole world became the eager audience of those who had something to say. The day when learning had been a monopoly of a privileged few came to an end. And the last excuse for ignorance was removed from this world, when Elzevier of Haarlem began to print his cheap and popular editions. Then Aristotle and Plato, Virgil and Horace and Pliny, all the goodly company of the ancient authors and philosophers and scientists, offered to become man's faithful friend in exhange for a few paltry pennies. Humanism had made all men free and equal before the printed word.

41

The Great Discoveries

But Now That People Had Broken Through the
Bonds of Their Narrow Mediæval Limitations,
They Had to Have More Room for Their
Wanderings. The European World Had Grown
Too Small for Their Ambitions. It Was
the Time of the Great Voyages of Discovery

The Crusades had been a lesson in the liberal art of travelling. But very few people had ever ventured beyond the well-known beaten track which led from Venice to Jaffa. In the thirteenth century the Polo brothers, merchants of Venice, had wandered across the great Mongolian desert and after climbing mountains as high as the moon, they had found their way to the court of the great Khan of Cathay, the mighty emperor of China. The son of one of the Polos, by the name of Marco, had written a book about their adventures, which covered a period of more than twenty years. The astonished world had gaped at his descriptions of the golden towers of the strange island of Zipangu, which was his Italian way of spelling Japan. Many people had wanted to go east, that they might find this gold-land and grow rich. But the trip was too far and too dangerous and so they stayed at home.

Of course, there was always the possibility of making the voyage by sea. But the sea was very unpopular in the Middle Ages and for many very good reasons. In the first place, ships were very small. The vessels on which Magellan made his famous trip around the world, which lasted many years, were not as large as a modern ferryboat. They carried from twenty to fifty men, who lived in dingy quarters (too low to allow any of them to stand up straight) and the sailors were obliged to eat poorly cooked food as the kitchen arrangements were very bad and no fire could be made whenever

Marco Polo

the weather was the least bit rough. The mediæval world knew how to pickle herring and how to dry fish. But there were no canned goods and fresh vegetables were never seen on the bill of fare as soon as the coast had been left behind. Water was carried in small barrels. It soon became stale and then tasted of rotten wood and iron rust and was full of slimy growing things. As the people of the Middle Ages knew nothing about microbes (Roger Bacon, the learned monk of the thirteenth century, seems to have suspected their existence, but he wisely kept his discovery to himself) they often drank unclean water and sometimes the whole crew died of typhoid fever. Indeed the mortality on board the ships of the earliest navigators was terrible. Of the two hundred sailors who in the year 1519 left Seville to accompany Magellan on his famous voyage around the world, only eighteen returned. As late as the seventeenth century when there was a brisk trade between western Europe and the Indies, a mortality of forty percent was nothing unusual for a trip from Amsterdam to Batavia and back. The greater part of these victims died of scurvy, a disease which is caused by lack of fresh vegetables and which affects the gums and poisons the blood until the patient dies of sheer exhaustion.

Under those circumstances you will understand that the sea did not attract the best elements of the population. Famous discoverers like Magellan and Columbus and Vasco da Gama travelled at the head of crews that were almost entirely composed of ex-jailbirds, future murderers and pickpockets out of a job.

These navigators certainly deserve our admiration for the courage and the pluck with which they accomplished their hopeless tasks in the face of difficulties of which the people of our own comfortable world can have no conception. Their ships were leaky. The rigging was clumsy. Since the middle of the thirteenth century they had possessed some sort of a compass (which had come to Europe from China by way of Arabia and the Crusades) but they had very bad and incorrect maps. They set their course by God and by guess. If luck was with them they returned after one or two or three years. In the other case, their bleached bones remained behind on some lonely beach. But they were true pioneers. They gambled with luck. Life to them was a glorious adventure. And all the suffering, the thirst and the hunger and the pain were forgotten when their eyes beheld the dim outlines of a new coast or the placid waters of an ocean that had lain forgotten since the beginning of time.

Again I wish that I could make this book a thousand pages long. The subject of the early discoveries is so fascinating. But history, to give you a true idea of past times, should be like those etchings which Rembrandt used to make. It should cast a vivid light on certain important causes, on those which are best and greatest. All the rest should be left in the shadow or should be indicated by a few lines. And in this chapter I can only give you a short list of the most important discoveries.

Keep in mind that all during the fourteenth and fifteenth centuries the navigators were trying to accomplish just *one thing*—they wanted to find a comfortable and safe road to the empire of Cathay (China), to the island of Zipangu (Japan) and to those mysterious islands where grew the spices which the mediæval world had come to like since the days of the Crusades, and which people needed in those days before the introduction of cold storage, when meat and fish spoiled very quickly and could only be eaten after a liberal sprinkling of pepper or nutmeg.

The Venetians and the Genoese had been the great navigators of the Mediterranean, but the honour for exploring the coast of the Atlantic goes to the Portuguese. Spain and Portugal were full of that patriotic energy which their age-old struggle against the Moorish invaders had developed. Such energy, once it exists, can easily be forced into new channels. In the thirteenth century, King Alphonso III had conquered the kingdom of Algarve in the southwestern corner of the Spanish peninsula and had added it to his dominions. In the next century, the Portuguese had turned the tables on the Mohammedans, had crossed the Strait of Gibraltar and had taken possession of Ceuta, opposite the Arabic city

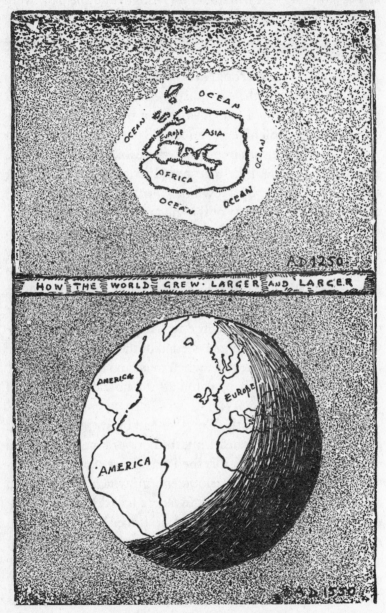

How the World Grew Larger

of Ta'Rifa (a word which in Arabic means "inventory" and which by way of the Spanish language has come down to us as "tariff") and Tangier, which became the capital of an African addition to Algarve.

They were ready to begin their career as explorers.

In the year 1415, Prince Henry, known as Henry the Navigator, the son of John I of Portugal and Philippa, the daughter of John of Gaunt (about whom you can read in "Richard II," a play by William Shakespeare), began to make preparations for the systematic exploration of north-western Africa. Before this, that hot and sandy coast had been visited by the Phœnicians and by the Norsemen, who remembered it as the home of the hairy "wild man" whom we have come to know as the gorilla. One after another, Prince Henry and his captains discovered the Canary Islands, re-discovered the island of Madeira, which a century before had been visited by a Genoese ship, carefully charted the Azores, which had been vaguely known to both the Portuguese and the Spaniards, and caught a glimpse of the mouth of the Senegal River on the west coast of Africa, which they supposed to be the western mouth of the Nile. At last, by the middle of the fifteenth century, they saw Cape Verde, or the Green Cape, and the Cape Verde Islands, which lie almost halfway between the coast of Africa and Brazil.

But Henry did not restrict himself in his investigations to the waters of the ocean. He was grand master of the Order of Christ. This was a Portuguese continuation of the Crusading order of the Templars which had been abolished by Pope Clement V in the year 1312 at the request of King Philip the Fair of France, who had improved the occasion by burning his own Templars at the stake and stealing all their possessions. Prince Henry used the revenues of the domains of his religious order to equip several expeditions which explored the hinterland of the Sahara and the coast of Guinea.

But he was still very much a son of the Middle Ages and spent a great deal of time and wasted a lot of money upon a search for the mysterious "Prester John," the mythical Christian priest who was said to be the emperor of a vast empire "situated somewhere in the east." The story of this strange potentate had first been told in Europe in the middle of the twelfth century. For three hundred years people had tried to find "Prester John" and his descendants. Henry took part in the search. Thirty years after his death, the riddle was solved.

In the year 1486 Bartholomew Diaz, trying to find the land of Prester John by sea, had reached the southernmost point of Africa. At first he called it the Storm Cape, on account of the strong winds which had prevented him from continuing his voyage toward the east, but the Lisbon pilots who understood the importance of this discovery in their quest for the India water route, changed the name into that of the Cape of Good Hope.

One year later, Pedro de Covilham, provided with letters of credit on the house of Medici, started upon a similar mission by land. He crossed the Mediterranean and after leaving Egypt, he travelled southward. He reached Aden, and from there, travelling through the waters of the Persian Gulf, which few white men had seen since the days of Alexander the Great, eighteen centuries before, he visited Goa and Calicut on the coast of India, where he got a great deal of news about the island of the Moon (Madagascar), which was supposed to lie halfway between Africa and India. Then he returned, paid a secret visit to Mecca and to Medina, crossed the Red Sea once more and in the year 1490 he discovered the realm of Prester John, who was no one less than the Black Negus (or king) of Abyssinia, whose ancestors had adopted Christianity in the fourth century, seven hundred years before the Christian missionaries had found their way to Scandinavia.

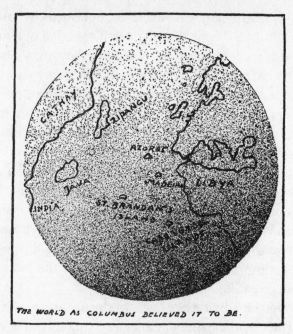

THE WORLD AS COLUMBUS BELIEVED IT TO BE.

The World of Columbus

These many voyages had convinced the Portuguese geographers and cartographers that while the voyage to the Indies by an eastern sea-route was possible, it was by no means easy. Then there arose a great debate. Some people wanted to continue the explorations east of the Cape of Good Hope. Others said, "No, we must sail west across the Atlantic and then we shall reach Cathay."

Let us state right here that most intelligent people of that day were firmly convinced that the earth was not as flat as a pancake but was round. The Ptolemæan system of the universe, invented and duly described by Claudius Ptolemy, the great Egyptian geographer, who had lived in the second century of our era, which had served the simple needs of the men of the Middle Ages, had long been discarded by the scientists of the Renaissance. They had accepted the doctrine of

the Polish mathematician Nicolaus Copernicus, whose studies had convinced him that the earth was one of a number
of round planets which turned around the sun, a discovery
which he did not venture to publish for thirty-six years (it
was printed in 1543, the year of his death) from fear of the
Holy Inquisition, a Papal court which had been established
in the thirteenth century when the heresies of the Albigenses
and the Waldenses in France and in Italy (very mild heresies of devoutly pious people who did not believe in private
property and preferred to live in Christ-like poverty) had for
a moment threatened the absolute power of the bishops of
Rome. But the belief in the roundness of the earth was common among the nautical experts and, as I said, they were
now debating the respective advantages of the eastern and
the western routes.

Among the advocates of the western route was a Genoese mariner by the name of Cristoforo Colombo. He was the
son of a wool merchant. He seems to have been a student at
the University of Pavia where he specialised in mathematics
and geometry. Then he took up his father's trade but soon
we find him in Chios in the eastern Mediterranean travelling on business. Thereafter we hear of voyages to England
but whether he went north in search of wool or as the captain of a ship we do not know. In February of the year 1477,
Colombo (if we are to believe his own words) visited Iceland,
but very likely he only got a far as the Färoe Islands which
are cold enough in February to be mistaken for Iceland by
any one. Here Colombo met the descendants of those brave
Norsemen who in the tenth century had settled in Greenland and who had visited America in the eleventh century,
when Leif's vessel had been blown to the coast of Vineland,
or Labrador.

What had become of those far western colonies no one
knew. The American colony of Thorfinn Karlsefne, the hus-

band of the widow of Leif's brother Thorstein, founded in the year 1003, had been discontinued three years later on account of the hostility of the Esquimaux. As for Greenland, not a word had been heard from the settlers since the year 1440. Very likely the Greenlanders had all died of the Black Death, which had just killed half the people of Norway. However that might be, the tradition of a "vast land in the distant west" still survived among the people of the Färoe and Iceland, and Colombo must have heard of it. He gathered further information among the fishermen of the northern Scottish islands and then went to Portugal where he married the daughter of one of the captains who had served under Prince Henry the Navigator.

From that moment on (the year 1478) he devoted himself to the quest of the western route to the Indies. He sent his

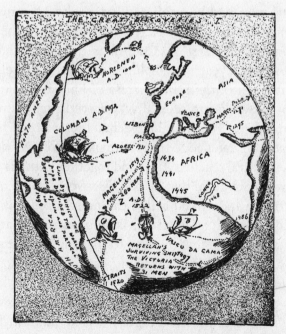

The Great Discoveries, Western Hemisphere

plans for such a voyage to the courts of Portugal and Spain. The Portuguese, who felt certain that they possessed a monopoly of the eastern route, would not listen to his plans. In Spain, Ferdinand of Aragon and Isabella of Castile, whose marriage in 1469 had made Spain into a single kingdom, were busy driving the Moors from their last stronghold, Granada. They had no money for risky expeditions. They needed every peseta for their soldiers.

Few people were ever forced to fight as desperately for their ideas as this brave Italian. But the story of Colombo (or Colon or Columbus, as we call him) is too well known to bear repeating. The Moors surrendered Granada on January 2 of the year 1492. In the month of April of the same year, Columbus signed a contract with the king and queen of Spain. On Friday, August 3, he left Palos with three little ships and a crew of eighty-eight men, many of whom were criminals who had been offered indemnity of punishment if they joined the expedition. At two o'clock in the morning of Friday, October 12, Columbus discovered land. On January 4 of the year 1493, Columbus waved farewell to the forty-four men of the little fortress of La Navidad (none of whom was ever again seen alive) and returned homeward. By the middle of February he reached the Azores where the Portuguese threatened to throw him into gaol. On March 15, 1493, the admiral reached Palos and together with his Indians (for he was convinced that he had discovered some outlying islands of the Indies and called the natives red Indians) he hastened to Barcelona to tell his faithful patrons that he had been successful and that the road to the gold and the silver of Cathay and Zipangu was at the disposal of Their Most Catholic Majesties.

Alas, Columbus never knew the truth. Towards the end of his life, on his fourth voyage, when he had touched the mainland of South America, he may have suspected that all was not well with his discovery. But he died in the firm belief

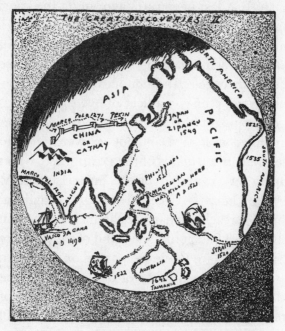

The Great Discoveries, Eastern Hemisphere

that there was no solid continent between Europe and Asia and that he had found the direct route to China.

Meanwhile, the Portuguese, sticking to their eastern route, had been more fortunate. In the year 1498, Vasco da Gama had been able to reach the coast of Malabar and return safely to Lisbon with a cargo of spice. In the year 1502 he had repeated the visit. But along the western route, the work of exploration had been most disappointing. In 1497 and 1498 John and Sebastian Cabot had tried to find a passage to Japan but they had seen nothing but the snowbound coasts and the rocks of Newfoundland, which had first been sighted by the Northmen, five centuries before. Amerigo Vespucci, a Florentine who became the pilot major of Spain, and who gave his name to our continent, had explored the coast of Brazil, but had found not a trace of the Indies.

In the year 1513, seven years after the death of Columbus, the truth at last began to dawn upon the geographers of Europe. Vasco Núñez de Balboa had crossed the isthmus of Panama, had climbed the famous peak in Darién and had looked down upon a vast expanse of water which seemed to suggest the existence of another ocean.

Finally in the year 1519 a fleet of five small Spanish ships under command of the Portuguese navigator Ferdinand Magellan sailed westward (and not eastward since that route was absolutely in the hands of the Portuguese, who allowed no competition) in search of the Spice Islands. Magellan crossed the Atlantic between Africa and Brazil and sailed southward. He reached a narrow channel between the southernmost point of Patagonia, the "land of the people with the big feet," and the Fire Island (so named on account of a fire, the only sign of the existence of natives, which the sailors watched one night). For almost five weeks the ships of Magellan were at the mercy of the terrible storms and blizzards which swept through the straits. A mutiny broke out among the sailors. Magellan suppressed it with terrible severity and sent two of his men on shore where they were left to repent of their sins at leisure. At last the storms quieted down, the channel broadened and Magellan entered a new ocean. Its waves were quiet and placid. He called it the Peaceful Sea, the Mare Pacifico. Then he continued in a western direction. He sailed for ninety-eight days without seeing land. His people almost perished from hunger and thirst and ate the rats that infested the ships, and when these were all gone they chewed pieces of sail to still their gnawing hunger.

In March of the year 1521 they saw land. Magellan called it the land of the Ladrones (which mean robbers) because the natives stole everything they could lay hands on. Then further westward to the Spice Islands!

Again land was sighted. A group of lonely islands. Magellan called them the Philippines, after Philip, the son of his

master Charles V, the Philip II of unpleasant historical memory. At first Magellan was well received, but when he used
the guns of his ships to make Christian converts he was killed
by the aborigines, together with a number of his captains
and sailors. The survivors burned one of the three remaining
ships and continued their voyage. They found the Moluccas,
the famous Spice Islands; they sighted Borneo and reached
Tidor. There, one of the two ships, too leaky to be of further
use, remained behind with her crew. The "Vittoria," under
Sebastian del Cano, crossed the Indian Ocean, missed seeing
the northern coast of Australia (which was not discovered
until the first half of the seventeenth century when ships of
the Dutch East India Company explored this flat and inhospitable land) and after great hardships reached Spain.

This was the most notable of all voyages. It had taken
three years. It had been accomplished at a great cost both of
men and money. But it had established the fact that the earth
was round and that the new lands discovered by Columbus
were not a part of the Indies but a separate continent. From
that time on, Spain and Portugal devoted all their energies
to the development of their Indian and American trade. To
prevent an armed conflict between the rivals, Pope Alexander VI (the only avowed heathen who was ever elected to
this most holy office) had obligingly divided the world into
two equal parts by a line of demarcation which followed the
fiftieth degree of longitude west of Greenwich, the so-called
division of Tordesillas of 1494. The Portuguese were to establish their colonies to the east of this line, the Spaniards were
to have theirs to the west. This accounts for the fact that
the entire American continent with the exception of Brazil
became Spanish and that all of the Indies and most of Africa
became Portuguese until the English and the Dutch colonists (who had no respect for Papal decisions) took these possessions away in the seventeenth and eighteenth centuries.

Magellan

When news of the discovery of Columbus reached the
Rialto of Venice, the Wall Street of the Middle Ages, there
was a terrible panic. Stocks and bonds went down forty
and fifty percent. After a short while, when it appeared that
Columbus had failed to find the road to Cathay, the Venetian merchants recovered from their fright. But the voyages
of da Gama and Magellan proved the practical possibilities
of an eastern water-route to the Indies. Then the rulers of
Genoa and Venice, the two great commercial centres of the
Middle Ages and the Renaissance, began to be sorry that they
had refused to listen to Columbus. But it was too late. Their
Mediterranean became an inland sea. The overland trade to
the Indies and China dwindled to insignificant proportions.
The old days of Italian glory were gone. The Atlantic became
the new centre of commerce and therefore the centre of civilisation. It has remained so ever since.

A New World

262 THE STORY OF MANKIND

See how strangely civilisation has progressed since those early days, fifty centuries before, when the inhabitants of the valley of the Nile began to keep a written record of history. From the River Nile, it went to Mesopotamia, the land between the rivers. Then came the turn of Crete and Greece and Rome. An inland sea became the centre of trade and the cities along the Mediterranean were the home of art and science and philosophy and learning. In the sixteenth century it moved westward once more and made the countries that border upon the Atlantic become the masters of the earth.

There are those who say that the World War and the suicide of the great European nations has greatly diminished the importance of the Atlantic Ocean. They expect to see civilisation cross the American continent and find a new home in the Pacific. But I doubt this.

The westward trip was accompanied by a steady increase in the size of ships and a broadening of the knowledge of the navigators. The flat-bottomed vessels of the Nile and the Euphrates were replaced by the sailing vessels of the Phœnicians, the Ægeans, the Greeks, the Carthaginians and the Romans. These in turn were discarded for the square-rigged vessels of the Portuguese and the Spaniards. And the latter were driven from the ocean by the full-rigged craft of the English and the Dutch.

At present, however, civilisation no longer depends upon ships. Aircraft has taken and will continue to take the place of the sailing vessel and the steamer. The next centre of civilisation will depend upon the development of aircraft and waterpower. And the sea once more shall be the undisturbed home of the little fishes, who once upon a time shared their deep residence with the earliest ancestors of the human race.

42

Buddha and Confucius

Concerning Buddha and Confucius

The discoveries of the Portuguese and the Spaniards had brought the Christians of western Europe into close contact with the people of India and of China. They knew of course that Christianity was not the only religion on this earth. There were the Mohammedans and the heathenish tribes of northern Africa who worshipped sticks and stones and dead trees. But in India and in China the Christian conquerors found new millions who had never heard of Christ and who did not want to hear of Him, because they thought their own religion, which was thousands of years old, much better than that of the West. As this is a story of mankind and not an exclusive history of the people of Europe and our western hemisphere, you ought to know something of two men whose teaching and whose example continue to influence the actions and the thoughts of the majority of our fellow-travellers on this earth.

In India, Buddha was recognised as the great religious teacher. His history is an interesting one. He was born in the sixth century before the birth of Christ, within sight of the mighty Himalaya Mountains, where four hundred years before Zarathustra (or Zoroaster), the first of the great leaders of the Aryan race (the name which the eastern branch of the Indo-European race had given to itself), had taught his people to regard life as a continuous struggle between Ahriman and Ormuzd, the gods of evil and good. Buddha's father was Suddhodana, a mighty chief among the tribe of the Sakiyas. His mother, Maha Maya, was the daughter of a neighbouring king. She had been married when she was a very young girl. But many moons had passed beyond the distant ridge of hills and still her husband was without an heir who should rule his lands after him. At last, when she was fifty years old, her day came and she went forth that she might be among her own people when her baby should come into this world.

It was a long trip to the land of the Koliyans, where Maha Maya had spent her earliest years. One night she was resting among the cool trees of the garden of Lumbini. There her son was born. He was given the name of Siddhartha, but we know him as Buddha, which means the Enlightened One.

In due time, Siddhartha grew up to be a handsome young prince and when he was nineteen years old, he was married to his cousin Yasodhara. During the next ten years he lived far away from all pain and all suffering, behind the protecting walls of the royal palace, awaiting the day when he should succeed his father as king of the Sakiyas.

But it happened that when he was thirty years old, he drove outside of the palace gates and saw a man who was old and worn out with labour and whose weak limbs could hardly carry the burden of life. Siddhartha pointed him out to his coachman, Channa, but Channa answered that there were lots of poor people in this world and that one more or less did not matter. The young prince was very sad but he did not say anything and went back to live with his wife and his father and his mother and tried to be happy. A little while later he left the palace a second time. His carriage met a man who suffered from a terrible disease. Siddhartha asked

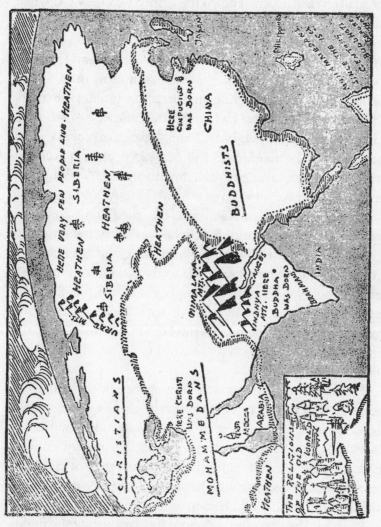

The Three Great Religions

Channa what had been the cause of this man's suffering, but the coachman answered that there were many sick people in this world and that such things could not be helped and did not matter very much. The young prince was very sad when he heard this but again he returned to his people.

A few weeks passed. One evening Siddhartha ordered his carriage in order to go to the river and bathe. Suddenly his horses were frightened by the sight of a dead man whose rotting body lay sprawling in the ditch beside the road. The young prince, who had never been allowed to see such things, was frightened, but Channa told him not to mind such trifles. The world was full of dead people. It was the rule of life that all things must come to an end. Nothing was eternal. The grave awaited us all and there was no escape.

That evening, when Siddhartha returned to his home, he was received with music. While he was away his wife had given birth to a son. The people were delighted because now they knew that there was an heir to the throne and they celebrated the event by the beating of many drums. Siddhartha, however, did not share their joy. The curtain of life had been lifted and he had learned the horror of man's existence. The sight of death and suffering followed him like a terrible dream.

That night the moon was shining brightly. Siddhartha woke up and began to think of many things. Never again could he be happy until he should have found a solution to the riddle of existence. He decided to find it far away from all those whom he loved. Softly he went into the room where Yasodhara was sleeping with her baby. Then he called for his faithful Channa and told him to follow.

Together the two men went into the darkness of the night, one to find rest for his soul, the other to be a faithful servant unto a beloved master.

The people of India among whom Siddhartha wandered

for many years were just then in a state of change. Their ancestors, the native Indians, had been conquered without great difficulty by the war-like Aryans (our distant cousins) and thereafter the Aryans had been the rulers and masters of tens of millions of people. To maintain themselves in the seat of the mighty, they had divided the population into different classes and gradually a system of "caste" of the most rigid sort had been enforced upon the natives. The descendants of the Indo-European conquerors belonged to the highest "caste," the class of warriors and nobles. Next came the caste of the priests. Below these followed the peasants and the business men. The ancient natives, however, who were called pariahs, formed a class of despised and miserable slaves and never could hope to be anything else.

Even the religion of the people was a matter of caste. The old Indo-Europeans, during their thousands of years of wandering, had met with many strange adventures. These had been collected in a book called the Veda. The language of this book was called Sanskrit, and it was closely related to the different languages of the European continent, to Greek and Latin and Russian and German and two-score others. The three highest castes were allowed to read these Holy Scriptures. The pariah, however, the despised member of the lowest caste, was not permitted to know its contents. Woe to the man of noble or priestly caste who should teach a pariah to study the sacred volume!

The majority of the Indian people, therefore, lived in misery. Since this planet offered them very little joy, salvation from suffering must be found elsewhere. They tried to derive a little consolation from meditation upon the bliss of their future existence.

Brahma, the all-creator who was regarded by the Indian people as the supreme ruler of life and death, was worshipped as the highest ideal of perfection. To become like Brahma, to lose all desires for riches and power, was recognised as the most exalted purpose of existence. Holy thoughts were regarded as more important than holy deeds, and many people went into the desert and lived upon the leaves of trees and starved their bodies that they might feed their souls with the glorious contemplation of the splendours of Brahma, the Wise, the Good and the Merciful.

Siddhartha, who had often observed these solitary wanderers who were seeking the truth far away from the turmoil of the cities and the villages, decided to follow their example. He cut his hair. He took his pearls and his rubies and sent them back to his family with a message of farewell, which the ever faithful Channa carried. Without a single follower, the young prince then moved into the wilderness.

Soon the fame of his holy conduct spread among the mountains. Five young men came to him and asked that they might be allowed to listen to his words of wisdom. He agreed to be their master if they would follow him. They consented, and he took them into the hills and for six years he taught them all he knew amidst the lonely peaks of the Vindhya Mountains. But at the end of this period of study, he felt that he was still far from perfection. The world that he had left continued to tempt him. He now asked that his pupils leave him and then he fasted for forty-nine days and nights, sitting upon the roots of an old tree. At last he received his reward. In the dusk of the fiftieth evening, Brahma revealed himself to his faithful servant. From that moment on, Siddhartha was called Buddha and he was revered as the Enlightened One who had come to save men from their unhappy mortal fate.

The last forty-five years of his life, Buddha spent within the valley of the Ganges River, teaching his simple lesson of submission and meekness unto all men. In the year 488 before our era, he died, full of years and beloved by millions of people. He had not preached his doctrines for the benefit of a single class. Even the lowest pariah might call himself his disciple.

This, however, did not please the nobles and the priests and the merchants who did their best to destroy a creed which recognised the equality of all living creatures and offered men the hope of a second life (a reincarnation) under happier circumstances. As soon as they could, they encouraged the people of India to return to the ancient doctrines of the Brahmin creed with its fasting and its tortures of the sinful body. But Buddhism could not be destroyed. Slowly the disciples of the Enlightened One wandered across the valleys of the Himalayas, and moved into China. They crossed the Yellow Sea and preached the wisdom of their master unto the people of Japan, and they faithfully obeyed the will of their great master, who had forbidden them to use force. To-day more people recognise Buddha as their teacher than ever before and their number surpasses that of the combined followers of Christ and Mohammed.

As for Confucius, the wise old man of the Chinese, his story is a simple one. He was born in the year 550 B.C. He led a quiet, dignified and uneventful life at a time when China was without a strong central government and when the Chinese people were at the mercy of bandits and robber-barons who went from city to city, pillaging and stealing and murdering and turning the busy plains of northern and central China into a wilderness of starving people.

Confucius, who loved his people, tried to save them. He did not have much faith in the use of violence. He was a very peaceful person. He did not think that he could make people over by giving them a lot of new laws. He knew that the only possible salvation would come from a change of heart, and he set out upon the seemingly hopeless task of changing the character of his millions of fellow-men who inhabited the wide plains of eastern Asia. The Chinese had never been

Buddha Goes into the Mountains

much interested in religion as we understand that word. They believed in devils and spooks as most primitive people do. But they had no prophets and recognised no "revealed truth." Confucius is almost the only one among the great moral leaders who did not see visions, who did not proclaim himself as the messenger of a divine power; who did not, at some time or another, claim that he was inspired by voices from above.

He was just a very sensible and kindly man, rather given to lonely wanderings and melancholy tunes upon his faithful flute. He asked for no recognition. He did not demand that any one should follow him or worship him. He reminds us of the ancient Greek philosophers, especially those of the Stoic school, men who believed in right living and righteous thinking without the hope of a reward but simply for the peace of the soul that comes with a good conscience.

Confucius was a very tolerant man. He went out of his way to visit Lao-Tse, the other great Chinese leader and the founder of a philosophic system called "Taoism," which was merely an early Chinese version of the Golden Rule.

Confucius bore no hatred to any one. He taught the virtue of supreme self-possession. A person of real worth, according to the teaching of Confucius, did not allow himself to be ruffled by anger and suffered whatever fate brought him with the resignation of those sages who understand that everything which happens, in one way or another, is meant for the best.

At first he had only a few students. Gradually the number increased. Before his death, in the year 478 B.C., several of the kings and the princes of China confessed themselves his disciples. When Christ was born in Bethlehem, the philosophy of Confucius had already become a part of the mental make-up of most Chinamen. It has continued to influence their lives ever since. Not however in its pure, original form.

The Great Moral Leaders

Most religions change as time goes on. Christ preached humility and meekness and absence from worldly ambitions, but fifteen centuries after Golgotha, the head of the Christian church was spending millions upon the erection of a building that bore little relation to the lonely stable of Bethlehem.

Lao-Tse taught the Golden Rule, and in less than three centuries the ignorant masses had made him into a real and very cruel god and had buried his wise commandments under a rubbish-heap of superstition which made the lives of the average Chinese one long series of frights and fears and horrors.

Confucius had shown his students the beauties of honouring their father and their mother. They soon began to be more interested in the memory of their departed parents than in the happiness of their children and their grandchildren. Deliberately they turned their backs upon the future and tried to peer into the vast darkness of the past. The worship of the ancestors became a positive religious system. Rather than disturb a cemetery situated upon the sunny and fertile side of a mountain, they would plant their rice and wheat upon the barren rocks of the other slope where nothing could possibly grow. And they preferred hunger and famine to the desecration of the ancestral grave.

At the same time the wise words of Confucius never quite lost their hold upon the increasing millions of eastern Asia. Confucianism, with its profound sayings and shrewd observations, added a touch of common-sense philosophy to the soul of every Chinaman and influenced his entire life, whether he was a simple laundryman in a steaming basement or the ruler of vast provinces who dwelt behind the high walls of a secluded palace.

In the sixteenth century the enthusiastic but rather uncivilised Christians of the western world came face to face with the older creeds of the east. The early Spaniards and Portu-

guese looked upon the peaceful statues of Buddha and contemplated the venerable pictures of Confucius and did not
in the least know what to make of those worthy prophets
with their far-away smile. They came to the easy conclusion that these strange divinities were just plain devils who
represented something idolatrous and heretical and did not
deserve the respect of the true sons of the church. Whenever
the spirit of Buddha or Confucius seemed to interfere with
the trade in spices and silks, the Europeans attacked the "evil
influence" with bullets and grapeshot. That system had certain very definite disadvantages. It has left us an unpleasant
heritage of ill-will which promises little good for the immediate future.

43

The Reformation

The Progress of the Human Race Is Best Compared
to a Gigantic Pendulum Which Forever
Swings Forward and Backward. The Religious
Indifference and the Artistic and Literary
Enthusiasm of the Renaissance Were Followed
by the Artistic and Literary Indifference and the
Religious Enthusiasm of the Reformation

Of course you have heard of the Reformation. You think of a small but courageous group of Pilgrims who crossed the ocean to have "freedom of religious worship." Vaguely in the course of time (and more especially in our Protestant countries) the Reformation has come to stand for the idea of "liberty of thought." Martin Luther is represented as the leader of the vanguard of progress. But when history is something more than a series of flattering speeches addressed to our own glorious ancestors, when to use the words of the German historian Ranke, we try to discover what "actually happened," then much of the past is seen in a very different light.

Few things in human life are either entirely good or entirely bad. Few things are either black or white. It is the duty of the honest chronicler to give a true account of all the good and bad sides of every historical event. It is very difficult to do this because we all have our personal likes and dislikes. But we ought to try and be as fair as we can be, and must not allow our prejudices to influence us too much.

Take my own case as an example. I grew up in the very Protestant centre of a very Protestant country. I never saw any Catholics until I was about twelve years old. Then I felt very uncomfortable when I met them. I was a little bit afraid. I knew the story of the many thousand people who had been burned and hanged and quartered by the Spanish Inquisition when the duke of Alba tried to cure the Dutch people of their Lutheran and Calvinistic heresies. All that was very real to me. It seemed to have happened only the day before. It might occur again. There might be another St. Bartholomew's Night, and poor little me would be slaughtered in my nightie and my body would be thrown out of the window, as had happened to the noble admiral de Coligny.

Much later I went to live for a number of years in a Catholic country. I found the people much pleasanter and much more tolerant and quite as intelligent as my former countrymen. To my great surprise, I began to discover that there was a Catholic side to the Reformation, quite as much as a Protestant.

Of course the good people of the sixteenth and seventeenth centuries, who actually lived through the Reformation, did not see things that way. They were always right and their enemy was always wrong. It was a question of hang or be hanged, and both sides preferred to do the hanging. Which was no more than human and for which they deserve no blame.

When we look at the world as it appeared in the year 1500, an easy date to remember, and the year in which the emperor Charles V was born, this is what we see. The feudal disorder of the Middle Ages has given way before the order of a number of highly centralised kingdoms. The most powerful of all sovereigns is the great Charles, then a baby in a cradle. He is the grandson of Ferdinand and Isabella and of Maximillian of Habsburg, the last of the mediæval knights, and of his wife, Mary, the daughter of Charles the Bold, the ambitious Burgundian duke who had made successful war upon France, but had been killed by the independent Swiss peasants. The child Charles therefore has fallen heir to the greater part of the map, to all the lands of his parents, grandparents, uncles, cousins and aunts in Germany, in Austria, in Holland, in Belgium, in Italy and in Spain, together with all their colonies in Asia, Africa and America. By a strange irony of fate, he has been born in Ghent, in that same castle of the counts of Flanders which the Germans used as a prison during their recent occupation of Belgium, and although a Spanish king and a German emperor, he receives the training of a Fleming.

As his father is dead (poisoned, so people say, but this is never proved), and his mother has lost her mind (she is travelling through her domains with the coffin containing the body of her departed husband), the child is left to the strict discipline of his aunt Margaret. Forced to rule Germans and Italians and Spaniards and a hundred strange races, Charles grows up a Fleming, a faithful son of the Catholic church, but quite averse to religious intolerance. He is rather lazy, both as a boy and as a man. But fate condemns him to rule the world when the world is in a turmoil of religious fervour. Forever he is speeding from Madrid to Innsbrück and from Bruges to Vienna. He loves peace and quiet and he is always at war. At the age of fifty-five, we see him turn his back upon the human race in utter disgust at so much hate and so much stupidity. Three years later he dies, a very tired and disappointed man.

So much for Charles the emperor. How about the church, the second great power in the world? The church has changed greatly since the early days of the Middle Ages, when it started out to conquer the heathen and show them the advantages of a pious and righteous life. In the first place, the church has grown too rich. The Pope is no longer the shepherd of a flock of humble Christians. He lives in a vast palace and surrounds himself with artists and musicians and famous literary men. His churches and chapels are covered with new pictures in which the saints look more like Greek gods than is strictly necessary. He divides his time unevenly between affairs of state and art. The affairs of state take ten percent of his time. The other ninety percent goes to an active interest in Roman statues, recently discovered Greek vases, plans for a new summer home, the rehearsal of a new play. The archbishops and the cardinals follow the example of their Pope. The bishops try to imitate the archbishops. The village priests, however, have remained faithful to their duties. They keep themselves aloof from the wicked world and the heathenish love of beauty and pleasure. They stay away from the monasteries where the monks seem to have forgotten their ancient vows of simplicity and poverty and live as happily as they dare without causing too much of a public scandal.

Finally, there are the common people. They are much better off than they have ever been before. They are more prosperous, they live in better houses, their children go to better schools, their cities are more beautiful than before, their firearms have made them the equal of their old enemies, the robber-barons, who for centuries have levied such heavy taxes upon their trade. So much for the chief actors in the Reformation.

Now let us see what the Renaissance has done to Europe, and then you will understand how the revival of learning and art was bound to be followed by a revival of religious interests. The Renaissance began in Italy. From there it spread to France. It was not quite successful in Spain, where five hundred years of warfare with the Moors had made the people very narrow minded and very fanatical in all religious matters. The circle had grown wider and wider, but once the Alps had been crossed, the Renaissance had suffered a change.

The people of northern Europe, living in a very different climate, had an outlook upon life which contrasted strangely with that of their southern neighbours. The Italians lived out in the open, under a sunny sky. It was easy for them to laugh and to sing and to be happy. The Germans, the Dutch, the English, the Swedes spent most of their time indoors, listening to the rain beating on the closed windows of their comfortable little houses. They did not laugh quite so much. They took everything more seriously. They were forever conscious of their immortal souls and they did not like to be funny about matters which they considered holy and sacred. The "humanistic" part of the Renaissance, the books, the studies of ancient authors, the grammar and the text-books, interested them greatly. But the general return to the old pagan civilisation of Greece and Rome, which was one of the chief results of the Renaissance in Italy, filled their hearts with horror.

But the Papacy and the College of Cardinals was almost entirely composed of Italians and they had turned the church into a pleasant club where people discussed art and music and the theatre, but rarely mentioned religion. Hence the split between the serious north and the more civilised but easy-going and indifferent south was growing wider and wider all the time and nobody seemed to be aware of the danger that threatened the church.

There were a few minor reasons which will explain

why the Reformation took place in Germany rather than in Sweden or England. The Germans bore an ancient grudge against Rome. The endless quarrels between emperor and Pope had caused much mutual bitterness. In the other European countries where the government rested in the hands of a strong king, the ruler had often been able to protect his subjects against the greed of the priests. In Germany, where a shadowy emperor ruled a turbulent crowd of little princelings, the good burghers were more directly at the mercy of their bishops and prelates. These dignitaries were trying to collect large sums of money for the benefit of those enormous churches which were a hobby of the Popes of the Renaissance. The Germans felt that they were being mulcted and quite naturally they did not like it.

And then there is the rarely mentioned fact that Germany was the home of the printing press. In northern Europe books were cheap and the Bible was no longer a mysterious manuscript owned and explained by the priest. It was a household book of many families where Latin was understood by the father and by the children. Whole families began to read it, which was against the law of the church. They discovered that the priests were telling them many things which, according to the original text of the Holy Scriptures, were somewhat different. This caused doubt. People began to ask questions. And questions, when they cannot be answered, often cause a great deal of trouble.

The attack began when the humanists of the north opened fire upon the monks. In their heart of hearts they still had too much respect and reverence for the Pope to direct their sallies against His Most Holy Person. But the lazy, ignorant monks, living behind the sheltering walls of their rich monasteries, offered rare sport.

The leader in this warfare, curiously enough, was a very faithful son of the church. Gerard Gerardzoon, or Desiderius

Erasmus, as he is usually called, was a poor boy, born in Rotterdam in Holland, and educated at the same Latin school of Deventer from which Thomas à Kempis had graduated. He had become a priest and for a time he had lived in a monastery. He had travelled a great deal and knew whereof he wrote. When he began his career as a public pamphleteer (he would have been called an editorial writer in our day) the world was greatly amused at an anonymous series of letters which had just appeared under the title of "Letters of Obscure Men." In these letters, the general stupidity and arrogance of the monks of the late Middle Ages was exposed in a strange German-Latin doggerel which reminds one of our modern limericks. Erasmus himself was a very learned and serious scholar, who knew both Latin and Greek and gave us the first reliable version of the New Testament, which he translated into Latin together with a corrected edition of the original Greek text. But he believed with Horace, the Roman poet, that nothing prevents us from "stating the truth with a smile upon our lips."

In the year 1500, while visiting Sir Thomas More in England, he took a few weeks off and wrote a funny little book, called the "Praise of Folly," in which he attacked the monks and their credulous followers with that most dangerous of all weapons, humour. The booklet was the best seller of the sixteenth century. It was translated into almost every language and it made people pay attention to those other books of Erasmus in which he advocated reform of the many abuses of the church and appealed to his fellow humanists to help him in his task of bringing about a great re-birth of the Christian faith.

But nothing came of these excellent plans. Erasmus was too reasonable and too tolerant to please most of the enemies of the church. They were waiting for a leader of a more robust nature.

Luther Translates the Bible

He came, and his name was Martin Luther.

Luther was a north German peasant with a first-class brain and possessed of great personal courage. He was ordained an Augustinian friar and was an important figure in the Saxon province of the Order of St. Augustine. Then he became a college professor at the theological school of Wittenberg and began to explain the Scriptures to the indifferent ploughboys of his Saxon home. He had a lot of spare time and this he used to study the original texts of the Old and New Testaments. Soon he began to see the great difference which existed between the words of Christ and those that were preached by the Popes and the bishops.

In the year 1511, he visited Rome on official business. Alexander VI, of the family of Borgia, who had enriched himself for the benefit of his son and daughter, was dead. But his successor, Julius II, a man of irreproachable personal character, was spending most of his time fighting and building and did not impress this serious minded German theologian with his piety. Luther returned to Wittenberg a much disappointed man. But worse was to follow.

The gigantic church of St. Peter which Pope Julius had wished upon his innocent successors, although only half begun, was already in need of repair. Alexander VI had spent every penny of the Papal treasury. Leo X, who succeeded

Julius in the year 1513, was on the verge of bankruptcy. He reverted to an old method of raising ready cash. He began to sell "indulgences." An indulgence was a piece of parchment which, in return for a certain sum of money, promised a sinner a decrease of the time which he would have to spend in Purgatory. It was a perfectly correct thing according to the creed of the late Middle Ages. Since the church had the power to forgive the sins of those who truly repented before they died, the church also had the right to shorten, through its intercession with the saints, the time during which the soul must be purified in the shadowy realms of Purgatory.

It was unfortunate that these indulgences must be sold for money. But they offered an easy form of revenue and besides, those who were too poor to pay received theirs for nothing.

Now it happened in the year 1517 that the exclusive territory for the sale of indulgences in Saxony was given to a Dominican monk by the name of Johan Tetzel. Brother Johan was a hustling salesman. To tell the truth he was a little too eager. His business methods outraged the pious people of the little duchy. And Luther, who was an honest fellow, got so angry that he did a rash thing. On October 31 of the year 1517, he went to the court church and upon the doors thereof he posted a sheet of paper with ninety-five statements (or theses), attacking the sale of indulgences. These statements had been written in Latin. Luther had no intention of starting a riot. He was not a revolutionist. He objected to the institution of the indulgences and he wanted his fellow-professors to know what he thought about them. But this was still a private affair of the clerical and professorial world and there was no appeal to the prejudices of the community of laymen.

Unfortunately, at that moment when the whole world had begun to take an interest in the religious affairs of the day, it was utterly impossible to discuss anything without at once creating a serious mental disturbance. In less than two

months, all Europe was discussing the ninety-five theses of
the Saxon monk. Every one must take sides. Every obscure
little theologian must print his own opinion. The Papal
authorities began to be alarmed. They ordered the Wittenberg professor to proceed to Rome and give an account of
his action. Luther wisely remembered what had happened
to Huss. He stayed in Germany and he was punished with
excommunication. Luther burned the Papal bull in the presence of an admiring multitude and from that moment, peace
between himself and the Pope was no longer possible.

Without any desire on his part, Luther had become the
leader of a vast army of discontented Christians. German
patriots like Ulrich von Hutten rushed to his defence. The
students of Wittenberg and Erfurt and Leipzig offered to
defend him should the authorities try to imprison him. The
elector of Saxony reassured the eager young men. No harm
would befall Luther as long as he stayed on Saxon ground.

All this happened in the year 1520. Charles V was twenty
years old and, as the ruler of half the world, was forced to
remain on pleasant terms with the Pope. He sent out calls
for a Diet or general assembly in the good city of Worms on
the Rhine and commanded Luther to be present and give
an account of his extraordinary behaviour. Luther, who now
was the national hero of the Germans, went. He refused to
take back a single word of what he had ever written or said.
His conscience was controlled only by the word of God. He
would live and die for his conscience.

The Diet of Worms, after due deliberation, declared
Luther an outlaw before God and man, and forbade all Germans to give him shelter or food or drink, or to read a single
word of the books which the dastardly heretic had written.
But the great reformer was in no danger. By the majority
of the Germans of the north the edict was denounced as a
most unjust and outrageous document. For greater safety,

Luther was hidden in the Wartburg, a castle belonging to the elector of Saxony, and there he defied all Papal authority by translating the entire Bible into the German language, that all the people might read and know the word of God for themselves.

By this time, the Reformation was no longer a spiritual and religious affair. Those who hated the beauty of the modern church building used this period of unrest to attack and destroy what they did not like because they did not understand it. Impoverished knights tried to make up for past losses by grabbing the territory which belonged to the monasteries. Discontented princes made use of the absence of the emperor to increase their own power. The starving peasants, following the leadership of half-crazy agitators, made the best of the opportunity and attacked the castles of their masters and plundered and murdered and burned with the zeal of the old Crusaders.

A veritable reign of disorder broke loose throughout the empire. Some princes became Protestants (as the "protesting" adherents of Luther were called) and persecuted their Catholic subjects. Others remained Catholic and hanged their Protestant subjects. The Diet of Speyer of the year 1526 tried to settle this difficult question of allegiance by ordering that "the subjects should all be of the same religious denomination as their princes." This turned Germany into a checkerboard of a thousand hostile little duchies and principalities and created a situation which prevented the normal political growth for hundreds of years.

In February of the year 1546 Luther died and was put to rest in the same church where twenty-nine years before he had proclaimed his famous objections to the sale of indulgences. In less than thirty years, the indifferent, joking and laughing world of the Renaissance had been transformed into the arguing, quarrelling, back-biting debating-society of the Reformation. The universal spiritual empire of the Popes came to a sudden end and the whole of western Europe was turned into a battlefield, where Protestants and Catholics killed each other for the greater glory of certain theological doctrines which are as incomprehensible to the present generation as the mysterious inscriptions of the ancient Etruscans.

44

Religious Warfare

The Age of the Great Religious Controversies

The sixteenth and seventeenth centuries were the age of religious controversy.

If you will notice you will find that almost everybody around you is forever "talking economics" and discussing wages and hours of labour and strikes in their relation to the life of the community, for that is the main topic of interest of our own time.

The poor little children of the year 1600 or 1650 fared worse. They never heard anything but "religion." Their heads were filled with "predestination," "transubstantiation," "free will" and a hundred other queer words, expressing obscure points of "the true faith," whether Catholic or Protestant. According to the desire of their parents they were baptised Catholics or Lutherans or Calvinists or Zwinglians or Anabaptists. They learned their theology from the Augsburg catechism, composed by Luther, or from the "Institutes of Christianity," written by Calvin, or they mumbled the Thirty-nine Articles of Faith which were printed in the English Book of Common Prayer, and they were told that these alone represented the "true faith."

They heard of the wholesale theft of church property perpetrated by King Henry VIII, the much-married monarch of

England, who made himself the supreme head of the English church, and assumed the old Papal rights of appointing bishops and priests. They had a nightmare whenever some one mentioned the Holy Inquisition, with its dungeons and its many torture chambers, and they were treated to equally horrible stories of how a mob of outraged Dutch Protestants had got hold of a dozen defenceless old priests and hanged them for the sheer pleasure of killing those who professed a different faith. It was unfortunate that the two contending parties were so equally matched. Otherwise the struggle would have come to a quick solution. Now it dragged on for eight generations, and it grew so complicated that I can only tell you the most important details, and must ask you to get the rest from one of the many histories of the Reformation.

The great reform movement of the Protestants had been followed by a thoroughgoing reform within the bosom of the church. Those Popes who had been merely amateur humanists and dealers in Roman and Greek antiquities disappeared from the scene and their place was taken by serious men who spent twenty hours a day administering those holy duties which had been placed in their hands.

The long and rather disgraceful happiness of the monasteries came to an end. Monks and nuns were forced to be up at sunrise, to study the church fathers, to tend the sick

The Inquisition

and console the dying. The Holy Inquisition watched day and night that no dangerous doctrines should be spread by way of the printing press. Here it is customary to mention poor Galileo, who was locked up because he had been a little too indiscreet in explaining the heavens with his funny little telescope and had muttered certain opinions about the behaviour of the planets which were entirely opposed to the official views of the church. But in all fairness to the Pope, the clergy and the Inquisition, it ought to be stated that the Protestants were quite as much the enemies of science and medicine as the Catholics and with equal manifestations of ignorance and intolerance regarded the men who investigated things for themselves as the most dangerous enemies of mankind.

And Calvin, the great French reformer and the tyrant (both political and spiritual) of Geneva, not only assisted the French authorities when they tried to hang Michael Servetus (the Spanish theologian and physician who had become famous as the assistant of Vesalius, the first great anatomist), but when Servetus had managed to escape from his French jail and had fled to Geneva, Calvin threw this brilliant man into prison and, after a prolonged trial, allowed him to be burned at the stake on account of his heresies, totally indifferent to his fame as a scientist.

And so it went. We have few reliable statistics upon the subject, but on the whole, the Protestants tired of this game long before the Catholics, and the greater part of honest men and women who were burned and hanged and decapitated on account of their religious beliefs fell as victims of the very energetic but also very drastic church of Rome.

For tolerance (and please remember this when you grow older) is of very recent origin and even the people of our own so-called "modern world" are apt to be tolerant only upon such matters as do not interest them very much. They are tolerant towards a native of Africa, and do not care whether he becomes a Buddhist or a Mohammedan, because neither Buddhism nor Mohammedanism means anything to them. But when they hear that their neighbour who was a Republican and believed in a high protective tariff has joined the Socialist party and now wants to repeal all tariff laws, their tolerance ceases and they use almost the same words as those employed by a kindly Catholic (or Protestant) of the seventeenth century, who was informed that his best friend whom he had always respected and loved had fallen a victim to the terrible heresies of the Protestant (or Catholic) church.

"Heresy" until a very short time ago was regarded as a disease. Nowadays when we see a man neglecting the personal cleanliness of his body and his home and exposing himself and his children to the dangers of typhoid fever or another preventable disease, we send for the board-of-health and the health officer calls upon the police to aid him in removing this person who is a danger to the safety of the entire community. In the sixteenth and seventeenth centuries, a heretic, a man or a woman who openly doubted the fundamental principles upon which his Protestant or Catholic religion had been founded, was considered a more terrible menace than a typhoid carrier. Typhoid fever might (very likely would) destroy the body. But heresy, according to them, would positively destroy the immortal soul. It was therefore the duty of all good and logical citizens to warn the police against the enemies of the established order of things and those who failed to do so were as culpable as a modern man who does not telephone to the nearest doctor when he discovers that his fellow-tenants are suffering from cholera or small-pox.

In the years to come you will hear a great deal about preventive medicine. Preventive medicine simply means that our doctors do not wait until their patients are sick, then step forward and cure them. On the contrary, they study the patient and the conditions under which he lives when he (the patient) is perfectly well and they remove every possible cause of illness by cleaning up rubbish, by teaching him what to eat and what to avoid and by giving him a few simple ideas of personal hygiene. They go even further than that, and these good doctors enter the schools and teach the children how to use toothbrushes and how to avoid catching colds.

The sixteenth century, which regarded (as I have tried to show you) bodily illness as much less important than sickness which threatened the soul, organised a system of spiritual preventive medicine. As soon as a child was old enough to spell his first words, he was educated in the true (and the "only true") principles of the faith. Indirectly this proved to be a good thing for the general progress of the people of Europe. The Protestant lands were soon dotted with schools. They used a great deal of very valuable time to explain the catechism, but they gave instruction in other things besides theology. They encouraged reading and they were responsible for the great prosperity of the printing trade.

But the Catholics did not lag behind. They too devoted much time and thought to education. The church, in this matter, found an invaluable friend and ally in the newly founded order of the Society of Jesus. The founder of this remarkable organisation was a Spanish soldier who after a life of unholy adventures had been converted and thereupon felt himself bound to serve the church just as many former sinners, who have been shown the errors of their way by the Salvation Army, devote the remaining years of their lives to the task of aiding and consoling those who are less fortunate.

The name of this Spaniard was Ignatius of Loyola. He was born in the year before the discovery of America. He had been wounded and lamed for life and while he was in the hospital he had seen a vision of the Holy Virgin and her Son, who bade him give up the wickedness of his former life. He

decided to go to the Holy Land and finish the task of the Crusades. But a visit to Jerusalem had shown him the impossibility of the task and he returned west to help in the warfare
upon the heresies of the Lutherans.

In the year 1534 he was studying in Paris at the Sorbonne.
Together with seven other students he founded a fraternity.
The eight men promised each other that they would lead
holy lives, that they would not strive after riches but after
righteousness, and would devote themselves, body and soul,
to the service of the church. A few years later this small
fraternity had grown into a regular organisation and was
recognised by Pope Paul III as the Society of Jesus.

Loyola had been a military man. He believed in discipline, and absolute obedience to the orders of the superior
dignitaries became one of the main causes for the enormous success of the Jesuits. They specialised in education.
They gave their teachers a most thorough-going education
before they allowed them to talk to a single pupil. They lived
with their students and they entered into their games. They
watched them with tender care. And as a result they raised a
new generation of faithful Catholics who took their religious
duties as seriously as the people of the early Middle Ages.

The shrewd Jesuits, however, did not waste all their efforts
upon the education of the poor. They entered the palaces of
the mighty and became the private tutors of future emperors and kings. And what this meant you will see for yourself
when I tell you about the Thirty Years War. But before this
terrible and final outbreak of religious fanaticism, a great
many other things had happened.

Charles V was dead. Germany and Austria had been left
to his brother Ferdinand. All his other possessions, Spain
and the Netherlands and the Indies and America, had gone
to his son, Philip. Philip was the son of Charles and a Portuguese princess who had been first cousin to her own hus-

band. The children that are born of such a union are apt to be rather queer. The son of Philip, the unfortunate Don Carlos (murdered afterwards with his own father's consent), was crazy. Philip was not quite crazy, but his zeal for the church bordered closely upon religious insanity. He believed that Heaven had appointed him as one of the saviours of mankind. Therefore, whosoever was obstinate and refused to share His Majesty's views proclaimed himself an enemy of the human race and must be exterminated lest his example corrupt the souls of his pious neighbours.

Spain, of course, was a very rich country. All the gold and silver of the new world flowed into the Castilian and Aragonian treasuries. But Spain suffered from a curious economic disease. Her peasants were hard working men and even harder working women. But the better classes maintained a supreme contempt for any form of labour, outside of employment in the army or navy or the civil service. As for the Moors, who had been very industrious artisans, they had been driven out of the country long before. As a result, Spain, the treasure chest of the world, remained a poor country because all her money had to be sent abroad in exchange for the wheat and the other necessities of life which the Spaniards neglected to raise for themselves.

Philip, ruler of the most powerful nation of the sixteenth century, depended for his revenue upon the taxes which were gathered in the busy commercial bee-hive of the Netherlands. But these Flemings and Dutchmen were devoted followers of the doctrines of Luther and Calvin and they had cleansed their churches of all images and holy paintings and they had informed the Pope that they no longer regarded him as their shepherd but intended to follow the dictates of their consciences and the commands of their newly translated Bible.

This placed the king in a very difficult position. He could not possibly tolerate the heresies of his Dutch subjects, but he needed their money. If he allowed them to be Protestants and took no measures to save their souls, he was deficient in his duty toward God. If he sent the Inquisition to the Netherlands and burned his subjects at the stake, he would lose the greater part of his income.

Being a man of uncertain will-power, he hesitated a long time. He tried kindness and sternness and promises and threats. The Hollanders remained obstinate, and continued to sing psalms and listen to the sermons of their Lutheran

The Night of St. Bartholomew

and Calvinist preachers. Philip in his despair sent his "man of iron," the duke of Alba, to bring these hardened sinners to terms. Alba began by decapitating those leaders who had not wisely left the country before his arrival. In the year 1572 (the same year that the French Protestant leaders were all killed during the terrible Night of St. Bartholomew), he attacked a number of Dutch cities and massacred the inhabitants as an example for the others. The next year he laid siege to the town of Leyden, the manufacturing center of Holland.

Meanwhile, the seven small provinces of the northern Netherlands had formed a defensive union, the so-called union of Utrecht, and had recognised William of Orange, a German prince who had been the private secretary of the emperor Charles V, as the leader of their army and as com-

mander of their freebooting sailors, who were known as the
Beggars of the Sea. William, to save Leyden, cut the dikes,
created a shallow inland sea and delivered the town with the
help of a strangely equipped navy consisting of scows and
flat-bottomed barges which were rowed and pushed and
pulled through the mud until they reached the city walls.

It was the first time that an army of the invincible Spanish king had suffered such a humiliating defeat. It surprised
the world just as the Japanese victory of Mukden, in the

Leyden Delivered by the Cutting of the Dikes

Russian-Japanese War, surprised our own generation. The
Protestant powers took fresh courage and Philip devised
new means for the purpose of conquering his rebellious subjects. He hired a poor half-witted fanatic to go and murder
William of Orange. But the sight of their dead leader did not
bring the seven provinces to their knees. On the contrary
it made them furiously angry. In the year 1581, the Estates

General (the meeting of the representatives of the seven provinces) came together at The Hague and most solemnly abjured their "wicked king Philip" and themselves assumed the burden of sovereignty which thus far had been invested in their "king by the Grace of God."

This is a very important event in the history of the great struggle for political liberty. It was a step which reached much further than the uprising of the nobles which ended with the signing of the Magna Carta. These good bur-ghers said: "Between a king and his subjects there is a silent understanding that both sides shall perform certain services and shall recognize certain definite duties. If either party fails to live up to this contract, the other has the right to con-sider it terminated." The American subjects of King George III in the year 1776 came to a similar conclusion. But they had three thousand miles of ocean between themselves and their ruler and the Estates General took their decision (which meant a slow death in case of defeat) within hearing of the Spanish guns and although in constant fear of an avenging Spanish fleet.

The stories about a mysterious Spanish fleet that was to conquer both Holland and England when Protestant Queen Elizabeth had succeeded Catholic "Bloody Mary" was an old one. For years the sailors of the waterfront had talked about

The Murder of William the Silent

it. In the eighties of the sixteenth century, the rumour took a definite shape. According to pilots who had been in Lisbon, all the Spanish and Portuguese wharves were building ships. And in the southern Netherlands (in Belgium) the duke of Parma was collecting a large expeditionary force to be carried from Ostend to London and Amsterdam as soon as the fleet should arrive.

In the year 1586 the Great Armada set sail for the north. But the harbours of the Flemish coast were blockaded by a Dutch fleet and the Channel was guarded by the English, and the Spaniards, accustomed to the quieter seas of the south, did not know how to navigate in this squally and bleak northern climate. What happened to the Armada once it was attacked by ships and by storms I need not tell you. A few ships, by sailing around Ireland, escaped to tell the terrible story of defeat. The others perished and lie at the bottom of the North Sea.

Turn about is fair play. The British and the Dutch Protestants now carried the war into the territory of the enemy. Before the end of the century, Houtman, with the help of a booklet written by Linschoten (a Hollander who had been in the Portuguese service), had at last discovered the route to the Indies. As a result the great Dutch East India Company was founded and a systematic war upon the Portuguese

The Armada Is Coming!

and Spanish colonies in Asia and Africa was begun in all
seriousness.

It was during this early era of colonial conquest that a
curious law-suit was fought out in the Dutch courts. Early
in the seventeenth century a Dutch captain by the name of
van Heemskerk, a man who had made himself famous as
the head of an expedition which had tried to discover the
north-eastern passage to the Indies and who had spent a
winter on the frozen shores of the island of Nova Zembla,
had captured a Portuguese ship in the Strait of Malacca.
You will remember that the Pope had divided the world
into two equal shares, one of which had been given to the
Spaniards and the other to the Portuguese. The Portuguese
quite naturally regarded the water which surrounded their
Indian islands as part of their own property and since, for the
moment, they were not at war with the United Seven Netherlands, they claimed that the captain of a private Dutch
trading company had no right to enter their private domain
and steal their ships. And they brought suit. The directors of
the Dutch East India Company hired a bright young lawyer,
by the name of De Groot or Grotius, to defend their case. He
made the astonishing plea that the ocean is free to all comers.
Once outside the distance which a cannon ball fired from the
land can reach, the sea is, or (according to Grotius) ought to
be, a free and open highway to all the ships of all nations. It
was the first time that this startling doctrine had been publicly pronounced in a court of law. It was opposed by all the
other seafaring people. To counteract the effect of Grotius'
famous plea for the "Mare Liberum," or "Open Sea," John
Selden, the Englishman, wrote his famous treatise upon the
"Mare Clausum" or "Closed Sea" which treated of the natural right of a sovereign to regard the seas which surrounded
his country as belonging to his territory. I mention this here
because the question had not yet been decided and during
the last war caused all sorts of difficulties and complications.

To return to the warfare between Spaniard and Hollander and Englishman, before twenty years were over the most valuable colonies of the Indies and the Cape of Good Hope and Ceylon and those along the coast of China and even Japan were in Protestant hands. In 1621 a West Indian Company was founded which conquered Brazil and in North America built a fortress called Nieuw Amsterdam at the mouth of the river which Henry Hudson had discovered in the year 1609.

These new colonies enriched both England and the Dutch Republic to such an extent that they could hire foreign soldiers to do their fighting on land while they devoted themselves to commerce and trade. To them the Protestant revolt meant independence and prosperity. But in many other parts of Europe it meant a succession of horrors compared to which the last war was a mild excursion of kindly Sunday-school boys.

The Thirty Years War which broke out in the year 1618 and which ended with the famous treaty of Westphalia in 1648 was the perfectly natural result of a century of ever increasing religious hatred. It was, as I have said, a terrible war. Everybody fought everybody else and the struggle ended only when all parties had been thoroughly exhausted and could fight no longer.

In less than a generation it turned many parts of central Europe into a wilderness, where the hungry peasants fought for the carcass of a dead horse with the even hungrier wolf. Five-sixths of all the German towns and villages were destroyed. The Palatinate, in western Germany, was plundered twenty-eight times. And a population of eighteen million people was reduced to four million.

The hostilities began almost as soon as Ferdinand II of the house of Habsburg had been elected emperor. He was the product of a most careful Jesuit training and was a most obedient and devout son of the church. The vow which he

The Death of Hudson

had made as a young man, that he would eradicate all sects and all heresies from his domains, Ferdinand kept to the best of his ability. Two days before his election, his chief opponent, Frederick, the Protestant elector of the Palatinate and a son-in-law of James I of England, had been made king of Bohemia, in direct violation of Ferdinand's wishes.

At once the Habsburg armies marched into Bohemia. The young king looked in vain for assistance against this formidable enemy. The Dutch Republic was willing to help, but, engaged in a desperate war of its own with the Spanish branch of the Habsburgs, it could do little. The Stuarts in England were more interested in strengthening their own absolute power at home than spending money and men upon a forlorn adventure in far away Bohemia. After a struggle of a few months, the elector of the Palatinate was driven away and his domains were given to the Catholic house of Bavaria. This was the beginning of the great war.

Then the Habsburg armies, under Tilly and Wallenstein, fought their way through the Protestant part of Germany until they had reached the shores of the Baltic. A Catholic neighbour meant serious danger to the Protestant king of Denmark. Christian IV tried to defend himself by attacking his enemies before they had become too strong for him. The Danish armies marched into Germany but were defeated. Wallenstein followed up his victory with such energy and violence that Denmark was forced to sue for peace. Only one town of the Baltic then remained in the hands of the Protestants. That was Stralsund.

There, in the early summer of the year 1630, landed King Gustavus Adolphus of the house of Vasa, king of Sweden, and famous as the man who had defended his country against the Russians. A Protestant prince of unlimited ambition, desirous of making Sweden the centre of a great northern empire, Gustavus Adolphus was welcomed by the Protestant princes of Europe as the saviour of the Lutheran cause. He defeated Tilly, who had just successfully butchered the Protestant inhabitants of Magdeburg. Then his troops began their great march through the heart of Germany in an attempt to reach the Habsburg possessions in Italy. Threatened in the rear by the Catholics, Gustavus suddenly veered around and defeated the main Habsburg army in the battle of Lützen. Unfortunately the Swedish king was killed when he strayed away from his troops. But the Habsburg power had been broken.

Ferdinand, who was a suspicious sort of person, at once began to distrust his own servants. Wallenstein, his commander-in-chief, was murdered at his instigation. When the Catholic Bourbons, who ruled France and hated their Habsburg rivals, heard of this, they joined the Protestant Swedes. The armies of Louis XIII invaded the eastern part of Germany, and Turenne and Condé added their fame to that of Baner and Weimar, the Swedish generals, by murdering, pillaging and burning Habsburg property. This brought great fame and riches to the Swedes and caused the Danes to become envious. The Protestant Danes thereupon declared war upon the Protestant Swedes who were the allies of the

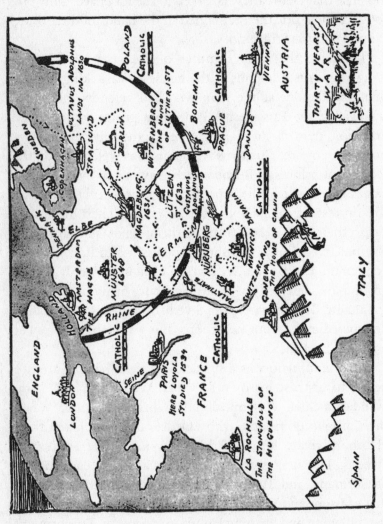

The Thirty Years War

Catholic French, whose political leader, the Cardinal de Richelieu, had just deprived the Huguenots (or French Protestants) of those rights of public worship which the Edict of Nantes of the year 1598 had guaranteed them.

The war, after the habit of such encounters, did not decide anything, when it came to an end with the treaty of Westphalia in 1648. The Catholic powers remained Catholic and the Protestant powers stayed faithful to the doctrines of Luther and Calvin and Zwingli. The Swiss and Dutch Protestants were recognised as independent republics. France kept the cities of Metz and Toul and Verdun and a part of Alsace. The Holy Roman Empire continued to exist as a sort of scarecrow state, without men, without money, without hope and without courage.

The only good the Thirty Years War accomplished was a negative one. It discouraged both Catholics and Protestants from ever trying it again. Henceforth they left each other in peace. This however did not mean that religious feeling and theological hatred had been removed from this earth. On the contrary. The quarrels between Catholic and Protestant came to an end, but the disputes between the different Protestant sects continued as bitterly as ever before. In Holland a difference of opinion as to the true nature of predestination

Amsterdam in 1648

(a very obscure point of theology, but exceedingly important in the eyes of your great-grandfather) caused a quarrel which ended with the decapitation of John of Oldenbarneveldt, the Dutch statesman who had been responsible for the success of the republic during the first twenty years of its independence, and who was the great organizing genius of her Indian trading company. In England, the feud led to civil war.

But before I tell you of this outbreak which led to the first execution by process-of-law of a European king, I ought to say something about the previous history of England. In this book I am trying to give you only those events of the past which can throw a light upon the conditions of the present world. If I do not mention certain countries, the cause is not to be found in any secret dislike on my part. I wish that I could tell you what happened to Norway and Switzerland and Serbia and China. But these lands exercised no great influence upon the development of Europe in the sixteenth and seventeenth centuries. I therefore pass them by with a polite and very respectful bow. England, however, is in a different position. What the people of that small island have done during the last five hundred years has shaped the course of history in every corner of the world. Without a proper knowledge of the background of English history, you cannot understand what you read in the newspapers. And it is therefore necessary that you know how England happened to develop a parliamentary form of government while the rest of the European continent was still ruled by absolute monarchs.

45

The English Revolution

How the Struggle Between the "Divine Right of
Kings" and the Less Divine but More Reasonable
"Right of Parliament" Ended Disastrously
for King Charles I

Cæsar, the earliest explorer of north-western Europe, had
crossed the Channel in the year 55 B.C. and had conquered
England. During four centuries the country then remained a
Roman province. But when the barbarians began to threaten
Rome, the garrisons were called back from the frontier that
they might defend the home country and Britannia was left
without a government and without protection.

As soon as this became known among the hungry Saxon
tribes of northern Germany, they sailed across the North Sea
and made themselves at home in the prosperous island. They
founded a number of independent Anglo-Saxon kingdoms (so
called after the original invaders, the Angles or English and
the Saxons) but these small states were forever quarrelling
with each other and no king was strong enough to establish
himself as the head of a united country. For more than five
hundred years, Mercia and Northumbria and Wessex and
Sussex and Kent and East Anglia, or whatever their names,
were exposed to attacks from various Scandinavian pirates.

Finally in the eleventh century, England, together with Norway and northern Germany, became part of the large Danish Empire of Canute the Great and the last vestiges of independence disappeared.

The Danes, in the course of time, were driven away but no sooner was England free than it was conquered for the fourth time. The new enemies were the descendants of another tribe of Norsemen who early in the tenth century had invaded France and had founded the duchy of Normandy. William, duke of Normandy, who for a long time had looked across the water with an envious eye, crossed the Channel in October of the year 1066. At the battle of Hastings, on October 14 of that year, he destroyed the weak forces of Harold of Wessex, the last of the Anglo-Saxon Kings, and established himself as king of England. But neither William nor his successors of the house of Anjou and Plantagenet regarded England as their true home. To them the island was

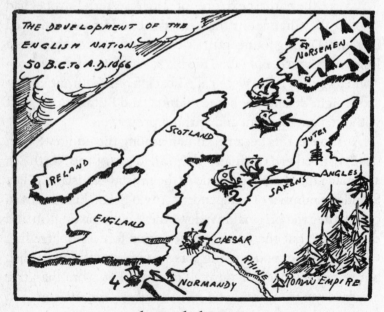

The English Nation

merely a part of their great inheritance on the continent—a
sort of colony inhabited by rather backward people upon
whom they forced their own language and civilisation. Gradually, however, the "colony" of England gained upon the
"mother country" of Normandy. At the same time the kings

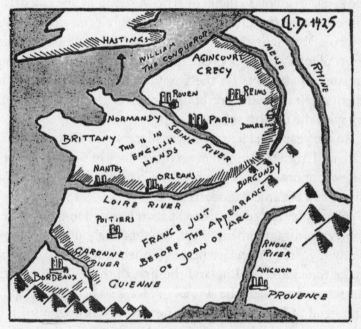

The Hundred Years War

of France were trying desperately to get rid of the powerful Norman-English neighbours who were in truth no more
than disobedient servants of the French crown. After a century of warfare the French people, under the leadership of a
young girl by the name of Joan of Arc, drove the "foreigners"
from their soil. Joan herself, taken a prisoner at the battle of
Compiègne in the year 1430 and sold by her Burgundian captors to the English soldiers, was burned as a witch. But the
English never gained foothold upon the continent and their
kings were at last able to devote all their time to their Brit-

ish possessions. As the feudal nobility of the island had been engaged in one of those strange feuds which were as common in the Middle Ages as measles and small-pox, and as the greater part of the old landed proprietors had been killed during these so-called Wars of the Roses, it was quite easy for the kings to increase their royal power. And by the end of the fifteenth century, England was a strongly centralized country, ruled by Henry VII of the house of Tudor, whose famous court of justice, the "Star Chamber" of terrible memory, suppressed all attempts on the part of the surviving nobles to regain their old influence upon the government of the country with the utmost severity.

In the year 1509 Henry VII was succeeded by his son Henry VIII, and from that moment on the history of England gained a new importance for the country ceased to be a mediæval island and became a modern state.

Henry had no deep interest in religion. He gladly used a private disagreement with the Pope about one of his many divorces to declare himself independent of Rome and make the church of England the first of those "nationalistic churches" in which the worldly ruler also acts as the spiritual head of his subjects. This peaceful reformation of 1534 not only gave the house of Tudor the support of the English clergy, who for a long time had been exposed to the violent attacks of many Lutheran propagandists, but it also increased the royal power through the confiscation of the former possessions of the monasteries. At the same time it made Henry popular with the merchants and tradespeople, who, as the proud and prosperous inhabitants of an island which was separated from the rest of Europe by a wide and deep channel, had a great dislike for everything "foreign" and did not want an Italian bishop to rule their honest British souls.

In 1547 Henry died. He left the throne to his small son, aged ten. The guardians of the child, favoring the modern

Lutheran doctrines, did their best to help the cause of Protestantism. But the boy died before he was sixteen, and was succeeded by his sister Mary, the wife of Philip II of Spain, who burned the bishops of the new "national church" and in other ways followed the example of her royal Spanish husband.

Fortunately she died, in the year 1558, and was succeeded by Elizabeth, the daughter of Henry VIII and Anne Boleyn, the second of his six wives, whom he had decapitated when she no longer pleased him. Elizabeth, who had spent some time in prison, and who had been released only at the request of the holy Roman emperor, was a most cordial enemy of everything Catholic and Spanish. She shared her father's indifference in the matter of religion but she inherited his ability as a very shrewd judge of character, and spent the forty-five years of her reign in strengthening the power of the dynasty and in increasing the revenue and possessions of her merry islands. In this she was most ably assisted by a number of men who gathered around her throne and made the Elizabethan age a period of such importance that you ought to study it in detail.

Elizabeth, however, did not feel entirely safe upon her throne. She had a rival and a very dangerous one. Mary, of the house of Stuart, daughter of a French duchess and a Scottish father, widow of King Francis II of France and daughter-in-law of Catherine of Medici (who had organised the murders of St. Bartholomew's Night), was the mother of a little boy who was afterwards to become the first Stuart king of England. She was an ardent Catholic and a willing friend to those who were the enemies of Elizabeth. Her own lack of political ability and the violent methods which she employed to punish her Calvinistic subjects caused a revolution in Scotland and forced Mary to take refuge on English territory. For eighteen years she remained in England, plotting forever and a day against the woman who had given her shelter and who was at last obliged to follow the advice of her trusted councilors "to cutte off the Scottish Queen's heade."

The head was duly "cutte off" in the year 1587 and caused a war with Spain. But the combined navies of England and Holland defeated Philip's Invincible Armada, as we have already seen, and the blow which had been meant to destroy the power of the two great anti-Catholic leaders was turned into a profitable business adventure.

For now at last, after many years of hesitation, the English as well as the Dutch thought it their good right to invade the Indies and America and avenge the ills which their Protestant brethren had suffered at the hands of the Spaniards. The English had been among the earliest successors of Columbus. British ships, commanded by the Venetian pilot Giovanni Caboto (or Cabot), had been the first to discover and explore the northern American continent in 1496. Labrador and Newfoundland were of little importance as a possible colony. But the banks of Newfoundland offered a rich reward to the English fishing fleet. A year later, in 1497, the same Cabot had explored the coast of Florida.

Then had come the busy years of Henry VII and Henry

John and Sebastian Cabot See the Coast of Newfoundland

VIII when there had been no money for foreign explorations. But under Elizabeth, with the country at peace and Mary Stuart in prison, the sailors could leave their harbour without fear for the fate of those whom they left behind. While Elizabeth was still a child, Willoughby had ventured to sail past the North Cape and one of his captains, Richard Chancellor, pushing further eastward in his quest of a possible road to the Indies, had reached Archangel, Russia, where he had established diplomatic and commercial relations with the mysterious rulers of this distant Muscovite empire. During the first years of Elizabeth's rule this voyage had been followed up by many others. Merchant adventurers, working for the benefit of a "joint stock company," had laid the foundations of trading companies which in later centuries were to become colonies. Half pirate, half diplomat, willing to stake everything on a single lucky voyage, smugglers of everything that could be loaded into the hold of a vessel, dealers in men and merchandise with equal indifference to everything except their profit, the sailors of Elizabeth had carried the English

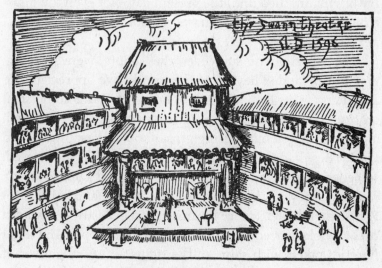

The Elizabethan Stage

flag and the fame of their Virgin Queen to the four corners of the seven seas. Meanwhile William Shakespeare kept Her Majesty amused at home, and the best brains and the best wit of England co-operated with the queen in her attempt to change the feudal inheritance of Henry VIII into a modern national state.

In the year 1603 the old lady died at the age of seventy. Her cousin, the great-grandson of her own grandfather Henry VII and son of Mary Stuart, her rival and enemy, succeeded her as James I. By the Grace of God, he found himself the ruler of a country which had escaped the fate of its continental rivals. While the European Protestants and Catholics were killing each other in a hopeless attempt to break the power of their adversaries and establish the exclusive rule of their own particular creed, England was at peace and "reformed" at leisure without going to the extremes of either Luther or Loyola. It gave the island kingdom an enormous advantage in the coming struggle for colonial possessions. It assured England a leadership in international affairs which that country has maintained until the present day. Not even the disastrous adventure with the Stuarts was able to stop this normal development.

The Stuarts, who succeeded the Tudors, were "foreigners" in England. They do not seem to have appreciated or understood this fact. The native house of Tudor could steal a horse, but the "foreign" Stuarts were not allowed to look at the bridle without causing great popular disapproval. Old Queen Bess had ruled her domains very much as she pleased. In general, however, she had always followed a policy which meant money in the pocket of the honest (and otherwise) British merchants. Hence the queen had been always assured of the wholehearted support of her grateful people. And small liberties taken with some of the rights and prerogatives of Parliament were gladly overlooked for the ulterior benefits which were derived from Her Majesty's strong and successful foreign policies.

Outwardly King James continued the same policy. But he lacked that personal enthusiasm which had been so very typical of his great predecessor. Foreign commerce continued to be encouraged. The Catholics were not granted any liberties. But when Spain smiled pleasantly upon England in an effort to establish peaceful relations, James was seen to smile back. The majority of the English people did not like this, but James was their king and they kept quiet.

Soon there were other causes of friction. King James and his son, Charles I, who succeeded him in the year 1625, both firmly believed in the principle of their "divine right" to administer their realm as they thought fit without consulting the wishes of their subjects. The idea was not new. The Popes, who in more than one way had been the successors of the Roman emperors (or rather of the Roman imperial ideal of a single and undivided state covering the entire known world), had always regarded themselves and had been publicly recognised as the "Vice-Regents of Christ upon Earth." No one questioned the right of God to rule the world as He saw fit. As a natural result, few ventured to doubt the right of the divine "Vice-Regent" to do the same thing and to demand the obedience of the masses because he was the direct representative of the Absolute Ruler of the Universe and responsible only to Almighty God.

When the Lutheran Reformation proved successful, those rights which formerly had been vested in the Papacy were taken over by the many European sovereigns who became Protestants. As head of their own national or dynastic churches they insisted upon being "Christ's Vice-Regents" within the limit of their own territory. The people did not question the right of their rulers to take such a step. They accepted it, just as we in our own day accept the idea of a representative system which to us seems the only reasonable and just form of government. It is unfair therefore to state that either Lutheranism or Calvinism caused the particular feeling of irritation which greeted King James's oft and loudly repeated assertion of his "divine right." There must have been other grounds for the genuine English disbelief in the divine right of kings.

The first positive denial of the "divine right" of sovereigns had been heard in the Netherlands when the Estates General abjured their lawful sovereign King Philip II of Spain, in the year 1581. "The king," so they said, "has broken his contract and the king therefore is dismissed like any other unfaithful servant." Since then, this particular idea of a king's responsibilities towards his subjects had spread among many of the nations who inhabited the shores of the North Sea. They were in a very favourable position. They were rich. The poor people in the heart of central Europe, at the mercy of their ruler's bodyguard, could not afford to discuss a problem which would at once land them in the deepest dungeon of the nearest castle. But the merchants of Holland and England who possessed the capital necessary for the maintenance of great armies and navies, who knew how to handle the almighty weapon called "credit," had no such fear. They were willing to pit the "divine right" of their own good money against the "divine right" of any Habsburg or Bourbon or Stuart. They knew that their guilders and shillings could beat the clumsy feudal armies which were the only weapons of the king. They dared to act, where others were condemned to suffer in silence or run the risk of the scaffold.

When the Stuarts began to annoy the people of England with their claim that they had a right to do what they pleased and never mind the responsibility, the English middle classes used the House of Commons as their first line of defence against this abuse of the royal power. The crown refused

to give in and the king sent Parliament about its own business. Eleven long years, Charles I ruled alone. He levied taxes
which most people regarded as illegal and he managed his
British kingdom as if it had been his own country estate. He
had capable assistants and we must say that he had the courage of his convictions.

Unfortunately, instead of assuring himself of the support
of his faithful Scottish subjects, Charles became involved in
a quarrel with the Scotch Presbyterians. Much against his
will, but forced by his need for ready cash, Charles was at
last obliged to call Parliament together once more. It met in
April of 1640 and showed an ugly temper. It was dissolved a
few weeks later. A new Parliament convened in November.
This one was even less pliable than the first one. The members understood that the question of "government by divine
right" or "government by Parliament" must be fought out
for good and all. They attacked the king in his chief councillors and executed half a dozen of them. They announced
that they would not allow themselves to be dissolved without their own approval. Finally on December 1, 1641, they
presented to the king a "Grand Remonstrance" which gave a
detailed account of the many grievances of the people against
their ruler.

Charles, hoping to derive some support for his own policy in the country districts, left London in January of 1642.
Each side organised an army and prepared for open warfare
between the absolute power of the crown and the absolute
power of Parliament. During this struggle, the most powerful religious element of England, called the Puritans (they
were Anglicans who had tried to purify their doctrines to
the most absolute limits), came quickly to the front. The regiments of "Godly men," commanded by Oliver Cromwell,
with their iron discipline and their profound confidence in
the holiness of their aims, soon became the model for the

entire army of the opposition. Twice Charles was defeated. After the battle of Naseby, in 1645, he fled to Scotland. The Scotch sold him to the English.

There followed a period of intrigue and an uprising of the Scotch Presbyterians against the English Puritan. In August of the year 1648 after the three days' battle of Preston Pans, Cromwell made an end to this second civil war, and took Edinburgh. Meanwhile his soldiers, tired of further talk and wasted hours of religious debate, had decided to act on their own initiative. They removed from Parliament all those who did not agree with their own Puritan views. Thereupon the "Rump," which was what was left of the old Parliament, accused the king of high treason. The House of Lords refused to sit as a tribunal. A special tribunal was appointed and it condemned the king to death. On January 30 of the year 1649, King Charles walked quietly out of a window of White Hall onto the scaffold. That day, the sovereign people, acting through their chosen representatives, for the first time executed a ruler who had failed to understand his own position in the modern state.

The period which followed the death of Charles is usually called after Oliver Cromwell. At first the unofficial dictator of England, he was officially made lord protector in the year 1653. He ruled five years. He used this period to continue the policies of Elizabeth. Spain once more became the arch enemy of England and war upon the Spaniard was made a national and sacred issue.

The commerce of England and the interests of the traders were placed before everything else, and the Protestant creed of the strictest nature was rigourously maintained. In maintaining England's position abroad, Cromwell was successful. As a social reformer, however, he failed very badly. The world is made up of a number of people and they rarely think alike. In the long run, this seems a very wise provision. A government of and by and for one single part of the entire community cannot possibly survive. The Puritans had been a great force for good when they tried to correct the abuse of the royal power. As the absolute rulers of England they became intolerable.

When Cromwell died in 1658, it was an easy matter for the Stuarts to return to their old kingdom. Indeed, they were welcomed as "deliverers" by the people who had found the yoke of the meek Puritans quite as hard to bear as that of autocratic King Charles. Provided the Stuarts were willing to forget about the divine right of their late and lamented father and were willing to recognise the superiority of Parliament, the people promised that they would be loyal and faithful subjects.

Two generations tried to make a success of this new arrangement. But the Stuarts apparently had not learned their lesson and were unable to drop their bad habits. Charles II, who came back in the year 1660, was an amiable but worthless person. His indolence and his constitutional insistence upon following the easiest course, together with his conspicuous success as a liar, prevented an open outbreak between himself and his people. By the Act of Uniformity in 1662 he broke the power of the Puritan clergy by banishing all dissenting clergymen from their parishes. By the so-called Conventicle Act of 1664 he tried to prevent the Dissenters from attending religious meetings by a threat of deportation to the West Indies. This looked too much like the good old days of divine right. People began to show the old and well-known signs of impatience, and Parliament suddenly experienced difficulty in providing the king with funds.

Since he could not get money from an unwilling Parliament, Charles borrowed it secretly from his neighbour and cousin, King Louis of France. He betrayed his Protestant allies in return for two hundred thousand pounds per year, and laughed at the poor simpletons of Parliament.

Economic independence suddenly gave the king great

faith in his own strength. He had spent many years of exile among his Catholic relations and he had a secret liking for their religion. Perhaps he could bring England back to Rome! He passed a Declaration of Indulgence which suspended the old laws against the Catholics and Dissenters. This happened just when Charles' younger brother James was said to have become a Catholic. All this looked suspicious to the man in the street. People began to fear some terrible Popish plot. A new spirit of unrest entered the land. Most of the people wanted to prevent another outbreak of civil war. To them royal oppression and a Catholic king—yea, even divine right—were preferable to a new struggle between members of the same race. Others however were less lenient. They were the much-feared Dissenters, who invariably had the courage of their convictions. They were led by several great noblemen who did not want to see a return of the old days of absolute royal power.

For almost ten years, these two great parties, the Whigs (the middle-class element, called by this derisive name because in the year 1640 a lot of Scottish Whiggamores or horse-drovers, headed by the Presbyterian clergy, had marched to Edinburgh to oppose the king) and the Tories (an epithet originally used against the royalist Irish adherents but now applied to the supporters of the king) opposed each other, but neither wished to bring about a crisis. They allowed Charles to die peacefully in his bed and permitted the Catholic James II to succeed his brother in 1685. But when James, after threatening the country with the terrible foreign invention of a "standing army" (which was to be commanded by Catholic Frenchmen), issued a second Declaration of Indulgence in 1688, and ordered it to be read in all Anglican churches, he went just a trifle beyond that line of sensible demarcation which can only be transgressed by the most popular of rulers under very exceptional circumstances. Seven bishops refused to comply with the royal command. They were accused of "seditious libel." They were brought before a court. The jury which pronounced the verdict of "not guilty" reaped a rich harvest of popular approval.

At this unfortunate moment, James (who in a second marriage had taken to wife Maria of the Catholic house of Modena-Este) became the father of a son. This meant that the throne was to go to a Catholic boy rather than to his older sisters, Mary and Anne, who were Protestants. The man in the street again grew suspicious. Maria of Modena was too old to have children! It was all part of a plot! A strange baby had been brought into the palace by some Jesuit priest that England might have a Catholic monarch. And so on. It looked as if another civil war would break out. Then seven well-known men, Whigs and Tories, wrote a letter asking the husband of James's oldest daughter, Mary, William III, the stadtholder or head of the Dutch Republic, to come to England and deliver the country from its lawful but entirely undesirable sovereign.

On November 5 of the year 1688, William landed at Torbay. As he did not wish to make a martyr out of his father-in-law, he helped him to escape safely to France. On January 22 of 1689 he summoned Parliament. On February 13 of the same year he and his wife, Mary, were proclaimed joint sovereigns of England and the country was saved for the Protestant cause.

Parliament, having undertaken to be something more than a mere advisory body to the king, made the best of its opportunities. The old Petition of Rights of the year 1628 was fished out of a forgotten nook of the archives. A second and more drastic Bill of Rights demanded that the sovereign of England should belong to the Anglican church. Furthermore it stated that the king had no right to suspend the laws or permit certain privileged citizens to disobey certain laws. It stipulated that "without consent of Parliament no taxes could be levied and no army could be maintained." Thus in the year 1689 did England acquire an amount of liberty unknown in any other country of Europe.

But it is not only on account of this great liberal measure that the rule of William in England is still remembered. During his lifetime, government by a "responsible" ministry first developed. No king of course can rule alone. He needs a few trusted advisers. The Tudors had their Great Council which was composed of nobles and clergy. This body grew too large. It was restricted to the small "Privy Council." In the course of time it became the custom of these councillors to meet the king in a cabinet in the palace. Hence they were called the "Cabinet Council." After a short while they were known as the "Cabinet."

William, like most English sovereigns before him, had chosen his advisers from among all parties. But with the increased strength of Parliament, he had found it impossible to direct the politics of the country with the help of the Tories while the Whigs had a majority in the house of Commons. Therefore the Tories had been dismissed and the Cabinet Council had been composed entirely of Whigs. A few years later when the Whigs lost their power in the House of Commons, the king, for the sake of convenience, was obliged to look for his support among the leading Tories. Until his death in 1702, William was too busy fighting Louis of France to bother much about the government of England. Practically all important affairs had been left to his Cabinet Council. When William's sister-in-law, Anne, succeeded him in 1702 this condition of affairs continued. When she died in 1714 (and unfortunately not a single one of her seventeen children survived her) the throne went to George I of the house of Hanover, the son of Sophie, granddaughter of James I.

This somewhat rustic monarch, who never learned a

word of English, was entirely lost in the complicated mazes of England's political arrangements. He left everything to his Cabinet Council and kept away from their meetings, which bored him as he did not understand a single sentence. In this way the Cabinet got into the habit of ruling England and Scotland (whose Parliament had been joined to that of England in 1707) without bothering the king, who was apt to spend a great deal of his time on the continent.

During the reign of George I and George II, a succession of great Whigs (of whom one, Sir Robert Walpole, held office for twenty-one years) formed the Cabinet Council of the king. Their leader was finally recognised as the official leader not only of the actual Cabinet but also of the majority party in power in Parliament. The attempts of George III to take matters into his own hands and not to leave the actual business of government to his Cabinet were so disastrous that they were never repeated. And from the earliest years of the eighteenth century on, England enjoyed representative government, with a responsible ministry which conducted the affairs of the land.

To be quite true, this government did not represent all classes of society. Less than one man in a dozen had the right to vote. But it was the foundation for the modern representative form of government. In a quiet and orderly fashion it took the power away from the king and placed it in the hands of an ever increasing number of popular representatives. It did not bring the millennium to England, but it saved that country from most of the revolutionary outbreaks which proved so disastrous to the European continent in the eighteenth and nineteenth centuries.

46

The Balance of Power

In France, on the Other Hand, the "Divine Right
of Kings" Continued with Greater Pomp and
Splendour Than Ever Before and the Ambition
of the Ruler Was Only Tempered by the Newly
Invented Law of the "Balance of Power"

As a contrast to the previous chapter, let me tell you what
happened in France during the years when the English people
were fighting for their liberty. The happy combination
of the right man in the right country at the right moment is
very rare in history. Louis XIV was a realisation of this ideal,
as far as France was concerned, but the rest of Europe would
have been happier without him.

The country over which the young king was called to
rule was the most populous and the most brilliant nation of
that day. Louis came to the throne when Mazarin and Richelieu, the two great cardinals, had just hammered the ancient
French kingdom into the most strongly centralised state of
the seventeenth century. He was himself a man of extraordinary ability. We, the people of the twentieth century, are still
surrounded by the memories of the glorious age of the Sun
King. Our social life is based upon the perfection of manners

and the elegance of expression attained at the court of Louis. In international and diplomatic relations, French is still the official language of diplomacy and international gatherings because two centuries ago it reached a polished elegance and a purity of expression which no other tongue had as yet been able to equal. The theatre of King Louis still teaches us lessons which we are only too slow in learning. During his reign the French Academy (an invention of Richelieu) came to occupy a position in the world of letters which other countries have flattered by their imitation. We might continue this list for many pages. It is no matter of mere chance that our modern bill-of-fare is printed in French. The very difficult art of decent cooking, one of the highest expressions of civilisation, was first practised for the benefit of the great monarch. The age of Louis XIV was a time of splendour and grace which can still teach us a lot.

Unfortunately this brilliant picture has another side which was far less encouraging. Glory abroad too often means misery at home, and France was no exception to this rule. Louis XIV succeeded his father in the year 1643. He died in the year 1715. That means that the government of France was in the hands of one single man for seventy-two years, almost two whole generations.

It will be well to get a firm grasp of this idea, "one single man." Louis was the first of a long list of monarchs who in many countries established that particular form of highly efficient autocracy which we call "enlightened despotism." He did not like kings who merely played at being rulers and turned official affairs into a pleasant picnic. The kings of that enlightened age worked harder than any of their subjects. They got up earlier and went to bed later than anybody else, and felt their "divine responsibility" quite as strongly as their "divine right" which allowed them to rule without consulting their subjects.

Of course, the king could not attend to everything in person. He was obliged to surround himself with a few helpers and councillors. One or two generals, some experts upon foreign politics, a few clever financiers and economists would do for this purpose. But these dignitaries could act only through their sovereign. They had no individual existence. To the mass of the people, the sovereign actually represented in his own sacred person the government of their country. The glory of the common fatherland became the glory of a single dynasty. It meant the exact opposite of our own American ideal. France was ruled of and by and for the house of Bourbon.

The disadvantages of such a system are clear. The king grew to be everything. Everybody else grew to be nothing at all. The old and useful nobility was gradually forced to give up its former shares in the government of the provinces. A little royal bureaucrat, his fingers splashed with ink, sitting behind the greenish windows of a government building in far away Paris, now performed the task which a hundred years before had been the duty of the feudal lord. The feudal lord, deprived of all work, moved to Paris to amuse himself as best he could at the court. Soon his estates began to suffer from that very dangerous economic sickness, known as "absentee landlordism." Within a single generation, the industrious and useful feudal administrators had become the well-mannered but quite useless loafers of the court of Versailles.

Louis was ten years old when the peace of Westphalia was concluded and the house of Habsburg, as a result of the Thirty Years War, lost its predominant position in Europe. It was inevitable that a man with his ambition should use so favourable a moment to gain for his own dynasty the honours which had formerly been held by the Habsburgs. In the year 1660 Louis had married Maria Theresa, daughter of the king of Spain. Soon afterward, his father-in-law, Philip

IV, one of the half-witted Spanish Habsburgs, died. At once
Louis claimed the Spanish Netherlands (Belgium) as part of
his wife's dowry. Such an acquisition would have been disastrous to the peace of Europe, and would have threatened the
safety of the Protestant states. Under the leadership of Jan
de Witt, "raadpensionaris" or foreign minister of the United
Seven Netherlands, the first great international alliance, the
Triple Alliance of Sweden, England and Holland, of the year
1664, was concluded. It did not last long. With money and
fair promises Louis bought up both King Charles and the
Swedish Estates. Holland was betrayed by her allies and was
left to her own fate. In the year 1672 the French invaded the
low countries. They marched to the heart of the country. For
a second time the dikes were opened and the Royal Sun of
France set amidst the mud of the Dutch marshes. The peace
of Nimwegen which was concluded in 1678 settled nothing
but merely anticipated another war.

A second war of aggression from 1689 to 1697, ending with

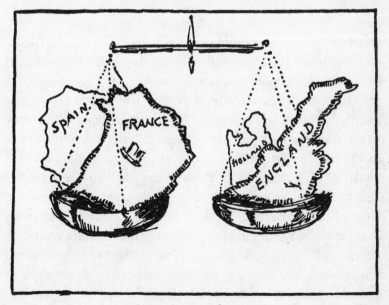

The Balance of Power

the peace of Ryswick, also failed to give Louis that position in the affairs of Europe to which he aspired. His old enemy, Jan de Witt, had been murdered by the Dutch rabble, but his successor, William III (whom you met in the last chapter), had checkmated all efforts of Louis to make France the ruler of Europe.

The great War for the Spanish Succession, begun in the year 1701, immediately after the death of Charles II, the last of the Spanish Habsburgs, and ended in 1713 by the peace of Utrecht, remained equally undecided, but it had ruined the treasury of Louis. On land the French king had been victorious, but the navies of England and Holland had spoiled all hope for an ultimate French victory; besides, the long struggle had given birth to a new and fundamental principle of international politics, which thereafter made it impossible for one single nation to rule the whole of Europe or the whole of the world for any length of time.

That was the so-called "balance of power." It was not a written law but for three centuries it has been obeyed as closely as are the laws of nature. The people who originated the idea maintained that Europe, in its nationalistic stage of development, could only survive when there should be an absolute balance of the many conflicting interests of the entire continent. No single power or single dynasty must ever be allowed to dominate the others. During the Thirty Years War, the Habsburgs had been the victims of the application of this law. They, however, had been unconscious victims. The issues during that struggle were so clouded in a haze of religious strife that we do not get a very clear view of the main tendencies of that great conflict. But from that time on, we begin to see how cold, economic considerations and calculations prevail in all matters of international importance. We discover the development of a new type of statesman, the statesman with the personal feelings of the slide-rule and the cash-register. Jan de Witt was the first successful exponent of this new school of politics. William III was the first great pupil. And Louis XIV, with all his fame and glory, was the first conscious victim. There have been many others since.

47

The Rise of Russia

The Story of the Mysterious Moscovite Empire
Which Suddenly Burst upon the Grand Political
Stage of Europe

In the year 1492, as you know, Columbus discovered America. Early in the year, a Tyrolese by the name of Schnups, travelling as the head of a scientific expedition for the archbishop of Tyrol, and provided with the best letters of introduction and excellent credit, tried to reach the mythical town of Moscow. He did not succeed. When he reached the frontiers of this vast Moscovite state which was vaguely supposed to exist in the extreme eastern part of Europe, he was firmly turned back. No foreigners were wanted. And Schnups went to visit the heathen Turk in Constantinople, in order that he might have something to report to his clerical master when he came back from his explorations.

Sixty-one years later, Richard Chancellor, trying to discover the north-eastern passage to the Indies, and blown by an ill wind into the White Sea, reached the mouth of the Dwina and found the Moscovite village of Kholmogory, a few hours from the spot where in 1584 the town of Archangel was founded. This time the foreign visitors were requested to come to Moscow and show themselves to the grand duke.

They went and returned to England with the first commercial treaty ever concluded between Russia and the western world. Other nations soon followed and something became known of this mysterious land.

Geographically, Russia is a vast plain. The Ural Mountains are low and form no barrier against invaders. The rivers are broad but often shallow. It was an ideal territory for nomads.

While the Roman Empire was founded, grew in power and disappeared again, Slavic tribes, who had long since left their homes in central Asia, wandered aimlessly through the forests and plains of the region between the Dniester and Dnieper rivers. The Greeks had sometimes met these Slavs and a few travellers of the third and fourth centuries mention them. Otherwise they were as little known as were the Nevada Indians in the year 1800.

Unfortunately for the peace of these primitive peoples, a very convenient trade-route ran through their country. This was the main road from northern Europe to Constantinople. It followed the coast of the Baltic until the Neva was reached. Then it crossed Lake Ladoga and went southward along the Volkhov River. Then through Lake Ilmen and up the small Lovat River. Then there was a short portage until the Dnieper was reached. Then down the Dnieper into the Black Sea.

The Norsemen knew of this road at a very early date. In the ninth century they began to settle in northern Russia, just as other Norsemen were laying the foundation for independent states in Germany and France. But in the year 862, three Norsemen, brothers, crossed the Baltic and founded three small dynasties. Of the three brothers, only one, Rurik, lived for a number of years. He took possession of the territory of his brothers, and twenty years after the arrival of this first Norseman, a Slavic state had been established with Kiev as its capital.

The Origin of Russia

From Kiev to the Black Sea is a short distance. Soon the existence of an organised Slavic state became known in Constantinople. This meant a new field for the zealous missionaries of the Christian faith. Byzantine monks followed the Dnieper on their way northward and soon reached the heart of Russia. They found the people worshipping strange gods who were supposed to dwell in woods and rivers and in mountain caves. They taught them the story of Jesus. There was no competition from the side of Roman missionaries. These good men were too busy educating the heathen Teutons to bother about the distant Slavs. Hence Russia received its religion and its alphabet and its first ideas of art and architecture from the Byzantine monks and as the Byzantine Empire (a relic of the eastern Roman Empire) had become very oriental and had lost many of its European traits, the Russians suffered in consequence.

Politically speaking these new states of the great Russian plains did not fare well. It was the Norse habit to divide every inheritance equally among all the sons. No sooner had a small state been founded but it was broken up among eight or nine heirs who in turn left their territory to an ever increasing number of descendants. It was inevitable that these small competing states should quarrel among themselves. Anarchy was the order of the day. And when the red glow of the eastern horizon told the people of the threatened invasion of a savage Asiatic tribe, the little states were too weak and too divided to render any sort of defence against this terrible enemy.

It was in the year 1224 that the first great Tartar invasion took place and that the hordes of Jenghiz Khan, the conqueror of China, Bokhara, Tashkent and Turkestan, made their first appearance in the west. The Slavic armies were beaten near the Kalka River and Russia was at the mercy of the Mongolians. Just as suddenly as they had come they disappeared.

Thirteen years later, in 1237, however, they returned. In less than five years they conquered every part of the vast Russian plains. Until the year 1380 when Dmitry Donskoi, grand duke of Moscow, beat them on the plains of Kulikovo, the Tartars were the masters of the Russian people.

All in all, it took the Russian two centuries to deliver themselves from this yoke. For a yoke it was and a most offensive and objectionable one. It turned the Slavic peasants into miserable slaves. It deprived the mass of the people of all feeling of honour and independence. It made hunger and misery and maltreatment and personal abuse the normal state of human existence. Until at last the average Russian, were he peasant or nobleman, went about his business like a neglected dog who has been beaten so often that his spirit has been broken and he dare not wag his tail without permission.

There was no escape. The horsemen of the Tartar Khan were fast and merciless. The endless prairie did not give a man a chance to cross into the safe territory of his neighbour. He must keep quiet and bear what his master decided to inflict upon him or run the risk of death. Of course, Europe might have interfered. But Europe was engaged upon business of its own, fighting the quarrels between the Pope and the emperor or suppressing this or that or the other heresy. And so Europe left the Slav to his fate, and forced him to work out his own salvation.

The final saviour of Russia was one of the many small states, founded by the early Norse rulers. It was situated in the heart of the Russian plain. Its capital, Moscow, was upon a steep hill on the banks of the Moskva River. This little principality, by dint of pleasing the Tartar (when it was necessary to please), and opposing him (when it was safe to do so), had during the middle of the fourteenth century made itself the leader of a new national life. It must be remembered that the Tartars were wholly deficient in constructive political ability.

They could only destroy. Their chief aim in conquering new territories was to obtain revenue. To get this revenue in the form of taxes, it was necessary to allow certain remnants of the old political organization to continue. Hence there were many little towns, surviving by the grace of the Great Khan, that they might act as tax-gatherers and rob their neighbours for the benefit of the Tartar treasury.

The state of Moscow, growing fat at the expense of the surrounding territory, finally became strong enough to risk open rebellion against its masters, the Tartars. It was successful and its fame as the leader in the cause of Russian independence made Moscow the natural centre for all those who still believed in a better future for the Slavic race. In the year 1453, Constantinople was taken by the Turks. Ten years later, under the rule of Ivan III, Moscow informed the western world that the Slavic state laid claim to the worldly and spiritual inheritance of the lost Byzantine Empire and such traditions of the Roman Empire as had survived in Constantinople. A generation afterwards, under Ivan the Terrible, the grand dukes of Moscow were strong enough to adopt the title of Cæsar, or tsar, and to demand recognition by the western powers of Europe.

In the year 1598, with Feodor I, the old Muscovite dynasty, descendants of the original Norseman Rurik, came to an end. For the next seven years, a Tartar half-breed, by the name of Boris Godunow, reigned as tsar. It was during this period that the future destiny of the large masses of the Russian people was decided. This empire was rich in land but very poor in money. There was no trade and there were no factories. Its few cities were dirty villages. It was composed of a strong central government and a vast number of illiterate peasants. This government, a mixture of Slavic, Norse, Byzantine and Tartar influences, recognised nothing beyond the interest of the state. To defend this state, it needed an army. To gather the taxes, which were necessary to pay the soldiers, it needed civil servants. To pay these many officials it needed land. In the vast wilderness on the east and west there was a sufficient supply of this commodity. But land without a few labourers to till the fields and tend the cattle has no value. Therefore the old nomadic peasants were robbed of one privilege after the other, until finally, during the first year of the seventeenth century, they were formally made a part of the soil upon which they lived. The Russian peasants ceased to be free men. They became serfs or slaves and they remained serfs until the year 1861, when their fate had become so terrible that they were beginning to die out.

In the seventeenth century, this new state with its growing territory which was spreading quickly into Siberia had become a force with which the rest of Europe was obliged to reckon. In 1613, after the death of Boris Godunow, the Russian nobles had elected one of their own number to be tsar. He was Michael, the son of Feodor, of the Moscow family of Romanow who lived in a little house just outside the Kremlin.

In the year 1672 his great-grandson, Peter, the son of another Feodor, was born. When the child was ten years old, his step-sister Sophia took possession of the Russian throne. The little boy was allowed to spend his days in the suburbs of the national capital, where the foreigners lived. Surrounded by Scotch barkeepers, Dutch traders, Swiss apothecaries, Italian barbers, French dancing teachers and German school-masters, the young prince obtained a first but rather extraordinary impression of that far away and mysterious Europe where things were done differently.

When he was seventeen years old, he suddenly pushed Sister Sophia from the throne. Peter himself became the ruler of Russia. He was not contented with being the tsar of a semi-barbarous and half-Asiatic people. He must be the sovereign head of a civilised nation. To change Russia overnight from a Byzantine-Tartar state into a European empire was no small undertaking. It needed strong hands and a capable head. Peter possessed both. In the year 1698, the great operation of grafting modern Europe upon ancient Russia was performed. The patient did not die. But he never got over the shock, as the events of the last five years have shown very plainly.

48

Russia vs. Sweden

Russia and Sweden Fought Many Wars
to Decide Who Shall Be the Leading Power
of North-Eastern Europe

In the year 1698, Tsar Peter set forth upon his first voyage to western Europe. He traveled by way of Berlin and went to Holland and to England. As a child he had almost been drowned sailing a homemade boat in the duck pond of his father's country home. This passion for water remained with him to the end of his life. In a practical way it showed itself in his wish to give his land-locked domains access to the open sea.

While the unpopular and harsh young ruler was away

Peter the Great in the Dutch Shipyard

from home, the friends of the old Russian ways in Moscow set to work to undo all his reforms. A sudden rebellion among his life-guards, the Streltsi Regiment, forced Peter to hasten home by the fast mail. He appointed himself executioner-in-chief and the Streltsi were hanged and quartered and killed to the last man. Sister Sophia, who had been the head of the rebellion, was locked up in a cloister and the rule of Peter began in earnest. This scene was repeated in the year 1716 when Peter had gone on his second western trip. That time the reactionaries followed the leadership of Peter's half-witted son, Alexis. Again the tsar returned in great haste. Alexis was beaten to death in his prison cell and the friends of the old-fashioned Byzantine ways marched thousands of dreary miles to their final destination in the Siberian lead mines. After that, no further outbreaks of popular discontent took place. Until the time of his death, Peter could reform in peace.

It is not easy to give you a list of his reforms in chronological order. The tsar worked with furious haste. He followed no system. He issued his decrees with such rapidity that it is difficult to keep count. Peter seemed to feel that everything that had ever happened before was entirely wrong. The whole of Russia therefore must be changed within the shortest possible time. When he died he left behind a well-trained army of two hundred thousand men and a navy of fifty ships. The old system of government had been abolished over night. The Duma, or convention of nobles, had been dismissed and in its stead, the tsar had surrounded himself with an advisory board of state officials, called the Senate.

Russia was divided into eight large "governments" or provinces. Roads were constructed. Towns were built. Industries were created wherever it pleased the tsar, without any regard for the presence of raw material. Canals were dug and mines were opened in the mountains of the east. In this land of illit-

erates, schools were founded and establishments of higher
learning, together with universities and hospitals and professional schools. Dutch naval engineers and tradesmen and
artisans from all over the world were encouraged to move to
Russia. Printing shops were established, but all books must
be first read by the imperial censors. The duties of each class
of society were carefully written down in a new law and the
entire system of civil and criminal laws was gathered into a
series of printed volumes. The old Russian costumes were
abolished by imperial decree, and policemen, armed with
scissors, watching all the country roads, changed the long-
haired Russian moujiks suddenly into a pleasing imitation of
smooth-shaven west Europeans.

In religious matters, the tsar tolerated no division of
power. There must be no chance of a rivalry between an
emperor and a Pope as had happened in Europe. In the year
1721, Peter made himself head of the Russian church. The
patriarchate of Moscow was abolished and the Holy Synod
made its appearance as the highest source of authority in all
matters of the established church.

Since, however, these many reforms could not be successful while the old Russian elements had a rallying point in the
town of Moscow, Peter decided to move his government to
a new capital. Amidst the unhealthy marshes of the Baltic
Sea the tsar built this new city. He began to reclaim the land
in the year 1703. Forty thousand peasants worked for years
to lay the foundations for this imperial city. The Swedes
attacked Peter and tried to destroy his town and illness and
misery killed tens of thousands of the peasants. But the work
was continued, winter and summer, and the ready-made
town soon began to grow. In the year 1712, it was officially
declared to be the "imperial residence." A dozen years later
it had 75,000 inhabitants. Twice a year the whole city was
flooded by the Neva. But the terrific will-power of the tsar

Peter the Great Builds His New Capital

created dikes and canals and the floods ceased to do harm.
When Peter died in 1725 he was the owner of the largest city
in northern Europe.

Of course, this sudden growth of so dangerous a rival had
been a source of great worry to all the neighbours. From his
side, Peter had watched with interest the many adventures
of his Baltic rival, the kingdom of Sweden. In the year 1654
Christina, the only daughter of Gustavus Adolphus, the hero
of the Thirty Years War, had renounced the throne and had
gone to Rome to end her days as a devout Catholic. A Protestant nephew of Gustavus Adolphus had succeeded the last
queen of the house of Vasa. Under Charles X and Charles XI,
the new dynasty had brought Sweden to its highest point of
development. But in 1697, Charles XI died suddenly and was
succeeded by a boy of fifteen, Charles XII.

This was the moment for which many of the northern
states had waited. During the great religious wars of the seventeenth century, Sweden had grown at the expense of her
neighbours. The time had come, so the owners thought, to
balance the account. At once war broke out between Russia,
Poland, Denmark and Saxony on the one side, and Sweden

Moscow

on the other. The raw and untrained armies of Peter were disastrously beaten by Charles in the famous battle of Narva in November of the year 1700. Then Charles, one of the most interesting military geniuses of that century, turned against his other enemies and for nine years he hacked and burned his way through the villages and cities of Poland, Saxony, Denmark and the Baltic provinces, while Peter drilled and trained his soldiers in distant Russia.

As a result, in the year 1709, in the battle of Poltawa, the Moscovites destroyed the exhausted armies of Sweden. Charles continued to be a highly picturesque figure, a wonderful hero of romance, but in his vain attempt to have his revenge, he ruined his own country. In the year 1718, he was accidentally killed or assassinated (we do not know which) and when peace was made in 1721, in the town of Nystadt, Sweden had lost all of her former Baltic possessions except Finland. The new Russian state, created by Peter, had become the leading power of northern Europe. But already a new rival was on the way. The Prussian state was taking shape.

49

The Rise of Prussia

<hr />

The Extraordinary Rise of a Little State in a Dreary
Part of Northern Germany, Called Prussia

The history of Prussia is the history of a frontier district. In the ninth century, Charlemagne had transferred the old centre of civilisation from the Mediterranean to the wild regions of north-western Europe. His Frankish soldiers had pushed the frontier of Europe further and further towards the east. They had conquered many lands from the heathenish Slavs and Lithuanians who were living in the plain between the Baltic Sea and the Carpathian Mountains, and the Franks administered those outlying districts just as the United States used to administer her territories before they achieved the dignity of statehood.

The frontier state of Brandenburg had been originally founded by Charlemagne to defend his eastern possessions against raids of the wild Saxon tribes. The Wends, a Slavic tribe which inhabited that region, were subjugated during the tenth century and their market-place, by the name of Brennabor, became the centre of and gave its name to the new province of Brandenburg.

During the eleventh, twelfth, thirteenth and fourteenth centuries, a succession of noble families exercised the functions of imperial governor in this frontier state. Finally in the fifteenth century, the house of Hohenzollern made its appearance and, as electors of Brandenburg, commenced to change a sandy and forlorn frontier territory into one of the most efficient empires of the modern world.

These Hohenzollerns, who have just been removed from the historical stage by the combined forces of Europe and America, came originally from southern Germany. They were of very humble origin. In the twelfth century a certain Frederick of Hohenzollern had made a lucky marriage and had been appointed keeper of the castle of Nuremberg. His descendants had used every chance and every opportunity to improve their power and after several centuries of watchful grabbing, they had been appointed to the dignity of elector, the name given to those sovereign princes who were supposed to elect the emperors of the old German Empire. During the Reformation they had taken the side of the Protestants and the early seventeenth century found them among the most powerful of the north German princes.

During the Thirty Years War, both Protestants and Catholics had plundered Brandenburg and Prussia with equal zeal. But under Frederick William, the Great Elector, the damage was quickly repaired and by a wise and careful use of all the economic and intellectual forces of the country, a state was founded in which there was practically no waste.

Modern Prussia, a state in which the individual and his wishes and aspirations have been entirely absorbed by the interests of the community as a whole—this Prussia dates back to the father of Frederick the Great. Frederick William I was a hard working, parsimonious Prussian sergeant, with a great love for bar-room stories and strong Dutch tobacco, an intense dislike of all frills and feathers (especially if they were of French origin) and possessed of but one idea. That idea was Duty. Severe with himself, he tolerated no weakness in his subjects, whether they be generals or common soldiers. The relation between himself and his son Frederick was never cordial, to say the least. The boorish manners of the father offended the finer spirit of the son. The son's love for French manners, literature, philosophy and music was rejected by the father as a manifestation of sissy-ness. There followed a terrible outbreak between these two strange temperaments. Frederick tried to escape to England. He was caught and court-martialed and forced to witness the decapitation of his best friend who had tried to help him. Thereupon as part of his punishment, the young prince was sent to a little fortress somewhere in the provinces to be taught the details of his future business of being a king. It proved a blessing in disguise. When Frederick came to the throne in 1740, he knew how his country was managed from the birth certificate of a pauper's son to the minutest detail of a complicated annual budget.

As an author, especially in his book called the "Anti-Machiavelli," Frederick had expressed his contempt for the political creed of the ancient Florentine historian, who had advised his princely pupils to lie and cheat whenever it was necessary to do so for the benefit of their country. The ideal ruler in Frederick's volume was the first servant of his people, the enlightened despot after the example of Louis XIV. In practice, however, Frederick, while working for his people twenty hours a day, tolerated no one to be near him as a counsellor. His ministers were superior clerks. Prussia was his private possession, to be treated according to his own wishes. And nothing was allowed to interfere with the interest of the state.

In the year 1740 the emperor Charles VI, of Austria, died. He had tried to make the position of his only daughter, Maria Theresa, secure through a solemn treaty, written black on white, upon a large piece of parchment. But no sooner had the old emperor been deposited in the ancestral crypt of the Habsburg family than the armies of Frederick were marching towards the Austrian frontier to occupy that part of Silesia for which (together with almost everything else in central Europe) Prussia clamoured, on account of some ancient and very doubtful rights of claim. In a number of wars, Frederick conquered all of Silesia, and although he was often very near defeat, he maintained himself in his newly acquired territories against all Austrian counter-attacks.

Europe took due notice of this sudden appearance of a very powerful new state. In the eighteenth century, the Germans were a people who had been ruined by the great religious wars and who were not held in high esteem by any one. Frederick, by an effort as sudden and quite as terrific as that of Peter of Russia, changed this attitude of contempt into one of fear. The internal affairs of Prussia were arranged so skillfully that the subjects had less reason for complaint than elsewhere. The treasury showed an annual surplus instead of a deficit. Torture was abolished. The judiciary system was improved. Good roads and good schools and good universities, together with a scrupulously honest administration, made the people feel that whatever services were demanded of them, they (to speak the vernacular) got their money's worth.

After having been for several centuries the battle field of the French and the Austrians and the Swedes and the Danes and the Poles, Germany, encouraged by the example of Prussia began to regain self-confidence. And this was the work of the little old man, with his hook-nose and his old uniforms covered with snuff, who said very funny but very unpleasant things about his neighbours, and who played the scandalous game of eighteenth century diplomacy without any regard for the truth, provided he could gain something by his lies. This in spite of his book, "Anti-Machiavelli." In the year 1786 the end came. His friends were all gone. Children he had never had. He died alone, tended by a single servant and his faithful dogs, whom he loved better than human beings because, as he said, they were never ungrateful and remained true to their friends.

50

The Mercantile System

How the Newly Founded National or Dynastic
States of Europe Tried to Make Themselves Rich
and What Was Meant by the Mercantile System

We have seen how, during the sixteenth and the seventeenth centuries, the states of our modern world began to
take shape. Their origins were different in almost every case.
Some had been the result of the deliberate effort of a single king. Others had happened by chance. Still others had
been the result of favourable natural geographic boundaries.
But once they had been founded, they had all of them tried
to strengthen their internal administration and to exert the
greatest possible influence upon foreign affairs. All this of
course had cost a great deal of money. The mediæval state
with its lack of centralised power did not depend upon a
rich treasury. The king got his revenues from the crown
domains and his civil service paid for itself. The modern centralised state was a more complicated affair. The old knights
disappeared and hired government officials or bureaucrats
took their place. Army, navy and internal administration
demanded millions. The question then became—where was
this money to be found?

Gold and silver had been a rare commodity in the Middle

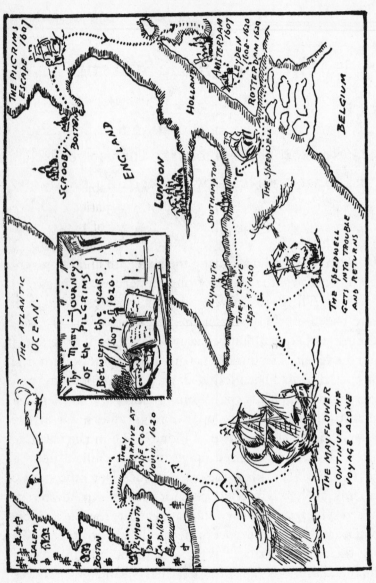

The Voyage of the Pilgrims

Ages. The average man, as I have told you, never saw a gold piece as long as he lived. Only the inhabitants of the large cities were familiar with silver coin. The discovery of America and the exploitation of the Peruvian mines changed all this. The centre of trade was transferred from the Mediterranean to the Atlantic seaboard. The old "commercial cities" of Italy lost their financial importance. New "commercial nations" took their place and gold and silver were no longer a curiosity.

Through Spain and Portugal and Holland and England, precious metals began to find their way to Europe. The sixteenth century had its own writers on the subject of political economy and they evolved a theory of national wealth which seemed to them entirely sound and of the greatest possible benefit to their respective countries. They reasoned that both gold and silver were actual wealth. Therefore they believed that the country with the largest supply of actual cash in the vaults of its treasury and its banks was at the same time the richest country. And since money meant armies, it followed that the richest country was also the most powerful and could rule the rest of the world.

We call this system the "mercantile system," and it was accepted with the same unquestioning faith with which the early Christians believed in miracles and many of the present-day American business men believe in the tariff. In practice, the mercantile system worked out as follows: To get the largest surplus of precious metals a country must have a favourable balance of export trade. If you can export more to your neighbour than he exports to your own country, he will owe you money and will be obliged to send you some of his gold. Hence you gain and he loses. As a result of this creed, the economic program of almost every seventeenth century state was as follows:

1. Try to get possession of as many precious metals as you can.
2. Encourage foreign trade in preference to domestic trade.
3. Encourage those industries which change raw materials into exportable finished products.
4. Encourage a large population, for you will need workmen for your factories and an agricultural community does not raise enough workmen.
5. Let the state watch this process and interfere whenever it is necessary to do so.

Instead of regarding international trade as something akin to a force of nature which would always obey certain natural laws regardless of man's interference, the people of the sixteenth and seventeenth centuries tried to regulate their commerce by the help of official decrees and royal laws and financial help on the part of the government.

In the sixteenth century Charles V adopted this mercantile system (which was then something entirely new) and introduced it into his many possessions. Elizabeth of England flattered him by her imitation. The Bourbons, especially King Louis XIV, were fanatical adherents of this doctrine and Colbert, his great minister of finance, became the prophet of mercantilism to whom all Europe looked for guidance.

The entire foreign policy of Cromwell was a practical application of the mercantile system. It was invariably directed against the rich rival republic of Holland. For the Dutch shippers, as the common-carriers of the merchandise of Europe, had certain leanings towards free-trade and therefore had to be destroyed at all cost.

It will be easily understood how such a system must affect the colonies. A colony under the mercantile system became merely a reservoir of gold and silver and spices, which was to be tapped for the benefit of the home country. The Asiatic,

How Europe Conquered the World

American and African supply of precious metals and the raw materials of these tropical countries became a monopoly of the state which happened to own that particular colony. No outsider was ever allowed within the precincts and no native was permitted to trade with a merchant whose ship flew a foreign flag.

Undoubtedly the mercantile system encouraged the development of young industries in certain countries where there never had been any manufacturing before. It built roads and dug canals and made for better means of transportation. It demanded greater skill among the workmen and gave the merchant a better social position, while it weakened the power of the landed aristocracy.

On the other hand, it caused very great misery. It made the natives in the colonies the victims of a most shameless exploitation. It exposed the citizens of the home country to an even more terrible fate. It helped in a great measure to

Sea Power

turn every land into an armed camp and divided the world into little bits of territory, each working for its own direct benefit, while striving at all times to destroy the power of its neighbours and get hold of their treasures. It laid so much stress upon the importance of owning wealth that "being rich" came to be regarded as the sole virtue of the average citizen. Economic systems come and go like the fashions in surgery and in the clothes of women, and during the nineteenth century the mercantile system was discarded in favor of a system of free and open competition. At least, so I have been told.

51

The American Revolution

At the End of the Eighteenth Century Europe
Heard Strange Reports of Something
Which Had Happened in the Wilderness
of the North American Continent. The
Descendants of the Men Who Had Punished
King Charles for His Insistence upon His "Divine
Rights" Added a New Chapter to the Old Story of
the Struggle for Self-Government

For the sake of convenience, we ought to go back a few centuries and repeat the early history of the great struggle for colonial possessions.

As soon as a number of European nations had been created upon the new basis of national or dynastic interests, that is to say, during and immediately after the Thirty Years War, their rulers, backed up by the capital of their merchants and the ships of their trading companies, continued the fight for more territory in Asia, Africa and America.

The Spaniards and the Portuguese had been exploring the Indian Sea and the Pacific Ocean for more than a century ere Holland and England appeared upon the stage. This proved

The Fight for Liberty

an advantage to the latter. The first rough work had already been done. What is more, the earliest navigators had so often made themselves unpopular with the Asiatic and American and African natives that both the English and the Dutch were welcomed as friends and deliverers. We cannot claim any superior virtues for either of these two races. But they were merchants before everything else. They never allowed religious considerations to interfere with their practical common sense. During their first relations with weaker races, all European nations have behaved with shocking brutality. The English and the Dutch, however, knew better where to draw the line. Provided they got their spices and their gold and silver and their taxes, they were willing to let the native live as it best pleased him.

It was not very difficult for them therefore to establish themselves in the richest parts of the world. But as soon as this had been accomplished, they began to fight each other for still further possessions. Strangely enough, the colonial wars were never settled in the colonies themselves. They were decided three thousand miles away by the navies of the contending countries. It is one of the most interesting principles of ancient and modern warfare (one of the few reliable laws of history) that "the nation which commands the sea is also the nation which commands the land." So far this

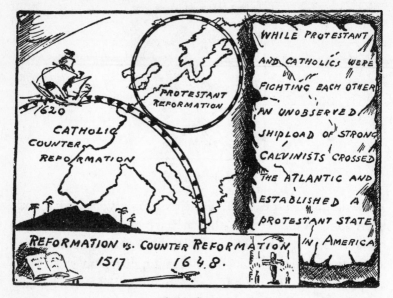

WHILE PROTESTANT AND CATHOLICS WERE FIGHTING EACH OTHER AN UNOBSERVED SHIPLOAD OF STRONG CALVINISTS CROSSED THE ATLANTIC AND ESTABLISHED A PROTESTANT STATE IN AMERICA

PROTESTANT REFORMATION

1620

CATHOLIC COUNTER REFORMATION

REFORMATION vs. COUNTER REFORMATION
1517   1648.

The Pilgrims

law has never failed to work, but the modern airplane may have changed it. In the eighteenth century, however, there were no flying machines and it was the British navy which gained for England her vast American and Indian and African colonies.

The series of naval wars between England and Holland in the seventeenth century does not interest us here. It ended as all such encounters between hopelessly ill-matched powers will end. But the warfare between England and France (her other rival) is of greater importance to us, for while the superior British fleet in the end defeated the French navy, a great deal of the preliminary fighting was done on our own American continent In this vast country, both France and England claimed everything which had been discovered and a lot more which the eye of no white man had ever seen. In 1497 Cabot had landed in the northern part of America and twenty-seven years later, Giovanni Verrazano had visited

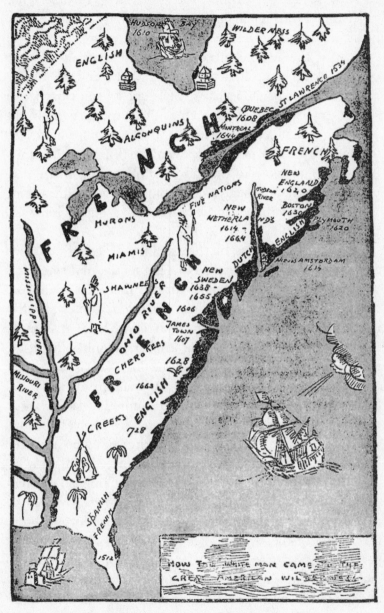

How the White Man Settled in North America

these coasts. Cabot had flown the English flag. Verrazano had sailed under the French flag. Hence both England and France proclaimed themselves the owners of the entire continent.

During the seventeenth century, some ten small English colonies had been founded between Maine and the Carolinas. They were usually a haven of refuge for some particular sect of English Dissenters, such as the Puritans, who in the year 1620 went to New England, or the Quakers, who settled in Pennsylvania in 1681. They were small frontier communities, nestling close to the shores of the ocean, where people had gathered to make a new home and begin life among happier surroundings, far away from royal supervision and interference.

The French colonies, on the other hand, always remained a possession of the crown. No Huguenots or Protestants were allowed in these colonies for fear that they might contaminate the Indians with their dangerous Protestant doctrines and would perhaps interfere with the missionary work of the Jesuit fathers. The English colonies, therefore, had been founded upon a much healthier basis than their French neighbours and rivals. They were an expression of the commercial energy of the English middle classes, while the French settlements were inhabited by people who had crossed the ocean as servants of the king and who expected to return to Paris at the first possible chance.

Politically, however, the position of the English colonies was far from satisfactory. The French had discovered the mouth of the St. Lawrence in the sixteenth century. From the region of the Great Lakes they had worked their way southward, had descended the Mississippi and had built several fortifications along the Gulf of Mexico. After a century of exploration, a line of sixty French forts cut off the English settlements along the Atlantic seaboard from the interior.

The English land grants, made to the different colonial

The Blockhouse in the Wilderness

In the Cabin of the "Mayflower"

companies, had given them "all land from sea to sea." This sounded well on paper, but in practice, British territory ended where the line of French fortifications began. To break through this barrier was possible but it took both men and money and caused a series of horrible border wars in which both sides murdered their white neighbours, with the help of the Indian tribes.

As long as the Stuarts had ruled England there had been no danger of war with France. The Stuarts needed the Bourbons in their attempt to establish an autocratic form of government and to break the power of Parliament. But in 1689 the last of the Stuarts had disappeared from British soil and Dutch William, the great enemy of Louis XIV, succeeded him. From that time on, until the treaty of Paris of 1763, France and England fought for the possession of India and North America.

The French Explore the West

During these wars, as I have said before, the English navies invariably beat the French. Cut off from her colonies, France lost most of her possessions, and when peace was declared, the entire North American continent had fallen into British hands and the great work of exploration of Cartier, Champlain, La Salle, Marquette and a score of others was lost to France.

Only a very small part of this vast domain was inhabited. From Massachusetts in the north, where the Pilgrims (a sect of Puritans who were very intolerant and who therefore had found no happiness either in Anglican England or Calvinist Holland) had landed in the year 1620, to the Carolinas and Virginia (the tobacco-raising provinces which had been founded entirely for the sake of profit) stretched a thin line of sparsely populated territory. But the men who lived in this new land of fresh air and high skies were very different from their brethren of the mother country. In the wilderness they had learned independence and self-reliance. They were the sons of hardy and energetic ancestors. Lazy and timorous people did not cross the ocean in those days. The American colonists hated the restraint and the lack of breathing space which had made their lives in the old country so very unhappy. They meant to be their own masters. This the

The First Winter in New England

ruling classes of England did not seem to understand. The government annoyed the colonists and the colonists, who hated to be bothered in this way, began to annoy the British government.

Bad feeling caused more bad feeling. It is not necessary to repeat here in detail what actually happened and what might have been avoided if the British king had been more intelligent than George III or less given to drowsiness and indifference than his minister, Lord North. The British colonists, when they understood that peaceful arguments would not settle the difficulties, took to arms. From being loyal subjects, they turned rebels, who exposed themselves to the punishment of death when they were captured by the German soldiers whom George hired to do his fighting after the pleasant custom of that day, when Teutonic princes sold whole regiments to the highest bidder.

The war between England and her American colonies lasted seven years. During most of that time, the final success of the rebels seemed very doubtful. A great number of the people, especially in the cities, had remained loyal to the king. They were in favour of a compromise, and would have been willing to sue for peace. But the great figure of Washington stood guard over the cause of the colonists.

Ably assisted by a handful of brave men, he used his stead-fast but badly equipped armies to weaken the forces of the king. Time and again when defeat seemed unavoidable, his strategy turned the tide of battle. Often his men were ill-fed. During the winter they lacked shoes and coats and were forced to live in unhealthy dug-outs. But their trust in their great leader was absolute and they stuck it out until the final hour of victory.

But more interesting that the campaigns of Washington or the diplomatic triumphs of Benjamin Franklin, who was in Europe getting money from the French government and the Amsterdam bankers, was an event which occurred early in the Revolution. The representatives of the different colonies had gathered in Philadelphia to discuss matters of common importance. It was the first year of the Revolution. Most of the big towns of the sea coast were still in the hands of the British. Reinforcements from England were arriving by the ship load. Only men who were deeply convinced of the righteousness of their cause would have found the courage

George Washington

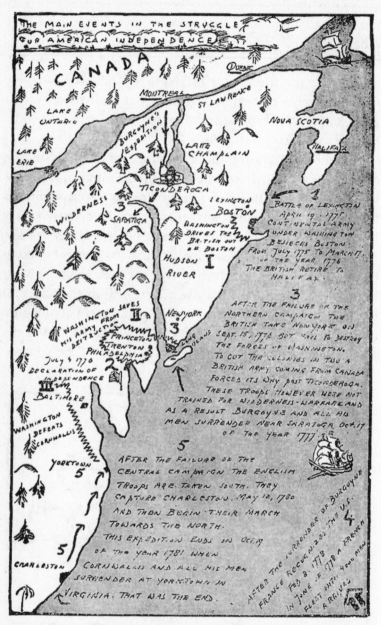

The Great American Revolution

to take the momentous decision of the months of June and
July of the year 1776.

In June, Richard Henry Lee of Virginia proposed a motion
to the Continental Congress that "these united colonies are,
and of right ought to be, free and independent states, that
they are absolved from all allegiance to the British crown,
and that all political connection between them and the state
of Great Britain is and ought to be, totally dissolved."

The motion was seconded by John Adams of Massachusetts. It was carried on July 2 and on July 4, it was followed by
an official Declaration of Independence, which was the work
of Thomas Jefferson, a serious and exceedingly capable student of both politics and government and destined to be one
of the most famous of our American presidents.

When news of this event reached Europe, and was followed by the final victory of the colonists and the adoption
of the famous Constitution of the year 1787 (the first of all
written constitutions) it caused great interest. The dynastic
system of the highly centralised states which had been developed after the great religious wars of the seventeenth century
had reached the height of its power. Everywhere the palace
of the king had grown to enormous proportions, while the
cities of the royal realm were being surrounded by rapidly
growing acres of slums. The inhabitants of those slums were
showing signs of restlessness. They were quite helpless. But
the higher classes, the nobles and the professional men, they
too were beginning to have certain doubts about the economic and political conditions under which they lived. The
success of the American colonists showed them that many
things were possible which had been held impossible only a
short time before.

According to the poet, the shot which opened the battle of
Lexington was "heard around the world." That was a bit of
an exaggeration. The Chinese and the Japanese and the Rus-

sians (not to speak of the Australians and the Hawaiians who had just been re-discovered by Captain Cook, whom they had killed for his trouble) never heard of it at all. But it carried across the Atlantic Ocean. It landed in the powder house of European discontent and in France it caused an explosion which rocked the entire continent from Petrograd to Madrid and buried the representatives of the old statecraft and the old diplomacy under several tons of democratic bricks.

52

The French Revolution

The Great French Revolution Proclaims the
Principles of Liberty, Fraternity and Equality
unto All the People of the Earth

Before we talk about a revolution it is just as well that we explain just what this word means. In the terms of a great Russian writer (and Russians ought to know what they are talking about in this field) a revolution is "a swift overthrow, in a few years, of institutions which have taken centuries to root in the soil, and seem so fixed and immovable that even the most ardent reformers hardly dare to attack them in their writings. It is the fall, the crumbling away in a brief period, of all that up to that time has composed the essence of social, religious, political and economic life in a nation."

Such a revolution took place in France in the eighteenth century when the old civilisation of the country had grown stale. The king in the days of Louis XIV had become EVERY-THING and was the state. The nobility, formerly the civil servant of the federal state, found itself without any duties and became a social ornament of the royal court.

This French state of the eighteenth century, however, cost incredible sums of money. This money had to be produced in the form of taxes. Unfortunately the kings of France had not been strong enough to force the nobility and the clergy to pay their share of these taxes. Hence the taxes were paid entirely by the agricultural population. But the peasants, living in dreary hovels, no longer in intimate contact with their former landlords, but victims of cruel and incompetent land agents, were going from bad to worse. Why should they work and exert themselves? Increased returns upon their land merely meant more taxes and nothing for themselves and therefore they neglected their fields as much as they dared.

Hence we have a king who wanders in empty splendour through the vast halls of his palaces, habitually followed by hungry office seekers, all of whom live upon the revenue obtained from peasants who are no better than the beasts of the fields. It is not a pleasant picture, but it is not exaggerated. There was, however, another side to the so-called "Ancien Régime" which we must keep in mind.

A wealthy middle class closely connected with the nobility (by the usual process of the rich banker's daughter marrying the poor baron's son) and a court composed of all the most entertaining people of France had brought the polite art of graceful living to its highest development. As the best brains of the country were not allowed to occupy themselves with questions of political economics, they spent their idle hours upon the discussion of abstract ideas.

As fashions in modes of thought and personal behaviour are quite as likely to run to extremes as fashion in dress, it was natural that the most artificial society of that day should take a tremendous interest in what they considered "the simple life." The king and the queen, the absolute and unquestioned proprietors of France, and all its colonies and dependencies, together with their courtiers, went to live in funny little country houses all dressed up as milk-maids and stable-boys and played at being shepherds in a happy vale of ancient Hellas. Around them, their courtiers danced attendance, their court-musicians composed lovely minuets, their court barbers devised more and more elaborate and costly headgear, until from sheer boredom and lack of real jobs, this whole artificial world of Versailles (the great show place which Louis XIV had built far away from his noisy and restless city) talked of nothing but those subjects which were furthest removed from their own lives, just as a man who is starving will talk of nothing except food.

When Voltaire, the courageous old philosopher, play-wright, historian and novelist, and the great enemy of all religious and political tyranny, began to throw his bombs of criticism at everything connected with the Established Order of Things, the whole French world applauded him and his theatrical pieces played to standing room only. When Jean Jacques Rousseau waxed sentimental about primitive man and gave his contemporaries delightful descriptions of the happiness of the original inhabitants of this planet (about whom he knew as little as he did about the children, upon whose education he was the recognised authority) all France read his "Social Contract" and this society, in which the king and the state were one, wept bitter tears when they heard Rousseau's appeal for a return to the blessed days when the real sovereignty had lain in the hands of the people and when the king had been merely the servant of his people.

When Montesquieu published his "Persian Letters" in which two distinguished Persian travellers turn the whole existing society of France topsy-turvy and poke fun at every-thing from the king down to the lowest of his six hundred pastry cooks, the book immediately went through four edi-tions and assured the writer thousands of readers for his famous discussion of the "Spirit of the Laws" in which the noble baron compared the excellent English system with the backward system of France and advocated instead of an absolute monarchy the establishment of a state in which the executive, the legislative and the judicial powers should be in separate hands and should work independently of each other. When Lebreton, the Parisian book-seller, announced that Messieurs Diderot, d'Alembert, Turgot and a score of other distinguished writers were going to publish an "Encyclopædia" which was to contain "all the new ideas and the new science and the new knowledge," the response from the side of the public was most satisfactory, and when after twenty-two years the last of the twenty-eight volumes had been finished, the somewhat belated interference of the police could not repress the enthusiasm with which French society received this most important but very dangerous contribution to the discussions of the day.

Here, let me give you a little warning. When you read a novel about the French Revolution or see a play or a movie, you will easily get the impression that the Revolution was the work of the rabble from the Paris slums. It was nothing of the kind. The mob appears often upon the revolutionary stage, but invariably at the instigation and under the leadership of those middle-class professional men who used the hungry multitude as an efficient ally in their warfare upon the king and his court. But the fundamental ideas which caused the Revolution were invented by a few brilliant minds, and they

The Guillotine

were at first introduced into the charming drawing-rooms of the "Ancien Régime" to provide amiable diversion for the much-bored ladies and gentlemen of His Majesty's court. These pleasant but careless people played with the dangerous fireworks of social criticism until the sparks fell through the cracks of the floor, which was old and rotten just like the rest of the building. Those sparks unfortunately landed in the basement where age-old rubbish lay in great confusion. Then there was a cry of fire. But the owner of the house, who was interested in everything except the management of his property, did not know how to put the small blaze out. The flame spread rapidly and the entire edifice was consumed by the conflagration, which we call the Great French Revolution.

For the sake of convenience, we can divide the French Revolution into two parts. From 1789 to 1791 there was a more or less orderly attempt to introduce a constitutional monarchy. This failed, partly through lack of good faith and stupidity on the part of the monarch himself, partly through circumstances over which nobody had any control.

From 1792 to 1799 there was a republic and a first effort to establish a democratic form of government. But the actual outbreak of violence had been preceded by many years of unrest and many sincere but ineffectual attempts at reform.

When France had a debt of four billion francs and the treasury was always empty and there was not a single thing upon which new taxes could be levied, even good King Louis (who was an expert locksmith and a great hunter but a very poor statesman) felt vaguely that something ought to be done. Therefore he called for Turgot, to be his minister of finance. Anne Robert Jacques Turgot, baron de l'Aulne, a man in the early sixties, a splendid representative of the fast disappearing class of landed gentry, had been a successful governor of a province and was an amateur political economist of great ability. He did his best. Unfortunately, he could not perform miracles. As it was impossible to squeeze more taxes out of the ragged peasants, it was necessary to get the necessary funds from the nobility and clergy who had never paid a centime. This made Turgot the best hated man at the court of Versailles. Furthermore he was obliged to face the enmity of Marie Antoinette, the queen, who was against everybody who dared to mention the word "economy" within her hearing. Soon Turgot was called an "unpractical visionary" and a "theoretical professor" and then of course his position became untenable. In the year 1776 he was forced to resign.

After the "professor" there came a man of Practical Business Sense. He was an industrious Swiss by the name of Necker who had made himself rich as a grain speculator and the partner in an international banking house. His ambitious wife had pushed him into the government service that she might establish a position for her daughter who afterwards as the wife of the Swedish minister in Paris, Baron de Staël, became a famous literary figure of the early nineteenth century.

Necker set to work with a fine display of zeal just as Turgot had done. In 1781 he published a careful review of the French finances. The king understood nothing of this "Compte Rendu." He had just sent troops to America to help the colonists against their common enemies, the English. This expedition proved to be unexpectedly expensive and Necker was asked to find the necessary funds. When instead of producing revenue, he published more figures and made statistics and began to use the dreary warning about "necessary economies" his days were numbered. In the year 1781 he was dismissed as an incompetent servant.

After the Professor and the Practical Business Man came the delightful type of financier who will guarantee everybody one hundred percent per month on their money if only they

Louis XVI

will trust his own infallible system. He was Charles Alexandre de Calonne, a pushing official, who had made his career both by his industry and his complete lack of honesty and scruples. He found the country heavily indebted, but he was a clever man, willing to oblige everybody, and he invented a quick remedy. He paid the old debts by contracting new ones. This method is not new. The result since time immemorial has been disastrous. In less than three years more than eight hundred million francs had been added to the French debt by this charming minister of finance who never worried and smilingly signed his name to every demand that was made by His Majesty and by his lovely queen, who had learned the habit of spending during the days of her youth in Vienna.

At last even the Parliament of Paris (a high court of justice and not a legislative body), although by no means lacking in loyalty to their sovereign, decided that something must be done. Calonne wanted to borrow another eighty million francs. It had been a bad year for the crops and the misery and hunger in the country districts were terrible. Unless something sensible were done, France would go bankrupt. The king as always was unaware of the seriousness of the situation. Would it not be a good idea to consult the representatives of the people? Since 1614 no Estates General had been called together. In view of the threatening panic there was a demand that the Estates be convened. Louis XVI, however, who never could take a decision, refused to go as far as that.

To pacify the popular clamour he called together a meeting of the Notables in the year 1787. This merely meant a gathering of the best families who discussed what could and should be done, without touching their feudal and clerical privilege of tax-exemption. It is unreasonable to expect that a certain class of society shall commit political and economic suicide for the benefit of another group of fellow-citizens. The 127 Notables obstinately refused to surrender a single one of their ancient rights. The crowd in the street, being now exceedingly hungry, demanded that Necker, in whom they had confidence, be reappointed. The Notables said "No." The crowd in the street began to smash windows and do other unseemly things. The Notables fled. Calonne was dismissed.

A new colourless minister of finance, the Cardinal Loménie de Brienne, was appointed and Louis, driven by the violent threats of his starving subjects, agreed to call together the old Estates General as "soon as practicable." This vague promise of course satisfied no one.

No such severe winter had been experienced for almost a century. The crops had been either destroyed by floods or had been frozen to death in the fields. All the olive trees of Provence had been killed. Private charity tried to do something but could accomplish little for eighteen million starving people. Everywhere bread riots occurred. A generation before these would have been put down by the army. But the work of the new philosophical school had begun to bear fruit. People began to understand that a shotgun is no effective remedy for a hungry stomach and even the soldiers (who came from among the people) were no longer to be depended upon. It was absolutely necessary that the king should do something definite to regain the popular goodwill, but again he hesitated.

Here and there in the provinces, little independent republics were established by followers of the new school. The cry of "no taxation without representation" (the slogan of the American rebels a quarter of a century before) was heard among the faithful middle classes. France was threatened with general anarchy. To appease the people and to increase the royal popularity, the government unexpectedly suspended the former very strict form of censorship of books. At once a flood of ink descended upon France. Everybody, high or low, criticised and was criticised. More than two thousand pamphlets were published. Loménie de Brienne was swept away by a storm of abuse. Necker was hastily called back to placate, as best he could, the nation-wide unrest. Immediately the stock market went up thirty percent. And by common consent, people suspended judgment for a little while longer. In May of 1789 the Estates General were to assemble and then the wisdom of the entire nation would speedily solve the difficult problem of re-creating the kingdom of France into a healthy and happy state.

This prevailing idea, that the combined wisdom of the people would be able to solve all difficulties, proved disastrous. It lamed all personal effort during many important months. Instead of keeping the government in his own hands at this critical moment, Necker allowed everything to drift. Hence there was a new outbreak of the acrimonious debate upon the best ways to reform the old kingdom. Everywhere the power of the police weakened. The people of the Paris suburbs, under the leadership of professional agitators, gradually began to discover their strength, and commenced to play the rôle which was to be theirs all through the years of the great unrest, when they acted as the brute force which was used by the actual leaders of the Revolution to secure those things which could not be obtained in a legitimate fashion.

As a sop to the peasants and the middle class, Necker decided that they should be allowed a double representation in the Estates General. Upon this subject, the Abbé Siéyès then wrote a famous pamphlet, "To What does the Third Estate Amount?," in which he came to the conclusion that the Third Estate (a name given to the middle class) ought to amount to everything, that it had not amounted to anything in the past and that it now desired to amount to something. He expressed the sentiment of the great majority of the people who had the best interests of the country at heart.

Finally the elections took place under the worst conditions imaginable. When they were over, 308 clergymen, 285 noblemen and 621 representatives of the Third Estate packed their trunks to go to Versailles. The Third Estate was obliged to carry additional luggage. This consisted of voluminous reports called "cahiers" in which the many complaints and

The Bastille

grievances of their constituents had been written down. The stage was set for the great final act that was to save France.

The Estates General came together on May 5, 1789. The king was in a bad humour. The Clergy and the Nobility let it be known that they were unwilling to give up a single one of their privileges. The king ordered the three groups of representatives to meet in different rooms and discuss their grievances separately. The Third Estate refused to obey the royal command. They took a solemn oath to that effect in a squash court (hastily put in order for the purpose of this illegal meeting) on June 20, 1789. They insisted that all three estates, Nobility, Clergy and Third Estate, should meet together and so informed His Majesty. The king gave in.

As the "National Assembly," the Estates General began to discuss the state of the French kingdom. The king got angry. Then again he hesitated. He said that he would never surrender his absolute power. Then he went hunting, forgot all about the cares of the state and when he returned from the chase he gave in. For it was the royal habit to do the right thing at the wrong time in the wrong way. When the people clamoured for A, the king scolded them and gave them nothing. Then, when the palace was surrounded by a howling multitude of poor people, the king surrendered and gave his subjects what they had asked for. By this time, however, the people wanted A plus B. The comedy was repeated. When the king signed his name to the royal decree which granted his beloved subjects A and B they were threatening to kill the entire royal family unless they received A plus B plus C. And so on, through the whole alphabet and up to the scaffold.

Unfortunately the king was always just one letter behind. He never understood this. Even when he laid his head under the guillotine, he felt that he was a much-abused man who had received a most unwarrantable treatment at the hands of people whom he had loved to the best of his limited ability.

Historical "ifs," as I have often warned you, are never of any value. It is very easy for us to say that the monarchy might have been saved "if" Louis had been a man of greater energy and less kindness of heart. But the king was not alone. Even "if" he had possessed the ruthless strength of Napoleon, his career during these difficult days might have been easily ruined by his wife, who was the daughter of Maria Theresa of Austria and who possessed all the characteristic virtues and vices of a young girl who had been brought up at the most autocratic and mediæval court of that age.

She decided that some action must be taken and planned a counter-revolution. Necker was suddenly dismissed and loyal troops were called to Paris. The people, when they heard of this, stormed the fortress of the Bastille prison, and on July 14 of the year 1789, they destroyed this familiar but much-hated symbol of autocratic power which had long since ceased to be a political prison and was now used as the city lock-up for pickpockets and second-story men. Many of the nobles took the hint and left the country. But the king as usual did nothing. He had been hunting on the day of the fall of the Bastille and he had shot several deer and felt very much pleased.

The National Assembly now set to work and on August 4, with the noise of the Parisian multitude in their ears, they abolished all privileges. This was followed on August 27 by the "Declaration of the Rights of Man," the famous preamble to the first French Constitution. So far so good, but the court had apparently not yet learned its lesson. There was a widespread suspicion that the king was again trying to interfere with these reforms and as a result, on October 5, there was a second riot in Paris. It spread to Versailles and the people were not pacified until they had brought the king back to his palace in Paris. They did not trust him in Versailles. They liked to have him where they could watch him and control his correspondence with his relatives in Vienna and Madrid and the other courts of Europe.

In the Assembly meanwhile, Mirabeau, a nobleman who had become leader of the Third Estate, was beginning to put order into chaos. But before he could save the position of the king he died, on April 2 of the year 1791. The king, who now began to fear for his own life, tried to escape on June 21. He was recognised from his picture on a coin, was stopped near the village of Varennes by members of the National Guard and was brought back to Paris.

In September of 1791, the first constitution of France was accepted, and the members of the National Assembly went home. On the first of October of 1791, the Legislative Assembly came together to continue the work of the National Assembly. In this new gathering of popular representatives there were many extremely revolutionary elements. The boldest among these were known as the Jacobins, after the old Jacobin cloister in which they held their political meetings. These young men (most of them belonging to the professional classes) made very violent speeches and when the newspapers carried these orations to Berlin and Vienna, the king of Prussia and the emperor decided that they must do something to save their good brother and sister. They were very busy just then dividing the kingdom of Poland, where rival political factions had caused such a state of disorder that the country was at the mercy of anybody who wanted to take a couple of provinces. But they managed to send an army to invade France and deliver the king.

Then a terrible panic of fear swept throughout the land of France. All the pent-up hatred of years of hunger and suffering came to a horrible climax. The mob of Paris stormed the palace of the Tuileries. The faithful Swiss body-guards tried to defend their master, but Louis, unable to make up his mind, gave order to "cease firing" just when the crowd was retiring. The people, drunk with blood and noise and cheap wine, murdered the Swiss to the last man, then invaded the palace, and went after Louis, who had escaped into the meeting hall of the Assembly, where he was immediately suspended of his office, and from where he was taken as a prisoner to the old castle of the Temple.

But the armies of Austria and Prussia continued their advance and the panic changed into hysteria and turned men and women into wild beasts. In the first week of September of the year 1792, the crowd broke into the jails and murdered all the prisoners. The government did not interfere. The Jacobins, headed by Danton, knew that this crisis meant either the success or the failure of the Revolution, and that only the most brutal audacity could save them. The Legislative Assembly was closed and on September 21 of the year 1792, a new National Convention came together. It was a body composed almost entirely of extreme revolutionists. The king was formally accused of high treason and was brought before the Convention. He was found guilty and by a vote of 361 to 360 (the extra vote being that of his cousin the Duke of Orleans) he was condemned to death. On January 21 of the year 1793, he quietly and with much dignity suffered himself to be taken to the scaffold. He had never understood what all the shooting and the fuss had been about. And he had been too proud to ask questions.

Then the Jacobins turned against the more moderate element in the convention, the Girondists, called after their southern district, the Gironde. A special revolutionary tribunal was instituted and twenty-one of the leading Girondists were condemned to death. The others committed suicide. They were capable and honest men but too philosophical and too moderate to survive during these frightful years.

In October of the year 1793 the Constitution was suspended by the Jacobins "until peace should have been declared." All power was placed in the hands of a small Committee of Public Safety, with Danton and Robespierre as its leaders. The Christian religion and the old chronology were abolished. The "Age of Reason" (of which Thomas Paine had written so eloquently during the American Revolution) had come and with it the "Terror" which for more than a year killed good and bad and indifferent people at the rate of seventy or eighty a day.

The autocratic rule of the king had been destroyed. It was succeeded by the tyranny of a few people who had such a passionate love for democratic virtue that they felt compelled to kill all those who disagreed with them. France was turned into a slaughter house. Everybody suspected everybody else. No one felt safe. Out of sheer fear, a few members of the old Convention, who knew that they were the next candidates for the scaffold, finally turned against Robespierre, who had already decapitated most of his former colleagues. Robespierre, "the only true and pure Democrat," tried to kill him-

The French Revolution Invades Holland

self but failed. His shattered jaw was hastily bandaged and he was dragged to the guillotine. On July 27 of the year 1794 (the ninth Thermidor of the year II, according to the strange chronology of the Revolution), the Reign of Terror came to an end, and all Paris danced with joy.

The dangerous position of France, however, made it necessary that the government remain in the hands of a few strong men, until the many enemies of the Revolution should have been driven from the soil of the French fatherland. While the half-clad and half-starved revolutionary armies fought their desperate battles of the Rhine and Italy and Belgium and Egypt, and defeated every one of the enemies of the Great Revolution, five Directors were appointed, and they ruled France for four years. Then the power was vested in the hands of a successful general by the name of Napoleon Bonaparte, who became "First Consul" of France in the year 1799. And during the next fifteen years, the old European continent became the laboratory of a number of political experiments, the like of which the world had never seen before.

53

Napoleon

Napoleon was born in the year 1769, the third son of Carlo Maria Buonaparte, an honest notary public of the city of Ajaccio in the island of Corsica, and his good wife, Letizia Ramolino. He therefore was not a Frenchman, but an Italian whose native island (an old Greek, Carthaginian and Roman colony in the Mediterranean Sea) had for years been struggling to regain its independence, first of all from the Genoese, and after the middle of the eighteenth century from the French, who had kindly offered to help the Corsicans in their struggle for freedom and had then occupied the island for their own benefit.

During the first twenty years of his life, young Napoleon was a professional Corsican patriot—a Corsican Sinn Feiner, who hoped to deliver his beloved country from the yoke of the bitterly hated French enemy. But the French Revolution had unexpectedly recognised the claims of the Corsicans and gradually Napoleon, who had received a good training at the military school of Brienne, drifted into the service of his adopted country. Although he never learned to spell French correctly or to speak it without a broad Italian accent, he became a Frenchman. In due time he came to stand as the highest expression of all French virtues. At present he is regarded as the symbol of the Gallic genius.

Napoleon was what is called a fast worker. His career does not cover more than twenty years. In that short span of time he fought more wars and gained more victories and marched more miles and conquered more square kilometers and killed more people and brought about more reforms and generally upset Europe to a greater extent than anybody (including Alexander the Great and Jenghis Khan) had ever managed to do.

He was a little fellow and during the first years of his life his health was not very good. He never impressed anybody by his good looks and he remained to the end of his days very clumsy whenever he was obliged to appear at a social function. He did not enjoy a single advantage of breeding or birth or riches. For the greater part of his youth he was desperately poor and often he had to go without a meal or was obliged to make a few extra pennies in curious ways.

He gave little promise as a literary genius. When he competed for a prize offered by the Academy of Lyons, his essay was found to be next to the last and he was number fifteen out of sixteen candidates. But he overcame all these difficulties through his absolute and unshakeable belief in his own destiny, and in his own glorious future. Ambition was the main-spring of his life. The thought of self, the workship of that capital letter N with which he signed all his letters, and which recurred forever in the ornaments of his hastily constructed palaces, the absolute will to make the name Napoleon the most important thing in the world next to the name of God, these desires carried Napoleon to a pinnacle of fame which no other man has ever reached.

When he was a half-pay lieutenant, young Bonaparte was very fond of the "Lives of Famous Men" which Plutarch, the Greek historian, had written. But he never tried to live up to the high standard of character set by these heroes of the older days. Napoleon seems to have been devoid of all those considerate and thoughtful sentiments which make men different from the animals. It will be very difficult to decide with any degree of accuracy whether he ever loved any one besides himself. He kept a civil tongue to his mother, but Letizia had the air and manners of a great lady and after the fashion of Italian mothers, she knew how to rule her brood of children and command their respect. For a few years he was fond of Josephine, his pretty Creole wife, who was the daughter of a French officer of Martinique and the widow of the vicomte de Beauharnais, who had been executed by Robespierre when he lost a battle against the Prussians. But the emperor divorced her when she failed to give him a son and heir and married the daughter of the Austrian emperor, because it seemed good policy.

During the siege of Toulon, where he gained great fame as commander of a battery, Napoleon studied Machiavelli with industrious care. He followed the advice of the Florentine statesman and never kept his word when it was to his advantage to break it. The word "gratitude" did not occur in his personal dictionary. Neither, to be quite fair, did he expect it from others. He was totally indifferent to human suffering. He executed prisoners of war (in Egypt in 1798) who had been promised their lives, and he quietly allowed his wounded in Syria to be chloroformed when he found it impossible to transport them to his ships. He ordered the duke of Enghien to be condemned to death by a prejudiced court-martial and to be shot contrary to all law on the sole ground that the "Bourbons needed a warning." He decreed that those German officers who were made prisoner while fighting for their country's independence should be shot against the nearest wall, and when Andreas Hofer, the Tyrolese hero, fell into his hands after a most heroic resistance, he was executed like a common traitor.

In short, when we study the character of the emperor, we

begin to understand those anxious British mothers who used
to drive their children to bed with the threat that "Bonaparte, who ate little boys and girls for breakfast, would come
and get them if they were not very good." And yet, having
said these many unpleasant things about this strange tyrant,
who looked after every other department of his army with
the utmost care, but neglected the medical service, and who
ruined his uniforms with Eau de Cologne because he could
not stand the smell of his poor sweating soldiers; having
said all these unpleasant things and being fully prepared to
add many more, I must confess to a certain lurking feeling
of doubt.

Here I am sitting at a comfortable table loaded heavily
with books, with one eye on my typewriter and the other on
Licorice the cat, who has a great fondness for carbon paper,
and I am telling you that the emperor Napoleon was a most
contemptible person. But should I happen to look out of the
window, down upon Seventh Avenue, and should the endless
procession of trucks and carts come to a sudden halt, and
should I hear the sound of the heavy drums and see the little
man on his white horse in his old and much-worn green uniform, then I don't know, but I am afraid that I would leave
my books and the kitten and my home and everything else to
follow him wherever he cared to lead. My own grandfather
did this and Heaven knows he was not born to be a hero. Millions of other people's grandfather did it. They received no
reward, but they expected none. They cheerfully gave legs
and arms and lives to serve this foreigner, who took them a
thousand miles away from their homes and marched them
into a barrage of Russian or English or Spanish or Italian or
Austrian cannon and stared quietly into space while they
were rolling in the agony of death.

If you ask me for an explanation, I must answer that I have
none. I can only guess at one of the reasons. Napoleon was

the greatest of actors and the whole European continent was his stage. At all times and under all circumstances he knew the precise attitude that would impress the spectators most and he understood what words would make the deepest impression. Whether he spoke in the Egyptian desert, before the backdrop of the Sphinx and the Pyramids, or addressed his shivering men on the dew-soaked plains of Italy, made no difference. At all times he was master of the situation. Even at the end, an exile on a little rock in the middle of the Atlantic, a sick man at the mercy of a dull and intolerable British governor, he held the centre of the stage.

After the defeat of Waterloo, no one outside of a few trusted friends ever saw the great emperor. The people of Europe knew that he was living on the island of St. Helena— they knew that a British garrison guarded him day and night—they knew that the British fleet guarded the garrison which guarded the emperor on his farm at Longwood. But he was never out of the mind of either friend or enemy. When illness and despair had at last taken him away, his silent eyes continued to haunt the world. Even to-day he is as much of a force in the life of France as a hundred years ago when people fainted at the mere sight of this sallow-faced man who stabled his horses in the holiest temples of the Russian Kremlin, and who treated the Pope and the mighty ones of this earth as if they were his lackeys.

To give you a mere outline of his life would demand a couple of volumes. To tell you of his great political reform of the French state, of his new codes of laws which were adopted in most European countries, of his activities in every field of public activity, would take thousands of pages. But I can explain in a few words why he was so successful during the first part of his career and why he failed during the last ten years. From the year 1789 until the year 1804, Napoleon was the great leader of the French Revolution. He was not merely fighting for the glory of his own name. He defeated Austria and Italy and England and Russia because he, himself, and his soldiers were the apostles of the new creed of "Liberty, Fraternity and Equality" and were the enemies of the courts while they were the friends of the people.

But in the year 1804, Napoleon made himself hereditary emperor of the French and sent for Pope Pius VII to come and crown him, even as Leo III, in the year 800 had crowned that other great king of the Franks, Charlemagne, whose example was constantly before Napoleon's eyes.

Once upon the throne, the old revolutionary chieftain became an unsuccessful imitation of a Habsburg monarch. He forgot his spiritual mother, the political club of the Jacobins. He ceased to be the defender of the oppressed. He became the chief of all the oppressors and kept his shooting squads ready to execute those who dared to oppose his imperial will. No one had shed a tear when in the year 1806 the sad remains of the Holy Roman Empire were carted to the historical dustbin and when the last relic of ancient Roman glory was destroyed by the grandson of an Italian peasant. But when the Napoleonic armies had invaded Spain, had forced the Spaniards to recognise a king whom they detested, had massacred the poor Madrilenes who remained faithful to their old rulers, then public opinion turned against the former hero of Marengo and Austerlitz and a hundred other revolutionary battles. Then and only then, when Napoleon was no longer the hero of the Revolution but the personification of all the bad traits of the Old Régime, was it possible for England to give direction to the fast-spreading sentiment of hatred which was turning all honest men into enemies of the French emperor.

The English people from the very beginning had felt deeply disgusted when their newspapers told them the gruesome details of the Terror. They had staged their own great

Revolution (during the reign of Charles I) a century before.
It had been a very simple affair compared to the upheaval of
Paris. In the eyes of the average Englishman a Jacobin was
a monster to be shot at sight and Napoleon was the Chief
Devil. The British fleet had blockaded France ever since the
year 1798. It had spoiled Napoleon's plan to invade India by
way of Egypt and had forced him to beat an ignominious
retreat, after his victories along the banks of the Nile. And
finally, in the year 1805, England got the chance it had waited
for so long.

Near Cape Trafalgar on the south-western coast of Spain,
Nelson annihilated the Napoleonic fleet, beyond a possible
chance of recovery. From that moment on, the emperor was
landlocked. Even so, he would have been able to maintain
himself as the recognised ruler of the continent had he understood the signs of the times and accepted the honourable
peace which the powers offered him. But Napoleon had been
blinded by the blaze of his own glory. He would recognise
no equals. He could tolerate no rivals. And his hatred turned
against Russia, the mysterious land of the endless plains with
its inexhaustible supply of cannon-fodder.

As long as Russia was ruled by Paul I, the half-witted son
of Catherine the Great, Napoleon had known how to deal
with the situation. But Paul grew more and more irresponsible until his exasperated subjects were obliged to murder
him, (lest they all be sent to the Siberian lead-mines) and the
son of Paul, the emperor Alexander, did not share his father's
affection for the usurper whom he regarded as the enemy
of mankind, the eternal disturber of the peace. He was a
pious man who believed that he had been chosen by God to
deliver the world from the Corsican curse. He joined Prussia
and England and Austria and he was defeated. He tried five
times and five times he failed. In the year 1812 he once more
taunted Napoleon until the French emperor, in a blind rage,

The Retreat from Moscow

vowed that he would dictate peace in Moscow. Then, from
far and wide, from Spain and Germany and Holland and
Italy and Portugal, unwilling regiments were driven northward, that the wounded pride of the great emperor might be
duly avenged.

The rest of the story is common knowledge. After a
march of two months, Napoleon reached the Russian capital and established his headquarters in the holy Kremlin. On
the night of September 15 of the year 1812, Moscow caught
fire. The town burned four days. When the evening of the
fifth day came, Napoleon gave the order for the retreat. Two
weeks later it began to snow. The army trudged through
mud and sleet until November 26 when the River Berezina
was reached. Then the Russian attacks began in all seriousness. The Cossacks swarmed around the "Grande Armée"
which was no longer an army but a mob. In the middle of
December the first of the survivors began to be seen in the
German cities of the east.

Then there were many rumours of an impending revolt.

"The time has come," the people of Europe said, "to free ourselves from this insufferable yoke." And they began to look for old shotguns which had escaped the eye of the ever-present French spies. But ere they knew what had happened, Napoleon was back with a new army. He had left his defeated soldiers and in his little sleigh had rushed ahead to Paris, making a final appeal for more troops that he might defend the sacred soil of France against foreign invasion.

Children of sixteen and seventeen followed him when he moved eastward to meet the allied powers. On October 16, 18 and 19 of the year 1813, the terrible battle of Leipzig took place where for three days boys in green and boys in blue fought each other until the Elster ran red with blood. On the afternoon of October 17, the massed reserves of Russian infantry broke through the French lines and Napoleon fled.

Back to Paris he went. He abdicated in favour of his small son, but the allied powers insisted that Louis XVIII, the brother of the late king Louis XVI, should occupy the French throne, and surrounded by Cossacks and Uhlans, the dull-eyed Bourbon prince made his triumphal entry into Paris.

As for Napoleon, he was made the sovereign ruler of the little island of Elba in the Mediterranean where he organised his stable boys into a miniature army and fought battles on a chess board.

But no sooner had he left France than the people began to realise what they had lost. The last twenty years, however costly, had been a period of great glory. Paris had been the capital of the world. The fat Bourbon king who had learned nothing and had forgotten nothing during the days of his exile disgusted everybody by his indolence.

On March 1 of the year 1815, when the representatives of the allies were ready to begin the work of unscrambling the map of Europe, Napoleon suddenly landed near Cannes. In less than a week the French army had deserted the Bourbons

and had rushed southward to offer their swords and bayo-
nets to the "little Corporal." Napoleon marched straight to
Paris where he arrived on March 20. This time he was more
cautious. He offered peace, but the allies insisted upon war.
The whole of Europe arose against the "perfidious Corsican." Rapidly the emperor marched northward that he might
crush his enemies before they should be able to unite their
forces. But Napoleon was no longer his old self. He felt sick.
He got tired easily. He slept when he ought to have been up
directing the attack of his advance-guard. Besides, he missed
many of his faithful old generals. They were dead.

Early in June his armies entered Belgium. On the sixteenth
of that month he defeated the Prussians under Blücher. But
a subordinate commander failed to destroy the retreating
army as he had been ordered to do.

Two days later, Napoleon met Wellington near Waterloo.

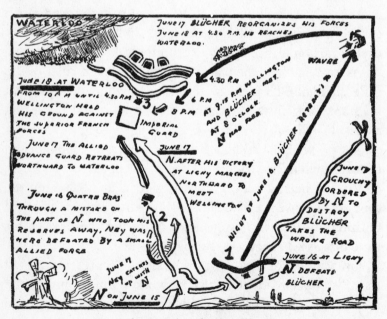

The Battle of Waterloo

Off for Trafalgar

It was June 18, a Sunday. At two o'clock of the afternoon, the battle seemed won for the French. At three a speck of dust appeared upon the eastern horizon. Napoleon believed that this meant the approach of his own cavalry who would now turn the English defeat into a rout. At four o'clock he knew better. Cursing and swearing, old Blücher drove his deathly tired troops into the heart of the fray. The shock broke the ranks of the guards. Napoleon had no further reserves. He told his men to save themselves as best they could, and he fled.

For a second time, he abdicated in favour of his son. Just one hundred days after his escape from Elba, he was making for the coast. He intended to go to America. In the year 1803, for a mere song, he had sold the French colony of Louisiana (which was in great danger of being captured by the English) to the young American Republic. "The Americans," so he said, "will be grateful and will give me a little bit of land and a house where I may spend the last days of my life in peace and quiet." But the English fleet was watching all French harbours. Caught between the armies of the allies and the ships of the British, Napoleon had no choice. The Prussians intended to shoot him. The English might be more generous. At Rochefort he waited in the hope that something might turn up. One month after Waterloo, he received orders from the new French government to leave French soil inside of twenty-four hours. Always the tragedian, he wrote a letter to the prince regent of England (George III, the king, was in an insane asylum) informing His Royal Highness of his intention to "throw himself upon the mercy of his enemies and like Themistocles, to look for a welcome at the fireside of his foes . . ."

On July 15 he went on board the "Bellerophon," and surrendered his sword to Admiral Hotham. At Plymouth he was transferred to the "Northumberland" which carried him

Napoleon Goes into Exile

to St. Helena. There he spent the last seven years of his life. He tried to write his memoirs, he quarreled with his keepers and he dreamed of past times. Curiously enough he returned (at least in his imagination) to his original point of departure. He remembered the days when he had fought the battles of the Revolution. He tried to convince himself that he had always been the true friend of those great principles of "Liberty, Fraternity and Equality" which the ragged soldiers of the convention had carried to the ends of the earth. He liked to dwell upon his career as commander-in-chief and consul. He rarely spoke of the empire. Sometimes he thought of his son, the duke of Reichstadt, the little eagle, who lived in Vienna, where he was treated as a "poor relation" by his young Habsburg cousins, whose fathers had trembled at the very mention of the name of Him. When the end came, he was leading his troops to victory. He ordered Ney to attack with the guards. Then he died.

But if you want an explanation of this strange career, if you really wish to know how one man could possibly rule so many people for so many years by the sheer force of his will, do not read the books that have been written about him. Their authors either hated the emperor or loved him. You will learn many facts, but it is more important to "feel history" than to know it. Don't read, but wait until you have a chance to hear a good artist sing the song called "The Two Grenadiers." The words were written by Heine, the great German poet who lived through the Napoleonic era. The music was composed by Schumann, a German, who saw the emperor, the enemy of his country, whenever he came to visit his imperial father-in-law. The song therefore is the work of two men who had every reason to hate the tyrant.

Go and hear it. Then you will understand what a thousand volumes could not possibly tell you.

54

The Holy Alliance

As Soon as Napoleon Had Been Sent to St. Helena
the Rulers Who So Often Had Been Defeated by
the Hated "Corsican" Met at Vienna and Tried to
Undo the Many Changes Which Had Been
Brought About by the French Revolution

The Imperial Highnesses, the Royal Highnesses, their
Graces the Dukes, the Ministers Extraordinary and Plenipo-
tentiary, together with the plain Excellencies and their army
of secretaries, servants and hangers-on, whose labours had
been so rudely interrupted by the sudden return of the terrible Corsican (now sweltering under the hot sun of St. Helena) went back to their jobs. The victory was duly celebrated
with dinners, garden parties and balls at which the new and
very shocking "waltz" was danced to the great scandal of the
ladies and gentlemen who remembered the minuet of the
Old Régime.

For almost a generation they had lived in retirement. At
last the danger was over. They were very eloquent upon the
subject of the terrible hardships which they had suffered.
And they expected to be recompensed for every penny they
had lost at the hands of the unspeakable Jacobins who had

dared to kill their anointed king, who had abolished wigs
and who had discarded the short trousers of the court of Versailles for the ragged pantaloons of the Parisian slums.

You may think it absurd that I should mention such a
detail. But, if you please, the Congress of Vienna was one
long succession of such absurdities and for many months
the question of "short trousers vs. long trousers" interested
the delegates more than the future settlement of the Saxon
or Spanish problems. His Majesty the king of Prussia went so
far as to order a pair of short ones, that he might give public
evidence of his contempt for everything revolutionary.

Another German potentate, not to be outdone in this
noble hatred for the Revolution, decreed that all taxes which
his subjects had paid to the French usurper should be paid a
second time to the legitimate ruler who had loved his people
from afar while they were at the mercy of the Corsican ogre.
And so on. From one blunder to another, until one gasps and
exclaims "but why in the name of high Heaven did not the
people object?" Why not indeed? Because the people were
utterly exhausted, were desperate, did not care what happened or how or where or by whom they were ruled, provided there was peace. They were sick and tired of war and
revolution and reform.

In the eighties of the previous century they had all danced
around the tree of liberty. Princes had embraced their cooks
and duchesses had danced the carmagnole with their lackeys
in the honest belief that the Millennium of Equality and Fraternity had at last dawned upon this wicked world. Instead
of the millennium they had been visited by the revolutionary
commissary who had lodged a dozen dirty soldiers in their
parlour and had stolen the family plate when he returned
to Paris to report to his government upon the enthusiasm
with which the "liberated country" had received the Constitution, which the French people had presented to their good
neighbours.

When they had heard how the last outbreak of revolutionary disorder in Paris had been suppressed by a young officer, called Bonaparte, or Buonaparte, who had turned his guns upon the mob, they gave a sigh of relief. A little less liberty, fraternity and equality seemed a very desirable thing. But ere long, the young officer called Buonaparte or Bonaparte became one of the three consuls of the French Republic, then sole consul and finally emperor. As he was much more efficient than any ruler that had ever been seen before, his hand pressed heavily upon his poor subjects. He showed them no mercy. He impressed their sons into his armies, he married their daughters to his generals and he took their pictures and their statues to enrich his own museums. He turned the whole of Europe into an armed camp and killed almost an entire generation of men.

Now he was gone, and the people (except a few professional military men) had but one wish. They wanted to be let alone. For a while they had been allowed to rule themselves, to vote for mayors and aldermen and judges. The system had been a terrible failure. The new rulers had been inexperienced and extravagant. From sheer despair the people turned to the representative men of the Old Régime. "You rule us," they said, "as you used to do. Tell us what we owe you for taxes and leave us alone. We are busy repairing the damage of the age of liberty."

The men who stage-managed the famous Congress certainly did their best to satisfy this longing for rest and quiet. The Holy Alliance, the main result of the Congress, made the policeman the most important dignitary of the state and held out the most terrible punishment to those who dared criticise a single official act.

Europe had peace, but it was the peace of the cemetery.

The three most important men at Vienna were the emperor Alexander of Russia, Metternich, who represented the interests of the Austrian house of Habsburg, and Talley-

The Spectre Which Frightened the Holy Alliance

rand, the erstwhile bishop of Autun, who had managed to live through the different changes in the French government by the sheer force of his cunning and his intelligence and who now travelled to the Austrian capital to save for his country whatever could be saved from the Napoleonic ruin. Like the gay young man of the limerick, who never knew when he was slighted, this unbidden guest came to the party and ate just as heartily as if he had been really invited. Indeed, before long, he was sitting at the head of the table entertaining everybody with his amusing stories and gaining the company's good will by the charm of his manner.

Before he had been in Vienna twenty-four hours he knew that the allies were divided into two hostile camps. On the one side were Russia, who wanted to take Poland, and Prussia, who wanted to annex Saxony; and on the other side were Austria and England, who were trying to prevent this grab because it was against their own interest that either Prussia or Russia should be able to dominate Europe. Talleyrand played the two sides against each other with great skill and it was due to his efforts that the French people were not made to suffer for the ten years of oppression which Europe had endured at the hands of the imperial officials. He argued that the French people had been given no choice in the matter. Napoleon had forced them to act at his bidding. But Napoleon was gone and Louis XVIII was on the throne. "Give him a chance," Talleyrand pleaded. And the allies, glad to see a legitimate king upon the throne of a revolutionary country, obligingly yielded and the Bourbons were given their chance, of which they made such use that they were driven out after fifteen years.

The second man of the triumvirate of Vienna was Metternich, the Austrian prime minister, the leader of the foreign policy of the house of Habsburg. Wenzel Lothar, prince of Metternich-Winneburg, was exactly what the name sug-

gests. He was a Grand Seigneur, a very handsome gentleman with very fine manners, immensely rich, and very able,
but the product of a society which lived a thousand miles
away from the sweating multitudes who worked and slaved
in the cities and on the farms. As a young man, Metternich
had been studying at the University of Strassburg when the
French Revolution broke out. Strassburg, the city which gave
birth to the "Marseillaise," had been a centre of Jacobin activities. Metternich remembered that his pleasant social life had
been sadly interrupted, that a lot of incompetent citizens had
suddenly been called forth to perform tasks for which they
were not fit, that the mob had celebrated the dawn of the
new liberty by the murder of perfectly innocent persons. He
had failed to see the honest enthusiasm of the masses, the ray
of hope in the eyes of women and children who carried bread
and water to the ragged troops of the Convention, marching through the city on their way to the front and a glorious
death for the French fatherland.

The whole thing had filled the young Austrian with disgust. It was uncivilised. If there were any fighting to be done
it must be done by dashing young men in lovely uniforms,
charging across the green fields on well-groomed horses. But
to turn an entire country into an evil-smelling armed camp
where tramps were overnight promoted to be generals, that
was both wicked and senseless. "See what came of all your
fine ideas," he would say to the French diplomats whom he
met at a quiet little dinner given by one of the innumerable
Austrian grand dukes. "You wanted liberty, equality and fraternity and you got Napoleon. How much better it would
have been if you had been contented with the existing order
of things." And he would explain his system of "stability."
He would advocate a return to the normalcy of the good old
days before the war, when everybody was happy and nobody
talked nonsense about "everybody being as good as every-

body else." In this attitude he was entirely sincere and as he was an able man of great strength of will and a tremendous power of persuasion, he was one of the most dangerous enemies of the revolutionary ideas. He did not die until the year 1859, and he therefore lived long enough to see the complete failure of all his policies when they were swept aside by the revolution of the year 1848. He then found himself the most hated man of Europe and more than once ran the risk of being lynched by angry crowds of outraged citizens. But until the very last, he remained steadfast in his belief that he had done the right thing.

He had always been convinced that people preferred peace to liberty and he had tried to give them what was best for them. And in all fairness, it ought to be said that his efforts to establish universal peace were fairly successful. The great

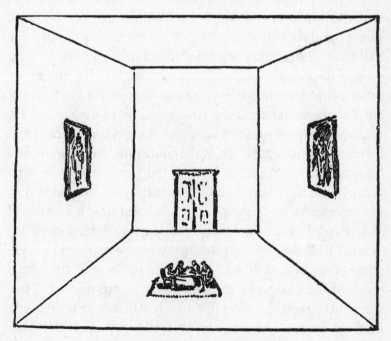

The Real Congress of Vienna

powers did not fly at each other's throat for almost forty
years, indeed not until the Crimean War between Russia and
England, France and Italy and Turkey, in the year 1854. That
means a record for the European continent.

The third hero of this waltzing congress was the emperor
Alexander. He had been brought up at the court of his grandmother, the famous Catherine the Great. Between the lessons of this shrewd old woman, who taught him to regard
the glory of Russia as the most important thing in life, and
those of his private tutor, a Swiss admirer of Voltaire and
Rousseau, who filled his mind with a general love of humanity, the boy grew up to be a strange mixture of a selfish
tyrant and a sentimental revolutionist. He had suffered great
indignities during the life of his crazy father, Paul I. He had
been obliged to witness the wholesale slaughter of the Napoleonic battle-fields. Then the tide had turned. His armies had
won the day for the allies. Russia had become the saviour of
Europe and the tsar of this mighty people was acclaimed as a
half-God who would cure the world of its many ills.

But Alexander was not very clever. He did not know
men and women as Talleyrand and Metternich knew them.
He did not understand the strange game of diplomacy. He
was vain (who would not be under the circumstances?) and
loved to hear the applause of the multitude and soon he had
become the main "attraction" of the Congress while Metternich and Talleyrand and Castlereagh (the very able British representative) sat around a table and drank a bottle of
Tokay and decided what was actually going to be done. They
needed Russia and therefore they were very polite to Alexander, but the less he had personally to do with the actual
work of the Congress, the better they were pleased. They
even encouraged his plans for a Holy Alliance that he might
be fully occupied while they were engaged upon the work
at hand.

Alexander was a sociable person who liked to go to parties and meet people. Upon such occasions he was happy and gay but there was a very different element in his character. He tried to forget something which he could not forget. On the night of March 23 of the year 1801 he had been sitting in a room of the St. Michael Palace in Petersburg, waiting for the news of his father's abdication. But Paul had refused to sign the document which the drunken officers had placed before him on the table, and in their rage they had put a scarf around his neck and had strangled him to death. Then they had gone downstairs to tell Alexander that he was emperor of all the Russian lands.

The memory of this terrible night stayed with the tsar who was a very sensitive person. He had been educated in the school of the great French philosophers who did not believe in God but in Human Reason. But Reason alone could not satisfy the emperor in his predicament. He began to hear voices and see things. He tried to find a way by which he could square himself with his conscience. He became very pious and began to take an interest in mysticism, that strange love of the mysterious and the unknown which is as old as the temples of Thebes and Babylon.

The tremendous emotion of the great revolutionary era had influenced the character of the people of that day in a strange way. Men and women who had lived through twenty years of anxiety and fear were no longer quite normal. They jumped whenever the door-bell rang. It might mean the news of the "death on the field of honour" of an only son. The phrases about "brotherly love" and "liberty" of the Revolution were hollow words in the ears of sorely stricken peasants. They clung to anything that might give them a new hold on the terrible problems of life. In their grief and misery they were easily imposed upon by a large number of impostors who posed as prophets and preached a strange new doctrine which they dug out of the more obscure passages of the Book of Revelation.

In the year 1814, Alexander, who had already consulted a large number of wonder-doctors, heard of a new seeress who was foretelling the coming doom of the world and was exhorting people to repent ere it be too late. The baroness von Krüdener, the lady in question, was a Russian woman of uncertain age and similar reputation who had been the wife of a Russian diplomat in the days of the emperor Paul. She had squandered her husband's money and had disgraced him by her strange love affairs. She had lived a very dissolute life until her nerves had given way and for a while she was not in her right mind. Then she had been converted by the sight of the sudden death of a friend. Thereafter she despised all gaiety. She confessed her former sins to her shoemaker, a pious Moravian brother, a follower of the old reformer John Huss, who had been burned for his heresies by the Council of Constance in the year 1415.

The next ten years the baroness spent in Germany making a specialty of the "conversion" of kings and princes. To convince Alexander, the Saviour of Europe, of the error of his ways was the greatest ambition of her life. And as Alexander, in his misery, was willing to listen to anybody who brought him a ray of hope, the interview was easily arranged. On the evening of June 4 of the year 1815, she was admitted to the tent of the emperor. She found him reading his Bible. We do not know what she said to Alexander, but when she left him three hours later, he was bathed in tears, and vowed that "at last his soul had found peace." From that day on the baroness was his faithful companion and his spiritual adviser. She followed him to Paris and then to Vienna and the time which Alexander did not spend dancing he spent at the Krüdener prayer-meetings.

You may ask why I tell you this story in such great detail?

Are not the social changes of the nineteenth century of greater importance than the career of an ill-balanced woman who had better be forgotten? Of course they are, but there exist any number of books which will tell you of these other things with great accuracy and in great detail. I want you to learn something more from this history than a mere succession of facts. I want you to approach all historical events in a frame of mind that will take nothing for granted. Don't be satisfied with the mere statement that "such and such a thing happened then and there." Try to discover the hidden motives behind every action and then you will understand the world around you much better and you will have a greater chance to help others, which (when all is said and done) is the only truly satisfactory way of living.

I do not want you to think of the Holy Alliance as a piece of paper which was signed in the year 1815 and lies dead and forgotten somewhere in the archives of state. It may be forgotten but it is by no means dead. The Holy Alliance was directly responsible for the promulgation of the Monroe Doctrine, and the Monroe Doctrine of America for the Americans has a very distinct bearing upon your own life. That is the reason why I want you to know exactly how this document happened to come into existence and what the real motives were underlying this outward manifestation of piety and Christian devotion to duty.

The Holy Alliance was the joint labour of an unfortunate man who had suffered a terrible mental shock and who was trying to pacify his much-disturbed soul, and of an ambitious woman who after a wasted life had lost her beauty and her attraction and who satisfied her vanity and her desire for notoriety by assuming the rôle self-appointed messiah of a new and strange creed. I am not giving away any secrets when I tell you these details. Such sober minded people as Castlereagh, Metternich and Talleyrand fully understood the limited abilities of the sentimental baroness. It would have been easy for Metternich to send her back to her German estates. A few lines to the almighty commander of the imperial police and the thing was done.

But France and England and Austria depended upon the good will of Russia. They could not afford to offend Alexander. And they tolerated the silly old baroness because they had to. And while they regarded the Holy Alliance as utter rubbish and not worth the paper upon which it was written, they listened patiently to the tsar when he read them the first rough draft of this attempt to create the Brotherhood of Men upon a basis of the Holy Scriptures. For this is what the Holy Alliance tried to do, and the signers of the document solemnly declared that they would "in the administration of their respective states and in their political relations with every other government take for their sole guide the precepts of that Holy Religion, namely the precepts of Justice, Christian Charity and Peace, which far from being applicable only to private concerns must have an immediate influence on the councils of princes, and must guide all their steps as being the only means of consolidating human institutions and remedying their imperfections." They then proceeded to promise each other that they would remain united "by the bonds of a true and indissoluble fraternity, and considering each other as fellow-countrymen, they would on all occasions and in all places lend each other aid and assistance." And more words to the same effect.

Eventually the Holy Alliance was signed by the emperor of Austria, who did not understand a word of it. It was signed by the Bourbons, who needed the friendship of Napoleon's old enemies. It was signed by the king of Prussia, who hoped to gain Alexander for his plans for a "greater Prussia," and by all the little nations of Europe who were at the mercy of Russia. England never signed, because Castlereagh thought the whole thing buncombe. The Pope did not sign because he resented this interference in his business by a Greek Orthodox and a Protestant. And the sultan did not sign because he never heard of it.

The general mass of the European people, however, soon were forced to take notice. Behind the hollow phrases of the Holy Alliance stood the armies of the Quintuple Alliance which Metternich had created among the great powers. These armies meant business. They let it be known that the peace of Europe must not be disturbed by the so-called liberals who were in reality nothing but disguised Jacobins, and hoped for a return of the revolutionary days. The enthusiasm for the great wars of liberation of the years 1812, 1813, 1814 and 1815 had begun to wear off. It had been followed by a sincere belief in the coming of a happier day. The soldiers who had borne the brunt of the battle wanted peace and they said so.

But they did not want the sort of peace which the Holy Alliance and the council of the European powers had now bestowed upon them. They cried that they had been betrayed. But they were careful lest they be heard by a secret-police spy. The reaction was victorious. It was a reaction caused by men who sincerely believed that their methods were necessary for the good of humanity. But it was just as hard to bear as if their intentions had been less kind. And it caused a great deal of unnecessary suffering and greatly retarded the orderly progress of political development.

55

The Great Reaction

They Tried to Assure the World an Era of
Undisturbed Peace by Suppressing All
New Ideas. They Made the Police Spy
the Highest Functionary in the State and Soon
the Prisons of All Countries Were Filled with
Those Who Claimed That People Have
the Right to Govern Themselves as They See Fit

To undo the damage done by the great Napoleonic flood
was almost impossible. Age-old fences had been washed
away. The palaces of two-score dynasties had been damaged
to such an extent that they had to be condemned as uninhab-
itable. Other royal residences had been greatly enlarged at
the expense of less fortunate neighbours. Strange odds and
ends of revolutionary doctrine had been left behind by the
receding waters and could not be dislodged without danger to the entire community. But the political engineers of
the Congress did the best they could and this is what they
accomplished.

France had disturbed the peace of the world for so many
years that people had come to fear that country almost

instinctively. The Bourbons, through the mouth of Talleyrand, had promised to be good, but the Hundred Days had
taught Europe what to expect should Napoleon manage to
escape for a second time. The Dutch Republic, therefore, was
changed into a kingdom, and Belgium (which had not joined
the Dutch struggle for independence in the sixteenth century
and since then had been part of the Habsburg domains, first
under Spanish rule and thereafter under Austrian rule) was
made part of this new kingdom of the Netherlands. Nobody
wanted this union either in the Protestant north or in the
Catholic south, but no questions were asked. It seemed good
for the peace of Europe and that was the main consideration.

Poland had hoped for great things because a Pole, Prince
Adam Czartoryski, was one of the most intimate friends of
Tsar Alexander and had been his constant adviser during the
war and at the Congress of Vienna. But Poland was made a
semi-independent part of Russia with Alexander as her king.
This solution pleased no one and caused much bitter feeling
and three revolutions.

Denmark, which had remained a faithful ally of Napoleon until the end, was severely punished. Seven years
before, an English fleet had sailed down the Kattegat and
without a declaration of war or any warning had bombarded
Copenhagen and had taken away the Danish fleet, lest it be
of value to Napoleon. The Congress of Vienna went one step
further. It took Norway (which since the union of Calmar
of the year 1397 had been united with Denmark) away from
Denmark and gave it to Charles XIV of Sweden as a reward
for his betrayal of Napoleon, who had set him up in the king
business. This Swedish king, curiously enough, was a former
French general by the name of Bernadotte, who had come
to Sweden as one of Napoleon's adjutants, and had been
invited to the throne of that good country when the last of
the rulers of the house of Holstein-Gottorp had died with-

out leaving either son or daughter. From 1815 until 1844 he ruled his adopted country (the language of which he never learned) with great ability. He was a clever man and enjoyed the respect of both his Swedish and his Norwegian subjects, but he did not succeed in joining two countries which nature and history had put asunder. The dual Scandinavian state was never a success and in 1905, Norway, in a most peaceful and orderly manner, set up as an independent kingdom and the Swedes bade her "good speed" and very wisely let her go her own way.

The Italians, who since the days of the Renaissance had been at the mercy of a long series of invaders, also had put great hopes in General Bonaparte. The emperor Napoleon, however, had grievously disappointed them. Instead of the united Italy which the people wanted, they had been divided into a number of little principalities, duchies, republics and the Papal State, which (next to Naples) was the worst governed and most miserable region of the entire peninsula. The Congress of Vienna abolished a few of the Napoleonic republics and in their place resurrected several old principalities, which were given to deserving members, both male and female, of the Habsburg family.

The poor Spaniards, who had started the great nationalistic revolt against Napoleon, and who had sacrificed the best blood of the country for their king, were punished severely when the Congress allowed His Majesty to return to his domains. This vicious creature, known as Ferdinand VII, had spent the last four years of his life as a prisoner of Napoleon. He had improved his days by knitting garments for the statues of his favourite patron saints. He celebrated his return by reintroducing the Inquisition and the torture-chamber, both of which had been abolished by the Revolution. He was a disgusting person, despised as much by his subjects as by his four wives, but the Holy Alliance maintained him upon his legitimate throne and all efforts of the decent Spaniards to get rid of this curse and make Spain a constitutional kingdom ended in bloodshed and executions.

Portugal had been without a king since the year 1807 when the royal family had fled to the colonies in Brazil. The country had been used as a base of supply for the armies of Wellington during the Peninsula War, which lasted from 1808 until 1814. After 1815 Portugal continued to be a sort of British province until the house of Braganza returned to the throne, leaving one of its members behind in Rio de Janeiro as emperor of Brazil, the only American empire which lasted for more than a few years, and which came to an end in 1889 when the country became a republic.

In the east, nothing was done to improve the terrible conditions of both the Slavs and the Greeks who were still subjects of the sultan. In the year 1804 Black George, a Serbian swine-herd (the founder of the Karageorgevich dynasty), had started a revolt against the Turks, but he had been defeated by his enemies and had been murdered by one of his supposed friends, the rival Serbian leader, called Milosh Obrenovich (who became the founder of the Obrenovich dynasty), and the Turks had continued to be the undisputed masters of the Balkans.

The Greeks, who since the loss of their independence, two thousand years before, had been subjects of the Macedonians, the Romans, the Venetians and the Turks, had hoped that their countryman Capo d'Istria, a native of Corfu, and together with Czartoryski, the most intimate personal friend of Alexander, would do something for them. But the Congress of Vienna was not interested in Greeks, but was very much interested in keeping all "legitimate" monarchs, Christian, Moslem and otherwise, upon their respective thrones. Therefore nothing was done.

The last but perhaps the greatest blunder of the Congress

was the treatment of Germany. The Reformation and the Thirty Years War had not only destroyed the prosperity of the country, but had turned it into a hopeless political rubbish heap, consisting of a couple of kingdoms, a few grand duchies, a large number of duchies and hundreds of margravates, principalities, baronies, electorates, free cities and free villages, ruled by the strangest assortment of potentates that was ever seen off the comic opera stage. Frederick the Great had changed this when he created a strong Prussia, but this state had not survived him by many years.

Napoleon had blue-penciled the demand for independence of most of these little countries, and only fifty-two out of a total of more than three hundred had survived the year 1806. During the years of the great struggle for independence, many a young soldier had dreamed of a new fatherland that should be strong and united. But there can be no union without a strong leadership, and who was to be this leader?

There were five kingdoms in the German speaking lands. The rulers of two of these, Austria and Prussia, were kings by the Grace of God. The rulers of three others, Bavaria, Saxony and Württemberg, were kings by the Grace of Napoleon, and as they had been the faithful henchmen of the emperor, their patriotic credit with the other Germans was therefore not very good.

The Congress had established a new German Confederation, a league of thirty-eight sovereign states, under the chairmanship of the king of Austria, who was now known as the emperor of Austria. It was the sort of make-shift arrangement which satisfied no one. It is true that a German Diet, which met in the old coronation city of Frankfurt, had been created to discuss matters of "common policy and importance." But in this Diet, thirty-eight delegates represented thirty-eight different interests and as no decision could be taken without a unanimous vote (a parliamentary rule which had in previous centuries ruined the mighty kingdom of Poland), the famous German Confederation became very soon the laughing stock of Europe and the politics of the old empire began to resemble those of our Central American neighbours in the forties and the fifties of the last century.

It was terribly humiliating to the people who had sacrificed everything for a national ideal. But the Congress was not interested in the private feelings of "subjects," and the debate was closed.

Did anybody object? Most assuredly. As soon as the first feeling of hatred against Napoleon had quieted down—as soon as the enthusiasm of the great war had subsided—as soon as the people came to a full realisation of the crime that had been committed in the name of "peace and stability" they began to murmur. They even made threats of open revolt. But what could they do? They were powerless. They were at the mercy of the most pitiless and efficient police system the world had ever seen.

The members of the Congress of Vienna honestly and sincerely believed that "the Revolutionary Principle had led to the criminal usurpation of the throne by the former emperor Napoleon." They felt that they were called upon to eradicate the adherents of the so-called "French ideas" just as Philip II had only followed the voice of his conscience when he burned Protestants or hanged Moors. In the beginning of the sixteenth century a man who did not believe in the divine right of the Pope to rule his subjects as he saw fit was a "heretic" and it was the duty of all loyal citizens to kill him. In the beginning of the nineteenth century, on the continent of Europe, a man who did not believe in the divine right of his king to rule him as he or his prime minister saw fit, was a "heretic," and it was the duty of all loyal citizens to denounce him to the nearest policeman and see that he got punished.

But the rulers of the year 1815 had learned efficiency in

the school of Napoleon and they performed their task much better than it had been done in the year 1517. The period between the year 1815 and the year 1860 was the great era of the political spy. Spies were everywhere. They lived in palaces and they were to be found in the lowest gin-shops. They peeped through the key-holes of the ministerial Cabinet and they listened to the conversations of the people who were taking the air on the benches of the municipal park. They guarded the frontier so that no one might leave without a duly visaed passport and they inspected all packages, that no books with dangerous "French ideas" should enter the realm of their royal masters. They sat among the students in the lecture hall and woe to the professor who uttered a word against the existing order of things. They followed the little boys and girls on their way to church lest they play hookey.

In many of these tasks they were assisted by the clergy. The church had suffered greatly during the days of the Revolution. The church property had been confiscated. Several priests had been killed and the generation that had learned its catechism from Voltaire and Rousseau and the other French philosophers had danced around the Altar of Reason when the Committee of Public Safety had abolished the worship of God in October of the year 1793. The priests had followed the "émigrés" into their long exile. Now they returned in the wake of the allied armies and they set to work with a vengeance.

Even the Jesuits came back in 1814 and resumed their former labours of educating the young. Their order had been a little too successful in its fight against the enemies of the church. It had established "provinces" in every part of the world, to teach the natives the blessings of Christianity, but soon it had developed into a regular trading company which was forever interfering with the civil authorities. During the reign of the marquis de Pombal, the great reforming minister of Portugal, they had been driven out of the Portuguese lands and in the year 1773 at the request of most of the Catholic powers of Europe, the order had been suppressed by Pope Clement XIV. Now they were back on the job, and preached the principles of "obedience" and "love for the legitimate dynasty" to children whose parents had hired shopwindows that they might laugh at Marie Antoinette driving to the scaffold which was to end her misery.

But in the Protestant countries like Prussia, things were not a whit better. The great patriotic leaders of the year 1812, the poets and the writers who had preached a holy war upon the usurper, were now branded as dangerous "demagogues." Their houses were searched. Their letters were read. They were obliged to report to the police at regular intervals and give an account of themselves. The Prussian drill master was let loose in all his fury upon the younger generation. When a party of students celebrated the tercentenary of the Reformation with noisy but harmless festivities on the old Wartburg, the Prussian bureaucrats had visions of an imminent revolution. When a theological student, more honest than intelligent, killed a Russian government spy who was operating in Germany, the universities were placed under police-supervision and professors were jailed or dismissed without any form of trial.

Russia, of course, was even more absurd in these anti-revolutionary activities. Alexander had recovered from his attack of piety. He was gradually drifting toward melancholia. He well knew his own limited abilities and understood how at Vienna he had been the victim both of Metternich and the Krüdener woman. More and more he turned his back upon the west and became a truly Russian ruler whose interests lay in Constantinople, the old holy city that had been the first teacher of the Slavs. The older he grew, the harder he worked and the less he was able to accomplish.

And while he sat in his study, his ministers turned the whole of Russia into a land of military barracks.

It is not a pretty picture. Perhaps I might have shortened this description of the Great Reaction. But it is just as well that you should have a thorough knowledge of this era. It was not the first time that an attempt had been made to set the clock of history back. The result was the usual one.

56

National Independence

The Love of National Independence, However, Was Too Strong to Be Destroyed in This Way. The South Americans Were the First to Rebel Against the Reactionary Measures of the Congress of Vienna. Greece and Belgium and Spain and a Large Number of Other Countries of the European Continent Followed Suit and the Nineteenth Century Was Filled with the Rumour of Many Wars of Independence

It will serve no good purpose to say "if only the Congress of Vienna had done such and such a thing instead of taking such and such a course, the history of Europe in the nineteenth century would have been different." The Congress of Vienna was a gathering of men who had just passed through a great revolution and through twenty years of terrible and almost continuous warfare. They came together for the purpose of giving Europe that "peace and stability" which they thought that the people needed and wanted. They were what we call reactionaries. They sincerely believed in the inability of the mass of the people to rule themselves. They re-arranged the map of Europe in such a way as seemed to promise the greatest possibility of a lasting success. They failed, but not through any premeditated wickedness on their part. They were, for the greater part, men of the old school who remembered the happier days of their quiet youth and ardently wished a return of that blessed period. They failed to recognise the strong hold which many of the revolutionary principles had gained upon the people of the European continent. That was a misfortune but hardly a sin. But one of the things which the French Revolution had taught not only Europe but America as well was the right of people to their own "nationality."

Napoleon, who respected nothing and nobody, was utterly ruthless in his dealing with national and patriotic aspirations. But the early revolutionary generals had proclaimed the new doctrine that "nationality was not a matter of political frontiers or round skulls and broad noses, but a matter of the heart and soul." While they were teaching the French children the greatness of the French nation, they encouraged Spaniards and Hollanders and Italians to do the same thing. Soon these people, who all shared Rousseau's belief in the superior virtues of Original Man, began to dig into their past and found, buried beneath the ruins of the feudal system, the bones of the mighty races of which they supposed themselves the feeble descendants.

The first half of the nineteenth century was the era of the great historical discoveries. Everywhere historians were busy publishing mediæval charters and early mediæval chronicles and in every country the result was a new pride in the old fatherland. A great deal of this sentiment was based upon the wrong interpretation of historical facts. But in practical politics, it does not matter what is true, but everything depends upon what the people believe to be true. And in most countries both the kings and their subjects firmly believed in the glory and fame of their ancestors.

The Congress of Vienna was not inclined to be sentimental. Their Excellencies divided the map of Europe according to the best interests of half a dozen dynasties and put "national aspirations" upon the Index, or list of forbidden books, together with all other dangerous "French doctrines."

But history is no respecter of congresses. For some reason or other (it may be an historical law, which thus far has escaped the attention of the scholars) "nations" seemed to be necessary for the orderly development of human society and the attempt to stem this tide was quite as unsuccessful as the Metternichian effort to prevent people from thinking.

Curiously enough the first trouble began in a very distant part of the world, in South America. The Spanish colonies of that continent had been enjoying a period of relative independence during the many years of the great Napoleonic Wars. They had even remained faithful to their king when he was taken prisoner by the French emperor and they had refused to recognise Joseph Bonaparte, who had in the year 1808 been made king of Spain by order of his brother.

Indeed, the only part of America to get very much upset by the Revolution was the island of Haiti, the Espagnola of Columbus' first trip. Here in the year 1791 the French Convention, in a sudden outburst of love and human brotherhood, had bestowed upon their black brethren all the privileges hitherto enjoyed by their white masters. Just as suddenly they had repented of this step, but the attempt to undo the original promise led to many years of terrible warfare between General Leclerc, the brother-in-law of Napoleon, and Toussaint l'Ouverture, the negro chieftain. In the year 1801, Toussaint was asked to visit Leclerc and discuss terms of peace. He received the solemn promise that he would not be molested. He trusted his white adversaries, was put on board a ship and shortly afterwards died in a French prison. But the negroes gained their independence all the same and founded a republic. Incidentally they were of great help to the first great South American patriot in his efforts to deliver his native country from the Spanish yoke.

Simon Bolivar, a native of Caracas in Venezuela, born in the year 1783, had been educated in Spain, had visited Paris, where he had seen the revolutionary government at work, had lived for a while in the United States and had returned to his native land where the widespread discontent against Spain, the mother country, was beginning to take a definite form. In the year 1811, Venezuela declared its independence and Bolivar became one of the revolutionary generals. Within two months, the rebels were defeated and Bolivar fled.

For the next five years he was the leader of an apparently lost cause. He sacrificed all his wealth and he would not have been able to begin his final and successful expedition without the support of the president of Haiti. Thereafter the revolt spread all over South America and soon it appeared that Spain was not able to suppress the rebellion unaided. She asked for the support of the Holy Alliance.

This step greatly worried England. The British shippers had succeeded the Dutch as the common-carriers of the world and they expected to reap heavy profits from a declaration of independence on the part of all South America. They had hopes that the United States of America would interfere but the Senate had no such plans and in the House, too, there were many voices which declared that Spain ought to be given a free hand.

Just then, there was a change of ministers in England. The Whigs went out and the Tories came in. George Canning became secretary of state. He dropped a hint that England would gladly back up the American government with all the might of her fleet, if said government would declare its disapproval of the plans of the Holy Alliance in regard to the rebellious colonies of the southern continent. President Monroe thereupon, on December 2 of the year 1823, addressed Congress and stated that: "America would consider any attempt on the part of the allied powers to extend their system to any portion of this western hemisphere as dangerous to our peace and safety," and gave warning that "the American government would consider such action on the part of the Holy Alliance as a manifestation of an unfriendly disposition toward the United States." Four weeks later, the text of the "Monroe Doctrine" was printed in the English newspapers and the members of the Holy Alliance were forced to make their choice.

Metternich hesitated. Personally he would have been willing to risk the displeasure of the United States (which had allowed both its army and navy to fall into neglect since the end of the Anglo-American war of the year 1812). But Canning's threatening attitude and trouble on the continent forced him to be careful. The expedition never took place and South America and Mexico gained their independence.

As for the troubles on the continent of Europe, they were coming fast and furious. The Holy Alliance had sent French troops to Spain to act as guardians of the peace in the year 1820. Austrian troops had been used for a similar purpose in Italy when the "Carbonari" (the secret society of the Charcoal Burners) were making propaganda for a united Italy and had caused a rebellion against the unspeakable Ferdinand of Naples.

Bad news also came from Russia where the death of Alexander had been the sign for a revolutionary outbreak in St. Petersburg, a short but bloody upheaval, the so-called Dekaberist revolt (because it took place in December), which ended with the hanging of a large number of good patriots who had been disgusted by the reaction of Alexander's last years and had tried to give Russia a constitutional form of government.

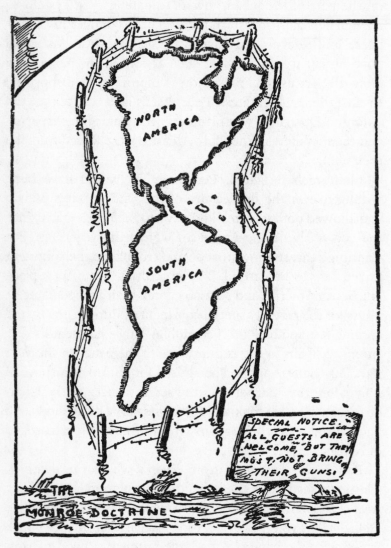

The Monroe Doctrine

But worse was to follow. Metternich had tried to assure himself of the continued support of the European courts by a series of conferences at Aix-la-Chapelle, at Troppau, at Laibach and finally at Verona. The delegates from the different powers duly travelled to these agreeable watering places where the Austrian prime minister used to spend his summers. They always promised to do their best to suppress revolt but they were none too certain of their success. The spirit of the people was beginning to be ugly and especially in France the position of the king was by no means satisfactory.

The real trouble, however, began in the Balkans, the gateway to western Europe through which the invaders of that continent had passed since the beginning of time. The first outbreak was in Moldavia, the ancient Roman province of Dacia which had been cut off from the empire in the third century. Since then, it had been a lost land, a sort of Atlantis, where the people had continued to speak the old Roman tongue and still called themselves Romans and their country Roumania. Here in the year 1821, a young Greek, Prince Alexander Ypsilanti, began a revolt against the Turks. He told his followers that they could count upon the support of Russia. But Metternich's fast couriers were soon on their way to St. Petersburg and the tsar, entirely persuaded by the Austrian arguments in favor of "peace and stability," refused to help. Ypsilanti was forced to flee to Austria where he spent the next seven years in prison.

In the same year, 1821, trouble began in Greece. Since 1815 a secret society of Greek patriots had been preparing the way for a revolt. Suddenly they hoisted the flag of independence in the Morea (the ancient Peloponnesus) and drove the Turkish garrisons away. The Turks answered in the usual fashion. They took the Greek patriarch of Constantinople, who was regarded as their Pope both by the Greeks and by many Russians, and they hanged him on Easter Sunday of the year 1821, together with a number of his bishops. The Greeks came back with a massacre of all the Mohammedans in Tripolitsa, the capital of the Morea, and the Turks retaliated by an attack upon the island of Chios, where they murdered twenty-five thousand Christians and sold forty-five thousand others as slaves into Asia and Egypt.

Then the Greeks appealed to the European courts, but Metternich told them in so many words that they could "stew in their own grease" (I am not trying to make a pun, but I am quoting His Serene Highness who informed the tsar that this "fire of revolt ought to burn itself out beyond the pale of civilisation") and the frontiers were closed to those volunteers who wished to go to the rescue of the patriotic Hellenes. Their cause seemed lost. At the request of Turkey, an Egyptian army was landed in the Morea and soon the Turkish flag was again flying from the Acropolis, the ancient stronghold of Athens. The Egyptian army then pacified the country "à la Turque," and Metternich followed the proceedings with quiet interest, awaiting the day when this "attempt against the peace of Europe" should be a thing of the past.

Once more it was England which upset his plans. The greatest glory of England does not lie in her vast colonial possessions, in her wealth or her navy, but in the quiet heroism and independence of her average citizen. The Englishman obeys the law because he knows that respect for the rights of others marks the difference between a dog-kennel and civilised society. But he does not recognize the right of others to interfere with his freedom of thought. If his country does something which he believes to be wrong, he gets up and says so and the government which he attacks will respect him and will give him full protection against the mob which to-day, as in the time of Socrates, often loves to destroy those who surpass it in courage or intelligence. There never has been a good cause, however unpopular or however distant, which has not counted a number of Englishmen among its staunchest adherents. The mass of the English people are not different from those in other lands. They stick to the business at hand and have no time for unpractical "sporting ventures." But they rather admire their eccentric neighbour who drops everything to go and fight for some obscure people in Asia or Africa and when he has been killed they give him a fine public funeral and hold him up to their children as an example of valour and chivalry.

Even the police spies of the Holy Alliance were powerless against this national characteristic. In the year 1824, Lord Byron, a rich young Englishman who wrote the poetry over which all Europe wept, hoisted the sails of his yacht and started south to help the Greeks. Three months later the news spread through Europe that their hero lay dead in Missolonghi, the last of the Greek strongholds. His lonely death caught the imagination of the people. In all countries, societies were formed to help the Greeks. Lafayette, the grand old man of the American Revolution, pleaded their cause in France. The king of Bavaria sent hundreds of his officers. Money and supplies poured in upon the starving men of Missolonghi.

In England, George Canning, who had defeated the plans of the Holy Alliance in South America, was now prime minister. He saw his chance to checkmate Metternich for a second time. The English and Russian fleets were already in the Mediterranean. They were sent by governments which dared no longer suppress the popular enthusiasm for the cause of the Greek patriots. The French navy appeared because France, since the end of the Crusades, had assumed the rôle of the defender of the Christian faith in Mohammedan lands. On October 20 of the year 1827, the ships of the three nations attacked the Turkish fleet in the Bay of Navarino and destroyed it. Rarely has the news of a battle been received with such general rejoicing. The people of western Europe and Russia who enjoyed no freedom at home consoled themselves by fighting an imaginary war of liberty on behalf of the oppressed Greeks. In the year 1829 they had their reward. Greece became an independent nation and the policy of reaction and stability suffered its second great defeat.

It would be absurd were I to try, in this short volume, to give you a detailed account of the struggle for national independence in all other countries. There are a large number of excellent books devoted to such subjects. I have described the struggle for the independence of Greece because it was the first successful attack upon the bulwark of reaction which the Congress of Vienna had erected to "maintain the stability of Europe." That mighty fortress of suppression still held out and Metternich continued to be in command. But the end was near.

In France the Bourbons had established an almost unbearable rule of police officials who were trying to undo the work of the French Revolution, with an absolute disregard of the regulations and laws of civilised warfare. When Louis XVIII died in the year 1824, the people had enjoyed nine years of "peace" which had proved even more unhappy than the ten years of war of the empire. Louis was succeeded by his brother, Charles X.

Louis had belonged to that famous Bourbon family which, although it never learned anything, never forgot anything. The recollection of that morning in the town of Hamm, when news had reached him of the decapitation of his brother, remained a constant warning of what might happen to those kings who did not read the signs of the times aright. Charles, on the other hand, who had managed to run up private debts of fifty million francs before he was twenty years of age, knew nothing, remembered nothing and firmly intended to learn nothing. As soon as he had succeeded his brother, he established a government "by priests, through priests and for priests," and while the duke of Wellington, who made this remark, cannot be called a violent liberal, Charles ruled in such a way that he disgusted even that trusted friend of law and order. When he tried to suppress the newspapers which dared to criticize his government, and dismissed the Parliament because it supported the Press, his days were numbered.

On the night of July 27 of the year 1830, a revolution took place in Paris. On the thirtieth of the same month, the king fled to the coast and set sail for England. In this way the "famous farce of fifteen years" came to an end and the Bourbons were at last removed from the throne of France. They were too hopelessly incompetent. France then might have returned to a republican form of government, but such a step would not have been tolerated by Metternich.

The situation was dangerous enough. The spark of rebellion had leaped beyond the French frontier and had set fire to another powder house filled with national grievances. The new kingdom of the Netherlands had not been a success. The Belgian and the Dutch people had nothing in common and their king, William of Orange (the descendant of an uncle of William the Silent), while a hard worker and a good business man, was too much lacking in tact and pliability to keep the peace among his uncongenial subjects. Besides, the horde of priests which had descended upon France had at once found its way into Belgium and whatever Protestant William tried to do was howled down by large crowds of excited citizens as a fresh attempt upon the "freedom of the Catholic church." On August 25 there was a popular outbreak against the Dutch authorities in Brussels. Two months later, the Belgians declared themselves independent and elected Leopold of Coburg, the uncle of Queen Victoria of England, to the throne. That was an excellent solution of the difficulty. The two countries, which never ought to have been united, parted their ways and thereafter lived in peace and harmony and behaved like decent neighbours.

News in those days when there were only a few short railroads travelled slowly, but when the success of the French and the Belgian revolutionists became known in Poland there was an immediate clash between the Poles and their Russian rulers which led to a year of terrible warfare and ended with a complete victory for the Russians who "established order along the banks of the Vistula" in the well-known Russian fashion. Nicholas I, who had succeeded his brother Alexander in 1825, firmly believed in the divine right of his own family, and the thousands of Polish refugees who had found shelter in western Europe bore witness to the fact that the principles of the Holy Alliance were still more than a hollow phrase in Holy Russia.

In Italy too there was a moment of unrest. Marie Louise, duchess of Parma and wife of the former emperor Napoleon, whom she had deserted after the defeat of Waterloo, was driven away from her country, and in the Papal State the exasperated people tried to establish an independent republic. But the armies of Austria marched to Rome and soon everything was as of old. Metternich continued to reside at the Ball Platz, the home of the foreign minister of the Habsburg dynasty, the police spies returned to their job and peace reigned supreme. Eighteen more years were to pass before a second and more successful attempt could be made to deliver Europe from the terrible inheritance of the Vienna Congress.

Again it was France, the revolutionary weather-cock of Europe, which gave the signal of revolt. Charles X had been succeeded by Louis Philippe, the son of that famous duke of Orleans who had turned Jacobin, had voted for the death of his cousin the king, and had played a rôle during the early days of the Revolution under the name of "Philippe Egalité" or "Equality Philip." Eventually he had been killed when Robespierre tried to purge the nation of all "traitors" (by which name he indicated those people who did not share his own views) and his son had been forced to run away from the revolutionary army. Young Louis Philippe thereupon had wandered far and wide. He had taught school in Switzerland and had spent a couple of years exploring the unknown "far west" of America. After the fall of Napoleon he had returned to Paris. He was much more intelligent than his Bourbon cousins. He was a simple man who went about in the public parks with a red cotton umbrella under his arm, followed by a brood of children like any good housefather. But France had outgrown the king business and Louis did not know this until the morning of February 24 of the year 1848, when a crowd stormed the Tuileries, and drove His Majesty away and proclaimed the republic.

When the news of this event reached Vienna, Metternich expressed the casual opinion that this was only a repetition of the year 1793 and that the allies would once more be obliged to march upon Paris and make an end to this very unseemly democratic row. But two weeks later his own Austrian capital was in open revolt. Metternich escaped from the mob through the back door of his palace, and the emperor Ferdinand was forced to give his subjects a constitution which embodied most of the revolutionary principles which his prime minister had tried to suppress for the last thirty-three years.

This time all Europe felt the shock. Hungary declared itself independent, and commenced a war against the Habsburgs under the leadership of Louis Kossuth. The unequal struggle lasted more than a year. It was finally suppressed by the armies of Tsar Nicholas who marched across the Carpathian Mountains and made Hungary once more safe for autocracy. The Habsburgs thereupon established extraordinary court-martials and hanged the greater part of the Hungarian patriots whom they had not been able to defeat in open battle.

As for Italy, the island of Sicily declared itself independent from Naples and drove its Bourbon king away. In the Papal States the prime minister, Rossi, was murdered and the Pope was forced to flee. He returned the next year at the head of a French army which remained in Rome to protect His Holiness against his subjects until the year 1870. Then it was called back to defend France against the Prussians, and Rome became the capital of Italy. In the north, Milan and Venice rose against their Austrian masters. They were supported by King Albert of Sardinia, but a strong Austrian army under old Radetzky marched into the valley of the Po, defeated the Sardinians near Custozza and Novara and forced Albert to abdicate in favour of his son, Victor Emmanuel, who a few years later was to be the first king of a united Italy.

In Germany the unrest of the year 1848 took the form of a great national demonstration in favour of political unity and a representative form of government. In Bavaria, the king who had wasted his time and money upon an Irish lady who posed as a Spanish dancer—(she was called Lola Montez and lies buried in New York's Potter's Field)—was driven away by the enraged students of the university. In Prussia, the king was forced to stand with uncovered head before the coffins of those who had been killed during the street fighting and to promise a constitutional form of government. And in March of the year 1849, a German Parliament, consisting of 550 delegates from all parts of the country, came together in Frankfurt and proposed that King Frederick William of Prussia should be the emperor of a united Germany.

Then, however, the tide began to turn. Incompetent Ferdinand had abdicated in favour of his nephew Francis Joseph. The well-drilled Austrian army had remained faithful to their war-lord. The hangman was given plenty of work and the Habsburgs, after the nature of that strangely cat-like family, once more landed upon their feet and rapidly strengthened their position as the masters of eastern and western Europe. They played the game of politics very adroitly and used the jealousies of the other German states to prevent the elevation of the Prussian king to the imperial dignity. Their long training in the art of suffering defeat had taught them the value of patience. They knew how to wait. They bided their time and while the liberals, utterly untrained in practical politics, talked and talked and talked and got intoxicated by their own fine speeches, the Austrians quietly gathered their forces, dismissed the Parliament of Frankfurt and re-established the old and impossible German Confederation which the Congress of Vienna had wished upon an unsuspecting world.

But among the men who had attended this strange Parliament of unpractical enthusiasts, there was a Prussian country squire by the name of Bismarck, who had made good use of his eyes and ears. He had a deep contempt for oratory. He knew (what every man of action has always known) that nothing is ever accomplished by talk. In his own way he was a sincere patriot. He had been trained in the old school of diplomacy and he could outlie his opponents just as he could outwalk them and outdrink them and outride them.

Bismarck felt convinced that the loose confederation of little states must be changed into a strong united country if it would hold its own against the other European powers. Brought up amidst feudal ideas of loyalty, he decided that the house of Hohenzollern, of which he was the most faithful servant, should rule the new state, rather than the incompetent Habsburgs. For this purpose he must first get rid of the Austrian influence, and he began to make the necessary preparations for this painful operation.

Italy in the meantime had solved her own problem, and had rid herself of her hated Austrian master. The unity of Italy was the work of three men, Cavour, Mazzini and Garibaldi. Of these three, Cavour, the civil-engineer with the short-sighted eyes and the steel-rimmed glasses, played the part of the careful political pilot. Mazzini, who had spent most of his days in different European garrets, hiding from the Austrian police, was the public agitator, while Garibaldi, with his band of red-shirted rough-riders, appealed to the popular imagination.

Mazzini and Garibaldi were both believers in the republican form of government. Cavour, however, was a monarchist, and the others, who recognised his superior ability in such matters of practical statecraft, accepted his decision and sacrificed their own ambitions for the greater good of their beloved fatherland.

Cavour felt towards the house of Sardinia as Bismarck did towards the Hohenzollern family. With infinite care and great shrewdness he set to work to jockey the Sardinian king into a position from which His Majesty would be able to assume the leadership of the entire Italian people. The unsettled political conditions in the rest of Europe greatly helped him in his plans and no country contributed more to the independence of Italy than her old and trusted (and often distrusted) neighbour, France.

In that turbulent country, in November of the year 1852, the republic had come to a sudden but not unexpected end. Napoleon III, the son of Louis Bonaparte, the former king of Holland, and the small nephew of a great uncle, had re-

Giuseppe Mazzini

established an empire and had made himself emperor "by the Grace of God and the Will of the People."

This young man, who had been educated in Germany and who mixed his French with harsh Teutonic gutturals (just as the first Napoleon had always spoken the language of his adopted country with a strong Italian accent), was trying very hard to use the Napoleonic tradition for his own benefit. But he had many enemies and did not feel very certain of his hold upon his ready-made throne. He had gained the friendship of Queen Victoria but this had not been a difficult task, as the good queen was not particularly brilliant and was very susceptible to flattery. As for the other European sovereigns, they treated the French emperor with insulting haughtiness and sat up nights devising new ways in which they could show their upstart "Good Brother" how sincerely they despised him.

Napoleon was obliged to find a way in which he could break this opposition, either through love or through fear. He well knew the fascination which the word "glory" still held for his subjects. Since he was forced to gamble for his throne he decided to play the game of empire for high stakes. He used an attack of Russia upon Turkey as an excuse for bringing about the Crimean War in which England and

France combined against the tsar on behalf of the sultan. It was a very costly and exceedingly unprofitable enterprise. Neither France nor England nor Russia reaped much glory.

But the Crimean War did one good thing. It gave Sardinia a chance to volunteer on the winning side and when peace was declared it gave Cavour the opportunity to lay claim to the gratitude of both England and France.

Having made use of the international situation to get Sardinia recognised as one of the more important powers of Europe, the clever Italian then provoked a war between Sardinia and Austria in June of the year 1859. He assured himself of the support of Napoleon in exchange for the provinces of Savoy and the city of Nice, which was really an Italian town. The Franco-Italian armies defeated the Austrians at Magenta and Solferino, and the former Austrian provinces and duchies were united into a single Italian kingdom. Florence became the capital of this new Italy until the year 1870 when the French recalled their troops from Rome to defend France against the Germans. As soon as they were gone, the Italian troops entered the eternal city and the house of Sardinia took up its residence in the old Palace of the Quirinal which an ancient Pope had built on the ruins of the baths of the emperor Constantine.

The Pope, however, moved across the River Tiber and hid behind the walls of the Vatican, which had been the home of many of his predecessors since their return from the exile of Avignon in the year 1377. He protested loudly against this high-handed theft of his domains and addressed letters of appeal to those faithful Catholics who were inclined to sympathise with him in his loss. Their number, however, was small, and it has been steadily decreasing. For, once delivered from the cares of state, the Pope was able to devote all his time to questions of a spiritual nature. Standing high above the petty quarrels of the European politicians, the Papacy assumed a new dignity which proved of great benefit to the church and made it an international power for social and religious progress which has shown a much more intelligent appreciation of modern economic problems than most Protestant sects.

In this way, the attempt of the Congress of Vienna to settle the Italian question by making the peninsula an Austrian province was at last undone.

The German problem, however, remained as yet unsolved. It proved the most difficult of all. The failure of the revolution of the year 1848 had led to the wholesale migration of the more energetic and liberal elements among the German people. These young fellows had moved to the United States of America, to Brazil, to the new colonies in Asia and America. Their work was continued in Germany but by a different sort of men.

In the new Diet which met at Frankfurt, after the collapse of the German Parliament and the failure of the liberals to establish a united country, the kingdom of Prussia was represented by that same Otto von Bismarck from whom we parted a few pages ago. Bismarck by now had managed to gain the complete confidence of the king of Prussia. That was all he asked for. The opinion of the Prussian Parliament or of the Prussian people interested him not at all. With his own eyes he had seen the defeat of the liberals. He knew that he would not be able to get rid of Austria without a war and he began by strengthening the Prussian army. The Landtag, exasperated at his high-handed methods, refused to give him the necessary credits. Bismarck did not even bother to discuss the matter. He went ahead and increased his army with the help of funds which the Prussian house of peers and the king placed at his disposal. Then he looked for a national cause which could be used for the purpose of creating a great wave of patriotism among all the German people.

In the north of Germany there were the duchies of Schleswig and Holstein which ever since the Middle Ages had been a source of trouble. Both countries were inhabited by a certain number of Danes and a certain number of Germans, but although they were governed by the king of Denmark, they were not an integral part of the Danish state and this led to endless difficulties. Heaven forbid that I should revive this forgotten question which now seems settled by the acts of the recent Congress of Versailles. But the Germans in Holstein were very loud in their abuse of the Danes and the Danes in Schleswig made a great ado of their Danishness, and all Europe was discussing the problem and German Männerchors and Turnvereins listened to sentimental speeches about the "lost brethren" and the different chancelleries were trying to discover what it was all about, when Prussia mobilised her armies to "save the lost provinces." As Austria, the official head of the German Confederation, could not allow Prussia to act alone in such an important matter, the Habsburg troops were mobilised too and the combined armies of the two great powers crossed the Danish frontiers and, after a very brave resistance on the part of the Danes, occupied the two duchies. The Danes appealed to Europe, but Europe was otherwise engaged and the poor Danes were left to their fate.

Bismarck then prepared the scene for the second number upon his imperial programme. He used the division of the spoils to pick a quarrel with Austria. The Habsburgs fell into the trap. The new Prussian army, the creation of Bismarck and his faithful generals, invaded Bohemia and in less than six weeks, the last of the Austrian troops had been destroyed at Königgrätz and Sadowa and the road to Vienna lay open. But Bismarck did not want to go too far. He knew that he would need a few friends in Europe. He offered the defeated Habsburgs very decent terms of peace, provided they would resign their chairmanship of the Confederation. He was less merciful to many of the smaller German states who had taken the side of the Austrians, and annexed them to Prussia. The greater part of the northern states then formed a new organization, the so-called North German Confederacy, and victorious Prussia assumed the unofficial leadership of the German people.

Europe stood aghast at the rapidity with which the work of consolidation had been done. England was quite indifferent but France showed signs of disapproval. Napoleon's hold upon the French people was steadily diminishing. The Crimean War had been costly and had accomplished nothing.

A second adventure in the year 1863, when a French army had tried to force an Austrian grand duke by the name of Maximilian upon the Mexican people as their emperor, had come to a disastrous end as soon as the American Civil War had been won by the north. For the government at Washington had forced the French to withdraw their troops and this had given the Mexicans a chance to clear their country of the enemy and shoot the unwelcome emperor.

It was necessary to give the Napoleonic throne a new coat of glory-paint. Within a few years the North German Confederation would be a serious rival of France. Napoleon decided that a war with Germany would be a good thing for his dynasty. He looked for an excuse and Spain, the poor victim of endless revolutions, gave him one.

Just then the Spanish throne happened to be vacant. It had been offered to the Catholic branch of the house of Hohenzollern. The French government had objected and the Hohenzollerns had politely refused to accept the crown. But Napoleon, who was showing signs of illness, was very much under the influence of his beautiful wife, Eugénie de Montijo, the daughter of a Spanish gentleman and the granddaughter of William Kirkpatrick, an American consul at Malaga, where the grapes come from. Eugénie, although shrewd enough, was as badly educated as most Spanish women of that day. She was at the mercy of her spiritual advisers and these worthy gentlemen felt no love for the Protestant king of Prussia. "Be bold," was the advice of the empress to her husband, but she omitted to add the second half of that famous Persian proverb, which admonishes the hero to "be bold but not too bold." Napoleon, convinced of the strength of his army, addressed himself to the king of Prussia and insisted that the king give him assurances that "he would never permit another candidature of a Hohenzollern prince to the Spanish crown." As the Hohenzollerns had just declined the honour, the demand was superfluous, and Bismarck so informed the French government. But Napoleon was not satisfied.

It was the year 1870 and King William was taking the waters at Ems. There one day he was approached by the French minister who tried to re-open the discussion. The king answered very pleasantly that it was a fine day and that the Spanish question was now closed and that nothing more remained to be said upon the subject. As a matter of routine, a report of this interview was telegraphed to Bismarck, who handled all foreign affairs. Bismarck edited the dispatch for the benefit of the Prussian and French press. Many people have called him names for doing this. Bismarck however could plead the excuse that the doctoring of official news, since time immemorial, had been one of the privileges of all civilised governments. When the "edited" telegram was printed, the good people in Berlin felt that their old and venerable king with his nice white whiskers had been insulted by an arrogant little Frenchman and the equally good people of Paris flew into a rage because their perfectly courteous minister had been shown the door by a royal Prussian flunkey.

And so they both went to war and in less than two months,

Napoleon and the greater part of his army were prisoners of the Germans. The Second Empire had come to an end and the Third Republic was making ready to defend Paris against the German invaders. Paris held out for five long months. Ten days before the surrender of the city, in the nearby palace of Versailles, built by that same King Louis XIV who had been such a dangerous enemy to the Germans, the king of Prussia was publicly proclaimed German emperor and a loud booming of guns told the hungry Parisians that a new German Empire had taken the place of the old harmless Confederation of Teutonic states and statelets.

In this rough way, the German question was finally settled. By the end of the year 1871, fifty-six years after the memorable gathering at Vienna, the work of the Congress had been entirely undone. Metternich and Alexander and Talleyrand had tried to give the people of Europe a lasting peace. The methods they had employed had caused endless wars and revolutions and the feeling of a common brotherhood of the eighteenth century was followed by an era of exaggerated nationalism which has not yet come to an end.

57

The Age of the Engine

But While the People of Europe Were Fighting for
Their National Independence, the World in Which
They Lived Had Been Entirely Changed by a Series
of Inventions, Which Had Made the Clumsy Old
Steam Engine of the Eighteenth Century the Most
Faithful and Efficient Slave of Man

The greatest benefactor of the human race died more than
half a million years ago. He was a hairy creature with a low
brow and sunken eyes, a heavy jaw and strong tiger-like teeth.
He would not have looked well in a gathering of modern scientists, but they would have honoured him as their master.
For he had used a stone to break a nut and a stick to lift up a
heavy boulder. He was the inventor of the hammer and the
lever, our first tools, and he did more than any human being
who came after him to give man his enormous advantage
over the other animals with whom he shares this planet.

Ever since, man has tried to make his life easier by the
use of a greater number of tools. The first wheel (a round
disc made out of an old tree) created as much stir in the communities of 100,000 B.C. as the flying machine did only a few
years ago.

In Washington, the story is told of a director of the Patent Office who in the early thirties of the last century suggested that the Patent Office be abolished, because "everything that possibly could be invented had been invented." A similar feeling must have spread through the prehistoric world when the first sail was hoisted on a raft and the people were able to move from place to place without rowing or punting or pulling from the shore.

Indeed one of the most interesting chapters of history is the effort of man to let some one else or something else do his work for him, while he enjoyed his leisure, sitting in the sun or painting pictures on rocks, or training young wolves and little tigers to behave like peaceful domestic animals.

Of course in the very olden days, it was always possible to enslave a weaker neighbour and force him to do the unpleasant tasks of life. One of the reasons why the Greeks and Romans, who were quite as intelligent as we are, failed to devise more interesting machinery was to be found in the wide-spread existence of slavery. Why should a great mathematician waste his time upon wires and pulleys and cogs and fill the air with noise and smoke when he could go to the market-place and buy all the slaves he needed at a very small expense?

And during the Middle Ages, although slavery had been abolished and only a mild form of serfdom survived, the guilds discouraged the idea of using machinery because they thought this would throw a large number of their brethren out of work. Besides, the Middle Ages were not at all interested in producing large quantities of goods. Their tailors and butchers and carpenters worked for the immediate needs of the small community in which they lived and had no desire to compete with their neighbours, or to produce more than was strictly necessary.

During the Renaissance, when the prejudices of the church

against scientific investigations could no longer be enforced as rigidly as before, a large number of men began to devote their lives to mathematics and astronomy and physics and chemistry. Two years before the beginning of the Thirty Years War, John Napier, a Scotchman, had published his little book which described the new invention of logarithms. During the war itself, Gottfried Leibnitz of Leipzig had perfected the system of infinitesimal calculus. Eight years before the peace of Westphalia, Newton, the great English natural philosopher, was born, and in that same year Galileo, the Italian astronomer, died. Meanwhile the Thirty Years War had destroyed the prosperity of central Europe and there was a sudden but very general interest in "alchemy," the strange pseudo-science of the Middle Ages by which people hoped to turn base metals into gold. This proved to be impossible but the alchemists in their laboratories stumbled upon many new ideas and greatly helped the work of the chemists who were their successors.

The work of all these men provided the world with a solid scientific foundation upon which it was possible to build even the most complicated of engines, and a number of practical men made good use of it. The Middle Ages had used wood for the few bits of necessary machinery. But wood wore out easily. Iron was a much better material, but iron was scarce except in England. In England therefore most of the smelting was done. To smelt iron, huge fires were needed. In the beginning, these fires had been made of wood, but gradually the forests had been used up. Then "stone coal" (the petrified trees of prehistoric times) was used. But coal as you know has to be dug out of the ground and it has to be transported to the smelting ovens and the mines have to be kept dry from the ever invading waters.

These were two problems which had to be solved at once. For the time being, horses could still be used to haul the coal-wagons, but the pumping question demanded the application of special machinery. Several inventors were busy trying to solve the difficulty. They all knew that steam would have to be used in their new engine. The idea of the steam engine was very old. Hero of Alexandria, who lived in the first century before Christ, has described to us several bits of machinery which were driven by steam. The people of the Renaissance had played with the notion of steam-driven war chariots. The marquis of Worcester, a contemporary of Newton, in his book of inventions, tells of a steam engine. A little later, in the year 1698, Thomas Savery of London applied for a patent for a pumping engine. At the same time, a Hollander, Christian Huygens, was trying to perfect an engine in which gun powder was used to cause regular explosions in much the same way as we use gasoline in our motors.

All over Europe, people were busy with the idea. Denis Papin, a Frenchman, friend and assistant of Huygens, was making experiments with steam engines in several countries. He invented a little wagon that was driven by steam, and a paddle wheel boat. But when he tried to take a trip in his vessel, it was confiscated by the authorities on a complaint of the boatmen's union, who feared that such a craft would deprive them of their livelihood. Papin finally died in London in great poverty, having wasted all his money on his inventions. But at the time of his death, another mechanical enthusiast, Thomas Newcomen, was working on the problem of a new steam-pump. Fifty years later his engine was improved upon by James Watt, a Glasgow instrument maker. In the year 1777, he gave the world the first steam engine that proved of real practical value.

But during the centuries of experiments with a "heat-engine," the political world had greatly changed. The British people had succeeded the Dutch as the common-carriers of the world's trade. They had opened up new colonies. They took the raw materials which the colonies produced to England, and there they turned them into finished products, and then they exported the finished goods to the four corners of the world. During the seventeenth century, the people of Georgia and the Carolinas had begun to grow a new shrub which gave a strange sort of woolly substance, the so-called "cotton wool." After this had been plucked, it was sent to England and there the people of Lancashire wove it into cloth. This weaving was done by hand and in the homes of the workmen. Very soon a number of improvements were made in the process of weaving. In the year 1730, John Kay invented the "fly shuttle." In 1770, James Hargreaves got a patent on his "spinning jenny." Eli Whitney, an American, invented the cotton-gin, which separated the cotton from its seeds, a job which had previously been done by hand at the rate of only a pound a day. Finally Richard Arkwright and the Reverend Edmund Cartwright invented large weaving machines, which were driven by waterpower. And then, in the eighties of the eighteenth century, just when the Estates General of France had begun those famous meetings which were to revolutionise the political system of Europe, the engines of Watt were arranged in such a way that they could drive the weaving machines of Arkwright, and this created an economic and social revolution which has changed human relationship in almost every part of the world.

As soon as the stationary engine had proved a success, the inventors turned their attention to the problem of propelling boats and carts with the help of a mechanical contrivance. Watt himself designed plans for a "steam locomotive," but ere he had perfected his ideas, in the year 1804, a locomotive made by Richard Trevithick carried a load of twenty tons at Pen-y-darran in the Wales mining district.

At the same time an American jeweller and portrait-painter by the name of Robert Fulton was in Paris, trying to

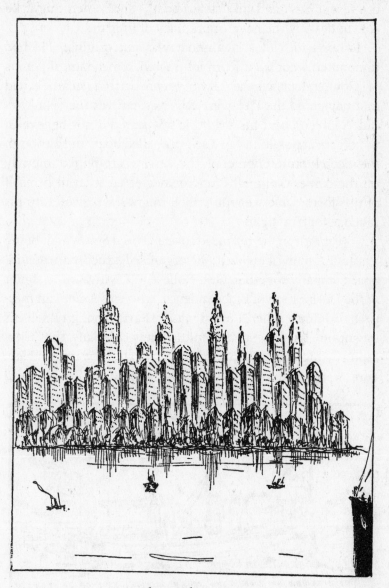

The Modern City

convince Napoleon that with the use of his submarine boat, the "Nautilus," and his "steam-boat," the French might be able to destroy the naval supremacy of England.

Fulton's idea of a steamboat was not original. He had undoubtedly copied it from John Fitch, a mechanical genius of Connecticut whose cleverly constructed steamer had first navigated the Delaware River as early as the year 1787. But Napoleon and his scientific advisers did not believe in the practical possibility of a self-propelled boat, and although the Scotch-built engine of the little craft puffed merrily on the Seine, the great emperor neglected to avail himself of this formidable weapon which might have given him his revenge for Trafalgar.

As for Fulton, he returned to the United States and, being a practical man of business, he organised a successful steamboat company together with Robert R. Livingston, a signer of the Declaration of Independence, who was American minister to France when Fulton was in Paris, trying to sell his invention. The first steamer of this new company, the "Clermont," which was given a monopoly of all the waters of New York State, equipped with an engine built by Boulton and

THIS STEAMER OF JOHN FITCH MADE A TRIAL TRIP OF 20 MILES IN 1788 IN 1790 IT WAS USED ON THE DELAWARE RIVER FOR RATES SEE PHILADELPHIA PAPERS OF THE YEAR 1790

The First Steamboat

THE AGE OF THE ENGINE

Watt of Birmingham in England, began a regular service between New York and Albany in the year 1807.

As for poor John Fitch, the man who long before any one else had used the "steam-boat" for commercial purposes, he came to a sad death. Broken in health and empty of purse, he had come to the end of his resources when his fifth boat, which was propelled by means of a screw-propeller, had been destroyed. His neighbours jeered at him as they were to laugh a hundred years later when Professor Langley constructed his funny flying machines. Fitch had hoped to give his country an easy access to the broad rivers of the west and his countrymen preferred to travel in flat-boats or go on foot. In the year 1798, in utter despair and misery, Fitch killed himself by taking poison.

But twenty years later, the "Savannah," a steamer of 1850 tons and making six knots an hour (the "Mauretania" goes just four times as fast), crossed the ocean from Savannah to Liverpool in the record time of twenty-five days. Then there was an end to the derision of the multitude and in their enthusiasm the people gave the credit for the invention to the wrong man.

Six years later, George Stephenson, an Englishman, who had been building locomotives for the purpose of hauling coal from the mine-pit to smelting ovens and cotton factories, built his famous "travelling engine" which reduced the price of coal by almost seventy percent and which made it possible to establish the first regular passenger service between Manchester and Liverpool, when people were whisked from city to city at the unheard-of speed of fifteen miles per hour. A dozen years later, this speed had been increased to twenty miles per hour. At the present time, any well-behaved fliv-ver (the direct descendant of the puny little motor-driven machines of Daimler and Levassor of the eighties of the last century) can do better than these early "Puffing Billies."

But while these practically minded engineers were improving upon their rattling "heat engines," a group of "pure" scientists (men who devote fourteen hours of each day to the study of those "theoretical" scientific phenomena without which no mechanical progress would be possible) were following a new scent which promised to lead them into the most secret and hidden domains of nature.

Two thousand years ago, a number of Greek and Roman philosophers (notably Thales of Miletus and Pliny who was killed while trying to study the eruption of Vesuvius of the year 79 when Pompeii and Herculaneum were buried beneath the ashes) had noticed the strange antics of bits of

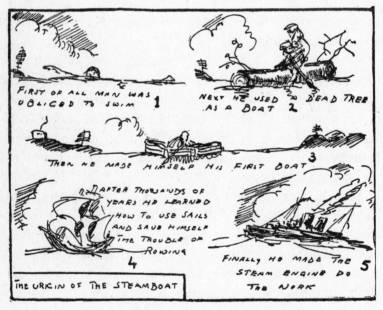

FIRST OF ALL MAN WAS OBLIGED TO SWIM 1

NEXT HE USED A DEAD TREE AS A BOAT 2

THEN HE MADE HIMSELF HIS FIRST BOAT 3

AFTER THOUSANDS OF YEARS HE LEARNED HOW TO USE SAILS AND SAVE HIMSELF THE TROUBLE OF ROWING 4

THE ORIGIN OF THE STEAMBOAT

FINALLY HE MADE THE STEAM ENGINE DO THE WORK 5

The Origin of the Steamboat

straw and of feather which were held near a piece of amber which was being rubbed with a bit of wool. The Schoolmen of the Middle Ages had not been interested in this mysterious "electric" power. But immediately after the Renaissance, William Gilbert, the private physician of Queen Elizabeth, wrote his famous treatise on the character and behaviour of magnets. During the Thirty Years War Otto von Guericke, the burgomaster of Magdeburg and the inventor of the air-pump, constructed the first electrical machine. During the next century a large number of scientists devoted them-

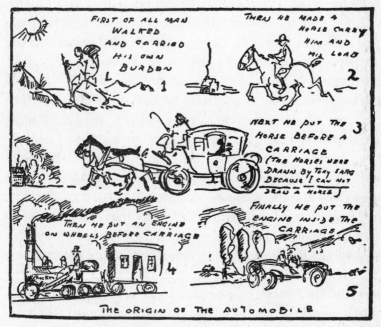

The Origin of the Automobile

selves to the study of electricity. Not less than three professors invented the famous Leyden jar in the year 1795. At the same time, Benjamin Franklin, the most universal genius of America next to Benjamin Thomson (who after his flight from New Hampshire on account of his pro-British sympathies became known as Count Rumford), was devoting his attention to this subject. He discovered that lightning and the electric spark were manifestations of the same electric power and continued his electric studies until the end of his busy and useful life. Then came Volta with his famous "electric pile" and Galvani and Day and the Danish professor Hans Christian Oersted and Ampère and Arago and Faraday, all of them diligent searchers after the true nature of the electric forces.

They freely gave their discoveries to the world and Samuel Morse (who like Fulton began his career as an artist) thought that he could use this new electric current to transmit messages from one city to another. He intended to use copper wire and a little machine which he had invented. People laughed at him. Morse therefore was obliged to finance his own experiments and soon he had spent all his money and then he was very poor and people laughed even louder. He then asked Congress to help him and a special Committee on Commerce promised him their support. But the members of Congress were not at all interested and Morse had to wait twelve years before he was given a small congressional appropriation. He then built a "telegraph" between Baltimore and Washington. In the year 1837 he had shown his first successful "telegraph" in one of the lecture halls of New York University. Finally, on May 24 of the year 1844 the first long-distance message was sent from Washington to Baltimore and to-day the whole world is covered with telegraph wires and we can send news from Europe to Asia in a few seconds. Twenty-three years later Alexander Graham Bell used the electric current for his telephone. And half a century afterwards Marconi improved upon these ideas by inventing a system of sending messages which did away entirely with the old-fashioned wires.

While Morse, the New Englander, was working on his "telegraph," Michael Faraday, the Yorkshire-man, had constructed the first "dynamo." This tiny little machine was completed in the year 1831 when Europe was still trembling as a result of the great July revolutions which had so severely upset the plans of the Congress of Vienna. The first dynamo grew and grew and grew and to-day it provides us with heat and with light (you know the little incandescent bulbs which Edison, building upon French and English experiments of the forties and fifties, first made in 1878) and with power for all sorts of machines. If I am not mistaken the electric engine will soon entirely drive out the "heat-engine" just as in the olden days the more highly organised prehistoric animals drove out their less efficient neighbours.

Personally (but I know nothing about machinery) this will make me very happy. For the electric engine which can be run by waterpower is a clean and companionable servant of mankind but the "heat-engine," the marvel of the eighteenth century, is a noisy and dirty creature forever filling the world with ridiculous smoke-stacks and with dust and soot and asking that it be fed with coal which has to be dug out of mines at great inconvenience and risk to thousands of people.

And if I were a novelist and not a historian, who must stick to facts and may not use his imagination, I would describe the happy day when the last steam locomotive shall be taken to the Museum of Natural History to be placed next to the skeleton of the dinosaur and the pterodactyl and the other extinct creatures of a by-gone age.

58

The Social Revolution

But the New Engines Were Very Expensive and
Only People of Wealth Could Afford Them. The
Old Carpenter or Shoemaker Who Had Been
His Own Master in His Little Workshop Was
Obliged to Hire Himself Out to the Owners of
the Big Mechanical Tools, and While He Made
More Money Than Before, He Lost His Former
Independence and He Did Not Like That

In the olden days the work of the world had been done by
independent workmen who sat in their own little workshops
in the front of their houses, who owned their tools, who
boxed the ears of their own apprentices and who, within the
limits prescribed by their guilds, conducted their business as
it pleased them. They lived simple lives, and were obliged to
work very long hours, but they were their own masters. If
they got up and saw that it was a fine day to go fishing, they
went fishing and there was no one to say "no."

But the introduction of machinery changed this. A
machine is really nothing but a greatly enlarged tool. A railroad train which carries you at the speed of a mile a minute is

in reality a pair of very fast legs, and a steam hammer which flattens heavy plates of iron is just a terrible big fist, made of steel.

But whereas we can all afford a pair of good legs and a good strong fist, a railroad train and a steam hammer and a cotton factory are very expensive pieces of machinery and they are not owned by a single man, but usually by a com-

Man Power and Machine Power

pany of people who all contribute a certain sum and then divide the profits of their railroad or cotton mill according to the amount of money which they have invested.

Therefore, when machines had been improved until they were really practicable and profitable, the builders of those large tools, the machine manufacturers, began to look for customers who could afford to pay for them in cash.

During the early Middle Ages, when land had been almost

the only form of wealth, the nobility were the only people who were considered wealthy. But as I have told you in a previous chapter, the gold and silver which they possessed was quite insignificant and they used the old system of barter, exchanging cows for horses and eggs for honey. During the Crusades, the burghers of the cities had been able to gather riches from the reviving trade between the east and the west, and they had been serious rivals of the lords and the knights.

The French Revolution had entirely destroyed the wealth of the nobility and had enormously increased that of the middle class or "bourgeoisie." The years of unrest which followed the Great Revolution had offered many middle-class people a chance to get more than their share of this world's goods. The estates of the church had been confiscated by the French Convention and had been sold at auction. There had been a terrific amount of graft. Land speculators had stolen thousands of square miles of valuable land, and during the Napoleonic Wars, they had used their capital to "profiteer" in grain and gun powder, and now they possessed more wealth than they needed for the actual expenses of their households and they could afford to build themselves factories and to hire men and women to work the machines.

This caused a very abrupt change in the lives of hundreds of thousands of people. Within a few years, many cities doubled the number of their inhabitants and the old civic centre which had been the real "home" of the citizens was surrounded with ugly and cheaply built suburbs where the workmen slept after their eleven or twelve hours, or thirteen hours, spent in the factories and from where they returned to the factory as soon as the whistle blew.

Far and wide through the countryside there was talk of the fabulous sums of money that could be made in the towns. The peasant boy, accustomed to a life in the open, went to the city. He rapidly lost his old health amidst the smoke and dust and dirt of those early and badly ventilated workshops, and the end, very often, was death in the poor-house or in the hospital.

Of course the change from the farm to the factory on the part of so many people was not accomplished without a certain amount of opposition. Since one engine could do as much work as a hundred men, the ninety-nine others who were thrown out of employment did not like it. Frequently they attacked the factory-buildings and set fire to the machines, but insurance companies had been organised as early as the seventeenth century and as a rule the owners were well protected against loss.

Soon, newer and better machines were installed, the factory was surrounded with a high wall and then there was

The Factory

an end to the rioting. The ancient guilds could not possibly survive in this new world of steam and iron. They went out of existence and then the workmen tried to organise regular labour unions. But the factory owners, who through their wealth could exercise great influence upon the politicians of the different countries, went to the legislature and had laws passed which forbade the forming of such trade unions because they interfered with the "liberty of action" of the working man.

Please do not think that the good members of Parliament who passed these laws were wicked tyrants. They were the true sons of the revolutionary period when everybody talked of "liberty" and when people often killed their neighbours because they were not quite as liberty-loving as they ought to have been. Since "liberty" was the foremost virtue of man, it was not right that labour unions should dictate to their members the hours during which they could work and the wages which they must demand. The workman must at all times be "free to sell his services in the open market," and the employer must be equally "free" to conduct his business as he saw fit. The days of the mercantile system, when the state had regulated the industrial life of the entire community, were coming to an end. The new idea of "freedom" insisted that the state stand entirely aside and let commerce take its course.

The last half of the eighteenth century had not merely been a time of intellectual and political doubt, but the old economic ideas, too, had been replaced by new ones which better suited the need of the hour. Several years before the French Revolution, Turgot, who had been one of the unsuccessful ministers of finance of Louis XVI, had preached the novel doctrine of "economic liberty." Turgot lived in a country which had suffered from too much red-tape, too many regulations, too many officials trying to enforce too many laws. "Remove this official supervision," he wrote, "let the people do as they please, and everything will be all right." Soon his famous advice of "laissez faire" became the battle-cry around which the economists of that period rallied.

At the same time in England, Adam Smith was working

on his mighty volumes on the "Wealth of Nations," which made another plea for "liberty" and the "natural rights of trade." Thirty years later, after the fall of Napoleon, when the reactionary powers of Europe had gained their victory at Vienna, that same freedom which was denied to the people in their political relations was forced upon them in their industrial life.

The general use of machinery, as I have said at the beginning of this chapter, proved to be of great advantage to the state. Wealth increased rapidly. The machine made it possible for a single country, like England, to carry all the burdens of the great Napoleonic Wars. The capitalists (the people who provided the money with which machines were bought) reaped enormous profits. They became ambitious and began to take an interest in politics. They tried to compete with the landed aristocracy which still exercised great influence upon the government of most European countries.

In England, where the members of Parliament were still elected according to a royal decree of the year 1265, and where a large number of recently created industrial centres were without representation, they brought about the passing of the Reform Bill of the year 1832, which changed the electoral system and gave the class of the factory-owners more influence upon the legislative body. This however caused great discontent among the millions of factory workers, who were left without any voice in the government. They too began an agitation for the right to vote. They put their demands down in a document which came to be known as the "People's Charter." The debates about this charter grew more and more violent. They had not yet come to an end when the revolutions of the year 1848 broke out. Frightened by the threat of a new outbreak of Jacobinism and violence, the English government placed the duke of Wellington, who was now in his eightieth year, at the head of the army, and called for volunteers. London was placed in a state of siege and preparations were made to suppress the coming revolution.

But the Chartist movement killed itself through bad leadership and no acts of violence took place. The new class of wealthy factory owners (I dislike the word "bourgeoisie," which has been used to death by the apostles of a new social order) slowly increased its hold upon the government, and the conditions of industrial life in the large cities continued to transform vast acres of pasture and wheat-land into dreary slums, which guard the approach of every modern European town.

59

Emancipation

The General Introduction of Machinery Did Not
Bring About the Era of Happiness and Prosperity
Which Had Been Predicted by the Generation
Which Saw the Stage Coach Replaced by the
Railroad. Several Remedies Were Suggested, But
None of These Quite Solved the Problem

In the year 1831, just before the passing of the first Reform
Bill Jeremy Bentham, the great English student of legislative
methods and the most practical political reformer of that day,
wrote to a friend: "The way to be comfortable is to make
others comfortable. The way to make others comfortable is
to appear to love them. The way to appear to love them is
to love them in reality." Jeremy was an honest man. He said
what he believed to be true. His opinions were shared by
thousands of his countrymen. They felt responsible for the
happiness of their less fortunate neighbours and they tried
their very best to help them. And Heaven knows it was time
that something be done!

The ideal of "economic freedom" (the "laissez faire" of
Turgot) had been necessary in the old society where mediæval
restrictions lamed all industrial effort. But this "liberty of

action" which had been the highest law of the land had led
to a terrible, yea, a frightful condition. The hours in the factory were limited only by the physical strength of the workers. As long as a woman could sit before her loom, without
fainting from fatigue, she was supposed to work. Children
of five and six were taken to the cotton mills, to save them
from the dangers of the street and a life of idleness. A law
had been passed which forced the children of paupers to go
to work or be punished by being chained to their machines.
In return for their services they got enough bad food to keep
them alive and a sort of pigsty in which they could rest at
night. Often they were so tired that they fell asleep at their
job. To keep them awake a foreman with a whip made the
rounds and beat them on the knuckles when it was necessary
to bring them back to their duties. Of course, under these
circumstances thousands of little children died. This was
regrettable and the employers, who after all were human
beings and not without a heart, sincerely wished that they
could abolish "child labour." But since man was "free" it followed that children were "free" too. Besides, if Mr. Jones had
tried to work his factory without the use of children of five
and six, his rival, Mr. Stone, would have hired an extra supply of little boys and Jones would have been forced into bankruptcy. It was therefore impossible for Jones to do without
child labour until such time as an act of Parliament should
forbid it for all employers.

But as Parliament was no longer dominated by the old
landed aristocracy (which had despised the upstart factory
owners with their money bags and had treated them with
open contempt), but was under control of the representatives
from the industrial centres, and as long as the law did not
allow workmen to combine in labour unions, very little was
accomplished. Of course the intelligent and decent people of
that time were not blind to these terrible conditions. They

were just helpless. Machinery had conquered the world by surprise and it took a great many years and the efforts of thousands of noble men and women to make the machine what it ought to be, man's servant, and not his master.

Curiously enough, the first attack upon the outrageous system of employment which was then common in all parts of the world was made on behalf of the black slaves of Africa and America. Slavery had been introduced into the American continent by the Spaniards. They had tried to use the Indians as labourers in the fields and in the mines, but the Indians, when taken away from a life in the open, had lain down and died and to save them from extinction a kind-hearted priest had suggested that negroes be brought from Africa to do the work. The negroes were strong and could stand rough treatment. Besides, association with the white man would give them a chance to learn Christianity and in this way, they would be able to save their souls, and so from every possible point of view, it would be an excellent arrangement both for the kindly white man and for his ignorant black brother. But with the introduction of machinery there had been a greater demand for cotton and the negroes were forced to work harder than ever before, and they too, like the Indians, began to die under the treatment which they received at the hands of the overseers.

Stories of incredible cruelty constantly found their way to Europe and in all countries men and women began to agitate for the abolition of slavery. In England, William Wilberforce and Zachary Macaulay (the father of the great historian whose history of England you must read if you want to know how wonderfully interesting a history-book can be) organised a society for the suppression of slavery. First of all they got a law passed which made "slave trading" illegal. And after the year 1840 there was not a single slave in any of the British colonies. The Revolution of 1848 put an end to slavery in the

French possessions. The Portuguese passed a law in the year 1858 which promised all slaves their liberty in twenty years from date. The Dutch abolished slavery in 1863 and in the same year Tsar Alexander II returned to his serfs that liberty which had been taken away from them more than two centuries before.

In the United States of America the question led to grave difficulties and a prolonged war. Although the Declaration of Independence had laid down the principle that "all men were created equal," an exception had been made for those men and women whose skins were dark and who worked on the plantations of the southern states. As time went on, the dislike of the people of the north for the institution of slavery increased and they made no secret of their feelings. The southerners, however, claimed that they could not grow their cotton without slave-labour, and for almost fifty years a mighty debate raged in both the Congress and the Senate.

The north remained obdurate and the south would not give in. When it appeared impossible to reach a compromise, the southern states threatened to leave the Union. It was a most dangerous point in the history of the Union. Many things "might" have happened. That they did not happen was the work of a very great and very good man.

On November 6 of the year 1860, Abraham Lincoln, an Illinois lawyer, and a man who had made his own intellectual fortune, had been elected president by the Republicans who were very strong in the anti-slavery states. He knew the evils of human bondage at first hand and his shrewd common-sense told him that there was no room on the northern continent for two rival nations. When a number of southern states seceded and formed the "Confederate States of America," Lincoln accepted the challenge. The northern states were called upon for volunteers. Hundreds of thousands of young men responded with eager enthusiasm and there followed four years of bitter civil war. The south, better prepared and following the brilliant leadership of Lee and Jackson, repeatedly defeated the armies of the north. Then the economic strength of New England and the west began to tell. An unknown officer by the name of Grant arose from obscurity and became the Charles Martel of the great slave war. Without interruption he hammered his mighty blows upon the crumbling defences of the South. Early in the year 1863, President Lincoln issued his "Emancipation Proclamation," which set all slaves free. In April of the year 1865 Lee surrendered the last of his brave armies at Appomattox. A few days later, President Lincoln was murdered by a lunatic. But his work was done. With the exception of Cuba, which was still under Spanish domination, slavery had come to an end in every part of the civilised world.

But while the black man was enjoying an increasing amount of liberty, the "free" workmen of Europe did not fare quite so well. Indeed, it is a matter of surprise to many contemporary writers and observers that the masses of workmen (the so-called proletariat) did not die out from sheer misery. They lived in dirty houses situated in miserable parts of the slums. They ate bad food. They received just enough schooling to fit them for their tasks. In case of death or an accident, their families were not provided for. But the brewery and distillery interests (who could exercise great influence upon the legislature) encouraged them to forget their woes by offering them unlimited quantities of whisky and gin at very cheap rates.

The enormous improvement which has taken place since the thirties and the forties of the last century is not due to the efforts of a single man. The best brains of two generations devoted themselves to the task of saving the world from the disastrous results of the all-too-sudden introduction of machinery. They did not try to destroy the capitalistic system. This would have been very foolish, for the accumulated wealth of other people, when intelligently used, may be of very great benefit to all mankind. But they tried to combat the notion that true equality can exist between the man who has wealth and owns the factories and can close their doors at will without the risk of going hungry, and the labourer who must take whatever job is offered, at whatever wage he can get, or face the risk of starvation for himself, his wife and his children.

They endeavoured to introduce a number of laws which regulated the relations between the factory owners and the factory workers. In this, the reformers have been increasingly successful in all countries. To-day, the majority of the labourers are well protected; their hours are being reduced to the excellent average of eight, and their children are sent to the schools instead of the mine pit and to the carding-room of the cotton mills.

But there were other men who also contemplated the sight of all the belching smoke-stacks, who heard the rattle of the railroad trains, who saw the store-houses filled with a surplus of all sorts of materials and who wondered to what ultimate goal this tremendous activity would lead in the years to come. They remembered that the human race had lived for hundreds of thousands of years without commercial and industrial competition. Could they change the existing order of things and do away with a system of rivalry which so often sacrificed human happiness to profits?

This idea—this vague hope for a better day—was not restricted to a single country. In England, Robert Owen, the owner of many cotton mills, established a so-called "socialistic community" which was a success. But when he died, the prosperity of New Lanark came to an end and an attempt of Louis Blanc, a French journalist, to establish "social workshops" all over France fared no better. Indeed, the increasing number of socialistic writers soon began to see that little individual communities which remained outside of the regular industrial life would never be able to accomplish anything at all. It was necessary to study the fundamental principles underlying the whole industrial and capitalistic society before useful remedies could be suggested.

The practical socialists like Robert Owen and Louis Blanc and François Fournier were succeeded by theoretical students of socialism like Karl Marx and Friedrich Engels. Of these two, Marx is the best known. He was a very brilliant man whose family had for a long time lived in Germany. He had heard of the experiments of Owen and Blanc, and he began to interest himself in questions of labour and wages and unemployment. But his liberal views made him very unpopular with the police authorities of Germany, and he was forced to flee to Brussels and then to London, where he lived a poor and shabby life as the correspondent of the "New York Tribune."

No one, thus far, had paid much attention to his books on economic subjects. But in the year 1864 he organized the first international association of working men and three years later, in 1867, he published the first volume of his well-known treatise called "Capital." Marx believed that all history was a long struggle between those who "have" and those who "don't have." The introduction and general use of machinery had created a new class in society, that of the capitalists who used their surplus wealth to buy the tools which were then used by the labourers to produce still more wealth, which was again used to build more factories and so on, until the end of time. Meanwhile, according to Marx, the third estate (the bourgeoisie) was growing richer and richer and the fourth estate (the proletariat) was growing poorer and poorer, and he predicted that in the end, one man would possess all the wealth of the world while the others would be his employees and dependent upon his good will.

To prevent such a state of affairs, Marx advised working

men of all countries to unite and to fight for a number of political and economic measures which he had enumerated in a Manifesto in the year 1848, the year of the last great European revolution.

These views of course were very unpopular with the governments of Europe; many countries, especially Prussia, passed severe laws against the socialists and policemen were ordered to break up the socialist meetings and to arrest the speakers. But that sort of persecution never does any good. Martyrs are the best possible advertisements for an unpopular cause. In Europe the number of socialists steadily increased and it was soon clear that the socialists did not contemplate a violent revolution but were using their increasing power in the different Parliaments to promote the interests of the labouring classes. Socialists were even called upon to act as Cabinet ministers, and they co-operated with progressive Catholics and Protestants to undo the damage that had been caused by the Industrial Revolution and to bring about a fairer division of the many benefits which had followed the introduction of machinery and the increased production of wealth.

60

The Age of Science

But the World Had Undergone Another Change
Which Was of Greater Importance Than Either
the Political or the Industrial Revolutions. After
Generations of Oppression and Persecution, the
Scientist Had at Last Gained Liberty of Action and
He Was Now Trying to Discover the Fundamental
Laws Which Govern the Universe

The Egyptians, the Babylonians, the Chaldeans, the Greeks and the Romans had all contributed something to the first vague notions of science and scientific investigation. But the great migrations of the fourth century had destroyed the classical world of the Mediterranean, and the Christian church, which was more interested in the life of the soul than in the life of the body, had regarded science as a manifestation of that human arrogance which wanted to pry into divine affairs which belonged to the realm of Almighty God, and which therefore was closely related to the seven deadly sins.

The Renaissance to a certain but limited extent had broken through this wall of mediæval prejudices. The Refor-

The Philosopher

mation, however, which had overtaken the Renaissance in
the early sixteenth century, had been hostile to the ideals
of the "new civilisation," and once more the men of science
were threatened with severe punishment, should they try to
pass beyond the narrow limits of knowledge which had been
laid down in holy Writ.

Our world is filled with the statues of great generals, atop
of prancing horses, leading their cheering soldiers to glorious
victory. Here and there, a modest slab of marble announces
that a man of science has found his final resting place. A
thousand years from now we shall probably do these things
differently, and the children of that happy generation shall
know of the splendid courage and the almost inconceivable
devotion to duty of the men who were the pioneers of that
abstract knowledge, which alone has made our modern
world a practical possibility.

Many of these scientific pioneers suffered poverty and
contempt and humiliation. They lived in garrets and died in
dungeons. They dared not print their names on the title-pages
of their books and they dared not print their conclusions in
the land of their birth, but smuggled the manuscripts to some
secret printing shop in Amsterdam or Haarlem. They were
exposed to the bitter enmity of the church, both Protestant
and Catholic, and were the subjects of endless sermons, incit-
ing the parishioners to violence against the "heretics."

Here and there they found an asylum. In Holland, where the spirit of tolerance was strongest, the authorities, while regarding these scientific investigations with little favour, yet refused to interfere with people's freedom of thought. It became a little asylum for intellectual liberty where French and English and German philosophers and mathematicians and physicians could go to enjoy a short spell of rest and get a breath of free air.

In another chapter I have told you how Roger Bacon, the great genius of the thirteenth century, was prevented for years from writing a single word, lest he get into new troubles with the authorities of the church. And five hundred years later, the contributors to the great philosophic "Encyclopædia" were under the constant supervision of the French gendarmerie. Half a century afterwards, Darwin, who dared to question the story of the creation of man, as revealed in the Bible, was denounced from every pulpit as an enemy of the human race. Even to-day, the persecution of those who venture into the unknown realm of science has not entirely come to an end. And while I am writing this Mr. Bryan is addressing a vast multitude on the "Menace of Darwinism," warning his hearers against the errors of the great English naturalist.

All this, however, is a mere detail. The work that has to be done invariably gets done, and the ultimate profit of the discoveries and the inventions goes to the mass of those same people who have always decried the man of vision as an unpractical idealist.

The seventeenth century had still preferred to investigate the far-off heavens and to study the position of our planet in relation to the solar system. Even so, the church had disapproved of this unseemly curiosity, and Copernicus, who first of all had proved that the sun was the centre of the universe, did not publish his work until the day of his death. Galileo spent the greater part of his life under the supervision of the

Galileo

clerical authorities, but he continued to use his telescope and provided Isaac Newton with a mass of practical observations, which greatly helped the English mathematician when he discovered the existence of that interesting habit of falling objects which came to be known as the law of gravitation.

That, for the moment at least, exhausted the interest in the heavens, and man began to study the earth. The invention of a workable microscope (a strange and clumsy little thing) by Anthony van Leeuwenhoek during the last half of the seventeenth century gave man a chance to study the "microscopic" creatures who are responsible for so many of his ailments. It laid the foundations of the science of "bacteriology" which in the last forty years has delivered the world from a great number of diseases by discovering the tiny organisms which cause the complaint. It also allowed the geologist to make a more careful study of different rocks and of the fossils (the petrified prehistoric plants) which they found deep below the surface of the earth. These investigations convinced them that the earth must be a great deal older than was stated in the book of Genesis and in the year 1830, Sir Charles Lyell published his "Principles of Geology" which denied the story of creation as related in the Bible and gave a far more wonderful description of slow growth and gradual development.

At the same time, the marquis de Laplace was working on a new theory of creation, which made the earth a little blotch in the nebulous sea out of which the planetary system had been formed, and Bunsen and Kirchhoff, by the use of the spectroscope, were investigating the chemical composition of the stars and of our good neighbour, the sun, whose curious spots had first been noticed by Galileo.

Meanwhile after a most bitter and relentless warfare with clerical authorities of Catholic and Protestant lands, the anatomists and physiologists had at last obtained permission to dissect bodies and to substitute a positive knowledge of our organs and their habits for the guesswork of the mediæval quack.

Within a single generation (between 1810 and 1840) more progress was made in every branch of science than in all the hundreds of thousands of years that had passed since man first looked at the stars and wondered why they were there. It must have been a very sad age for the people who had been educated under the old system. And we can understand their feeling of hatred for such men as Lamarck and Darwin, who did not exactly tell them that they were "descended from monkeys" (an accusation which our grandfathers seemed to regard as a personal insult) but who suggested that the proud human race had evolved from a long series of ancestors who could trace the family-tree back to the little jelly-fishes who were the first inhabitants of our planet.

The dignified world of the well-to-do middle class, which dominated the nineteenth century, was willing to make use of the gas or the electric light, of all the many practical applications of the great scientific discoveries, but the mere investigator, the man of the "scientific theory" without whom no progress would be possible, continued to be distrusted until very recently. Then, at last, his services were recognised. To-day the rich people who in past ages donated their wealth for the building of a cathedral construct vast laboratories

The Airplane

where silent men do battle upon the hidden enemies of mankind and often sacrifice their lives that coming generations may enjoy greater happiness and health.

Indeed it has come to pass that many of the ills of this world, which our ancestors regarded as inevitable "acts of God," have been exposed as manifestations of our own ignorance and neglect. Every child nowadays knows that he can keep from getting typhoid fever by a little care in the choice of his drinking water. But it took years and years of hard work before the doctors could convince the people of this fact. Few of us now fear the dentist chair. A study of the microbes that live in our mouth has made it possible to keep our teeth from decay. Must perchance a tooth be pulled, then we take a sniff of gas, and go our way rejoicing. When the newspapers of the year 1846 brought the story of the "painless operation" which had been performed in America with the help of ether, the good people of Europe shook their heads. To them it seemed against the will of God that man should escape the pain which was the share of all mortals, and it took a long time before the practice of taking ether and chloroform for operations became general.

But the battle of progress had been won. The breach in the old walls of prejudice was growing larger and larger, and as time went by, the ancient stones of ignorance came crumbling down. The eager crusaders of a new and happier social order rushed forward. Suddenly they found themselves facing a new obstacle. Out of the ruins of a long-gone past, another citadel of reaction had been erected, and millions of men had to give their lives before this last bulwark was destroyed.

61

Art

A Chapter of Art

When a baby is perfectly healthy and has had enough to eat and has slept all it wants, then it hums a little tune to show how happy it is. To grown-ups this humming means nothing. It sounds like "goo-zum, goo-zum, goo-o-o-o-o," but to the baby it is perfect music. It is his first contribution to art.

As soon as he (or she) gets a little older and is able to sit up, the period of mud-pie making begins. These mud-pies do not interest the outside world. There are too many million babies, making too many million mud-pies at the same time. But to the small infant they represent another expedition into the pleasant realm of art. The baby is now a sculptor.

At the age of three or four, when the hands begin to obey the brain, the child becomes a painter. His fond mother gives him a box of coloured chalks and every loose bit of paper is rapidly covered with strange pothooks and scrawls which represent houses and horses and terrible naval battles.

Soon, however, this happiness of just "making things" comes to an end. School begins and the greater part of the day is filled up with work. The business of living, or rather the business of "making a living," becomes the most important event in the life of every boy and girl. There is little time left for "art" between learning the tables of multiplication and the past participles of the irregular French verbs. And unless the desire for making certain things for the mere pleasure of creating them without any hope of a practical return be very strong, the child grows into manhood and forgets that the first five years of his life were mainly devoted to art.

Nations are not different from children. As soon as the caveman had escaped the threatening dangers of the long and shivering ice-period, and had put his house in order, he began to make certain things which he thought beautiful, although they were of no earthly use to him in his fight with the wild animals of the jungle. He covered the walls of his grotto with pictures of the elephants and the deer which he hunted, and out of a piece of stone, he hacked the rough figures of those women he thought most attractive.

As soon as the Egyptians and the Babylonians and the Persians and all the other people of the east had founded their little countries along the Nile and the Euphrates, they began to build magnificent palaces for their kings, invented bright pieces of jewellery for their women and planted gardens which sang happy songs of colour with their many bright flowers.

Our own ancestors, the wandering nomads from the distant Asiatic prairies, enjoying a free and easy existence as fighters and hunters, composed songs which celebrated the mighty deeds of their great leaders and invented a form of poetry which has survived until our own day. A thousand years later, when they had established themselves on the Greek mainland, and had built their "city-states," they expressed their joy (and their sorrows) in magnificent temples, in statues, in comedies and in tragedies, and in every conceivable form of art.

The Romans, like their Carthaginian rivals, were too busy administering other people and making money to have much love for "useless and unprofitable" adventures of the spirit. They conquered the world and built roads and bridges but they borrowed their art wholesale from the Greeks. They invented certain practical forms of architecture which answered the demands of their day and age. But their statues and their histories and their mosaics and their poems were mere Latin imitations of Greek originals. Without that vague and hard-to-define something which the world calls "personality," there can be no art and the Roman world distrusted that particular sort of personality. The empire needed efficient soldiers and tradesmen. The business of writing poetry or making pictures was left to foreigners.

Then came the Dark Ages. The barbarian was the proverbial bull in the china-shop of western Europe. He had no use for what he did not understand. Speaking in terms of the year 1921, he liked the magazine covers of pretty ladies, but threw the Rembrandt etchings which he had inherited into the ashcan. Soon he came to learn better. Then he tried to undo the damage which he had created a few years before. But the ashcans were gone and so were the pictures.

But by this time, his own art, which he had brought with him from the east, had developed into something very beautiful and he made up for his past neglect and indifference by the so-called "art of the Middle Ages" which as far as northern Europe is concerned was a product of the Germanic mind and had borrowed but little from the Greeks and the Latins and nothing at all from the older forms of art of Egypt and Assyria, not to speak of India and China, which simply did not exist, as far as the people of that time were concerned. Indeed, so little had the northern races been influenced by their southern neighbours that their own architectural products were completely misunderstood by the people of Italy and were treated by them with downright and unmitigated contempt.

You have all heard the word "Gothic." You probably asso-
ciate it with the picture of a lovely old cathedral, lifting its
slender spires towards high Heaven. But what does the word
really mean?

It means something "uncouth" and "barbaric"—something which one might expect from an "uncivilised Goth,"
a rough backwoods-man who had no respect for the established rules of classical art and who built his "modern horrors" to please his own low tastes without a decent regard for
the examples of the Forum and the Acropolis.

And yet for several centuries this form of Gothic architecture was the highest expression of the sincere feeling for art
which inspired the whole northern continent. From a previous chapter, you will remember how the people of the late
Middle Ages lived. Unless they were peasants and dwelt in
villages, they were citizens of a "city" or "civitas," the old
Latin name for a tribe. And indeed, behind their high walls
and their deep moats, these good burghers were true tribesmen who shared the common dangers and enjoyed the common safety and prosperity which they derived from their
system of mutual protection.

In the old Greek and Roman cities the market-place, where
the temple stood, had been the centre of civic life. During the
Middle Ages, the church, the House of God, became such a
centre. We modern Protestant people, who go to our church
only once a week, and then for a few hours only, hardly know
what a mediæval church meant to the community. Then,
before you were a week old, you were taken to the church
to be baptised. As a child, you visited the church to learn the
holy stories of the Scriptures. Later on you became a member of the congregation, and if you were rich enough you
built yourself a separate little chapel sacred to the memory of
the patron saint of your own family. As for the sacred edifice,
it was open at all hours of the day and many of the night. In a

certain sense it resembled a modern club, dedicated to all the inhabitants of the town. In the church you very likely caught a first glimpse of the girl who was to become your bride at a great ceremony before the high altar. And finally, when the end of the journey had come, you were buried beneath the stones of this familiar building, that all your children and their grandchildren might pass over your grave until the Day of Judgement.

Because the church was not only the House of God but also the true centre of all common life, the building had to be different from anything that had ever been constructed by the hands of man. The temples of the Egyptians and the Greeks and the Romans had been merely the shrine of a local divinity. As no sermons were preached before the images of Osiris or Zeus or Jupiter, it was not necessary that the interior offer space for a great multitude. All the religious processions of the old Mediterranean peoples took place in the open. But in the north, where the weather was usually bad, most functions were held under the roof of the church.

During many centuries the architects struggled with this problem of constructing a building that was large enough. The Roman tradition taught them how to build heavy stone walls with very small windows lest the walls lose their strength. On the top of this they then placed a heavy stone roof. But in the twelfth century, after the beginning of the Crusades, when the architects had seen the pointed arches of the Mohammedan builders, the western builders discovered a new style which gave them their first chance to make the sort of building which those days of an intense religious life demanded. And then they developed this strange style upon which the Italians bestowed the contemptuous name of "Gothic" or barbaric. They achieved their purpose by inventing a vaulted roof which was supported by "ribs." But such a roof, if it became too heavy, was apt to break the

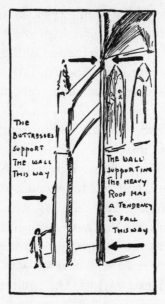

Gothic Architecture

walls, just as a man of three hundred pounds sitting down upon a child's chair will force it to collapse. To overcome this difficulty, certain French architects then began to re-enforce the walls with "buttresses" which were merely heavy masses of stone against which the walls could lean while they supported the roof. And to assure the further safety of the roof they supported the ribs of the roof by so-called "flying buttresses," a very simple method of construction which you will understand at once when you look at our picture.

This new method of construction allowed the introduction of enormous windows. In the twelfth century, glass was still an expensive curiosity, and very few private buildings possessed glass windows. Even the castles of the nobles were without protection and this accounts for the eternal drafts and explains why people of that day wore furs in-doors as well as out.

Fortunately, the art of making coloured glass, with which

the ancient people of the Mediterranean had been familiar, had not been entirely lost. There was a revival of stained glass-making and soon the windows of the Gothic churches told the stories of the Holy Book in little bits of brilliantly coloured window-pane, which were caught in a long framework of lead.

Behold, therefore, the new and glorious house of God, filled with an eager multitude, "living" its religion as no people have ever done either before or since! Nothing is considered too good or too costly or too wondrous for this House of God and Home of Man. The sculptors, who since the destruction of the Roman Empire have been out of employment, haltingly return to their noble art. Portals and pillars and buttresses and cornices are all covered with carven images of our Lord and the blessed saints. The embroiderers too are set to work to make tapestries for the walls. The jewellers offer their highest art that the shrine of the altar may be worthy of complete adoration. Even the painter does his best. Poor man, he is greatly handicapped by lack of a suitable medium.

And thereby hangs a story.

The Romans of the early Christian period had covered the floors and the walls of their temples and houses with mosaics, pictures made of coloured bits of glass. But this art had been exceedingly difficult. It gave the painter no chance to express all he wanted to say, as all children know who have ever tried to make figures out of coloured blocks of wood. The art of mosaic painting therefore died out during the late Middle Ages except in Russia, where the Byzantine mosaic painters had found a refuge after the fall of Constantinople and continued to ornament the walls of the Orthodox churches until the day of the Bolsheviki, when there was an end to the building of churches.

Of course, the mediæval painter could mix his colours with the water of the wet plaster which was put upon the walls of the churches. This method of painting upon "fresh plaster" (which was generally called "fresco" or "fresh" painting) was very popular for many centuries. To-day, it is as rare as the art of painting miniatures in manuscripts and among the hundreds of artists of our modern cities there is perhaps one who can handle this medium successfully. But during the Middle Ages there was no other way and the artists were "fresco" workers for lack of something better. The method, however, had certain great disadvantages. Very often the plaster came off the walls after only a few years, or dampness spoiled the pictures, just as dampness will spoil the pattern of our wall paper. People tried every imaginable expedient to get away from this plaster background. They tried to mix their colours with wine and vinegar and with honey and with the sticky white of egg, but none of these methods were satisfactory. For more than a thousand years these experiments continued. In painting pictures upon the parchment leaves of manuscripts the mediæval artists were very successful. But when it came to covering large spaces of wood or stone with paint which would stick, they did not succeed very well.

At last, during the first half of the fifteenth century, the problem was solved in the southern Netherlands by Jan and Hubert van Eyck. The famous Flemish brothers mixed their paint with specially prepared oils and this allowed them to use wood and canvas or stone or anything else as a background for their pictures.

But by this time the religious ardour of the early Middle Ages was a thing of the past. The rich burghers of the cities were succeeding the bishops as patrons of the arts. And as art invariably follows the full dinner-pail, the artists now began to work for these worldly employers and painted pictures for kings, for grand dukes and for rich bankers. Within a very short time, the new method of painting with oil spread through Europe and in every country there developed a school of special painting which showed the characteristic tastes of the people for whom these portraits and landscapes were made.

In Spain, for example, Velasquez painted court-dwarfs and the weavers of the royal tapestry-factories, and all sorts of persons and subjects connected with the king and his court. But in Holland, Rembrandt and Frans Hals and Vermeer painted the barnyard of the merchant's house, and they painted his rather dowdy wife and his healthy but bumptious children and the ships which had brought him his wealth. In Italy, on the other hand, where the Pope remained the largest patron of the arts, Michelangelo and Correggio continued to paint Madonnas and saints, while in England, where the aristocracy was very rich and powerful, and in France, where the kings had become uppermost in the state, the artists painted distinguished gentlemen who were members of the government, and very lovely ladies who were friends of His Majesty.

The great change in painting, which came about with the neglect of the old church and the rise of a new class in society, was reflected in all other forms of art. The invention of printing had made it possible for authors to win fame and reputation by writing books for the multitudes. In this way arose the profession of the novelist and the illustrator. But the people who had money enough to buy the new books were not the sort who liked to sit at home of nights, looking at the ceiling or just sitting. They wanted to be amused. The few minstrels of the Middle Ages were not sufficient to cover the demand for entertainment. For the first time since the early Greek city-states of two thousand years before, the professional playwright had a chance to ply his trade. The Middle Ages had known the theatre merely as part of certain church celebrations. The tragedies of the thirteenth and fourteenth centuries had told the story of the suffering of our Lord. But during the sixteenth century the worldly theatre made its reappearance. It is true that, at first, the position of the professional playwright and actor was not a very high one. William Shakespeare was regarded as a sort of circus-fellow who amused his neighbours with his tragedies and comedies. But when he died in the year 1616 he had begun to enjoy the respect of his neighbours and actors were no longer subjects of police supervision.

William's contemporary, Lope de Vega, the incredible Spaniard who wrote no less than eighteen hundred worldly and four hundred religious plays, was a person of rank who received the Papal approval upon his work. A century later, Molière, the Frenchman, was deemed worthy of the companionship of none less than King Louis XIV.

Since then, the theatre has enjoyed an ever increasing affection on the part of the people. To-day a "theatre" is part of every well-regulated city, and the "silent drama" of the movies has penetrated to the tiniest of our prairie hamlets.

Another art, however, was to become the most popular of all. That was music. Most of the old art-forms demanded a great deal of technical skill. It takes years and years of practice before our clumsy hand is able to follow the commands of the brain and reproduce our vision upon canvas or in marble. It takes a lifetime to learn how to act or how to write a good novel. And it takes a great deal of training on the part of the public to appreciate the best in painting and writing and sculpture. But almost any one, not entirely tone-deaf, can follow a tune and almost everybody can get enjoyment out of some sort of music. The Middle Ages had heard a little music but it had been entirely the music of the church. The holy chants were subject to very severe laws of rhythm and harmony and soon these became monotonous. Besides, they could not well be sung in the street or in the market-place.

The Renaissance changed this. Music once more came into its own as the best friend of man, both in his happiness and in his sorrows.

The Egyptians and the Babylonians and the ancient Jews had all been great lovers of music. They had even combined different instruments into regular orchestras. But the Greeks had frowned upon this barbaric foreign noise. They liked to hear a man recite the stately poetry of Homer and Pindar. They allowed him to accompany himself upon the lyre (the poorest of all stringed instruments). That was as far as any one could go without incurring the risk of popular disapproval. The Romans, on the other hand, had loved orchestral music at their dinners and parties and they had invented most of the instruments which (in *very* modified form) we use to-day. The early church had despised this music which smacked too much of the wicked pagan world which had just been destroyed. A few songs rendered by the entire congregation were all the bishops of the third and fourth centuries would tolerate. As the congregation was apt to sing dreadfully out of key without the guidance of an instrument, the church had afterwards allowed the use of an organ, an invention of the second century of our era which consisted of a combination of the old pipes of Pan and a pair of bellows.

Then came the great migrations. The last of the Roman musicians were either killed or became tramp-fiddlers going from city to city and playing in the street, and begging for pennies like the harpist on a modern ferry boat.

But the revival of a more worldly civilisation in the cities of the late Middle Ages had created a new demand for musicians. Instruments like the horn, which had been used only as signal-instruments for hunting and fighting, were remodelled until they could reproduce sounds which were agreeable in the dance-hall and in the banqueting room. A bow strung with horse-hair was used to play the old-fashioned

The Troubadour

guitar and before the end of the Middle Ages this six-stringed instrument (the most ancient of all string-instruments which dates back to Egypt and Assyria) had grown into our modern four-stringed fiddle which Stradivarius and the other Italian violin-makers of the eighteenth century brought to the height of perfection.

And finally the modern piano was invented, the most widespread of all musical instruments, which has followed man into the wilderness of the jungle and the ice-fields of Greenland. The organ had been the first of all keyed instruments but the performer always depended upon the co-operation of some one who worked the bellows, a job which nowadays is done by electricity. The musicians therefore looked for a handier and less circumstantial instrument to assist them in training the pupils of the many church choirs. During the great eleventh century, Guido, a Benedictine monk of the town of Arezzo (the birthplace of the poet Petrarch), gave us our modern system of musical annotation. Some time during that century, when there was a great deal of popular interest in music, the first instrument with both keys and strings was built. It must have sounded as tinkly as one of those tiny children's pianos which you can buy at every toy-shop. In the city of Vienna, the town where the strolling musicians of the

Middle Ages (who had been classed with jugglers and card sharps) had formed the first separate guild of musicians in the year 1288, the little monochord was developed into something which we can recognise as the direct ancestor of our modern Steinway. From Austria the "clavichord" as it was usually called in those days (because it had "claves" or keys) went to Italy. There it was perfected into the "spinet" which was so called after the inventor, Giovanni Spinetti of Venice. At last during the eighteenth century, some time between 1709 and 1720, Bartolomeo Cristofori made a "clavier" which allowed the performer to play both loudly and softly or, as it was said in Italian, "piano" and "forte." This instrument with certain changes became our "pianoforte" or piano.

Then for the first time the world possessed an easy and convenient instrument which could be mastered in a couple of years and did not need the eternal tuning of harps and fiddles and was much pleasanter to the ears than the mediæval tubas, clarinets, trombones and oboes. Just as the phonograph has given millions of modern people their first love of music so did the early "pianoforte" carry the knowledge of music into much wider circles. Music became part of the education of every well-bred man and woman. Princes and rich merchants maintained private orchestras. The musicians ceased to be a wandering "jongleur" and became a highly valued member of the community. Music was added to the dramatic performances of the theatre and out of this practice grew our modern opera. Originally only a few very rich princes could afford the expenses of an "opera troupe." But as the taste for this sort of entertainment grew, many cities built their own theatres where Italian and afterwards German operas were given to the unlimited joy of the whole community with the exception of a few sects of very strict Christians who still regarded music with deep suspicion as something which was too lovely to be entirely good for the soul.

By the middle of the eighteenth century the musical life
of Europe was in full swing. Then there came forward a man
who was greater than all others, a simple organist of the
Thomas Church of Leipzig, by the name of Johann Sebastian
Bach. In his compositions for every known instrument, from
comic songs and popular dances to the most stately of sacred
hymns and oratorios, he laid the foundation for all our modern music. When he died in the year 1750 he was succeeded
by Mozart, who created musical fabrics of sheer loveliness
which remind us of lace that has been woven out of harmony
and rhythm. Then came Ludwig van Beethoven, the most
tragic of men, who gave us our modern orchestra, yet heard
none of his greatest compositons because he was deaf, as the
result of a cold contracted during his years of poverty.

Beethoven lived through the period of the great French
Revolution. Full of hope for a new and glorious day, he had
dedicated one of his symphonies to Napoleon. But he lived
to regret the hour. When he died in the year 1827, Napoleon
was gone and the French Revolution was gone, but the steam
engine had come and was filling the world with a sound
that had nothing in common with the dreams of the Third
Symphony.

Indeed, the new order of steam and iron and coal and
large factories had little use for art, for painting and sculpture and poetry and music. The old protectors of the arts,
the church and the princes and the merchants of the Middle
Ages and the seventeenth and eighteenth centuries, no longer existed. The leaders of the new industrial world were too
busy and had too little education to bother about etchings
and sonatas and bits of carved ivory, not to speak of the men
who created those things, and who were of no practical use
to the community in which they lived. And the workmen
in the factories listened to the drone of their engines until
they too had lost all taste for the melody of the flute or fiddle

of their peasant ancestry. The arts became the step-children of the new industrial era. Art and life became entirely separated. Whatever paintings had been left, were dying a slow death in the museums. And music became a monopoly of a few "virtuosi" who took the music away from the home and carried it to the concert-hall.

But steadily, although slowly, the arts are coming back into their own. People begin to understand that Rembrandt and Beethoven and Rodin are the true prophets and leaders of their race and that a world without art and happiness resembles a nursery without laughter.

62

Colonial Expansion and War

A Chapter Which Ought to Give You a Great
Deal of Political Information About the Last
Fifty Years, But Which Really Contains Several
Explanations and a Few Apologies

If I had known how difficult it was to write a history of the
world, I should never have undertaken the task. Of course,
any one possessed of enough industry to lose himself for half
a dozen years in the musty stacks of a library can compile
a ponderous tome which gives an account of the events in
every land during every century. But that was not the purpose of the present book. The publishers wanted to print a
history that should have rhythm—a story which galloped
rather than walked. And now that I have almost finished I
discover that certain chapters gallop, that others wade slowly
through the dreary sands of long-forgotten ages—that a
few parts do not make any progress at all, while still others
indulge in a veritable jazz of action and romance. I did not
like this and I suggested that we destroy the whole manuscript and begin once more from the beginning. This, however, the publishers would not allow.

As the next best solution of my difficulties, I took the

typewritten pages to a number of charitable friends and asked them to read what I had said, and give me the benefit of their advice. The experience was rather disheartening. Each and every man had his own prejudices and his own hobbies and preferences. They all wanted to know why, where and how I dared to omit their pet nation, their pet statesman or even their most beloved criminal. With some of them, Napoleon and Jenghiz Khan were candidates for high honours. I explained that I had tried very hard to be fair to Napoleon, but that in my estimation he was greatly inferior to such men as George Washington, Gustavus Wasa, Augustus, Hammurabi or Lincoln, and a score of others, all of whom were obliged to content themselves with a few paragraphs, from sheer lack of space. As for Jenghiz Khan, I only recognise his

The Pioneer

superior ability in the field of wholesale murder and I did not intend to give him any more publicity than I could help.

"This is very well as far as it goes," said the next critic, "but how about the Puritans? We are celebrating the tercentenary of their arrival at Plymouth. They ought to have more space." My answer was that if I were writing a history of America, the Puritans would get fully one-half of the first twelve chapters; that, however, this was a history of mankind and that the event on Plymouth Rock was not a matter of far-reaching international importance until many centuries later; that the United States had been founded by thirteen colonies and not by a single one; that the most prominent leaders of the first twenty years of our history had been from Virginia, from Pennsylvania and from the island of Nevis, rather than from Massachusetts, and that therefore the Puritans ought to content themselves with a page of print and a special map.

Next came the prehistoric specialist. Why in the name of the great Tyrannosaur had I not devoted more space to the wonderful race of Cro-Magnon men, who had developed such a high stage of civilisation ten thousand years ago?

Indeed, and why not? The reason is simple. I do not take as much stock in the perfection of these early races as some of our most noted anthropologists seem to do. Rousseau and the philosophers of the eighteenth century created the "noble savage" who was supposed to have dwelt in a state of perfect happiness during the beginning of time. Our modern scientists have discarded the "noble savage," so dearly beloved by our grandfathers, and they have replaced him by the "splendid savage" of the French valleys who thirty-five thousand years ago made an end to the universal rule of the low-browed and low-living brutes of the Neanderthal and other Germanic neighbourhoods. They have shown us the elephants the Cro-Magnon painted and the statues he carved and they have surrounded him with much glory.

I do not mean to say that they are wrong. But I hold that we know by far too little of this entire period to re-construct that early west European society with any degree (however humble) of accuracy. And I would rather not state certain things than run the risk of stating certain things that were not so.

Then there were other critics, who accused me of direct

unfairness. Why did I leave out such countries as Ireland and Bulgaria and Siam while I dragged in such other countries as Holland and Iceland and Switzerland? My answer was that I did not drag in any countries. They pushed themselves in by main force of circumstances, and I simply could not keep them out. And in order that my point may be understood, let me state the basis upon which active membership to this book of history was considered.

There was but one rule. "Did the country or the person in question produce a new idea or perform an original act without which the history of the entire human race would have been different?" It was not a question of personal taste. It was a matter of cool, almost mathematical judgement. No race ever played a more picturesque rôle in history than the Mongolians, and no race, from the point of view of achievement or intelligent progress, was of less value to the rest of mankind.

The career of Tiglath-Pileser, the Assyrian, is full of dramatic episodes. But as far as we are concerned, he might just as well never have existed at all. In the same way, the history of the Dutch Republic is not interesting because once upon a time the sailors of de Ruyter went fishing in the River Thames, but rather because of the fact that this small mud-bank along the shores of the North Sea offered a hospitable asylum to all sorts of strange people who had all sorts of queer ideas upon all sorts of very unpopular subjects.

It is quite true that Athens or Florence, during the hey-day of their glory, had only one-tenth of the population of Kansas City. But our present civilisation would be very different had neither of these two little cities of the Mediterranean basin existed. And the same (with due apologies to the good people of Wyandotte County) can hardly be said of this busy metropolis on the Missouri River.

And since I am being very personal, allow me to state one other fact.

When we visit a doctor, we find out before hand whether he is a surgeon or a diagnostician or a homeopath or a faith healer, for we want to know from what angle he will look at our complaint. We ought to be as careful in the choice of our historians as we are in the selection of our physicians. We think, "Oh well, history is history," and let it go at that. But the writer who was educated in a strictly Presbyterian household somewhere in the backwoods of Scotland will look differently upon every question of human relationships from his neighbour who as a child was dragged to listen to the brilliant exhortations of Robert Ingersoll, the enemy of all revealed devils. In due course of time, both men may forget their early training and never again visit either church or lecture hall. But the influence of these impressionable years stays with them and they cannot escape showing it in whatever they write or say or do.

In the preface to this book, I told you that I should not be an infallible guide and now that we have almost reached the end, I repeat the warning. I was born and educated in an atmosphere of the old-fashioned liberalism which had followed the discoveries of Darwin and the other pioneers of the nineteenth century. As a child, I happened to spend most of my waking hours with an uncle who was a great collector of the books written by Montaigne, the great French essayist of the sixteenth century. Because I was born in Rotterdam and educated in the city of Gouda, I ran continually across Erasmus and for some unknown reason this great exponent of tolerance took hold of my intolerant self. Later I discovered Anatole France and my first experience with the English language came about through an accidental encounter with Thackeray's "Henry Esmond," a story which made more impression upon me than any other book in the English language.

If I had been born in a pleasant middle western city I probably should have a certain affection for the hymns which

I had heard in my childhood. But my earliest recollection of music goes back to the afternoon when my mother took me to hear nothing less than a Bach fugue. And the mathematical perfection of the great Protestant master influenced me to such an extent that I cannot hear the usual hymns of our prayer-meetings without a feeling of intense agony and direct pain.

Again, if I had been born in Italy and had been warmed by the sunshine of the happy valley of the Arno, I might love many colourful and sunny pictures which now leave me indifferent because I got my first artistic impressions in a country where the rare sun beats down upon the rain-soaked land with almost cruel brutality and throws everything into violent contrasts of dark and light. I state these few facts deliberately that you may know the personal bias of the man who wrote this history and may understand his point-of-view.

After this short but necessary excursion, we return to the history of the last fifty years. Many things happened during this period but very little occurred which at the time seemed to be of paramount importance. The majority of the greater

The Conquest of the West

powers ceased to be mere political agencies and became large business enterprises. They built railroads. They founded and subsidized steam-ship lines to all parts of the world. They connected their different possessions with telegraph wires. And they steadily increased their holdings in other continents. Every available bit of African or Asiatic territory was claimed by one of the rival powers. France became a colonial nation with interests in Algiers and Madagascar and Annam and Tonkin (in eastern Asia). Germany claimed parts of south-west and east Africa, built settlements in Kameroon on the west coast of Africa and in New Guinea and many of the islands of the Pacific, and used the murder of a few missionaries as a welcome excuse to take the harbour of Kiaouchau on the Yellow Sea in China. Italy tried her luck in Abyssinia, was disastrously defeated by the soldiers of the Negus and consoled herself by occupying the Turkish possessions in Tripoli in northern Africa. Russia, having occupied all of Siberia, took Port Arthur away from China. Japan, having defeated China in the war of 1895, occupied the island of Formosa and in the year 1905 began to lay claim to the entire empire of Corea. In the year 1883 England, the largest colonial empire the world has ever seen, undertook to "protect" Egypt. She performed this task most efficiently and to the great material benefit of that much-neglected country, which ever since the opening of the Suez Canal in 1868 had been threatened with a foreign invasion. During the next thirty years she fought a number of colonial wars in different parts of the world and in 1902 (after three years of bitter fighting) she conquered the independent Boer republics of the Transvaal and the Orange Free State. Meanwhile she had encouraged Cecil Rhodes to lay the foundations for a great African state, which reached from the Cape almost to the mouth of the Nile, and had faithfully picked up such islands or provinces as had been left without a European owner.

The shrewd king of Belgium, by name Leopold, used the discoveries of Henry Stanley to found the Congo Free State in the year 1885. Originally this gigantic tropical empire was an "absolute monarchy." But after many years of scandalous mismanagement, it was annexed by the Belgian people who made it a colony (in the year 1908) and abolished the terrible abuses which had been tolerated by this very unscrupulous Majesty, who cared nothing for the fate of the natives as long as he got his ivory and rubber.

As for the United States, they had so much land that they desired no further territory. But the terrible misrule of Cuba, one of the last of the Spanish possessions in the western hemisphere, practically forced the Washington government to take action. After a short and rather uneventful war, the Spaniards were driven out of Cuba and Puerto Rico and the Philippines, and the two latter became colonies of the United States.

This economic development of the world was perfectly natural. The increasing number of factories in England and France and Germany needed an ever increasing amount of raw materials and the equally increasing number of European workers needed an ever increasing amount of food. Everywhere the cry was for more and for richer markets, for more easily accessible coal mines and iron mines and rubber plantations and oil-wells, for greater supplies of wheat and grain.

The purely political events of the European continent dwindled to mere insignificance in the eyes of men who were making plans for steamboat lines on Victoria Nyanza or for railroads through the interior of Shantung. They knew that many European questions still remained to be settled, but they did not bother, and through sheer indifference and carelessness they bestowed upon their descendants a terrible inheritance of hate and misery. For untold centuries the

south-eastern corner of Europe had been the scene of rebellion and bloodshed. During the seventies of the last century
the people of Serbia and Bulgaria and Montenegro and Roumania were once more trying to gain their freedom and the
Turks (with the support of many of the western powers) were
trying to prevent this.

After a period of particularly atrocious massacres in Bulgaria in the year 1876, the Russian people lost all patience. The
government was forced to intervene just as President McKin-
ley was obliged to go to Cuba and stop the shooting-squads
of General Weyler in Havana. In April of the year 1877 the
Russian armies crossed the Danube, stormed the Shipka pass
and, after the capture of Plevna, marched southward until
they reached the gates of Constantinople. Turkey appealed
for help to England. There were many English people who
denounced their government when it took the side of the sultan. But Disraeli (who had just made Queen Victoria empress
of India and who loved the picturesque Turks while he hated
the Russians who were brutally cruel to the Jewish people
within their frontiers) decided to interfere. Russia was forced
to conclude the peace of San Stefano (1878) and the question
of the Balkans was left to a congress which convened at Berlin in June and July of the same year.

This famous conference was entirely dominated by the
personality of Disraeli. Even Bismarck feared the clever old
man with his well-oiled curly hair and his supreme arrogance, tempered by a cynical sense of humour and a marvellous gift for flattery. At Berlin the British prime minister
carefully watched over the fate of his friends the Turks.
Montenegro, Serbia and Roumania were recognised as independent kingdoms. The principality of Bulgaria was given
a semi-independent status under Prince Alexander of Bat-
tenberg, a nephew of Tsar Alexander II. But none of those
countries were given the chance to develop their powers

and their resources as they would have been able to do, had England been less anxious about the fate of the sultan, whose domains were necessary to the safety of the British Empire as a bulwark against further Russian aggression.

To make matters worse, the congress allowed Austria to take Bosnia and Herzegovina away from the Turks to be "administered" as part of the Habsburg domains. It is true that Austria made an excellent job of it. The neglected provinces were as well managed as the best of the British colonies, and that is saying a great deal. But they were inhabited by many Serbians. In older days they had been part of the great Serbian empire of Stephan Dushan, who early in the fourteenth century had defended western Europe against the invasions of the Turks and whose capital of Uskub had been a centre of civilisation 150 years before Columbus discovered the new lands of the west. The Serbians remembered their ancient glory as who would not? They resented the presence of the Austrians in two provinces which, so they felt, were theirs by every right of tradition.

And it was in Sarajevo, the capital of Bosnia, that the archduke Ferdinand, heir to the Austrian throne, was murdered on June 28 of the year 1914. The assassin was a Serbian student who had acted from purely patriotic motives.

But the blame for this terrible catastrophe which was the immediate though not the only cause of the Great World War did not lie with the half-crazy Serbian boy or his Austrian victim. It must be traced back to the days of the famous Berlin Conference when Europe was too busy building a material civilisation to care about the aspirations and the dreams of a forgotten race in a dreary corner of the old Balkan peninsula.

63

A New World

The Great War, Which Was Really the Struggle for a New and Better World

The marquis de Condorcet was one of the noblest charac-ters among the small group of honest enthusiasts who were responsible for the outbreak of the great French Revolution. He had devoted his life to the cause of the poor and the unfortunate. He had been one of the assistants of d'Alembert and Diderot when they wrote their famous "Encyclopédie." During the first years of the Revolution he had been the leader of the moderate wing of the Convention.

His tolerance, his kindliness, his stout common sense had made him an object of suspicion when the treason of the king and the court clique had given the extreme radicals their chance to get hold of the government and kill their oppo-nents. Condorcet was declared "hors de loi," or outlawed, an outcast who was henceforth at the mercy of every true patriot. His friends offered to hide him at their own peril. Condorcet refused to accept their sacrifice. He escaped and tried to reach his home, where he might be safe. After three nights in the open, torn and bleeding, he entered an inn and asked for some food. The suspicious yokels searched him and in his pockets they found a copy of Horace, the Latin poet.

This showed that their prisoner was a man of gentle breeding and had no business upon the highroads at a time when every educated person was regarded as an enemy of the revolutionary state. They took Condorcet and they bound him and they gagged him and they threw him into the village lock-up, but in the morning when the soldiers came to drag him back to Paris and cut his head off, behold! he was dead.

This man who had given all and had received nothing had good reason to despair of the human race. But he has written a few sentences which ring as true to-day as they did one hundred and thirty years ago. I repeat them here for your benefit.

"Nature has set no limits to our hopes," he wrote, "and the picture of the human race, now freed from its chains and marching with a firm tread on the road of truth and virtue and happiness, offers to the philosopher a spectacle which consoles him for the errors, for the crimes and the injustices which still pollute and afflict this earth."

The world has just passed through an agony of pain compared to which the French Revolution was a mere incident. The shock has been so great that it has killed the last spark of hope in the breasts of millions of men. They were chanting a hymn of progress, and four years of slaughter followed their prayers for peace. "Is it worth while," so they ask, "to work and slave for the benefit of creatures who have not yet passed beyond the stage of the earliest cave-men?"

War

There is but one answer.

That answer is "Yes!"

The World War was a terrible calamity. But it did not mean the end of things. On the contrary it brought about the coming of a new day.

It is easy to write a history of Greece and Rome or the Middle Ages. The actors who played their parts upon that long-forgotten stage are all dead. We can criticize them with a cool head. The audience that applauded their efforts has dispersed. Our remarks cannot possibly hurt their feelings.

But it is very difficult to give a true account of contemporary events. The problems that fill the minds of the people with whom we pass through life are our own problems, and they hurt us too much or they please us too well to be described with that fairness which is necessary when we are writing history and not blowing the trumpet of propaganda. All the same I shall endeavour to tell you why I agree with poor Condorcet when he expressed his firm faith in a better future.

Often before have I warned you against the false impression which is created by the use of our so-called historical epochs which divide the story of man into four parts, the ancient world, the Middle Ages, the Renaissance and the Reformation, and Modern Time. The last of these terms is the most dangerous. The word "modern" implies that we, the people of the twentieth century, are at the top of human achievement. Fifty years ago the liberals of England who followed the leadership of Gladstone felt that the problem of a truly representative and democratic form of government had been solved forever by the second great Reform Bill, which gave workmen an equal share in the government with their employers. When Disraeli and his conservative friends talked of a dangerous "leap in the dark" they answered "No." They felt certain of their cause and trusted that henceforth all classes of society would co-operate to make the government of their common country a success. Since then many things have happened, and the few liberals who are still alive begin to understand that they were mistaken.

There is no definite answer to any historical problem.

Every generation must fight the good fight anew or perish as those sluggish animals of the prehistoric world have perished.

If you once get hold of this great truth you will get a new and much broader view of life. Then, go one step further and try to imagine yourself in the position of your own great-great-grandchildren who will take your place in the year 10,000. They too will learn history. But what will they think of those short 4,000 years during which we have kept a written record of our actions and of our thoughts? They will think of Napoleon as a contemporary of Tiglath-Pileser, the Assyrian conqueror. Perhaps they will confuse him with Jenghiz Khan or Alexander the Macedonian. The Great War which has just come to an end will appear in the light of that long commercial conflict which settled the supremacy of the Mediterranean when Rome and Carthage fought during 128 years for the mastery of the sea. The Balkan troubles of the nineteenth century (the struggle for freedom of Serbia and Greece and Bulgaria and Montenegro) to them will seem a continuation of the disordered conditions caused by the great migrations. They will look at pictures of the Reims cathedral which only yesterday was destroyed by German guns as we look upon a photograph of the Acropolis ruined 250 years ago during a war between the Turks and the Venetians. They will regard the fear of death, which is still common among many people, as a childish superstition which was perhaps natural in a race of men who had burned witches as late as the year 1692. Even our hospitals and our laboratories and our operating rooms of which we are so proud will look like slightly improved workshops of alchemists and mediæval surgeons.

And the reason for all this is simple. We modern men and women are not "modern" at all. On the contrary we still belong to the last generations of the cave-dwellers. The foundation for a new era was laid but yesterday. The human race was given its first chance to become truly civilised when it took courage to question all things and made "knowledge and understanding" the foundation upon which to create a more reasonable and sensible society of human beings. The Great War was the "growing-pain" of this new world.

For a long time to come people will write mighty books to prove that this or that or the other person brought about the war. The socialists will publish volumes in which they will accuse the "capitalists" of having brought about the war for "commercial gain." The capitalists will answer that they lost infinitely more through the war than they made—that their children were among the first to go and fight and be killed— and they will show how in every country the bankers tried their very best to avert the outbreak of hostilities. French historians will go through the register of German sins from the days of Charlemagne until the days of William of Hohenzollern and German historians will return the compliment and will go through the list of French horrors from the days of Charlemagne until the days of President Poincaré. And then they will establish to their own satisfaction that the other fellow was guilty of "causing the war." Statesmen, dead and not yet dead in all countries will take to their typewriters and they will explain how they tried to avert hostilities and how their wicked opponents forced them into it.

The historian, a hundred years hence, will not bother about these apologies and vindications. He will understand the real nature of the underlying causes and he will know that personal ambitions and personal wickedness and personal greed had very little to do with the final outburst. The original mistake, which was responsible for all this misery, was committed when our scientists began to create a new

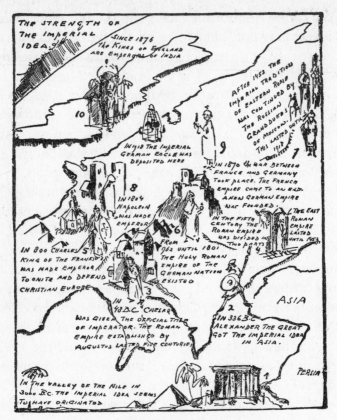

The Spread of the Imperial Idea

world of steel and iron and chemistry and electricity and forgot that the human mind is slower than the proverbial turtle, is lazier than the well-known sloth, and marches from one hundred to three hundred years behind the small group of courageous leaders.

A wolf in sheep's clothing is still a wolf. A dog trained to ride a bicycle and smoke a pipe is still a dog. And a human being with the mind of a sixteenth century tradesman driving a 1921 Rolls-Royce is still a human being with the mind of a sixteenth century tradesman.

If you do not understand this at first, read it again. It will become clearer to you in a moment and it will explain many things that have happened these last six years.

Perhaps I may give you another, more familiar, example to show you what I mean. In the movie theatres, jokes and funny remarks are often thrown upon the screen. Watch the audience the next time you have a chance. A few people seem almost to inhale the words. It takes them but a second to read the lines. Others are a bit slower. Still others take from twenty to thirty seconds. Finally those men and women who do not read any more than they can help get the point when the brighter ones among the audience have already begun to decipher the next cut-in. It is not different in human life, as I shall now show you.

In a former chapter I have told you how the idea of the Roman Empire continued to live for a thousand years after the death of the last Roman emperor. It caused the establishment of a large number of "imitation empires." It gave the bishops of Rome a chance to make themselves the head of the entire church, because they represented the idea of Roman world-supremacy. It drove a number of perfectly harmless barbarian chieftains into a career of crime and endless warfare because they were forever under the spell of this magic word "Rome." All these people, Popes, emperors and plain fighting men, were not very different from you or me. But they lived in a world where the Roman tradition was a vital issue—something living—something which was remembered clearly both by the father and the son and the grandson. And so they struggled and sacrificed themselves for a cause which to-day would not find a dozen recruits.

In still another chapter I have told you how the great religious wars took place more than a century after the first open act of the Reformation and if you will compare the chapter on the Thirty Years War with that on inventions, you will see that this ghastly butchery took place at a time when the first clumsy steam engines were already puffing in the laboratories of a number of French and German and English scientists. But the world at large took no interest in these strange contraptions, and went on with a grand theological discussion which to-day causes yawns, but no anger.

And so it goes. A thousand years from now, the historian will use the same words about Europe of the out-going nineteenth century, and he will see how men were engaged upon terrific nationalistic struggles while the laboratories all around them were filled with serious folk who cared not one whit for politics as long as they could force nature to surrender a few more of her million secrets.

You will gradually begin to understand what I am driving at. The engineer and the scientist and the chemist, within a single generation, filled Europe and America and Asia with their vast machines, with their telegraphs, their flying machines, their coal-tar products. They created a new world in which time and space were reduced to complete insignificance. They invented new products and they made these so cheap that almost every one could buy them. I have told you all this before but it certainly will bear repeating.

To keep the ever increasing number of factories going, the owners, who had also become the rulers of the land, needed raw materials and coal. Especially coal. Meanwhile the mass of the people were still thinking in terms of the sixteenth and seventeenth centuries and clinging to the old notions of the state as a dynastic or political organisation. This clumsy mediæval institution was then suddenly called upon to handle the highly modern problems of a mechanical and industrial world. It did its best, according to the rules of the game which had been laid down centuries before. The different states created enormous armies and gigantic navies which were used for the purpose of acquiring new possessions in distant lands. Wherever there was a tiny bit of land left, there arose an English or a French or a German or a Russian colony. If the natives objected, they were killed. In most cases they did not object, and were allowed to live peacefully, provided they did not interfere with the diamond mines or the coal mines or the oil mines or the gold mines or the rubber plantations, and they derived many benefits from the foreign occupation.

Sometimes it happened that two states in search of raw materials wanted the same piece of land at the same time. Then there was a war. This occurred fifteen years ago when Russia and Japan fought for the possession of certain territories which belonged to the Chinese people. Such conflicts, however, were the exception. No one really desired to fight. Indeed, the idea of fighting with armies and battleships and submarines began to seem absurd to the men of the early twentieth century. They associated the idea of violence with the long-ago age of unlimited monarchies and intriguing dynasties. Every day they read in their papers of still further inventions, of groups of English and American and German scientists who were working together in perfect friendship for the purpose of an advance in medicine or in astronomy. They lived in a busy world of trade and of commerce and factories. But only a few noticed that the development of the state (of the gigantic community of people who recognise certain common ideals) was lagging several hundred years behind. They tried to warn the others. But the others were occupied with their own affairs.

I have used so many similes that I must apologise for bringing in one more. The Ship of State (that old and trusted expression which is ever new and always picturesque) of the Egyptians and the Greeks and the Romans and the Venetians and the merchant adventurers of the seventeenth century had been a sturdy craft, constructed of well-seasoned wood, and commanded by officers who knew both their crew and their vessel and who understood the limitations of the art of navigating which had been handed down to them by their ancestors.

Then came the new age of iron and steel and machinery. First one part, then another of the old Ship of State was changed. Her dimensions were increased. The sails were discarded for steam. Better living quarters were established, but more people were forced to go down into the stoke-hole, and while the work was safe and fairly remunerative, they did not like it as well as their old and more dangerous job in the rigging. Finally, and almost imperceptibly, the old wooden square-rigger had been transformed into a modern ocean liner. But the captain and the mates remained the same. They were appointed or elected in the same way as a hundred years before. They were taught the same system of navigation which had served the mariners of the fifteenth century. In their cabins hung the same charts and signal flags which had done service in the days of Louis XIV and Frederick the Great. In short, they were (through no fault of their own) completely incompetent.

The sea of international politics is not very broad. When those imperial and colonial liners began to try and outrun each other, accidents were bound to happen. They did happen. You can still see the wreckage if you venture to pass through that part of the ocean.

And the moral of the story is a simple one. The world is in dreadful need of men who will assume the new leadership—who will have the courage of their own visions and who will recognise clearly that we are only at the beginning of the voyage, and have to learn an entirely new system of seamanship.

They will have to serve for years as mere apprentices. They will have to fight their way to the top against every possible form of opposition. When they reach the bridge, mutiny of an envious crew may cause their death. But some day, a man will arise who will bring the vessel safely to port, and he shall be the hero of the ages.

64

As It Ever Shall Be

"The more I think of the problems of our lives, the more I am persuaded that we ought to choose Irony and Pity for our assessors and judges as the ancient Egyptians called upon the Goddess Isis and the Goddess Nephtys on behalf of their dead.

Irony and Pity are both of good counsel; the first with her smiles makes life agreeable; the other sanctifies it with her tears.

The Irony which I invoke is no cruel Deity. She mocks neither love nor beauty. She is gentle and kindly disposed. Her mirth disarms and it is she who teaches us to laugh at rogues and fools, whom but for her we might be so weak as to despite and hate."

65

After Seven Years

The treaty of Versailles was writ with the point of a bayonet. And however useful the invention of Colonel Fuysegur may have been in a close scrimmage, as an instrument of peace it has never been considered a success.

To make matters worse, the people who handled this deadly weapon were all of them old men. It is one thing when a band of young fellows get into a scrap. They will fight each other with a deadly hatred. But once they have got rid of their pent-up anger, they can return to the affairs of the day without any great personal resentment toward those who only a short while before were their enemies. But it is something very different when half a dozen smooth-shaven graybeards, filled with the futile rage of a lifetime of frustrated ambitions, sit down around a green table and make ready to judge half a dozen defenceless opponents who in the heyday of their victory disregarded every principle of law and international decency.

On such an occasion may Heaven have mercy upon us!

Alas! the good Lord, whose name had been so terribly abused during the previous four years, was in no mood to extend his merciful hand to his undeserving children.

The carnage was of their own making. Now let them settle their difficulties as best they could!

A World in Flames

What that "best" was, we have since then had occasion to learn. And the story of the last seven years is an almost uninterrupted recital of ignominious blunders, of greed, of cruelty and short-sighted meanness—an epoch of such hair-raising imbecility that it stands unique among the dreary annals of human stupidity, which (if I may be permitted this aside) is saying a great deal.

It is of course quite impossible to predict what the people of the year 2500 will have to say about the underlying causes of the great upheaval that destroyed the civilisation of Europe and bestowed upon the unsuspecting American people the leadership of the human race. But in the light of what had gone before, ever since nations had become highly organised business organisations, they will probably come to the conclusion that an outbreak of some sort between the two great contending commercial factions was absolutely unavoidable, and was bound to occur sooner or later. In plain English, they will recognise that Germany had become too much of a menace to the prosperity of the British Empire to be allowed any further development as the general purveyor of the world's manifold wants and needs.

We who lived through the struggle find it much more difficult to estimate the events of the last decade at their true light, but now after seven years it is possible to draw a few fairly definite conclusions without causing too much commotion among our peaceful neighbours and friends.

The history of the last five hundred years is really the record of a gigantic struggle between the so-called "leading powers" and those who hoped to deprive them of their fortunate position and become their successors as the recognized masters of the seas. Spain came to glory across the dead bodies of the great Italian commercial republics and of Portugal. As soon as Spain had established that far-famed empire upon which the sun (for reasons of geography or honesty) was never known to set, Holland tried to rob her of her riches and in view of the difference in size of the two countries, the Dutch Republic achieved a very remarkable success. But no sooner had Holland acquired those parts of the world which then seemed to offer the biggest chance of immediate profit than France and England appeared upon the scene to despoil the Dutch people of their newly acquired possessions. When this had been accomplished, France and England fought for the spoils and after a long and costly struggle, England came out on top. Thereafter England dominated the world for more than a century. She brooked no rivalry. Small nations that came in her path were run under foot. Large ones which could not be tackled single handedly suddenly found themselves confronted by one of those mysterious political alliances of which the rulers of England (past masters in the craft of foreign politics) seemed to possess the secret.

In view of these well-known economic developments

(faithfully described in every primary textbook of history) the policies which the rulers of Germany followed during the first two decades of the twentieth century seem little short of naïve. Some people claim that the former kaiser was to blame and their argument deserves our close attention. William II was an honest man, of very restricted ability and a victim of that strange form of self-delusion which is so common among those who are by birth lifted into the seats of the mighty and who contemplate the rest of the world from such a high pinnacle of anointed superiority that they soon lose all touch with the ordinary run of humanity. This much is certain: that no man ever tried so hard to gain the good will

Sea Power

of the British people and that no foreigner ever failed quite so ignominiously to understand the true nature of the English character.

That curious island on the other side of the North Sea lives by and of and for just one thing—trade. Those who do not interfere with British commerce are, if not exactly "friends," at least "tolerated strangers." Those, on the other hand, who, however remotely, might become a menace to the imperial hegemony are "enemies" and they must be destroyed at the first possible opportunity. And all the lovely speeches and all the obvious manifestations of good will and friendship on the part of the anglophile Teuton emperor never even for a single moment made the average Englishman forget that the Germans were his most dangerous competitors and would sooner or later try to dump their own cheaper wares upon every part of the civilised and uncivilised world.

But that was only one side of the question. A most important one but not sufficient to account for the wholesale slaughter that was so characteristic of the late war.

In the happy days before the railroad and the telegraph, when each country was more or less of a definite entity which proceeded upon its own career with the plodding determination of an elephant pushing a circus truck, the quarrel between the two contending candidates for commercial supremacy would have proceeded slowly and the wily diplomats of the old school would probably have succeeded in localising the quarrel. Unfortunately in the year 1914 the whole world was one large international workshop. A strike in the Argentine was apt to cause suffering in Berlin. A raise in the price of certain raw materials in London might spell disaster to tens of thousands of long-suffering Chinese coolies who never even had heard of the existence of the big city on the Thames. The invention of some obscure "Privat-Dozent" in a third-rate German university would often force dozens of Chilean banks to close their doors, while bad management on the part of an old commercial house in Gothenburg might deprive hundreds of little boys and girls in Australia of a chance to go to college.

Of course, not all nations had reached the same stage

of industrial development. A few of them were still wholly
agricultural and others were only just emerging from a
state of almost mediæval feudalism. This, however, did not
make them undesirable allies in the eyes of their industri-
alised neighbors. On the contrary. Such states, as a rule, are
possessed of almost unlimited reservoirs of man power and
as sheer cannon-fodder the Russian peasant had never had
a rival.

How and in what way all these different and conflicting
interests were marshalled into one gigantic group of associated nations and why for more than four years they consented to fight for a common purpose—these are questions
the solution of which we had better leave to our grandchildren. The world will have to know a great deal more about
the preliminaries of the war than it does to-day before it can
pass judgement upon those misguided patriots who turned
the continent of Europe into one vast shambles.

All we can hope to do this hot day of August in the year
of Grace 1926 is to draw attention to one salient fact which is
almost invariably overlooked by those who call themselves

Man Power

historians, to wit: that the great European conflict which began as a world-wide war ended as a world-wide revolution and that it did not mean a short interruption of the normal development of affairs (as all the wars of the last three hundred years had done) but marked the beginning of an entirely new social and economic epoch. The old men who were responsible for the peace treaty of Versailles were too much a product of their own original surroundings to be able to recognise this.

They thought and talked and acted in terms of a by-gone age.

That probably is the reason why their labours proved such a curse to the rest of humanity. But still one other element which contributed greatly to the disastrous outcome of the war for democracy and the rights of small nations was the belated participation in the struggle on the part of the United States of America.

As a nation the American people, feeling themselves safely entrenched behind three thousand miles of ocean, had never taken any deep interest in foreign politics. Accustomed to think in terms of slogans and captions and head-lines and cheerfully ignorant of the historical development of Europe (or for that matter of any other part of the world) during the last two thousand years, the majority of President Wilson's fellow-citizens were obliged to get their historical information second-hand. Aided and abetted by certain colossal crimes on the part of the German military and naval leaders, it was an easy task for the manufacturers of allied propaganda to make their American friends see the war as a definite struggle between right and wrong, a clash between white and black, a duel to the death between the angels of Anglo-Saxon self-determination and the devils of Teutonic autocracy, until the American people, kind-hearted and senti-mental (and therefore apt to run to certain curious extremes of emotionalism and cruelty) felt that they could not possibly keep out of the struggle without becoming unfaithful to all that was good and decent in their own manhood. A hot wave of a crusade-like zeal and eagerness swept across the country. Slowly but steadily the gigantic mills of American industry began to grind and ere long two million men were hastening to the battlefields of Europe to put a stop to the intolerable depravities of the Hun.

Now it was only natural that these millions of serious minded and earnest young men should try and revaluate their fighting ideals into terms that should be comprehensible to all of their fellow-countrymen. Hence the slogan of "a war to end war." Hence the famous fourteen points of President Wilson—the new decalogue of international righteousness. Hence the enthusiasm for the self-determination of small nations, the hilariously expressed desire to "make the world safe for democracy."

To the Balfours and the Poincarés and the Churchills (not to mention the exiled leaders of the old Russian régime) such words must have sounded like rank heresy. If any of their own people had undertaken to parade such battle-cries they would have been sent before a firing-squad at very short notice. But the commander-in-chief of two million men, the trusted gatekeeper of all the treasures of the world, must be listened to with an outward semblance of respect. Hence the leaders of the different European nations, during the last year and a half of the war, fought for certain ideals for which they had no more use than for those fantastic economic innovations which were now being shouted in a hundred different tongues from the battlements of the old Kremlin. And as soon as the Germans, agreeably surprised by the reasonable terms of their much-feared American antagonists, had thrown their emperor overboard, had changed the name of their country from an "empire" to that of a "republic," and

Propaganda

adorned with red cockades and singing the popular song of international brotherhood had started upon their famous backward march to the Rhine, the allied chieftains hastened to rid themselves of those foolish and embarrassing American ideals and made ready to conclude a peace upon that well-known principle of "woe to the loser" which ever since the days of the cave-man had been accepted as the logical conclusion to a well-regulated physical encounter.

Their task would have been a great deal less complicated if President Wilson had not hit upon the unfortunate plan of taking a direct and personal part in the diplomatic negotiations of the year 1919. Had he remained at home, the European powers would have concluded peace according to their own terms of right and wrong. From an American point of view they would have been wrong, but right or wrong, their decisions would have been an honest expression of a definite school of thought. Now, however, American and European ideals (which never have mixed) got so horribly interwoven that nothing was definitely settled, that every one of the allies was left with a grievance, and that the peace proved infinitely more costly than the war.

But there was still another element which contributed greatly to the chaos caused by the treaty of Versailles. President Wilson, himself the head of a federation of semi-independent nations, had visions of a federated world-state. The thing had proved possible on the American continent. For more than a century it had given an ever increasing number of sovereign states a degree of political liberty and economic well-being which had made the nation as a whole the most prosperous and the richest country on the entire planet. Why should not the people of Europe learn the lesson which Virginia and Pennsylvania and Massachusetts had taken to heart in the year 1776?

Why not, indeed?

And so the allied leaders bowed low and listened respectfully when Mr. Wilson explained his scheme for a League of Nations. Under the press of circumstances they even agreed to incorporate the principles of a United States of the World into their treaty of peace. But just as soon as the presidential ship had hoisted anchor and had set course for the western hemisphere, they began to undo the work that had been closest to the heart of the great president and returned to the old diplomatic ideals of secret treaties and surreptitious alliances.

Meanwhile a very definite revulsion of feeling had taken place in America itself. It is, of course, very easy to blame certain personal characteristics of Mr. Wilson for this changed attitude towards the League of Nations on the part of so many of his contemporaries. But other forces, infinitely more subtle, were at work.

In the first place, the soldiers who had taken part in the

fight were returning to their homes. Their first-hand acquaintance with European conditions had not made them over-anxious to continue the close intimacy of the last two years.

In the second place, the people at large were beginning to recover from the mad fury of the war. They were no longer in fear for the lives of their beloved sons and daughters and once more were able to think soberly. The traditional distrust of Europe began to reassert itself. Soon it became clear that George Washington's ominous warning against "entangling alliances" had as much of a hold upon the mass of the people of the year 1918 as it had had a century before.

In the third place, after two years of parades and four-minute speeches and liberty loans, it was very pleasant to go back to the quiet routine of a profitable business career.

In short, the infant League of Nations which President Wilson had dumped so unceremoniously upon the threshold of Europe was now repudiated by its own spiritual parents. The child did not die. But it lived a precarious existence and grew up to be a weak and emaciated creature, too feeble to make its influence felt in any decisive way and merely irritating those who were its friends by an occasional futile scolding and the waving of a naughty, naughty finger.

ONCE MORE WE are confronted by an ominous historical "if."

"If the League of Nations had really turned the whole of the civilized world into a successful United States of the World. . . ."

I don't know, but even under the most favorable circumstances, the plan of President Wilson had only a slender chance of success.

For the war, as we are now beginning to understand, was not so much a war as a revolution and it was a revolution in which the victory was carried away by an unsuspected third party, who since then has been identified as the grandson of

America Goes Abroad

one James Watt, and who is coming to be known in wider and wider circles as "the Iron Man."

Originally the steam engine (like his younger brother, the electric engine) had been a welcome addition to the family of civilized human beings because he was a willing slave and ever ready to lighten the tasks of man and beast.

But soon it became clear that this inanimate factotum was full of cunning and devilment and the war with its temporary suspension of all the decencies of life gave the iron contraption a chance to enslave those who in reality were meant to be his masters.

Here and there some wise men of science may have foreseen the danger that threatened the race from the side of this unruly servant but as soon as such an unfortunate prophet opened his mouth and issued a word of warning, he was denounced as an enemy of society, as a rank Bolshevik and a seditious radical and he was bade to hold his tongue or take the consequences. For the politicians and the diplomats who had been responsible for the war were now engaged upon the serious task of fabricating a suitable peace and they must not be interrupted in these holy endeavours. Unfortunately, as a class such worthies are almost always completely ignorant of those elementary principles of natural science and political economy which happen to dominate our present indus-

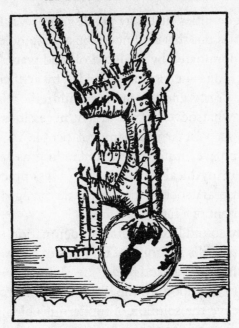

The Iron Man

trialised and mechanical form of society and they are less
fit to handle complicated modern problems than any other
group of men of whom I can think at the present moment.
The plenipotentiaries of Paris were no exception. They met
in the shadow of the Iron Man, they talked of a world that
was dominated by the Iron Man, yet never became aware of
his presence and until the very end talked in words and symbols that represented the mentality of the eighteenth century
but not that of the twentieth.

The result was inevitable. It is impossible to think in
terms of the year 1719 and prosper in terms of the year 1919.
But that, it is becoming increasingly evident, is exactly what
the old men of Versailles did.

Now BEHOLD THE world as it has been left in the wake of
this orgy of hatred and unreason—a crazy quilt of phantas-

tic new nationalities that may possess some value as historical curiosities but that will never be able to hold their own in a world dominated by coal and oil and water power and wholesale credits—a continent divided by artificial frontiers which look pretty enough upon a children's atlas but bear no relation whatsoever to the urgent necessities of modern civilisation—a vast armed camp of people in yellow and green and purple uniforms masquerading as feeble imitations of their mythical ancestors but of less practical use to our contemporary society than any little cash-girl that works in the basement of a ten-cent store.

This may sound like a brutal condemnation of a state of affairs that still fills the souls of millions of honest European patriots with gratitude and pride.

I am sorry but not until the statesmen of Europe shall be willing to leave the solution of modern problems to people with modern minds can there be any lasting improvement. Meanwhile in their agony and distress the people will turn to the cure-alls offered by Bolshevism and fascism.

INCIDENTALLY THIS outburst of rhetoric will explain the most dangerous and regrettable of all recent political developments—the rapidly increasing dislike between the people of Europe and those of America. Since I am trying to write for the children of all races and not merely for those who live on the fortunate patch of land that stretches from the Atlantic to the Pacific, this apparent waving of the stars and stripes may be considered as an exhibition of very doubtful taste. But this is a time for plain speech and even at the risk of being mistaken for a hundred percent patriot (the very last honour to which I aspire) I shall try to make my point clear.

I do not for a moment claim that man for man and woman for woman the Americans as a nation are superior to any of their cousins of the old world. But fortunately for themselves they have little consciousness of the past and therefore they are more able to approach the problems of the present with an open eye towards the future than the members of almost any other race. As a result they have accepted the modern world without any reservations and having accepted it with all its good and all its evil, they are rapidly reaching a "modus vivendi" whereby animate man and his inanimate servant shall be able to exist on terms of peace and mutual respect. It sounds absurd yet it is true that the country which has achieved the greatest mechanical perfection is also the first to bring the Iron Man to terms. In order to do this the American people have been forced to throw overboard a great deal of ancestral ballast. They have sacrificed hundreds of ideas and prejudices and ideals that served a highly useful purpose two hundred or two thousand years ago but which to-day are of no more value than a stage coach or a miracle-working image. As far as I can see there will be no hope for Europe until the mass of Germans and Englishmen and Spaniards and Heaven-only-knows-what-they-are-called do likewise.

In a chapter like this it would be so easy to deliver noble harangues upon the accomplishments of Locarno; the unfeasibility of a Marxian programme of applied economics; to discuss the follies of those small-town French politicians who have not yet learned that the days of Louis XIV and Napoleon have long since been relegated to the era of the Stone Age. But it would be a waste of energy and printer's ink.

The misery that has come over the world during the last ten years (hastened along by the Great War but by no means caused by that sanguinary conflict) is in reality due to a profound change in the economic and social structure of the entire world. But Europe, steeped in the lore of the past, has thus far been unwilling or unable to realise this fact.

The peace of Versailles, the last great gesture of the Old

Régime, was meant as a final stronghold against the inevitable approach of the modern era. In less than eight years it has become an obsolete ruin. It would have been considered a sublime piece of statecraft in the year of Grace 1700. To-day not one out of ten thousand people has ever bothered to read it. For the twentieth century is dominated by certain economic and industrial principles which recognise no political boundaries and tend with absolute inevitableness to turn the entire world into a single large and prosperous workshop regardless of language, race or previous condition of ancestral glory.

WHAT EVENTUALLY WILL come out of this workshop, what form of civilisation will be developed by an intelligent and willing cooperation between man and his machines—that I do not know and it really does not matter so very much. Life means change and this is not the first time that the human race has been faced by a similar emergency.

Our remote and our less distant ancestors have lived through such crises.

No doubt our children and grandchildren will do the same.

But for us, who are alive to-day, the one and only serious problem is a world-wide reorganisation along economic rather than worn-out political lines.

Seven years ago, our ears deafened by the noise of the big guns, our eyes blinded by the flash of the searchlights, we were still too dazed to understand whither the great upheaval had carried us. At that moment any fairly honourable and sincere man who pretended that he could guide us back to the happy days of 1914 was welcomed as a leader and was assured of our willing loyalty.

To-day we know better.

We have begun to understand that the comfortable old world in which we dwelled so unsuspectingly until the outbreak of the war had in reality outlived its usefulness by several decades.

This does not mean that we are absolutely certain about the road that now lies before us. Most likely we will follow a dozen wrong tracks before we find the right direction. And in the meantime we are fast learning one very important lesson—that the future belongs to the living and that the dead ought to mind their own business.

66

The United States Comes of Age

Being the First of Several Chapters on
Current History Written by Their Uncle Willem
for Piet, Jan, Dirk and Jane van Loon
and Their Contemporaries

Like most busy men, your grandfather left a lot of work unfinished. "The Story of Mankind" had been written for your father and myself when we were small boys. He had always planned to make it your book too by bringing it up to date. But up to what date? That was the question.

If you were trying to describe something very big, something like, let us say, an ocean storm, you would sit on a high hill from where you could see far in every direction. In this way you would be able to view things "in their true perspective." If, on the other hand, you were out on the sea in a boat you could only describe those waves that were bouncing you about.

The same applies to writing about history. The past we can view from the high hill of the present. We can see "the whole picture." But as for current history—and by current I mean the history of the past twenty or thirty years—there we are still very much "at sea." While trying to steer a safe course our "Ship of State" is being buffeted by wind and waves from every side. We don't know how big a storm it is or when it will be over. We can simply try to take our bearings and hope for the best.

People used to speak of "lulls" in history, periods when "nothing happened." Today we know better. These lulls were, like the weather, purely local. Prior to the development of the telegraph, the telephone and the radio, such major historical events as wars, revolutions and changes of government could take place in one country without even its neighbors knowing much about them. This is no longer the case. Thanks to modern communications and our free press, every turn in events in Lhasa, Rome or Cape Town can be known the very next day by every citizen of Kansas City, New Orleans or Vancouver. I say *can* be. There are, of course, those who do not wish to be informed.

The last time the people of the United States deliberately tried to ignore the rumblings of history elsewhere on this planet was after World War I. (This was the lull in which "The Story of Mankind" was written as a word of warning.) Having helped our erstwhile allies win the war against Germany, we felt we had done all that could be expected of us. Still blithely unaware of the responsibility that history was to toss into our lap, we turned our backs on the League of Nations and left Europe to stew in its own juices.

The "Roaring Twenties" were upon us. Under President Harding's slogan of "a return to normalcy" this country embarked on a wild scramble to exploit all forms of enterprise. Wastefulness, lawlessness and corruption were to be found in high places as well as low. Harding's sudden death, under ambiguous circumstances, gave rise to the rumor that, had he lived, he would have faced impeachment. Although the present generation chooses to look upon this "Jazz Age" with rose-colored glasses, the picture it painted of prosperity was on very rotten canvas.

If it seems odd that I should mention such a purely local development in what is essentially a history of the world, I do so with a purpose. Just as it takes a long time for a person or a nation to build up a reputation, so it also takes a long time for them to live one down. Although the 1920s saw us grow immensely rich and powerful our prestige as a nation of responsible citizens sank calamitously low. While many were paying little or no attention to developments beyond our borders, the eyes and ears of the rest of the world were focused on us.

Novelists like Sinclair Lewis and Theodore Dreiser, whose works mirrored the American scene, were being widely translated and much discussed. American plays found a new audience abroad and, even more important, there was that new great export commodity, the "movies." No history of America's role in world affairs can overlook the Judas kiss given this country by our motion pictures. By portraying and glorifying our riches and our free-and-easy ways these pictures built in the minds of the common people every-where an exaggerated concept of America that was to come home to roost. Just one example will show you what I mean. In every foreign language today you will find at least one American word: "Gangster."

Nobody was interested when in 1922 the former editor of the socialist paper "Avanti" marched on Rome carrying a banner bearing the "Fasces," an ax enclosed in a bundle of rods which was the symbol of authority in ancient Rome. When this same Benito Mussolini became "dictator" of Italy, Americans simply said, "Thank goodness, now the Italian trains will run on time." This was true. They did. The thou-sands of tourists who now flocked to Rome, Florence, Venice and Naples often had to stop at the street corners while a phalanx of black-shirted youths went marching along singing "Giovinezza." But these sightseers never stopped to realize what those singing boys and their bull-necked little "Duce" were up to. (See Chapter 24.)

Nor did the world pay much attention to an unfortunate incident which took place on the Odeonsplatz in Munich in 1923. There a strangely assorted group of men calling themselves the National Socialist German Workers party tried to stage a "Putsch" to overthrow the Bavarian government. They were fired on by the police. Since one of these "Nazis," as they later came to be known, was old General Erich Friedrich Wilhelm Ludendorff, everyone felt most apologetic. The Nazi ringleader, an Austrian of uncertain profession, was sentenced to five years in Landsberg prison but served only nine months. He put this time to good use. Having both unlimited supplies of paper and a devoted cell-mate and secretary named Rudolf Hess, this irascible little man dictated a book. Not being a man of much education his German usage was embarrassingly bad. Ghost writers soon remedied this and "Mein Kampf" (My Battle) by Adolf Hitler was translated for all the world to read.

Few people troubled to see what was in this dull, bombastic work. It is a pity they didn't. If they had they might have paid more attention to the efforts of a Frenchman named Aristide Briand and a German named Gustav Stresemann. As representatives of their two countries they signed a very conciliatory pact. In 1926 they were jointly awarded the Nobel Peace Prize. That was that.

Then there was Russia. It was easy not to know much about Russia. The Russians wanted it that way. They always had. Their distrust of the west, from which they had borrowed everything including the art of ballet dancing, existed even under the tsars. This, like many other things, the Soviet government saw no reason to change. On the contrary, if it was important that outsiders not know how well, or how poorly, each successive Soviet Five Year Plan was faring, it was even more important that the citizens of the Soviet Union learn as little as possible about the outside world.

Nevertheless, observant readers could note the gradual disappearance of the name Trotsky in all Soviet news reports and its replacement by the name Joseph Stalin. That this also meant a shift in the policy and aims of this potentially powerful nation was clear to those interested in the foreign news section of their daily papers. The others hopped from the murders on page 1 to the stock market reports and there settled down to do some serious reading. But on October 29, 1929, the stock market hit the front page.

The big Wall Street pot that had been bubbling so merrily finally boiled over and put out the flame. The roar of the twenties became a panic-stricken shriek. Harding's successor, "Cautious Cal" Coolidge, a president who prided himself on his ability to say nothing and do less, stepped down and made way for Herbert Hoover. In his attempts to rekindle the financial flame even this great economist was as helpless as a city-ite on a picnic trying to light wet wood without matches. He applied every known formula but unemployment and hysteria only increased.

The stock market crash did not bring an era to an end. This era, the era of exploitation, had died quite some time before and the crash simply revealed to what extent rot had set in. In America, the nineteenth century had lasted till 1929.

Unfortunately, few of the men who had waxed prosperous and influential in this period ever found time to read their history books. If they had they would have learned that those who wish to enjoy greater privilege must also assume greater responsibility. Otherwise the national apple-cart overturns. Such an incident is usually followed by a revolution. We had our "revolution" and it was known as "The Depression."

During the next few years we were far too preoccupied with our own troubles to notice what explosions our financial crackup had set off elsewhere. But certain events were taking place which were to shift global responsibilities onto our youthful shoulders. Whether it liked it or not, the United States had come of age.

67

The "Axis" Partners

The "Crash That Was Felt Around the World"
Hastens the Collapse of a Peace
That Was Built on Medieval Foundations

One day, many years ago, someone wanted to borrow a great deal of money. In return he offered the moneylender or "banker" some "shares of stock" in his business. The banker, being a bit of a gambler, decided to auction off these stocks to the highest bidder. Thus he became a "stockbroker." Such stock markets, of which the Bourse in Paris is one of the oldest, at first did business on a small local scale. Then a broker got the idea of employing couriers to carry "quotations" from one town to another. Finally, with the coming of the telegraph, stock market transactions became international. Today every important bid made on Wall Street sets ticker tape machines going in London, Cape Town and Buenos Aires.

During this final boom of the 1920s, stock prices on Wall Street went up and up. A gambling fever gripped the nation. By 1929 many important companies had overexpanded. Suddenly they went bankrupt. Their stocks became worthless. Some banks which had speculated in these stocks went bankrupt too. Many people whose money was invested in these banks became destitute.

Now place dominoes on end, one in front, two behind the two, four behind the three, etc. Push the front one over and as it falls it knocks the next two over. Soon they will have all gone down. This will explain what happened all over the world in 1929. One bank failed, then two, then three. Everywhere, in America, in Europe, in Asia, banks began to close their doors. The smaller ones went first, then the bigger ones. Because business had become international the disaster was universal. In 1931 the powerful Austrian Credit-Anstalt collapsed. But worse was yet to come.

For centuries the English pound sterling had been accepted as the standard and all other currencies were valued accordingly. But on September 21, 1931, the Bank of England, that symbol of British prosperity and reliability, slipped off the gold standard. You will have to read a book on banking to know exactly what that means. Till then you must take my word for it that this was a severe jolt to the stability of national economy everywhere. It was also the first real crack in the structure of the British Empire.

There were other signs which pointed to a general dissolution of "the empire on which the sun never sets." In India a soft-spoken Hindu named Mohandas Karamchand Gandhi, and called the "Mahatma" or "Great Souled" by his followers, was repeatedly imprisoned by British authorities. He kept urging his countrymen to achieve home rule through "passive resistance."

And then there was Palestine. The British had taken it away from the Turks after World War I. By the Balfour Declaration of 1917 they designated it as a Jewish homeland. The sudden increase in Jewish migration was met by severe opposition on the part of the local Arabs. Unfortunately it was also important to England to be on good terms with the Arabs. It was they who controlled the land close to the Suez Canal and the great oil fields of the Near East which were then beginning to be exploited. With a change of heart the British took steps to stem the flow of Zionists to their biblical homeland. How completely they failed in this is proven by the existence of the state of Israel today.

If you will now spin the globe around halfway (something everyone should do once in a while), you will observe a relatively small string of islands off the China coast. That is the Empire of Japan. Said to have been founded by Emperor Jimmu Tenno in the year 660 B.C., little of Japan's early history is definitely known. Accidentally discovered by the Portuguese in 1542, Japan was openly hostile to western traders and the missionaries they brought with them. In 1663 she closed her ports to all except the Dutch. Then in 1853 Commodore Matthew Perry, bearing a letter from President Fillmore, sailed into Tokyo Bay. Six years later Japan signed a commercial treaty first with the United States and then with other nations. Seemingly overnight this feudal empire became a modern industrial and military power.

In 1895 Japan took Formosa from China; in 1905 she won a brief war with Russia for port and rail rights in Manchuria; in 1910 she annexed Korea. Japan was now ready to embark on one of the greatest schemes of Asiatic imperialism since the days of Genghis Khan. She had everything that was needed for such an exploit—wealth, industry, vast man power reserves due to over population and a religion in which the emperor was God and to die for him was an honor. Cannily she bided her time.

With American prestige at a low ebb and most of Europe in a state of financial and political turmoil, Japan chose 1931 as the year in which to send her troops across the Korean border into Manchuria. It was a quick victory. The League of

Nations sent out a commission to investigate the "Manchu-kuo Incident" and the United States refused to recognize the Japanese puppet state under Emperor Henry Pu-Yi. Feigning hurt feelings, Japan indignantly withdrew from the League but continued to do business with the U.S.A. The "incident" was closed.

One man was watching Japan's defiance of the League of Nations with interest. He was the author of "Mein Kampf" and runner-up in the recent German presidential elections. His name was Adolf Hitler.

The Weimar Republic, although culturally one of the most brilliant periods in history, was a political failure. Unused to the privilege of forming their own political parties, the German people found themselves split up into as many as 125 different, and very weak, factions. Under these circumstances it was almost impossible to elect a president. The German Republic had only two: Friedrich Ebert, by profession a saddle-maker, and Paul Ludwig Hans Anton von Beneckendorff und von Hindenburg, a twice retired general.

Seventy-eight when he took office in 1925, the venerable hero of both the Franco-Prussian War and World War I looked excellent on postage stamps but was no longer the man for the job. Although reelected in 1932, defeating Adolf Hitler at the polls, the aged field marshal was no match for the upstart ex-corporal and his Nazi party. With bankruptcy jitters shaking the young German Republic to its foundations, Hitler made the most of the situation. His only serious rivals were the German Communists. Their tactics and his were far too similar for comfort. In 1933 the Nazis secretly set fire to the Berlin Reichstag building and "framed" an ex-Communist, Marinus van der Lubbe, as arsonist. This time the "Putsch" succeeded. With his own son a Nazi, Hindenburg yielded to pressure and named Adolf Hitler chancellor.

On Hindenburg's death in 1934, Hitler became both chancellor and president of Germany. Following the example of Italy's Mussolini, who had dubbed himself "Il Duce" (the Commander), Hitler became the "Führer" or Leader of the German people.

How can one explain Hitler's astonishing rise to power? He, or in any event his advisers, possessed an uncanny knowledge of "popular psychology." To the German military clique, smarting under the provisions of the Versailles treaty, Hitler promised rehabilitation. To the man-in-the-street he promised the return of German power and prestige. From Nordic mythology and the writings of Friedrich Nietzsche he concocted the theory of a so-called "Herrenrasse" or Germanic Master Race. But if they were so strong, why then had the Germans taken such a licking in the World War? They had been betrayed! By whom? Hitler needed a scape-goat. Taking an example from the Slavic countries, where discontent of any sort was apt to end in a pogrom, he pointed to the Jews. Although they formed less than 1 percent of the total population, Hitler maintained that the Jewish minority had caused the downfall of peace-loving, hard-working "Aryan" Germany.

Did people actually believe this nonsense? Unfortunately, yes. Nor were all of Hitler's supporters within Germany itself. Like Mussolini before him, Hitler was widely hailed as the man-of-the-people who had established order out of chaos. Still ignorant of the unthinkable excesses to which Hitler's "Master Race" theories would lead, everyone seemed quite willing to let him make the Third Reich into an arsenal. He was fulfilling his promise to provide the world with a convenient bulwark against Communism.

Once in the saddle Hitler wasted no time. He rode roughshod over any individual or group which stood in his way. The old military clique, now seeking its reward for supporting him, found itself bypassed in the remobilization program.

Needing the cooperation of German industry Hitler wooed the traditionally conservative industrialists by "purging" the more radically socialistic of his followers. With Machiavellian thoroughness he used a trumped-up plot against his life as the excuse to murder General von Schleicher, Ernst Röhm and other former friends. The Enabling Act, passed in 1934, took from the German people those democratic freedoms they had enjoyed under the Weimar Republic but apparently had never appreciated. Instead they were permitted to take part in an all-out campaign against Jews, Catholics, intellectuals and Communists.

Future generations may wonder at Hitler's campaign against the Communists. "Weren't Nazism and Communism both related ideologies?" they will ask. "Wasn't Germany the land of the National *Socialists* and Russia the Union of Soviet *Socialist* Republics?"

Similar ideologies do not prevent conflicts any more than divergent ones bring them about. The real issues in history lie deeper. Germany under Hitler was still Germany and Russia under Stalin was still Russia. The age-old power struggle between them had never ceased. On the contrary. In Hitler's opinion it had now been given a logical and "scientific" basis. That basis he found in geopolitics.

Proclaiming to have established a definite interrelation between politics and geography, geopoliticians divide the Eurasian land mass into "heart-land" and "rim-land." According to their teachings, whoever dominates the heart-land and gains access to the sea will dominate the world. This heart-land is in Russia. With Germany's leading geopolitician, Karl Haushofer, as his political adviser, Hitler pointed to the danger of a world dominated by Russia through Communism. But in point of truth he coveted the Russian heart-land himself and set his sights accordingly.

It is therefore understandable that Soviet Russia took a

dim view of the events in 1933. Already nervous about the Japanese activity, the Soviets had concluded nonaggression pacts with Poland, the Baltic States and France. Now, with the Nazi landslide in Germany, the Soviets began looking around for new friends. When Hitler, in his first test of strength, undid the work of Stresemann by withdrawing from the League of Nations, the Soviet Union became a member.

Although Mussolini undoubtedly joined his countrymen in their traditional contempt for the barbarians to the north, he reached a paternal hand to Hitler and bade him welcome. There followed any number of short diplomatic courtesy calls by both their foreign ministers until finally in 1934, amid an atmosphere of well-rehearsed enthusiasm, Hitler traveled to Rome. Despite the parades and banquets the visit resulted in friction, for someone kept bringing up the thorny question of Austria.

The crash of 1929 had not left Italy unscathed. Fear of bankruptcy caused Mussolini to impose increasingly rigid controls. The enthusiastic cheers with which Il Duce's first proclamations had been received took on a hollow ring. Mussolini diagnosed the symptoms of dissatisfaction correctly. The time had come to create a new cause, a diversion.

He too had been watching the League of Nations falter and took note. Italy, Il Duce pondered, was only a kingdom. Rome had been an empire. What was the most defenseless country he could find some reason to attack? His acquisitive eye fell on Abyssinia.

By always minding its own business, "the mysterious kingdom of Prester John" (see page 252) had managed to survive almost sixteen centuries of human progress. Its rugged terrain and its even more rugged fighters were legendary. They served as a deterrent to would-be empire builders. Not only did these dark-skinned Christians throw a lethal spear but they also had a habit of mutilating their prisoners of war.

Italy, as you read on page 497, had once before attempted to annex Abyssinia, or Ethiopia as it is now called. She had suffered a humiliating defeat at Adua in 1887, a defeat she may have forgiven but never forgot. Both countries signed a solemn treaty of friendship in 1928.

In December 1934, Italian and Ethiopian troops clashed at Ualual, on the disputed frontier of Italian Somaliland. Mussolini, pretending outrage, demanded reparations and refused to arbitrate. The Ethiopian Negus, Haile Selassie, laid his case before the League of Nations. Just as Mussolini expected, the League listened attentively and did nothing. Then Mussolini let it be known that he would arbitrate after all. The ruse worked.

As soon as he was ready, Mussolini invaded Ethiopia. With naked feet and armed with spears Haile Selassie's troops displayed the courage for which they were famous. They were no match for Italy's tanks, machine guns and bombing planes. Italy's fliers, among them the Duce's own son, gloatingly reported what "good sport" it was to achieve a direct hit on unarmed Ethiopians and watch the burst "open up like a flower."

The League of Nations, in a final effort, branded Italy an "aggressor" and voted to apply sanctions. But England was loath to close the Suez Canal to Italy, lest this "precipitate a war." On May 9, 1936, Mussolini was able to proclaim the king of Italy emperor of Ethiopia and the League of Nations was as good as dead.

The next move was Hitler's. Having already violated the Versailles Treaty by reinstituting military conscription, he now scrapped the Stresemann-Briand Locarno Pact and sent German troops into the Rhineland. The stage was set for the Führer and the Duce to act in unison. The scene was Spain.

In 1936 death came to Antonia Mercé, a Spanish dancer known as "La Argentina." Through her superb artistry and dignity of bearing this Argentine-born woman seemed, to all who saw her, a living symbol of the glory that was Spain. Spain's only other public symbol, her king, had in the meantime been doing his best to create just the opposite impression. Like many another Bourbon before him, Alfonso XIII was not very bright.

Preferring dalliance abroad to duties at home, Alfonso had left the running of his government to the marqués de Estella, also called Primo de Rivera. In 1925 this nobleman assumed the powers of a dictator and, by jamming the lid down hard, managed to preserve a semblance of order. But he antagonized his fellow aristocrats and in 1930 they persuaded the king to get rid of him. In 1931 the Spanish people also got rid of their king. Spain became a "Worker's Republic." But the Spaniards, like the Germans, had neither the education nor the patience necessary for self-government. They soon were split up into many impotent factions and the social unrest which followed everywhere in the wake of our Depression swept over Spain.

In July 1936, the news spotlight jumped from Abyssinia to Melilla in Spanish Morocco. Here a group of generals, among them the former governor of the Canary Islands, Francisco Franco, fomented a revolt against the recently formed *Frente Popular*. This leftist coalition had achieved a peaceful victory in the Cortes, or Parliament, over the monarchists, republicans and clerics.

The struggle which followed lasted almost three years. When it ended Spain's treasury was bankrupt, her citizens exhausted and her cities shattered by Europe's first taste of bomb warfare. Emerging victorious, General Franco became dictator or "El Caudillo." The resemblance to Hitler and Mussolini was no accident. What had began as a civil war between "Nationalists" and "Loyalists" had become, through armed intervention, the first test of strength between Berlin and Rome on one side and Moscow on the other. And Berlin and Rome had won.

Again I must ask you to forget "ideologies" and study geography. Then it will become more apparent to you what a "Loyalist" (meaning Communist) victory in Spain would have meant. A sudden projection of Soviet influence into this key spot of western Europe would have come at a time when France was corrupt and weak, and England, following the abdication of Edward VIII, decidedly shaken. Therefore both countries welcomed Franco's victory as the lesser of two evils. The 1937 Neutrality Act, which was aimed at keeping the western hemisphere out of European conflicts, still permitted the United States to sell arms to Portugal. These arms then conveniently found their way into Franco's hands.

Lack of modern equipment and military discipline hamstrung the Loyalists from the start. Aided by Soviet strategists and an international group of volunteers (the "Lincoln Brigade" was composed of Americans), these unfortunate pawns on the chess board of European power politics quickly lost ground but put up a spirited defense of Madrid and Valencia against Nazi bombing and "Fifth Column" strategy.

While some newspapers were trying to warn the world that the tactical lessons learned by the intervening powers in the "Spanish manoeuvres" might soon be applied elsewhere, others were reporting on the activity, or lack thereof, of a Nonintervention Committee composed of twenty-one nations, among them Germany, Italy and the Soviet Union.

It was against this background that the Axis came into being.

If anyone believed that Hitler's racial theories were more than a trumped-up expedient, the events of November 26, 1936, must have given him a serious shock. For on this date Nazi Germany welcomed the Japanese people (to whom Kaiser Wilhelm had once referred as "the Yellow

Peril") as "honorary Aryans" and allies. Known as the Anti-
Comintern or Anti-Communist Pact this scrap of paper created the Berlin-Tokyo arm of the Axis. The following year
Japan embarked on an undeclared but all-out war against
the Chinese.

In 1937 Mussolini also signed this document. The hand-
writing of history was on the wall for anyone who cared
to read.

68

Isolationism and Appeasement

How the Axis Partners Began to
Divide the World Among Themselves
and Why They Got as Far as They Did

World War I had not actually been a global struggle.
It was called a "World War" at the time mainly because
improved communications had brought the struggle in
Europe and the Near East to the attention of everyone capable of reading a newspaper. It was also the first conflict in
which an American Expeditionary Force had gone into battle on European soil.

The fighting had been going on for almost three years
when the United States came to the aid of the Allies,
England, France and Belgium; and American troops moved
into the trenches under the slogan "To make the world safe
for Democracy." (See page 520.)

Hardly had the last shot been fired when the emptiness
of this became apparent. The European allies, republics and
kingdoms alike, were little concerned with ideological aims.
Maintaining the European "balance of power" was the sole
issue which interested them. They thanked the United States
for its aid and promised in return to go on doing business
with us.

In the interest of honest historical reporting that is all we should have expected, for that is all we actually went into the war to achieve. But some Americans seemed loath to take such a realistic or, as they called it, "cynical" attitude. Hence they were disillusioned. They felt themselves betrayed and duped. Loudly they inveighed against any further "foreign entanglements." Thus "Isolationism" in America became a political issue.

Undoubtedly patriotic in their motives, these isolationists were soon to find themselves duped and betrayed in earnest. From the time he came to power in 1933, Hitler made use of America's isolationist sentiment to assure himself a free hand in Europe. His Propaganda Ministry, under Joseph Goebbels, used every medium at its disposal to dissuade the United States, burdened with its own internal affairs, from "meddling" in those of Germany. Several congressmen and members of such organizations as "The German-American Bund," "The America First Organization" and the Ku Klux Klan willingly joined in echoing this sentiment. (In homage to Hitler the Klan added anti-Semitism to its roster of "desirable American attributes.")

The United States did have troubles, that is true. Replacing Hoover as president in 1932, Franklin D. Roosevelt fell heir to the task of legislating the country out of economic chaos. By declaring a "bank holiday" and by passage of the Glass-Steagall Banking Act, the National Industrial Recovery Act (declared unconstitutional in 1935) and other unprecedented measures, Roosevelt finally managed to bring the depression to an end.

These new laws were bitter medicine to a people unused to any sort of government control in private enterprise. But the world was then, and still is, in the grip of that social revolution which began when man made himself master of the machine. (See page 454.) Like trees in a hurricane, old, rigid

governments were toppled by it while others bowed before
the storm but did not break. What had brought communism
to Russia, fascism to Central Europe and unrest to Asia,
Africa and South America brought only social legislation to
the United States. For that we must be very grateful. The
restrictions this country now felt were simply those everyone feels the day he finds out he is "growing up." And as we
have said before, the United States had come of age.

One of the surest signs of our growing maturity was the
fact that, for the first time in its history, the United States
began to take an interest in that vast continent in the southern hemisphere to which ours is linked by name, history and
geography. Despite their political independence, the majority of the Central and South American countries still maintain the language and many of the traditions of their Spanish
motherland. (Brazil, the one exception, is similarly bound
to Portugal.) The Civil War in Spain was therefore destined
to have serious repercussions from Tierra del Fuego to the
Rio Grande.

Hard hit by the Depression of the thirties, the Latin American republics had suffered economic unrest, which was followed by increased political activity. Just as in Spain, two
major factions eventually formed, each seeking to gain full
control of their country's government. Though never identi-
cal, the line-up usually looked much the same. On one side
was a "Worker's party," whose members made up for their
lack of education, discipline and financial backing by their
vast enthusiasm for the achievements of the Soviet Union.
Opposing them was a faction that was "Nationalist" (sometimes "National Socialist") in character. Headed by conservative politicians, army men and industrialists, this party had
everything its rival lacked, with one exception. Both parties
had an equal disposition to brutality and lack of scruple.

For a while each side would jockey for position. In some

countries the outcome of the contest almost seemed in doubt. But the Nationalist parties nearly always managed to out-manoeuvre and "outputsch" their adversaries, and a strong man stepped from the wings and took the center of the stage.

If one of these men had let his admiration for Franco mis-lead him into lending the insurgents military aid, the west-ern hemisphere would have become entangled in what was still, theoretically, a civil war in Spain. In order to forestall such a move President Roosevelt suggested a meeting of the Americas in Buenos Aires. It was here that the 1937 Neutral-ity Pact was signed. In the next few years several other agree-ments were signed which drew North and South America together for the first time.

In Europe meanwhile the Axis program was going ahead on schedule. Basing his audacity on the premise that "people don't like to get excited about things till they have to and by that time it is usually too late," Hitler was meeting with marked success. The fact that his anti-communism, anti-Semitism and anti-intellectualism was sending Germany's leading scientists, musicians and writers elsewhere, and *not* as enthusiastic spokesmen for the fatherland, seemingly slipped his mind. The loss of men like Thomas Mann, Stefan Zweig, Kurt Weill and Arnold Schönberg was not a matter of con-cern to one of Hitler's limited education. But that Albert Ein-stein was also among the exiles should have given him pause. Along with Einstein went the formula which was to place the atomic bomb in American and not in German hands.

Having Germany well in hand, the time had come for Hit-ler's "logical expansion." (*"Heute gehört uns Deutschland, Mor-gen die ganze Welt"*—"Today Germany is ours, tomorrow the world.") The annexation of Austria, or *Anschluss* (attempted first in 1934 but blocked by Mussolini), was planned and car-ried out with cold-blooded precision.

The Austrian chancellor, Dr. Kurt Schuschnigg, was

invited to be a guest at Hitler's home in Berchtesgaden. Within twenty-four hours this confident statesman had been reduced to political helplessness. Exposed to every form of psychological intimidation, Schuschnigg agreed to legalize the Austrian Nazi Party, pardon imprisoned Nazis, appoint Artur von Seyss-Inquart as minister of public safety and attach one hundred German officers to the Austrian Army.

Once back at home Schuschnigg regretted his timidity and twelve days later defied Hitler and demanded a plebiscite. This "act of perfidy" was just the excuse Hitler had been waiting for. When he massed troops at the Austrian border, Schuschnigg resigned and fled the country. On March 13, 1938, Seyss-Inquart proclaimed the *Anschluss* an established fact. On March 14 Hitler marched into Vienna.

Next on his list was Czechoslovakia.

Now flanked on three sides by "Grossdeutschland," this fortress state with its munitions works, its wealth of resources and its strategic location was a tempting morsel. It was also easy prey. Along Czechoslovakia's northern border, in the Sudetenland, lived almost three million people of German origin. "Suddenly" they developed a great desire for stationary repatriation. That is to say, they felt the Reich should expand and envelop them. Thus was the "Fifth Column" tactic of the Spanish War coming into its own.

Under the leadership of Konrad Henlein these Sudeten Germans took advantage of the freedom granted them by Czech democracy to form their own military organizations, whose similarity to those of the Nazis was obvious. Finally on April 24, 1938, in the Karlsbad Declaration, Henlein openly demanded autonomy for the Sudeten Germans.

Again the historic "if." IF those governments which helped create the Czech Republic after World War I had really been interested in its survival, could they not have saved it? Could Hitler have been stopped before he became

too strong? The answer is very probably yes. We know now
that in 1938 Hitler was bluffing, that he was not prepared to
back his demands with a full-scale war. But neither at the
time were France and England ready for armed conflict.
The United States was a neutral and Russia, though bound
diplomatically to France, was unwelcome to England as
an ally. Therefore England and France adopted a policy of
"appeasement."

On September 12, after a summer of uncertainty punc-
tuated by diplomatic activity, increased French mobilization
and the expansion of the British fleet, Hitler flatly demanded
self-determination for the Sudeten Germans. Rioting broke
out in Czechoslovakia and martial law was proclaimed.

It was then that Britain's prime minister traveled to Berchtesgaden. Carrying his well-known umbrella, which newspaper cartoonists later used as a symbol of appeasement,
Neville Chamberlain agreed that Czechoslovakia had no
right to demand arbitration. Like Schuschnigg before him,
Chamberlain did not realize till he returned home what had
been put over on him. But it was too late. Having won this
first concession, Hitler now demanded not only the surrender of the Sudeten territory with factories and military establishments intact, but a plebiscite to be held by November for
those areas of Czechoslovakia with a large German minority.
This time Chamberlain and France's Premier Edouard Daladier did confer with Russia while the United States appealed
to Hitler for a meeting of European powers. At the eleventh
hour Mussolini came up with a plan for a four-power meeting, held in Munich.

One of the most shameful betrayals in history was cheered
at the time by millions with sighs of relief. Chamberlain,
returning from the meeting where he had joined Daladier
in selling out Czechoslovakia, stepped from the plane which

brought him home and announced, "I believe it is peace for our time."

Hitler's "last territorial demand" was soon carried out. While Germany annexed Czechoslovakia's well-fortified western frontier, Poland and Hungary chewed off chunks in the east. In March 1939 the remaining core of this short-lived republic placed itself under "German protection."

Japanese troops meanwhile were sweeping across great areas of Chinese territory. To the "incidents" of Lukuchiao and Shanghai were added those of Soochow, Nanking and Hangchow. Under Generalissimo Chiang Kai-shek the well-trained Chinese army fought a dogged and defensive battle against an even better trained and ruthless adversary. And here, as in Spain and Ethiopia, it was the unarmed civilian population which suffered. Although civilian suffering was as old as warfare itself, never before had it been inflicted with such impersonal and mechanized brutality—nor had it ever been so thoroughly documented. This documentation, in the form of newsreels and on-the-spot reports, was not only condoned but encouraged by the Axis partners with the idea of striking fear in the heart of anyone who might seek to oppose them. To a certain extent this plan succeeded. But in many countries this "terror propaganda" had just the opposite effect. Shown in the United States, the Japanese newsreels, coupled with reports of renewed Nazi anti-Semitic activity, went a long way toward enabling President Roosevelt to combat American complacency and inaugurate his 1938 preparedness program. By 1939, "isolationism" in the United States was a dying issue. In Europe "appeasement" was also soon to die in the only way it could, by violence.

69

The Atlantic Charter

How the "War of Nerves" Gave Way to
"Total War" and How Hitler
Made Some Serious Miscalculations

On March 22, 1939, Hitler demanded the Baltic port of Memel: it had been ceded by Germany to Lithuania after World War I. The city was immediately yielded. Turning now to his former ally, Poland, Hitler demanded the city of Danzig and the right to build a motor highway and a railroad across the "Polish Corridor." Poland demurred and looked to Britain and France to back her up. Realizing, at long last, the outcome of appeasement, Britain and France pledged mutual aid to Poland in the event of German aggression.

Poland now also hoped for the Soviet government's support. But the Soviet Union suddenly began to shift her course. The first hint of this came when Foreign Minister Vyacheslav Molotov opened a verbal attack on Britain. Then, in August 1939, the unimaginable happened. Even Communist sympathizers were speechless with astonishment when Nazi Germany and the Soviet Union signed mutual trade and non-aggression pacts. (One of the stipulations the Nazis made, and which Stalin granted, was that the Soviet Union surrender to Hitler those former German Communists who had fled to Russia in 1933.)

With German "volunteers" already marching into Danzig and creating "border incidents," the British government was voted wartime powers. On August 31, 1939, Hitler announced that the Poles had rejected *his* sixteen-point peace proposal, a document which in reality they never saw. At dawn Nazi troops crossed the Polish frontier.

That day Albert Forster, leader of the Nazi Fifth Column in Poland, proclaimed the return of Danzig to the German Reich. With Nazi tanks rolling across Poland and the "Luftwaffe" (Air Force) displaying its startling, new "Blitzkrieg" (Lightning War) tactics, England and France sent Hitler an ultimatum demanding the withdrawal of German troops from Polish soil. Hitler rejected it. On September 2, 1939, Britain and France made a joint declaration of war. The "war of nerves" was over and in its stead began that global struggle called World War II.

With the western powers unable to lend immediate aid, Poland was carved up on schedule. On September 12 Soviet troops marched across her eastern border. The battered city of Warsaw surrendered to the Nazis.

For about six months, western Europe now experienced "the phony war," one of those deceptive lulls of which we spoke before. Having sent an expeditionary force to cool its heels in France, the English dug shelters at home and waited. Nonetheless pressure was brought to bear on the other members of the British Empire. Australia, New Zealand and India declared war on Germany immediately. On September 5, when Jan Christiaan Smuts became prime minister, the Union of South Africa defeated a proposal to remain neutral. Canada joined England on September 12. Only Ireland, remembering past grievances, remained "neutral" and provided a cooperative and convenient listening-post for Hitler's espionage.

In France the "Maginot mentality" still prevailed. Following the advice of her minister of war, André Maginot, France had built massive and supposedly tank-proof fortifications along her eastern borders. Costing two million dollars a mile this Maginot Line was never completed and thereby rendered useless. (The money appropriated to extend the fortifications along the Belgian frontier found its way into certain politicians' pockets.) Despite this fact a large portion of the French army manned the pill-boxes and lived for months in moist subterranean barracks.

Across the Rhine Hitler's answer to M. Maginot had been the "Siegfried Line." From here his troops did little that winter but use loudspeakers to hurl insults at their ancient enemies while the French retaliated in kind.

On the high seas, however, Nazi submarines were very active. Their threat to world shipping caused the Pan-American Conference, held in Panama, to declare a "safety zone" around the western hemisphere. The United States forbade its ships to enter belligerent waters but Roosevelt repealed the arms embargo and placed exports to belligerents on a cash-and-carry basis.

In eastern Europe the Soviet Union had quietly gone about securing fortified bases in Estonia, Latvia and Lithuania. Now the same demand was made of the Finns. When the Finns balked Soviet troops attacked.

Thus Europe was faced with the spectacle of a "war within a war." Italy considered itself sufficiently neutral to join Britain and France in sending planes, supplies and technical advisers to the aid of General von Mannerheim and his brave little army. Also neutral, the United States lent Finland ten million dollars. For a while it seemed as if Finland would be able to hold off the invaders indefinitely. But after three months of intense winter warfare Finland's "Mannerheim Line" was breached. In March 1940, Finland sued for peace and yielded ten percent of its territory, including the Karelian isthmus, to the Soviet Union.

What was the reason for this seemingly arbitrary move on Soviet Russia's part? Again I must refer you to your map. If you look at it closely you will discover that, despite their treaty with Hitler, the Soviet leaders were providing themselves with "buffer territory" all along the frontier. History was to prove them very wise indeed.

With the arrival of spring a new song was becoming popular in Germany. It was called *"Wir fahren gegen England"* ("We go against England"). As a first step toward the realization of this plan, Hitler ordered the invasion of Denmark and Norway. In this way he hoped to outflank England and secure bases and ports in the North Sea. Denmark was quickly overrun. Norway, despite extensive propaganda and Fifth Column preparation, put up a stiff fight. Now, too, for the first time English and French troops went into action. The Germans were driven out of Bergen and Trondheim. But in Norway's rugged terrain only one factor counted, air superiority. The Germans had it. When, on June 7, 1940, King Haakon fled to London, a Norwegian Nazi named Vidkun Quisling was made minister president and a new word for "traitor" found its way into every language of the world.

Tragic as it was, the debacle in Norway had one fortunate result. At No. 10 Downing Street, traditional residence of British prime ministers, Neville Chamberlain's appeasing umbrella made way for Winston Churchill's defiant cigar. Long called a "war monger," this great statesman and leader of Britain's Conservative party now was hailed as "the man of the hour." An eloquent orator and man of letters, Churchill promised the British people nothing but "blood, sweat and tears" and summed up the new British policy and goal with the words "Victory—victory at all costs, victory in spite of all terror, victory no matter how long and hard the road may be; for without victory there is no survival." (By coincidence the opening measures of Beethoven's Fifth Symphony were

found to have the same rhythmic beat as the letter "V" in
Morse Code. Aired over the BBC for the first time on July 20,
1941, this became the symbol of victory for all who opposed
the Axis.)

The darkest days for England were yet to come. On May
10, 1940, the day Churchill became prime minister, Hitler
out-flanked the Maginot Line by invading Belgium, Luxembourg and the Netherlands. Despite the arrival of French
and British troops Holland surrendered in four days and Belgium in eighteen. Outnumbered and outmaneuvered, the
Allies retreated towards the vicinity of Dunkerque where
the Nazis encircled them and drove them literally into
the sea. But Hitler had not reckoned with Britain's sea-going
citizenry. In one of the most heroic rescues ever undertaken
a fleet of nine hundred destroyers, launches, fishing craft,
river tugs and pleasure yachts braved the Blitzkrieg and took
three-fourths of the British army off the beaches.

Hitler's air force having rendered the Maginot Line as
obsolete as the cross-bow, France crumbled quickly. To protect it from bombing, Paris was declared an open city. When
the government quit Paris and fled to Tours and finally to
Bordeaux it reflected the panic which had seized the French
as a whole. Goaded by Nazi Fifth Columnists, civilians
clogged the radial roads leading out of Paris and impeded
the movement of troops going towards the front. On June 10,
Mussolini dropped his mask of neutrality and, in the words
of President Roosevelt, "plunged the dagger into the back of
his neighbor." On June 15 the Nazis entered Paris. A week
later Hitler performed a little dance of triumph in the Forest
of Compiègne for the benefit of the newsreels. Then, in the
same railway car in which the Armistice of 1918 had been
signed, France surrendered. Germany occupied two-thirds
of France, and the remaining territory was ruled by a puppet
government in Vichy under Marshal Henri Pétain. Britain
now stood alone.

For once Hitler's schedule was wrong. France fell almost two months sooner than he had expected. He was not yet ready for the next and logical step, the invasion of the British Isles. The necessary invasion barges and other equipment were on order but were not completed till August. But by that time the era of German air superiority had passed. Hitler's hopes of finishing up in the west before turning to the east were to be shattered by "The Few."

In August of 1940 the "Battle of Britain" began. Wave upon wave of German planes flew across the English Channel, displaying over Coventry, Manchester and London the same skill and precision they had shown over Warsaw, Oslo and Rotterdam. Much to their surprise a handful of British planes rose to meet them. These were "The Few," those RAF fliers who in that fateful winter manifested a courage matched only by that of Britain's civilian population. These were the days when one city after another was being "Coventryized," and Hitler boasted that not even U.S. aid could save England from her fate. But as more and more Nazi planes were destroyed and as RAF bombers began their raids over Germany, the invaders' hopes grew dimmer. Then, beginning in 1942, the American Eighth Air Force joined the RAF and the embattled island became an "unsinkable aircraft carrier."

Again an "if." If the British Isles had become a Nazi air base, would American cities have felt the Nazi Blitz? Knowing what we do now of Germany's pioneer work in guided missiles and jet propulsion, the answer is undoubtedly yes. Fortunately in December 1940 Roosevelt called for full air aid to England and termed the United States the "Arsenal of Democracy." In March 1941 he signed his name to a bill numbered HR 1776 and lend-lease came into being. In August of that same year, meeting aboard American and British warships anchored off Newfoundland, Roosevelt and Churchill drew up the Atlantic Charter. This eight-point document finally placed the United States squarely behind Great Britain in her battle with the Axis and in so doing gave the world the basic tenets of the future United Nations Charter.

While this Anglo-American friendship was prospering the Italian-German one was running into difficulties. Whereas Roosevelt and Churchill had both repudiated all desire for territorial expansion, Mussolini was finding his Axis partner far more expert at land-grabbing than he had bargained for. Then too, although Italy had annexed Albania in 1939, on every subsequent move Mussolini was forced to rely on Hitler to help him out.

Setting out from Libya in September 1940, the Italians pushed eastward along the coast into Egypt before the English had a chance to strike back. When they did, they threatened to make short work of Mussolini's half-hearted conquerors. It was then that the German Afrika Korps, under the leadership of General Erwin Rommel, arrived on the scene, recaptured Tobruk and pushed the British back to El Alamein.

The Italian fiasco in Greece was also no doubt prompted by Mussolini's urge to emulate his more successful Axis partner. Late in October 1940 he sent his troops from Albania into Greece. By mid-November they were soundly trounced. This Greek victory not only dealt a stunning blow to Axis prestige but also gave Britain the excuse she needed to come to Greece's aid and enter Europe by "the back door of the Balkans." In Hitler's anticipated eastward thrust an Allied army marching north could have caught him from the flank. Although the necessity for protecting Italy delayed his impending invasion of Soviet Russia for one fatal month, Hitler headed south. German instead of Italian tanks rolled into Athens in April 1941.

That Hitler had his eye on the Balkans had long been obvious. In June 1940, Soviet Russia again anticipated a German move and seized Bessarabia from Romania. By August the remainder of the country was demobilizing and the Nazis walked in. Thus Hungary and Bulgaria joined the Axis. But when the same action was taken by the Yugoslav government, rioting broke out and King Peter was forced to flee. This was Hitler's cue to march. Nor did he stop till he had taken Greece and surprised the British by an airborne invasion of the island of Crete. The date was May 20, 1941. To make Mussolini's ignominy all the more complete, British troops were in possession of Ethiopia, which they had liberated the day before.

That same month Rudolf Hess, Germany's third deputy Führer, parachuted to earth in Scotland in the hope of achieving, through personal contacts, what Hitler's bombing strategy had failed to bring about, an end to the German war with England. Hess was made prisoner of war but the reason for his mission soon became obvious. On June 22 Hitler invaded the U.S.S.R.

The Soviet Union was not completely taken by surprise. For three weeks the two huge, well-matched armies clashed at the border. Then the "Stalin Line" broke and the Germans fanned out. Now Hitler made the greatest mistake of his career. He allowed his "Master Race" theories to cost him a victory.

Many Russians looked upon the invading Germans as liberators. Under the leadership of the Russian General Andrei Vlassov six anti-Communist divisions placed themselves at Hitler's disposal. Ready to join them were two million men to whom the overthrow of the Kremlin meant the fulfillment of a dream. But according to Alfred Rosenberg, Hitler's racial theorist, the Russians were "Untermenschen" in the Nazi scheme of things, a people fit only for slave labor in the nefarious Organization Todt. Hitler was out to conquer Russia, not to liberate it. He thereby sealed his doom. Passionate nationalists, the Russians loved their country more than they disliked the Politburo. Disgusted with Hitler, they deserted Vlassov's cause.

Having committed themselves, the others fought on with him, retreated with the Germans and were finally captured in Germany. Handed over to the Soviets by the Americans, Vlassov and his followers met traitors' deaths in 1945.

Heading north, Hitler besieged Leningrad in September 1941, and in November he overran the Crimea and attacked Sevastopol. Regardless of losses, the embittered Russians made the Germans pay for every inch of ground. Then, on the road to Moscow, the month that Hitler had lost in taking Greece caught up with him. His troops ran into Russia's eternal ally, "General Winter." Undernourished because of the Soviet "scorched earth" policy and lacking adequate winter clothing, the German army was brought to a standstill outside Moscow and was forced to wait till spring. By then two things had changed; the Russians had a new ally and the Wehrmacht a new commander-in-chief. The latter, who now conducted the war by "intuition," was none other than the ex-Corporal Adolf Hitler, who had promoted himself to the rank of field marshal. Russia's new ally was the United States.

Between Japan and the United States relations had been growing increasingly strained. A full Axis partner since September 1940, Japan had suffered a curtailment in American war materials. Japanese assets in America were frozen. One by one the more cautious elements in the Japanese government were replaced by men of the temper of General Hideki Tojo, who became premier on October 16, 1941.

On December 7, while the Japanese peace envoy Saburo Kurusu was in Washington to continue negotiations, Japanese planes made a surprise attack on Pearl Harbor in the Hawaiian Islands.

70

Global War

How the Axis Was Defeated in the "Battle of
Production" But Final Victory Was Scored by
American and British Scientists and
a New Era Dawned for All Mankind

The more you look at the map the more incredible it seems.
In December 1941 the Japanese held northeastern China. By
June of 1942 they had also overrun the Philippines, Guam
and the Netherlands East Indies. They dominated French
Indo-China and Thailand and threatened India by way of
Burma. They landed on Attu in the Aleutians. At Pearl Har-
bor their bombers had crippled a major portion of the U.S.
Pacific Fleet.

This was indeed the "year of agony" for those who
opposed the Axis. Yet in one respect it was a year of triumph too. Twenty-six nations, many of them represented by
"governments-in-exile," committed themselves to the principles of the Atlantic Charter and thereby formed the nucleus
of what was to become the United Nations.

When the American declaration of war on Japan was followed by counter-declarations on the part of Germany and
Italy, the United States geared its entire industrial capacity

for war. In this era of highly mechanized warfare it was necessary not only to outfight but also to outproduce the enemy. As in other countries, women now joined the men in the defense factories and were inducted as auxiliaries into the army, the navy and the Marine Corps. Every technical skill, every branch of science and medicine was brought into play. Radar, penicillin, plastic materials are but a few of the discoveries whose development was hastened by the "defense effort." Overnight, trans-oceanic flying became commonplace. And now too the United States government allotted millions of dollars for research into a hitherto obscure branch of science, that of atomic fission.

The first all-American bombing raids over Germany did not take place till 1943. But on November 8, 1942, barely two weeks after General Sir Bernard Montgomery's decisive victory over Rommel at El Alamein, U.S. and British forces landed in French North Africa. Germany immediately occupied all of France yet failed to secure the French fleet. Part of it set sail for North Africa. The rest was scuttled in the harbor of Toulon.

That autumn was a crucial one on every front. In September the Red Army dealt a crushing defeat to the Germans at Stalingrad and thereby blocked their thrust towards the Caspian oil fields. In November the Japanese, still smarting under the April bombing of Tokyo and Yokohama by carrier-based U.S. planes, suffered their first defeat at sea. A three day naval engagement in the Solomon Islands ended in victory for the United States.

It was in a spirit of optimism that Churchill and Roosevelt met at Casablanca in January 1943. With Stalin unable to attend and France represented by the rival Free French leaders, Giraud and de Gaulle, the Allies felt certain enough of victory to press for the "unconditional surrender" of the Axis partners.

The next few months brought that victory nearer. In all of Russia the German forces had now begun a slow retreat. In the Pacific, General Douglas MacArthur reported a hard-won victory over the Japanese on Guadalcanal in the Solomons. Under General Dwight D. Eisenhower, the American Second Army, moving eastward along North Africa, met the British Eighth Army in Tunisia. A month later, on May 12, 1943, the last remnants of the once-proud Afrika Korps surrendered at Cape Bon.

With the Allied victory in North Africa, Mussolini's prestige collapsed. An Allied landing on Sicily was followed by the overthrow of Mussolini and his imprisonment. The Italian government, now headed by King Victor Emmanuel III and Marshal Pietro Badoglio, surrendered unconditionally on September 8. But a week later Mussolini was rescued by German troops and taken to northern Italy, where he proclaimed the establishment of a Republican Fascist party. Fighting in Italy continued until 1945 with German troops retreating inch by inch the length of the peninsula. The destruction of the beautiful Monte Cassino monastery which the Germans used as an observation post, the bombing of German-held Rome, the havoc wrought by the Allied landing at Anzio, the demolition of the bridges of Florence, these were Mussolini's legacy. His friendship with the Führer ended in making Italy a German "buffer-territory." Disguised in a Wehrmacht uniform, the onetime Duce attempted to escape to Germany in April 1945. He was captured by partisans and shot.

The Second World War was the war of global conferences. Air travel made it possible for the wartime leaders and their aides to meet and discuss informally the problems of mutual concern. Twice Churchill crossed the Atlantic to meet Roosevelt, once in Washington in 1941, once in Quebec in 1943. Late in November of that year Generalissimo Chiang Kai-shek flew to Cairo to confer with Roosevelt and Churchill on far eastern strategy and two days later the British and the American leaders met with Premier Stalin at Teheran.

With the exception of those troops on occupation duty in Nazi-held territories and those facing the Allies in Italy, the bulk of Hitler's armies was deployed along the eastern front. To relieve this pressure it is understandable that the Soviet Union clamored for the opening of a "second front." On June 6, 1944, with the invasion of Normandy, their wish was realized. D-Day had arrived.

As a result of the daring strategy, detailed planning and precise coordination achieved by the Supreme Headquarters of the Allied Expeditionary Force (SHAEF), the troops which crossed the Channel or parachuted from the skies to storm the heavily defended Atlantic Wall were able to capture both Cherbourg and Caen within a month. Under the leadership of General Eisenhower the liberation of France soon became a reality. On August 15 another landing was made, this one on the Riviera. Ten days later the other Allies halted outside of Paris to accord French troops the honor of joining the underground as French Forces of the Interior in the job of clearing the last remaining Germans from the French capital. Sweeping south of Paris, the American Third Army, under the command of General George S. Patton, made a swift armored thrust toward the River Rhine. But to the north, in Belgium and Holland, geography and the weather aided the Germans in making one last determined stand.

Allied airborne troops dropped at Arnhem failed to receive the ground support they needed from the south. They were encircled and all but wiped out. Breaking the dikes to flood the low-lying country was undertaken by German and Allies alike, thereby turning much of the land in the Rhine Delta into impassable swamps. This prevented German troops from sweeping south as they had done in 1940. It also prevented an Allied northward thrust to outflank the west wall. The Allies stopped to consolidate their gains. Then came the "Battle of the Bulge."

The amazing thing about this last great German counterattack was its degree of success. That, in turn, was due to the fact that the Allies were taken by surprise. No one, not even the German generals themselves, believed their armies still capable of taking such a stand. But Field Marshal Karl R. G. von Rundstedt who commanded the German forces in the west had received an order from the Führer. He was in no position to quibble. Since the events of July 1944 Wehrmacht generals were expendable.

Friction between Hitler and the German general staff had been of long standing. Out of the nucleus of Hitler's personal pre-1933 bodyguard had come the "SS," short for "Schutzstaffel" or Protective Echelon. Again and again Hitler had promised the Wehrmacht hierarchy that the SS would not be armed. Then he had promptly turned around and formed SS divisions, providing them with the finest equipment and such high sounding names as "Totenkopf" (Death's Head), "Leibstandarte Adolf Hitler" and so on. When Wehrmacht soldiers faltered, SS officers would be sent in to keep them in line. But Hitler's self-appointment as commander-in-chief of the armed forces was the last straw. The Wehrmacht plotted a revolt. On July 20 a bomb planted in a briefcase injured Hitler only slightly, and his escape convinced him more than ever of his league with destiny. After General von Witzleban and several co-plotters had been brutally strangled Hitler held the reins firmly in his hand. It was he who ordered a German breakthrough to the sea.

Coming at a time when Brussels, Antwerp and Aachen were already in Allied hands, the attack by twenty-four divisions began on December 16 and lasted eight days. Under orders to take no prisoners, the SS and Wehrmacht troops swarmed over an area of about one hundred square miles.

At Bastogne the American 101st Airborne Division was encircled and its surrender demanded. As answer the Germans received from General McAuliffe the now classic monosyllable "Nuts." Elements of the Third Army lifted the siege of Bastogne. On December 24 a raid by seven thousand planes brought the Germans to a halt. It was not until early the following February that the last of them were driven from Belgian soil.

While the allies were preparing to cross the Rhine in force, American troops luckily discovered an undestroyed railway bridge at Remagen, south of Bonn. Other crossings by boat brought the bulk of the Allied armies over the river in March.

From the east meanwhile the Soviet advance was steadily progressing. Finland, which had sided with Germany in 1941, suffered a second Soviet attack shortly after D-Day. In the south the Red Army reached the Romanian border by March of 1944. The invasion of Hungary and Czechoslovakia followed, and with the ultimate surrender of Budapest in February 1945, the Soviet conquest of the Balkans was complete.

In April 1943 the Soviet government had broken off diplomatic relations with the Polish government-in-exile. In the capture of Warsaw in January 1945 the reflection of a new but as yet veiled pattern of power politics could be seen. Later that month the Red Army crossed the River Oder and on February 7 was rolling toward the outskirts of Berlin.

On that day Stalin was playing host to Churchill and Roosevelt at Yalta in the Crimea. From this, their last meeting, came the Yalta agreement, postwar plans for Germany and Austria and an arrangement for the Soviet participation in the war against Japan.

Elected for a fourth term of office in 1944, Roosevelt was not a well man when he went to Yalta. Two months later, on April 12, 1945, he died at Warm Springs, Georgia, and his vice

president, Harry S. Truman, was sworn into office that afternoon. The following day the Red Army marched into Vienna
and at the first United Nations parley in San Francisco on
April 25 came the announcement that Soviet and American
troops had met on the River Elbe. Before the signing of the
United Nations Charter brought the two-month session to a
close the war in Europe was over. On May 1 an announcement was made by Grand Admiral Karl von Dönitz that Hitler had committed suicide in his bomb-shelter beneath the
ruined Chancellery in Berlin. A week later came the German
unconditional surrender at Reims. V-E Day was May 7, 1945.

Anti-German feeling ran high as Stalin met with Truman and Churchill in Potsdam in July to discuss the postwar
plans. British ire had been particularly aroused by the sudden
appearance of jet-propelled long range bombs and rockets
which the Germans launched after D-Day from the French,
Belgian and Dutch coasts. (Known as "V-Weapons," the "V"
was the Nazi answer to the "V for Victory" of the Allies. In
German it stood for "Vergeltung" or retaliation.) The Soviet
Union, as has been mentioned, deeply resented the wholesale deportation of its citizens to work as slave labor in the
Organization Todt. Worldwide indignation was aroused by
the discovery of the Nazi concentration camps where Jews,
political prisoners and all "enemies of the state" were herded
together to die of disease and starvation, or in the highly efficient gas chambers.

For their wanton "war crimes" those Nazi leaders who
had not followed their Führer into death were tried before a
four power tribunal in Nuremberg. One, Martin Bormann,
was never captured and was condemned *in absentia*. Two
died awaiting trial, three were acquitted, seven imprisoned
for life and ten hanged. On the eve of the hanging Hermann
Göring committed suicide in his cell.

During the Potsdam Conference a British election swept

the socialist leader Clement Attlee into office. As the new
prime minister he took Winston Churchill's place at the conference table. Now, with two of the Axis partners defeated,
the Allies turned their entire interest to the war with Japan.

A possible Japanese invasion of Australia had been fore-
stalled in 1942. Over a vast expanse of ocean, much of it
thirty-five hundred miles from Japan itself, American, British, Australian and Philippine troops began a new kind of
amphibious warfare known as "island hopping."

Initiating a concerted offensive in July 1943, the Allies
bypassed certain of the larger Japanese-held islands completely and attacked those which could provide air bases
from which planes could harass the Japanese shipping of supplies. In this way it was possible to starve the Japanese from
many islands without a fight. But a look at the map will show
you the magnitude of this operation. If only one island in
every hundred was invaded you can still see why the Pacific
war took such a terrific toll on lives.

The offensive began with the taking of tiny Rendova
Island in the Solomons. By the year's end Bougainville Island
and the air base at Munda on New Georgia Island had been
secured. On New Guinea Salamaua had fallen and the Japanese in Lae were encircled. The Allies now struck out toward
the Gilbert Islands and began a great encircling move.

In the year 1944 the Japanese discovered how difficult it
was to chew what they had bitten off. Though many of these
islands were no more than coral atolls, their possession by
the Allies was a vital necessity. In an outer arc, landings were
made at Kwajalein and Eniwetok in the Marshall group and
a bold thrust was made into the Marianas. With the recap-
ture of the bypassed island of Guam in August the Allies had
a base from which superfortresses could bomb Kyushu, the
southernmost of the Japanese islands. Moving up the New
Guinea coast Aitape and then Hollandia were taken as well

as Admiralty and Schouten Island. Landings were also made in the Carolines and the Moluccas. On October 19 General Douglas MacArthur was able to fulfill a promise when he stepped ashore at Leyte in the Philippines.

On the Asiatic continent, meanwhile, Chiang Kai-shek's troops were scoring victories and the Japanese had been driven out of India. With the Burma Road to China still in Japanese hands a regular Allied air-freight service had been initiated from India over "the hump" to Chiang Kai-shek's provisional capital at Chungking. Then began the grueling but successful campaign to force the Japanese out of the Burmese jungle.

The last phase of the Pacific war began late in 1944 when Saipan in the Marianas became the base for an all-out air offensive against Japanese industrial targets. It was an extremely hazardous undertaking: Japan was still more than 1,000 miles away. In March 1945 the month-long battle for the fortress island of Iwo Jima gave American bombers a base within 750 miles of Yokohama. This was followed in April by the invasion of Okinawa. Coinciding with the defeat of Germany, the greatest air offensive of the war could be unleashed on cities only 325 miles away. In southeast Asia, meanwhile, Admiral Lord Louis Mountbatten was able to announce a complete victory of British, American and Chinese forces over the no longer "Banzai-ing" Japanese.

Already aghast at the toll on lives the war had taken, the Allies knew that the contemplated invasion of Japan itself would take still more. While re-deployed troops were on their way from the European battlefronts, science stepped in to bring the war to a speedy and terrifying conclusion.

Physicists the world over had long been aware that the atom was not, as the Greeks had believed, a basic and unchanging entity. Research into the problem of converting "matter" into "energy" by splitting the atom had been hampered only by the need for securing "fissionable" material in sufficient quantities to make experimentation possible. The basic or key formula on which these experiments would be based was, as you know, carried from Germany to America in the head of the exiled German scientist, Albert Einstein.

The Allies knew that the Nazis had appropriated large sums of money to continue research along atomic lines. A daring British sabotage raid on a "heavy water" plant at Rjukan in Nazi-held Norway was made with this knowledge in mind. It was now clear to such scientists as Enrico Fermi, Lisa Meitner and Einstein himself that the discovery of atomic energy could place a powerful weapon in the hands of those who came upon it first. The urgency of this matter was pressed upon President Roosevelt and in greatest secrecy an atomic laboratory—which became a town in itself—was set up at Oak Ridge in Tennessee.

Working together, British and American scientists were able to witness, on July 16, 1945, the first atomic explosion ever seen by man. It took place in the desert at White Sands, New Mexico. On August 6, a second explosion took place, this one over the Japanese city of Hiroshima. In one devastating blast three-fifths of the city was destroyed, many thousands of people killed and as many injured. Three days later a third and even more devastating atom bomb was dropped at Nagasaki.

These events, coupled with a Soviet declaration of war upon Japan and a simultaneous invasion of Manchuria, brought Japan to her knees. Assured that their emperor, Hirohito, could remain, the Japanese surrendered formally aboard the U.S. battleship "Missouri" anchored in Tokyo Bay. This was V-J Day, September 2, 1945.

The nightmare of global war was over. Yet, as detailed reports of what had taken place in Hiroshima and Nagasaki filled the news, all mankind realized that a new and disturbing era had begun. What had been discovered could not be kept a secret by the United States and Great Britain forever. What was to be the future of the world now that this terrifying force was at man's disposal? For an answer the world now turned to the United Nations.

71

The United Nations

How the United States Fell Heir to World
Leadership and Played Host to the Participants
in a Great Experiment in International Relations

Oscar Wilde once quipped, "As long as war is regarded as wicked it will always have its fascination. When it is looked upon as vulgar, it will cease to be popular." If he had substituted the word "unprofitable" for "vulgar" he would have come even closer to the truth. Armies march not only "on their stomachs," as the saying goes, but on hope; the hope of a victor's recompense—riches, new territory, a better life or, ironically, peace. Take away this hope and armies will cease to march.

The havoc wrought by World War I seemed to have done just that. Calling it "the war to end war," optimists maintained that another such mechanized slaughter would be totally unfeasible and unprofitable even for the winner. But mankind is a creature of habit and slow to learn by his mistakes. Two decades later another war broke out. Those who started it hoped for a quick, violent and profitable victory. Instead they were defeated and their cities suffered great destruction and their governments bankruptcy. But the victors suffered as much if not more. Large portions of the Soviet

Union lay in ruins. China was racked with internal strife. The British Empire partially disintegrated and its burden of leadership shifted to the United States. In order to maintain its economy and have nations to do business with, the United States had to begin lending financial support to former allies and enemies alike. (This aid soon served another and almost more vital purpose, of which more later.)

The mushroom-shaped atomic cloud over Nagasaki had done more than bring Japan's dream of an Asiatic "Co-prosperity Sphere" to an abrupt end. Like a finger pointing to the sky it seemed to warn that warfare with atomic weapons would spell out "Winner take nothing." The alternative was arbitration of some new kind.

Even before the atom bomb was dropped, Winston Churchill had suggested that the United States, the British Commonwealth and the U.S.S.R. band together to create an organization as unprecedented in history as had been the creation of the United States of America itself. The urgency was so great that, despite the fiasco of the League of Nations, the idea took hold.

Anticipating the havoc and the misery the war would leave, the United Nations Relief and Rehabilitation Administration held its first session in Atlantic City in November 1943 and a second one in Montreal the following September. (UNRRA, as it was known, became the International Refugee Organization in 1947.)

In April 1944 the formation of a U.N. Organization for Educational and Cultural Reconstruction was proposed at a meeting of Allied Ministers in London. At the Bretton Woods Conference in July of that year forty-four nations participated in the first U.N. Monetary and Financial Conference, aimed at improving world-wide economic conditions through the creation of an International Monetary Fund and an International Bank for Reconstruction and Development.

Finally, after the Dumbarton Oaks Conference held in October, the "Big Three" published the proposals for a permanent international organization to be called the United Nations. This proposal was endorsed by Churchill, Roosevelt and Stalin at Yalta and worked out in detail in San Francisco in 1945. The Charter of the United Nations provided for the representation of all peace-loving nations in a General Assembly, and for a more powerful Security Council comprising five permanent members—the United States, Great Britain, the U.S.S.R., China and France—plus six other members elected for a term of two years each. Also there were created an Economic and Social Council and an International Court of Justice. The administrative work was to be undertaken by the Secretariat headed by a secretary-general. The first man to hold this post was the Norwegian Trygve Lie.

The question of how the Security Council members were to vote created difficulties from the start. As finally arranged at the Crimea Conference, a negative vote or "veto" by one of the five permanent members would be enough to defeat any proposal except one concerning procedure.

Through making excessive use of the veto the Soviet Union soon displayed its former truculence and its proverbial distrust of the western world. It became evident that the U.S.S.R. had little intention of attempting an honest settlement of the postwar problems in which it was involved. Whereas in 1943 the Soviet Union had voluntarily dissolved the "Comintern"—its international propaganda organization—as a gesture of friendship to its "fellow democracies," its delegates now accused their recent allies of "economic imperialism," thereby seeking to mask the Soviets' own increasingly imperialistic intentions. These, however, were rapidly becoming obvious.

At the Potsdam Conference it had been agreed to partition Germany and Austria. The capital cities of these two countries, although now both within the zones accorded the Soviets, were themselves divided into four parts. At the time when the U.S.S.R. lowered an "Iron Curtain" between its territories and those held by the other three occupying powers, England, France and the United States still maintained military government headquarters in Vienna and Berlin. This arrangement the Soviet Union found irksome. In order to force the Allies out of Berlin, in 1948 the Soviet government adopted the policy of blocking all road, rail and canal traffic from the west. The American answer to this was the "airlift," an air shuttle service from Frankfurt to Berlin that provided the French, British and American sectors with such vital necessities as food and coal. After a year and a half of mounting tension, during which the matter was referred to the United Nations, the Soviet Union lifted the blockade in May 1949. Instead of withdrawing from those Balkan countries they had overrun, the Soviets drew them closer and closer into their orbit. Finally, by means of a neatly staged *coup d'état*, they placed Czechoslovakia behind the Iron Curtain in 1948.

Elsewhere in Europe Soviet strong-arm tactics were meeting with less success. In Italy King Victor Emmanuel III stepped down in favor of his son, Umberto. He, in turn, bowed to a referendum held in 1946 and Italy became a republic. Amid the existing chaos of this disillusioned, impoverished country the threat of a Communist "Putsch" loomed large on the horizon. It was then that American Marshall Plan aid, under the European Recovery Program, yielded its first benefits. This plan, suggested by the wartime chief of staff and later secretary of state General George C. Marshall, was designed to lend financial aid to those countries not under Communist control—thus becoming America's realistic answer to Soviet expansion. Emerging from World War II as a powerful champion of the cause of self-government, the

United States became the logical protector of those countries resisting totalitarian domination.

The American policy of "Soviet containment" also helped curb the spread of Soviet influence in France. Following a substantial gain by the Communist faction in the French national elections in 1946, France was in turmoil. For the next few years French governments rose and fell. Still, during this time the Council of Europe was formed, consisting of the Benelux countries (Belgium, the Netherlands and Luxembourg), France, Italy, England and Ireland and the three Scandinavian kingdoms. By 1950, thanks to the Marshall Plan, France was once more in a condition stable enough so that it no longer feared communism, and put forward the "Schuman Plan," which called for a pooling of west European coal and steel production. Britain, invited to join in this, held herself aloof.

In one of the Balkan countries Joseph Stalin now met with unexpected resistance. Under Marshal Tito, the wartime guerilla leader, Yugoslavia at first seemed content to become just another Soviet satellite. Suddenly, in 1948, Tito bolted and established himself as a Communist dictator without benefit of the Soviet Union. Though Tito did not openly turn to the western powers for support they welcomed the breach he had made in the Iron Curtain. Late in 1950 Yugoslavia received substantial Marshall Plan aid from the United States.

To the south, Greece was the only European country where liberation did not bring the fighting to an end. When the British overcame the Nazi invaders in 1944, pro-Communist resistance forces immediately attacked the liberators in order to forestall the restoration of the monarchy. When in 1946 a plebiscite brought about the recall of King George II, antiroyalist guerillas, aided by Communists infiltrating from the north, increased their depredations by way of protest. On King George's death in 1947 his brother Paul came to the throne. That same year the United States appropriated three hundred million dollars for Greek aid, and U.S. supplies enabled the Greek forces to bring hostilities to an end in 1949.

With the Zionists insisting on the creation of an independent Jewish state in Palestine, and with the newly formed Arab League threatening to meet such a move with armed resistance, in April of 1947 Great Britain handed the problem over to the United Nations. On May 15, 1949, the British mandate over Palestine ended and the new republic of Israel was proclaimed. War broke out immediately, but the Arab League was no match for the Israeli forces. A temporary truce was arranged through the Swedish U.N. mediator Count Folke Bernadotte, the same man who had acted as go-between in arranging the German surrender in 1945. After Bernadotte was assassinated at the hands of a political extremist, Dr. Ralph Bunche, an American, continued the mediation. He succeeded in obtaining an Israeli-Egyptian armistice. For the first time in two thousand years the Jewish people had a nation and a flag of their own. In 1949 Israel was voted into the U.N.

In India too nationalism had long been asserting itself. Independence had been one condition demanded of the British in return for participation in the war against Japan. Now, however, the Moslem League under Mohammed Ali Jinnah sought the creation of a separate Moslem state of Pakistan. The Hindus opposed this plan firmly and Great Britain became more and more reluctant to take sides. Bringing matters to a head, early in 1947 the English announced the imminent transfer of authority to "responsible Indian hands" and bade the Hindus and Moslems reach an understanding. Yet despite the partition of British India into the republics of Pakistan and India, religious strife and bloodshed followed the actual withdrawal of the British in August 1949. Mahatma Gandhi, the Hindu lawyer whose doctrine of "passive resistance" had contributed so much toward Indian independence, was assassinated in 1948. His disciple Pandit Nehru soon placed India in a position of leadership in Asiatic affairs. Both India and Pakistan are members of the U.N.

Elsewhere in the east the Japanese war cry of "Asia for the Asiatics" had aroused many a nationalistic echo. Abiding by its promise, the United States granted the Philippines their independence in 1947. In the Netherlands East Indies a revolt broke out which ended only when, through U.N. intervention, the United States of Indonesia was formed. Similar rebellions faced the British in Burma and Malaya, and the French in Indochina found themselves embroiled in a full-scale jungle war against well-armed guerrillas from the province of Vietnam.

It was no coincidence that all these insurrections bore a similar, Communist stamp. The spread of Soviet influence, though momentarily checked in Europe, was made easy in the Orient by the exploitation suffered at the hands of western empire builders by the native populations. Although they had much to be thankful for in the field of medical help and education, in their eagerness to throw off the yoke of the west they failed to realize that by merely exchanging one form of imperialism for another they had less to gain than to lose.

The most tragic example of this was China. Though the war with Japan had temporarily healed old political antagonisms, its end brought a new eruption of them. Chiang Kai-shek's reactionary and dictatorial government relied on the support of its western allies to keep it in power, but at a crucial moment it failed. Soviet-backed Communist forces under the veteran Communist leader Mao Tse-tung attacked the Nationalist forces in October 1945. Chiang appealed to the United States for aid and was rebuffed. He was forced to give ground and finally, in January 1949, he resigned and fled to the island of Formosa. There he proceeded to build the largest anti-Communist force in all Asia.

Once in control of the Chinese mainland, the Chinese Communists established a new capital at Peiping. Afterward, their forces invaded the province of Tibet, high in the Himalayas. India, which had seemed friendly toward Mao Tsetung, viewed this latest move with great concern. In French Indochina, Chinese Communist aid to the Vietminh troops now caused the French to withdraw their forces from frontier positions. It was against this troubled background that the Korean War was waged.

As agreed at Yalta, Korea was divided at the thirty-eighth parallel into two zones, the northern to be occupied by the Soviet Union, the southern by the United States. Friction between these two rival powers was reflected in the violence which broke out during the elections held in 1946 and 1948 in the American zone. After the creation there of the Democratic Republic of Korea both sides mobilized, the South Koreans with the aid of American officers, the North Koreans with Soviet aid. On June 25, 1950, without warning or provocation, the North Korean army marched across the thirty-eighth parallel. Taken by surprise, the South Koreans fell back. Then, for the first time, the United Nations flag went into battle. Using Japan as a spring-board, General Douglas MacArthur took command of the U.N. forces fighting in Korea.

With amazing speed American troops in Korea were augmented by others called from Japanese occupation duty and from the United States. They were soon joined by contingents from England, Australia, Canada, the Philippines, France and Turkey. The U.N. forces succeeded in driving the North Koreans back across the thirty-eighth parallel and reached the Manchurian border in November 1950. Then Communist China intervened. Severely outnumbered, the U.N. troops fell back along the road they had come. At the port of Hungnam the largest troop evacuation since Dunkerque was successfully carried out and the troops were put ashore further down the peninsula, ready to fight again. The bitter Korean winter seemed to agree with the Chinese troops even less than it did with the U.N. forces, and by spring the Chinese were retreating once more toward the north.

Realizing now that the Soviet government would be deterred from further aggression only by a show of strength, the United States initiated a program of full-scale mobilization and war production. At the same time it promised close support and cooperation to the twelve European nations that had signed the North Atlantic Pact in 1949. On an American proposal to rearm western Germany, bitter opposition was voiced by France. On the other hand, Konrad Adenauer, chancellor of the newly formed Bonn republic, made use of the strong bargaining position of western Germany to insist that rearmament be accompanied by full equality of western Germany with the other Atlantic Pact nations.

Then on December 19, 1950, the twelve Atlantic Pact nations met in Brussels and appointed General Dwight D. Eisenhower as supreme commander of the proposed western European army.

72

A Turbulent Peace

How the Cold War Has Developed in Europe as
Open Conflict Erupts in Other Lands

The Korean War did not end the way that wars usually end, with a victory and a peace treaty. After many months of confused and bitter fighting between the forces of the United Nations and those of the Communists, armistice negotiations were begun on July 5, 1951. These talks dragged on for more than two years while the fighting continued intermittently. The stumbling block which caused most of the trouble was the repatriation of prisoners. The representatives of the United Nations wanted a program of voluntary repatriation, but the North Koreans insisted that all prisoners should be returned to their native countries whether they wanted to go or not. This would have resulted in the executions of many thousands of unwilling Communist returnees. Finally, however, compromises were worked out and, on July 27, 1953, an armistice was formally concluded and political conditions reverted to what they had been before the aggression began.

The war had been unpopular in the United States (which had supplied the great majority of the men for the fifteen-nation forces of the United Nations) and it had been costly—billions of dollars had been expended and almost two million casualties had been suffered. What had really been accomplished? For the first time in history, an armed force representing an international group of nations had succeeded in turning back a military thrust against a peaceful country. The United Nations had passed its first great test. To the multitudes of Asia though, something even more remarkable had taken place. These millions, subjected to indignities by Europeans for centuries, saw the conflict as a blunting of American imperialist desires in the far east by an emerging China. Western power and influence had been frustrated by an oriental power awakened from a sleep of centuries. Whether for good or evil, out of the ashes of Korea had emerged a "new" force in world politics and things would never again be quite the same. Today, the embattled nation of Korea remains a divided and potentially dangerous area where no permanent peace agreement has ever been effected.

While the fighting along the thirty-eighth parallel in Korea had continued, the nations which had created the North Atlantic Treaty Organization carried out their plans to secure western Europe from Communist attack. The original twelve signatories to the pact (Belgium, Canada, Denmark, France, Iceland, Italy, Luxembourg, the Netherlands, Norway, Portugal, the United Kingdom and the United States) were joined, by 1954, by Greece, Turkey and West Germany. The war in Korea had heightened American fears of Russian expansion and the United States had taken the lead in advocating a rearming of West Germany. The French, however, showed considerable anxiety over the rearming of their recent conqueror and also voiced displeasure at the rather lukewarm British commitment to the organization. Despite these internal difficulties, the Western European Union came into existence in 1954 as an indication of the determination of the nations of the West to oppose further Soviet expansion. The Russians could not view these moves with anything but alarm. They countered by creating, in 1955, the Warsaw Treaty Organization in an attempt to imitate the western program. The eight members of this pact (Albania, Bulgaria, Czechoslovakia, East Germany, Hungary, Poland, Romania and the U.S.S.R.) have shown considerable differences of opinion on many issues and revealed severe internal stresses—political, economic and ideological. The disagreements between the members of the two groups that do exist cannot hide the fact that Europe is once again, as so often before, divided into armed camps. But, hopefully, other forces are at work which might, in the somewhat distant future, put an end to the nationalistic bickerings and squabblings which have been the bane of European life for so many centuries.

On August 10, 1952, a proposal developed by Jean Monnet and Robert Schuman of France was put into operation. This was the Schuman Plan by which six industrial nations (Belgium, France, Italy, Luxembourg, the Netherlands and West Germany) banded together to form a European Coal and Steel Community to make possible a pooling of their mineral resources. This arrangement was quite successful and the cooperative agencies which had been set up to supervise its workings became the basis for further cooperation between these nations. On January 1, 1958, the European Economic Community, or Common Market, was formed. The goals of this organization include: a plan to develop economic activities throughout the European community by eliminating tariff barriers, the establishment of a free movement of labor and capital across political borders and the hope that eventual political unity can be achieved through economic cooperation. The structure has been a great success even though Great Britain's bid for membership was blocked several times by France. These were only temporary delays, however, and Great Britain was finally accepted for membership in 1971.

With all this economic cooperation, western Europe slowly moves toward the day when individual nations would forget their differences in a common cause.

Twenty years after the most horrible of wars, Europe was (thanks in great part to American aid) more prosperous than it had ever been. It was still far from complete political unity and it had to live with the American-Soviet rivalry which could explode into war at any time. Even so, western Europe was more optimistic and aware of its responsibilities and opportunities than ever before. Nineteenth-century autocrats like Napoleon I and Tsar Alexander I had dreamed of uniting Europe by conquering the other nations but had failed. Now there was a chance that the twentieth-century statesmen, elected to their offices and responsible to their electors, could succeed where their predecessors had failed. Who would dare compare Robert Schuman to the great Corsican and yet, someday when there is something like a United States of Europe, might not the name of the first be as famous as that of the second? Stranger things have happened.

It is recorded that on the tomb of Timur the Lame (whom we call Tamerlane) there is an inscription, "If I were alive, you would tremble." The terror that this man inspired in his lifetime shines through this awful warning. Only a few men who have lived in the centuries since Timur have used fear so effectively as he did. One such man was Josif Vissarionovich Dzhugashvili, whom the world calls Stalin, the "man of steel." This one-time theological student from Georgia near the Black Sea ended his life as the terror of millions. When, on March 5, 1953, a strange death ended his thirty-year rule as all-powerful leader of the Soviets, few tears were shed over his passing. Once he was safely dead, the usual power struggle took place and Georgi Malenkov became the leader of Russia. Since that time, Russia's attitude toward the west, and especially the United States, has been characterized by rapid changes of policy which, while confusing and irritating, have added up to an improvement over the inflexibility of Stalin. If the world has been kept in a state of tension, it has been less charged with danger than before, and we can perhaps begin to think of the possibility that competition and "peaceful coexistence" will someday replace fear. The "thaw" in the Cold War that has developed has not resulted in any major Soviet concessions to the west, but it has been evidence of the fact that the Soviets no longer follow the "hard" Stalin line which taught that war between them and the west was inevitable. They seemed to believe that they could conquer the world by "peaceful" means and were willing to try to do so with political and economic instead of military tools.

Malenkov, who concentrated upon increasing the flow of consumer goods to the Russian people at the expense of war production, was ousted from office on February 8, 1955, when these policies did not find favor with certain of the ruling elements. He was followed in office by Nikolai Bulganin, a marshal of the Soviet army, and Nikita Khrushchev, a party functionary and one of the most remarkable political figures of this century. Bulganin, who was a rather drab figure, was gradually eased from power by the clever Khrushchev, who remained as the Russian leader until his overthrow in 1964. It is worth nothing that neither Malenkov nor Bulganin was executed. They were simply "demoted." This is, in itself, representative of the quite remarkable change that has come over Russia since the death of Stalin. For almost a decade, Khrushchev occupied the center of the world stage and gave a truly memorable (if sometimes a bit incredible) performance. Whatever his faults and idiosyncrasies, he was responsible, in great measure, for the fact that relations between Russia and the western nations at the end of his tenure of office were much better than they ever could have been under Stalin. Perhaps he recognized that inflexibility was not the easy road to success. Stalin had believed it was. Or perhaps he believed that it was really possible for the Communist system to outdo the capitalist nations in open economic competition. We don't know what went on in his mind. It may have been for another reason entirely.

The first crack in the Communist monolith had appeared as early as the defection of Tito in 1948. When, on June 28 of that year, Yugoslavia was expelled from the Cominform, it was evident that all was not well in the Communist bloc. Unrest, chiefly caused by nationalistic feelings antagonistic to Soviet directives that all must look to Moscow as the final loyalty, was near the surface in many places. On June 17, 1953, workers in East Berlin rioted against conditions in their sector of the divided city. All too obvious to their eyes was the fact that life in western-occupied West Berlin was superior in every way to life in Soviet-occupied East Berlin. The West Germans had, with generous American help, performed the miracle of rebuilding their shattered land and now enjoyed a standard of living equal to that of any other European nation, and Berlin was a kind of shining light in the darkness of East Germany. The drab and regimented existence of the East Berliners showed up and contributed greatly to the discontent of the people. Trouble broke out. For several days an incredulous world was treated to scenes of fighting between stone-throwing German youths and massive Russian tanks but, and inevitably, the tanks won out. Order, if not contentment, was restored. Again, on June 28, 1956, similar riots broke out in the Polish city of Poznan. Here long-standing resentment against Russian occupation was coupled with Roman Catholic protests over state interference with religious affairs and together they produced an explosive situation. After some angry demonstrations an uneasy truce was effected and Poland has remained within the Russian orbit (although its ties to the west have been considerably strengthened in recent years). Even these Russian difficulties with the satellites were dwarfed by the revolt that began in Budapest on October 24, 1956. Thousands of Hungarians, led by Imre Nágy, participated in a nationwide uprising, centered in Budapest, against the Russian masters of their country. An amazed world watched as Russian puppets were hurled out of office and revolutionary officers installed. The Russian occupying army had withdrawn to observe the progress of the revolution and to determine whether or not it could be quelled by the Hungarian police and army. On November 4 they had decided that things could not be allowed to continue in the direction in which they were going and the Red Army returned to Budapest, and crushed the revolt. Thousands were killed and thousands more were imprisoned, placed in internment camps or deported to Siberia. Almost a quarter of a million Hungarians fled their homeland to take refuge in the west. The revolt, though unsuccessful, showed plainly the degree of dissatisfaction that existed in the satellite nations and left many wondering whether the puppets of eastern Europe might not turn out to be millstones instead of jewels about the Russians' necks. The revolt also showed that the new "peaceful coexistence" policy of the Kremlin could be pushed only so far and no further. When the anti-Stalinist Wladyslaw Gomulka had come to power as a result of the Polish unrest, Khrushchev had not intervened directly because he saw the difficulties only as an extension of Polish nationalism and independence and he accepted Gomulka as an alternative to armed intervention. But Hungary was a different story. There, the threat of a complete overthrow of the Red regime brought down the Russian wrath. Gomulka remained in power until the riots in 1970, while Nágy was treacherously murdered. Thus, though all has not been well for the Russians in these unhappy areas, there have been no further successful defections from Communist rule. Yugo-slavia remains a "Communist neutral" and has maintained a precarious national communism; Albania no longer serves as the mouthpiece of Red China and remains isolated; Catholic Poland is the only Communist nation to give legal recognition to the Common Market; Romania has closer economic ties to France than she does to her neighbors and so on. Even so, no man or nation can live in the shadow of the Red Army and be completely independent of Russian influence, but the events in the satellites have shown that even rigid adherence to Marxist principles has not been enough to stifle completely the independence of mind that makes man the highest of the animals.

Russia is not the only center of communism. The growing part in international affairs that Red China has been playing since Chiang fled to Formosa at the end of 1949 has been mentioned before. Neither the despots of antiquity nor the dictators of the modern world succeeded in imposing the degree of control upon their peoples that Chairman Mao and his followers have accomplished. Family life, so dear to Chinese civilization, has been almost obliterated and replaced by unquestioning loyalty to the state. A program of forced communization was begun that dwarfed the efforts of the Russians in this direction a quarter of a century before. Too, the Chinese began to play more and more of a part in the affairs of Asia. Their intervention in Korea was only the first of many such adventures. Tibet, which they had long claimed, was invaded and crushed in 1951. Indian territory was annexed in 1959 and again in 1962. To millions of people in the underdeveloped areas of the world who have long been accustomed to the aggressive moves of the white man, similar actions on the part of the Chinese have been accepted and even applauded. To these people, the Chinese Revolution, based as it is on the uprising of the peasants (as contrasted with the Russian emphasis upon the industrial working class), has had a considerable attraction. Their needs and their desires are met by the beliefs and action of Mao (or so they profess to believe) and China has taken its place as a leader of world politics to a degree exceeded only by the U.S.S.R. and the United States. This rise to eminence has been accompanied by terrible suffering. Families have been uprooted and whole cities have been moved or re-created without regard for human life. Internally, opposition to the new programs has usually meant death. Chairman Mao admitted in 1958 that eight hundred thousand "enemies of the Revolution" had been liquidated, but experts in the United Nations calculated the number of executions at an even higher figure. In 1956, Mao gave a celebrated speech in which he ordered that China should "Let one hundred flowers bloom. Let one hundred schools of thought contend." He did not foresee that his invitation to more intellectual freedom would result in widespread denunciation of the excesses of his regime. When this happened, the old curbs were returned and they have remained since. Although much hardship and many reverses have been suffered, the face of China has been redone. A tottering nation has become a giant, albeit one with enormous difficulties to overcome. China exhibited a fanatical anti-westernism especially in the late sixties during "the Cultural Revolution." Other developments have shown that serious differences between China and the Soviet Union also exist. As early as 1956, it became clear that all was not well in Sino-Soviet relations. The reason for this trouble (besides the ideological difference already mentioned) include the rivalry for leadership of the Communist world between the two Red giants and a Chinese belief in the inevitability of atomic war with the west which the Russians, with their hard-won industrial progress at stake, will not accept. There have been small battles along the border, and the future may well see a complete split between the Communist leaders but whether this will bode good or evil for the world is impossible to see. Meanwhile, a nation in which one-fifth of the population of the world lives is engaged in a rapid industrialization that will, with its virtually unlimited resources of people and minerals, make it one of the world's leaders for many years to come. The Chinese have, despite much hardship and the reverses suffered during the excesses of the Great Leap Forward, as they called their industrial movement in 1958, made great industrial advances, including the production of nuclear weapons.

Although China finally joined the United Nations in 1971, her exact destiny is still unclear. Yet it is certain that this huge country is awake and will play a major role in the future of mankind.

Another power has also risen again in the far east. The damage done by Japan's utter defeat—symbolized by the atomic fire balls of Hiroshima and Nagasaki—was repaired under the firm guidance of General MacArthur. The emperor of Japan has divested himself of his former "divinity," the Mitsubishi and other big business dynasties were dissolved and a new constitution was put into effect which permitted the establishment of strong labor unions and democratic political institutions. Whether or not this democratization will be permanent remains to be seen.

Japan was soon making giant strides toward economic recovery and economic expansion through cooperation with the west. Thanks to "the Japanese Economic Miracle," the hardworking, intelligent Japanese people were again making goods that were sold throughout the world. Tokyo became the most populous city in the world, and Japan became a place where old ways crossed and blended with the new. Cherry blossoms, kimonos and Shinto shrines remained, but in the large cities, a forest of television antennas appeared above the roofs of quaint Japanese houses. Automobiles crowded the narrow streets. Billboards and neon signs advertised everything from the latest American motion picture to the newest Toyota automobile to come off the Japanese assembly line. Japanese guitar-playing cowboys strummed in night spots while modern Japanese department stores in Tokyo's shopping district—the Ginza—displayed English ties and French gowns.

The greatest changes may have taken place in Japanese social life. Women play a greater role in business, education and political life. The modern democratic family is replacing the all powerful father. Perhaps these changes are but a prelude to the dimming, if not the destruction, of the old military values which the Japanese people have inherited from their feudal past.

The continued position of the United States as the world's greatest power has been one of the realities of the world picture since the capitulation of the Axis partners in 1945. Except for the Soviet Union, no nation on earth has ever dared to challenge seriously the military power of the United States. Prosperous as no other nation has ever been (though they are but one-twentieth of the world's population, Americans enjoy almost one-third of the world's estimated income), its citizens believe themselves committed to the protection of the free world. America's participation in the Korean venture had shown her determination to fill the requirements of this new role. The old spirit of isolation (or neutrality) was gone forever. As early as 1949, the United States had helped to create NATO as a bulwark against Russian expansion in Europe and in doing so had pledged herself to a constant involvement in European affairs. A similar commitment was made in Asiatic affairs when, on September 8, 1954, the South East Asia Treaty Organization (SEATO) was formed. This agreement, sometimes referred to as the Manila Pact, included Australia, France, Great Britain, New Zealand, Pakistan, the Philippine Republic and the United States as members. This pact was signed only a year after the conservative Dwight Eisenhower had taken over the reins of American government from Harry Truman, and was an indication that no fundamental change in American foreign policy had taken place. Eisenhower, who could speak from a position of incredible military strength because the United States had added the most powerful of all weapons, the hydrogen bomb, to its arsenal on November 1, 1952, carried out the policy of "containment" of communism that his predecessors had inaugurated with the Truman Doctrine. A pact guaranteeing the safety of Formosa was signed in 1955 and a program to combat Red inroads in the Middle East (the Eisenhower Doctrine) was announced on January 5, 1957. While pursuing these policies which were aimed at stopping communism's spread, Eisenhower also attempted to improve diplomatic relations between the United States and Russia. In the summer of 1955 he met with the Soviet leaders in a "summit conference" at Geneva, Switzerland. Later, in 1959, he played host to the first visit of a Russian ruler to the United States as Nikita Khrushchev and American Vice President Richard Nixon exchanged visits. The furthering of understanding that took place as a result of these meetings was shattered on May 5, 1960, when an American reconnaissance plane was shot down deep over Russian home territory (the U-2 incident). The handling of the affair by the administration (the United States claimed at first that the craft was merely a weather ship that had strayed off-course and this crude attempt at a cover-up was gleefully exploited by the wily Khrushchev) resulted in a considerable loss of American prestige. America did not regain "face" until October 1962 when the new president, John F. Kennedy, instituted a naval blockade of Cuba to prevent the Soviet government from supplying "offensive" rockets to Cuba's revolutionary leader, Fidel Castro. The resolute and courageous fashion in which this explosive affair was handled evoked admiration and confidence in the American nation and its new leader. Tragically, President Kennedy was murdered on November 22, 1963, and the presidency passed into the hands of Lyndon B. Johnson.

In 1956 there were only three independent nations in Africa south of the Sahara (Liberia, Ethiopia and the Union of South Africa). After the passage of a decade there were thirty-seven. This emergence of the African areas into the world's political arena has been a phenomenon of great importance. "Uhuru," a Swahili word meaning freedom or independence, has resounded throughout the continent since the terrible Mau Mau uprising in British Kenya that began in 1952. The first of the new African states to become free was the former British colony of the Gold Coast, which achieved independence as Ghana on March 6, 1957. It was soon followed by Guinea, Nigeria, Gabon, the Ivory Coast and, eventually, more than thirty others. Some of the periods of transition from colony to independent nation were marked by relative tranquility (as in most of the former British colonies where some degree of native participation in government had been encouraged). In other areas, this was not the case. The great Belgian colony in the Congo, for example, was granted independence on July 1, 1960. Within hours, an army revolt began that soon turned into anarchy and atrocity. Europeans fled for their lives and only the intervention of United Nations troops, mostly from the African nations, prevented what could have become disastrous civil war. However, so weak and inept was the new Congolese government and so strong were the ancient tribal divisions within the country that the tensions were not eased for several years. The experience in the Congo illustrated the new nations' lack of many of the characteristics of government that provide economic and political stability and these needs will continue to exist for years to come. The emerging areas are handicapped by religious and tribal disunity and are sorely lacking in trained and responsible leadership. Too often, political adventurers possessed of charisma (that indefinable attraction which made Hendrick van Loon's grandfather forget his Dutch hatred for the French and follow the banner of Napoleon) have caused great harm to their nations by reckless or misguided actions. Kwame Nkrumah, the dictatorial first leader of Ghana, and Patrice Lumumba, the rather unstable leftist who led the Congo until his abduction and murder six months after the achieving of independence, are prime examples of this kind of irresponsible leadership. The more farsighted African leaders have tried to build a federated Africa and, although the problems to be found in such a project are immense, a start has been made. In 1961, an Inter-Africa and Malagasy Organization was formed to promote African unity. This group was succeeded by the Organization of African Unity in 1963. The purposes of these organizations have been to promote the unity and development of Africa and to attempt to erase the traces of European colonialism. Today, however, everywhere in Africa there is dictatorship, corruption and inefficiency—the heritages of a European colonialism much more interested in economic gain than in the social or cultural advancement of the subject peoples. Too, everywhere there is an awareness of the developing power of the black man and an interest in his problems no matter where they exist. Pride in the black heritage has been continually stressed by leaders such as Julius Nyerere of Tanzania and leads many Africans to become interested in racial and civil rights problems in the United States. It is not too much to say that every movement in American race relations is followed by the residents of Nairobi, Lagos and Conakry. Nor is it too much to say that racial discord in the United States might have a definite bearing on the outcome of the contest between the United States and the Soviet Union for political favor in black Africa. However this problem is resolved, we can only hope that the peoples of Africa will accept cautious long range programs for their own betterment and will not fall prey to Utopian schemes offered to them by self-interested leaders and agitators from the outside.

North of the Sahara, there have been problems, too. Many Palestinian Arabs, who had lived on lands out of which Israel had been carved, were refugees living in the Gaza Strip along the Mediterranean Sea or on the west bank of the Jordan River. The impoverished refugees, who endured wretched conditions in refugee camps, plotted to destroy Israel so that they could return to their former homes, and were a source of serious concern to the Israelis. Indeed, the Arab nations of the Middle East and of North Africa refused to recognize the new Jewish state, and vowed to drive the Israelis back to the sea. Egypt (which was renamed the United Arab Republic in 1958) assumed a leading role in the Arab world. Egypt's leader in this venture was Gamal Abdel Nasser, who had been one of the leaders of the 1952 revolt which overthrew the corrupt reign of the notorious King Farouk.

Although the first Arab-Israeli War (1948) had been stopped by United Nations action, tensions continued to mount in the Middle East. Under an agreement with Egypt, Great Britain had guarded the Suez Canal for many years. In 1956, the British troops withdrew. In the same year, Nasser seized the canal and closed it to Israeli shipping. Israel sent an army to take over the canal, and British and French troops landed in the canal area in order to keep it open to ships of all nations. When the United Nations met, both the United States and the Soviet Union supported a United Nations condemnation of the military actions, and Great Britain, France and Israel withdrew their forces. In recompense for Israel's withdrawal to her old borders, the United States guaranteed free passage for Israeli ships into the Red Sea through the previously blockaded Strait of Tiran.

Until his death in 1970, Nasser was the undisputed leader of the Arab world. He had successfully removed the Suez Canal from foreign control in 1956 and, as a result, his prestige and potential as a leader was almost unlimited. After the Israeli-Egyptian War of 1956, the bitter dispute over Israel's right to exist and occasional raids continued. When the Egyptians reimposed the blockade of the Strait of Tiran, the Israelis realized that eventual war was inevitable. The Israelis took the initiative and powerful Israeli forces waged campaigns simultaneously against Egypt, Jordan and Syria, winning resounding victories. After six days of combat, a cease-fire left the Israelis occupying all of the Sinai Peninsula, the Gaza Strip, the east bank of the Suez Canal, all of the west bank of Jordan, and the strategic Golan Heights in western Syria. After the Six-Day War, the Arab nations were more bitter than ever and began sending trained guerrilla fighters into Israel, and the Israelis continued to strike back. In 1969, while guerrilla activity continued, Prime Minister Levi Eshkol died. He was succeeded by Mrs. Golda Meir, who, in her younger years, had taught school in the United States.

Why is the Middle East such a tinder box where a single spark could ignite a conflict that might possibly become the dreaded World War III?

Israel began as a neutral nation, willing to accept aid from the Communists as well as from the west. The Soviet Union, however, soon turned from Israel to the Arabs with a covetous eye toward the Arabs' oil and the possibility of establishing its naval power in the Mediterranean Sea. The United States, and many other western nations, do not want Russia's hopes of dominating the area to become a reality. Hence the United States, which tried to help both the Arabs and the Israelis, was forced to become Israel's firmest supporter among the great powers.

The Arabs say that oil is often mixed with blood and sand. This is sadly true. The area is divided into two armed camps, and at stake are the great oil fields of the Arabian peninsula and North Africa, the control of the Suez Canal and military dominance in the Mediterranean basin.

These nations of the Middle East and Africa have much in common with their Asiatic and our Latin American neighbors. They share the terrible problem of overpopulation. It is estimated, for instance, that the populations of the United Arab Republic and Costa Rica will double in less than twenty years and China adds between fifteen and twenty-five million people to her masses every year. All suffer from want of capital and skilled workers. The differences in the living standards of these underdeveloped areas and the highly industrialized nations of the west are immense. While the per capita income in the United States was over $3,000 in the mid-sixties, the average Bolivian worker earned about $130 and the average Indian worker received $55 for his year's labor. The gulf between these peoples is obviously great. Programs to aid these nations, such as the Alliance for Progress that is sponsored by the United States in Latin America, are trying to remedy the effects of centuries of exploitation but the problems, despite tremendous expenditure, remain acute. Five hundred million dollars in American aid goes to the nations of Africa every year, and double that is given annually to help the people of Latin America. The French, the British and the Russians have also contributed aid to these new countries and will continue to compete for the favor of the former colonies. These new nations have understood all too clearly their advantages and disadvantages in this political tug-of-war between east and west and have been quite content to accept aid from both sides without committing themselves politically to either. Money and goods flow to these new nations in much greater amounts than they ever received while they were colonies and we can observe the spectacle of the former masters competing for the favors of peoples who were their virtual slaves only a decade ago.

Europe's recovery from World War II has been almost complete. Britain no longer rules the waves but she is still a force in European politics and her commonwealth is a major factor in the world's economy. France, which was suffering from domestic ills and colonial uprisings in 1951, has righted herself. Charles de Gaulle, who helped to create the Fifth French Republic and bring order out of chaos in 1958, returned France to prominence. Her colonies are gone—some by bloody revolt (Algeria and Indochina) and some by amicable parting of the ways (the members of the French Community such as Chad and Gabon)—but France's stature has returned. De Gaulle convinced Frenchmen that theirs is a mighty destiny and he led the difficult way to economic stability and international prestige. By the time de Gaulle retired from politics in 1969 France had become one of the world's nuclear powers and now sees herself as the leader of a new Europe where she hopes to replace the United States as the determining factor in politics. Many Frenchmen suffered agonies over the losses of Algeria and Indochina, but these losses had to be endured. France is a better nation because of them.

In 1963, France and West Germany signed a treaty of mutual friendship. With this declaration, signed by de Gaulle and Konrad Adenauer, some of the hatred and distrust of centuries was removed. Of all the strange and wonderful events of the recent past this is certainly one of the most encouraging. Perhaps it is not too much to hope that other men and other nations, profiting by the example of these two ancient foes, might resolve their differences in ways other than war.

The world today is threatened as never before with total destruction. The spark to set off World War III might come from an incident in divided Berlin (divided by an actual wall since 1961!) or from another Israeli-Arab clash. It could come from one of the periodic battles between Pakistan and India; the latest Indian victory over Pakistan and the creation of Bangladesh in 1972 certainly stirred up Moslem-Hindu hatred. Or it might come from Cuba or Cyprus or the Soviet-Chinese border. Or it might come from Vietnam or elsewhere in Southeast Asia. With all these potentially explosive situations, it is obvious that the United Nations has not solved all of the world's problems. But it has accomplished much—aggressions have been stopped in Korea and in the Middle East, order has been brought out of disorder in the Congo and on Cyprus and much has been accomplished of a humanitarian nature. It is a far-from-perfect body, but it remains, in the words of the American president John Kennedy, "The last hope of the world."

73

An Old Order Gives Way

As Memories of the Wars of the First Half
of the Twentieth Century Fade Away,
New Generations Strive "to Tame the Savageness
of Man and Make Gentle the Life of the World"

By 1971, all of the great leaders of World War II—Franklin D. Roosevelt, Winston Churchill, Dwight D. Eisenhower, Charles de Gaulle and Douglas MacArthur—were dead. The torch, in the words of John Fitzgerald Kennedy, had been passed to a new generation born in this century, tempered by war, and disciplined by a hard and bitter peace. The younger generation, vigorous and impatient, looked at old problems with critical eyes.

To many of the people of the world John Kennedy represented the new activism and high idealism that marked the troubled sixties. In January 1961, the youthful Kennedy took over the burdens of the presidency from the fatherly and very popular Dwight David Eisenhower. He devoted his brief inaugural address to explaining his country's role in a hungry and divided world. The United States, he said, had been summoned "to bear the burden of a long twilight struggle . . . against the common enemies of man: tyranny, poverty, disease, and war itself." He pleaded with both parties in the Cold War to "begin anew the quest for peace, before the dark powers of destruction unleashed by science engulf all humanity in planned or accidental destruction." On numerous other occasions, he said: "It's time to get America moving again. We can do better, we must do better . . ."

Surrounded by bright young men, President Kennedy saw a "New Frontier" both at home and abroad, and Americans were thrilled by his idealism. "Ask not what your country can do for you," he said, "ask what you can do for your country." Inspired by his words, thousands of young Americans—and many older ones too—joined the Peace Corps or as "Freedom Riders" aided impoverished and unschooled people in the deep south or in Appalachia, where, among other things, they taught the forgotten men and women to exercise their right as American citizens to vote.

To bring equality of opportunity and more freedom to his people, Dr. Martin Luther King, Jr., a young black Baptist minister, fought segregation in buses in Montgomery, Alabama, and in school, jobs, and housing all over the nation. He told us about his "dream of equality of opportunity . . . a dream of a land where men will not argue that the color of a man's skin determines the content of his character."

Discrimination was not a new problem. In the 1940s, President Truman made civil rights a national issue. During his administration, a historic report, "To Secure These Rights," denounced religious and racial discrimination as twin evils frustrating the achievement of the ideal of American democracy. And, in the 1950s, President Eisenhower had completed desegregation of the armed forces, and vigorously enforced the Supreme Court's school desegregation decision in a dramatic confrontation in Little Rock, Arkansas.

After President Kennedy's untimely death, Lyndon Johnson pledged to carry on the New Frontier policies. Indeed, the new president assured the nation in his State of the Nation Address that, if the social needs of the nation were met, the "Great Society" would emerge. In the "Great Society," President Johnson felt, it was the responsibility of the federal government to plan for and cope with national problems such as poverty, discrimination, inadequate medical care, the problems of the cities and so on. He especially wanted to make life in the cities more livable, to provide good educations for all the children and job opportunities for everyone. Until the dream of the Great Society was obliterated by the war in Vietnam, he made some progress toward his goals by securing the passage of civil rights and voting rights acts and inaugurating his war on poverty.

There was an ugly side to the decade of the 1960s, too. The political assassinations of Dr. King and the two Kennedy brothers, John F. and Robert, and the riots and campus unrest, not to mention several vicious wars in Asia and Africa—all cast a shadow over the decade's accomplishments. Life in our large cities became more dangerous, unhealthful and unpleasant by the day. Tons of pollution were dumped into our skies and our waters; crime and the drug menace threatened our lives; slums grew dirtier and increasingly unsafe.

During his brief "thousand days" in office, President Kennedy had shown the way to meet these challenges from home and abroad. In foreign policy he set the style for himself and his successors when he said: "Let us never negotiate out of fear. But let us never fear to negotiate." He also attempted to promote better understanding through personal contacts with heads of states. He found Nikita Khrushchev a "hard nut to crack." After a two day session in Vienna President Kennedy described the difficulties he encountered in negotiating with the Russians in the following words. "The Soviets and ourselves give totally different meanings to the same words: war, peace, democracy, and popular will. We have different views of right and wrong, of what is an internal affair, and of what is aggression. And above all, we have totally different concepts of where the world is and where it is going." Despite such difficulties, however, the United States and the Soviet Union took a first step toward preventing nuclear war by negotiating a treaty to prevent the spread of nuclear weapons to other nations. The treaty was badly needed. Communist China and France were already manufacturing and testing nuclear weapons and other nations like Israel and India were thinking of doing the same. The treaty was drawn up by the Johnson administration and approved by the United States Senate shortly after Richard Nixon became president. Most of the nations of the world would have signed it.

To slow down the arms race, which was not only monstrously expensive but dangerous as well (on the theory that if a little boy has a firecracker he will be tempted to explode it), the two superpowers negotiated the Limited Nuclear Test Ban treaty in 1963 by which they agreed to stop the testing of nuclear weapons in the air, under the water or in space. In 1968, the United States and the Soviet Union joined with other nations in banning the use of nuclear weapons in space. Finally, President Nixon sent representatives to Helsinki, Finland, to begin discussions known as SALT (Strategic Arms Limitation Talks).

In the sixties men and women of this century had grappled with old problems and had met with some success. Yet, during these years, mankind became aware of some very grave problems that had been scarcely noticed at the start of the decade.

74

Spaceship Earth

We Must Maintain the Earth's Life-Support Systems or Pay the Penalty

In the space age, twentieth-century man is probing the unknown with the same curiosity and spirit of adventure as did his ancestors during the Age of Discovery. Like the explorers of the sixteenth century, spacemen take great risks, seek fame, court disaster and are rewarded by being the first to see whole new worlds "swim into their ken." But there is a big difference, too. Whereas months, often years, passed before discoveries became generally known four centuries ago, instant communication by television, press and wire make it possible today for the whole world to see as they occur the fiery take-offs of spaceships, men walking in space, space-vehicles docking and men actually landing on the moon.

On April 12, 1961, in a craft named "Vostok I," a Russian named Yuri Gagarin became the first man to enter the great realm of outer space. For as long as man has lived on this planet, he dreamed of leaving to explore the heavens above him. This dream became a reality as Gagarin's ship soared to an altitude of 203 miles above the earth at a speed of more than 17,000 miles per hour. This flight was a milestone in the race for space leadership between the Soviet Union and the United States that had been accelerated when the Russians launched their first artifical satellite, "Sputnik I," on October 4, 1957. The eyes of men are now on the stars in a way different from they have ever been before. When World War II ended, man was still tied to the earth. Now the whole universe beckons to us.

When Gherman Titov, the second of Russia's "cosmonauts" to orbit the earth, was in flight around the globe, he called back to earth, "I am an eagle! I am an eagle!" The exhilaration he felt is shared by many of us as we realize that, although the awful threat of nuclear war is constantly with us, our potential as creators of our destinies has only begun to be tapped. We stand on the threshold of wonders our ancestors never dreamed of attaining. The world is indeed a most wonderful and dangerous place.

Putting a man on the moon was the ultimate triumph of "the Iron Man," the term Hendrik van Loon applied to the Industrial Revolution. The feat was accomplished by courageous men and the technical skill of "ground control." But there was more to it than this. Actually the tiny spaceship, with its closed life-support system, was backed up by America's mighty industrial power. In a sense, too, the round-trip to the moon, accomplished by Neil A. Armstrong, Edwin E. Aldrin, Jr., and Michael Collins, was motivated by national pride and possible military and commercial advantages that accrue from "getting there first."

Yet, as exciting as their fantastic adventures in the heavens are, all cosmonauts and astronauts must inevitably return to earth from whence they were rocketed into space.

Until very recently, we have taken it for granted that the capacity of the earth's life-support systems was limitless. Since we have started monitoring them, however, we have learned to our dismay that we are in deep trouble. Scientists throughout the world are warning us that, unless we stop abusing its vital life-support systems, the earth's future is grim indeed. Astronauts contrast the awesome beauty of the earth spinning in the velvet blackness of space with the cold grayness of the moon. From space, the surface of the earth is alive with color of incredible beauty—vivid blues, bright greens and swirly whites. From earth, on closer scrutiny, our landscape is scarred and marred, mutilated over the years by the thoughtless excesses of its human inhabitants.

According to Genesis, God told man: "Be fruitful and multiply and replenish the earth and subdue it; and have dominion over the fish of the sea and the fowl of the air and over every living thing that moveth upon the earth." This is one commandment that man has obeyed faithfully and greatly to his peril. In a sense, the whole story of mankind has been the story of how man has been changing his surroundings to suit his growing physical and spiritual needs. He killed deer for food and wolves for safety; he felled forests for shelter, cropland and building materials; he mined the earth for fuels and metals; he dammed and diverted rivers for irrigation, and he used chemicals to combat pests and disease and to lessen the toil of farming. Eventually man's efforts to tame nature and to shape his needs seriously affected the earth's ecology. (Ecology is the relationship of all living things to their surroundings and to other forms of life.)

The problems of ecology began in the Garden of Eden. When Adam cast aside the first apple core, he began the process of despoiling "the good earth." Until quite recently, the earth's resources of water, air and soil seemed inexhaustible. From the dawn of civilization, the life-support systems of earth had kept its air, pressure and temperature in delicate balance so that life could be maintained. While men lived in traditional societies, their lives were bound by custom and limited by the primitive tools at their disposal. Under such circumstances, mankind lacked the power to destroy its environment on a global level. Nonetheless, men did make a desert out of much of the "Fertile Crescent"—valleys of the Euphrates, the Tigris and the Nile, which had served as "cradles of civilization" at the dawn of recorded history. Like the early settlers in the New World, men could always escape the consequences of their ignorance, however; by moving on to greener pastures and to untouched lands.

There is no Garden of Eden on earth today. The careless days of innocence and plenty are now over. Man's power today is such that he can destroy, and, indeed, he is destroying or at least very seriously impairing his environment on a global scale. Today we are gathering in the bitter fruit of unplanned development, ruthless exploitation of natural resources and just plain ignorance. Once clear, pure streams are now rainbow-colored, reflecting not the glow of the sky after a shower, but the only film formed by wastes dumped into them. We are slicing up woodlands for freeways, paving over farmlands for shopping center parking lots, fouling lakes and rivers, disturbing the balance of life in those waters on which human welfare depends. Even more insidious and dangerous is a new and horrifying threat unleashed by man's genius, the power of atomic energy not only to annihilate but also to pollute and destroy life—human, animal and inanimate.

The problems of environment are worldwide. On the arid plain of Castile in Spain, there is a magnificent park of ancient oak trees. The wood is one of the few left of the immense oak forests that once grew in Spain. It has survived because it was the hunting preserve of Spanish kings. The harsh, dry plains of Spain, and of the entire Mediterranean basin for that matter, are a tragic example of what happens when people ignore ecology. In Greece, Italy, as well as Spain, wealthy sheep owners turned their huge flocks loose on the countryside during the Middle Ages, and thus upset the delicate balance of nature. In India, polluted water annually causes two million deaths and fifty million serious illnesses.

Now man is beginning to understand that each advance to a better life has almost invariably come at the expense of his environment. Automobiles have enabled us to travel short and long distances comfortably, but automobile exhausts poison the air. Pesticides improve crop yields, and chemical weed killers eliminate backbreaking hand labor, but they also pollute the streams and the atmosphere.

We can never get rid of all pollution. To return our natural surroundings to their original purity would involve a return to Stone Age living conditions. Man can, however, improve the quality of his surroundings if he is willing to pay the costs involved. He may have to forgo rapid growth; his taxes may rise; and some of the products he buys, now produced cheaply at the expense of his environment, will cost more. At present, our ever-growing population and the increasing quantity of goods produced put "altered resources" or pollutants back into our skies, waterways and lands at a rate so fast that they cannot be assimilated without creating harmful effects.

Another global worry is the increase in the world's population. The population of the earth, now 3.6 billion persons, is growing at a rate that will double the number of persons inhabiting this earth in thirty years. Our own population of 205 million will be more than 305 million in that same period of time. With at least one-third of the world undernourished, ill-housed and poorly clothed now, starvation and universal misery become a stark possibility. Population growth will—indeed, must—end soon because Spaceship Earth, to which humanity is clinging, is a sphere only eight thousand miles in diameter shrouded in a thin film of air and clouds.

In the first century A.D., when Augustus was the Roman

emperor, the population of the world was estimated to be 250 million people. Sixteen hundred years were required to double that figure. Today, the more than 3 billion people on earth will double in thirty years' time, and the world's population will then be increasing at the rate of an additional billion every eight years. Your little brother, born in 1972, living into his seventies, would know a world of 15 billion inhabitants. His grandson might share Spaceship Earth with 60 billion fellow humans. Even now half of humanity is hungry. There is actually less food per person on the planet today than during the Great Depression of the 1930s. Thousands of people are dying each year of malnutrition, if not outright starvation, right now.

In short, scientists have warned us that we are following a primrose path leading to the imminent collapse of civilization because we are destroying the life-support systems of Spaceship Earth by doubling the number of passenger (the world population) every thirty years, by increasing our demands on our limited natural resources and by polluting the planet in the process.

75

The Earth as a Global Village

How the Marvels of Science and Technology
Have Made Our Planet a Shrinking World
and All Men Brothers

What can one say about the gloomy predictions of the world's scientific prophets of doom? Should we dismiss their findings and warnings about population and pollution as scientific fiction?

Perhaps it is best to remember that people have always thought that no previous generation had ever seen so many awful or wonderful events as they did. We are no different from our ancestors in this respect. We believe that we are living in a world whose threats are more terrible and whose promises are greater than any that have existed before. We forget that the atomic holocaust is no more terrifyingly real to us than were the hordes of Attila to frightened peoples of fifth-century Europe and that the material blessings of our civilization seem no more fabulous to us than those of China did to the contemporaries of Li-Po many centuries before Christ was born. On an occasion when the dark clouds of war had lifted just a wee bit, Winston Churchill remarked that, perhaps after all, mankind might soon be "moving along a broad, smooth causeway of peace and plenty, instead of roaming and peering around the rim of hell."

Indeed, the United States and other highly industrialized nations are moving into a more humane postindustrial age. More people are engaged in providing services for their fellowmen in fields such as teaching, medicine and recreation. It is estimated that per capita incomes in postindustrial societies will be fifty times greater than in preindustrial economies. In the future there will probably be guaranteed minimum incomes and basic welfare services for all people. In postindustrial lands education will be a lifelong process. Throughout your mature years, you will probably undergo periodic retraining for other careers, perhaps as many as four in a lifetime. This will be essential because increased leisure will open up new opportunities for self-fulfillment.

The success of the "Apollo 11" mission made the moon man's province. But, psychologically it did more. People now believe that nothing should be allowed to stand in the way of achieving a better world with all of the earth's inhabitants enjoying "the good life," that is, more leisure, economic security, social justice and a clean, healthful environment. Of course, the technological and scientific skills that put men on the moon cannot be converted to working similar miracles with human beings who cannot be programmed mathematically. But many people now think that a country that is able to explore the moon is also certainly capable of making life on earth safe, comfortable and more satisfying.

Today, many people are worrying less about the scarcity of material goods and more about the quality of their lives. The quality of one's life is determined by beauty and cleanliness of one's natural surroundings and one's freedom to pursue leisuretime pleasures even at the expense of lost income and reduced production. Workers are looking forward to a shorter work week so that they can enjoy more leisure hours in doing what they like to do. We have seen the many technological miracles of the past generation: television, space exploration computer science, the conquest of some diseases and space age technology.

Of the many achievements of the Industrial Revolution, the progress made in electronics may well be the most significant for world civilization. It made the space age possible. Starting in the mid-nineteenth century, the human voice was amplified by telegraph, telephone and radio until it could reach every corner of the earth. After photography was invented, photographs could also be sent by wire, made to move and, by means of television, to record events as they were taking place. Without the persuasive spoken words pouring from radio loudspeakers, the new nationalism of black Africans, the Southeast Asians or the Arabs would have been greatly hindered.

With the development of communications satellites, starting with Early Bird in 1965, the world for the first time can be bound together by spoken words. Hitherto such instant news existed only on the level of the village. Farseeing men think that instantaneous communication will, in fact, bring about a global village, and that national boundaries will ultimately fade away and become obsolete. The problems of other countries will become so intimate as to appear to be one's own. Differences among men, which create suspicion and hostility, will tend to lessen. Indeed, soon we may all be speaking a second global language. The benefits of education, news events, even symphonies played in great urban centers, can be shared by people from the Arctic to the tropics.

It seems clear that while the world is threatened as never before, mankind does have the means to work together to avert any great disaster—a new world war, overpopulation or irreparable pollution. The alarm has been sounded in the United Nations and carried by our modern means of communications to the four corners of the world. With courage and determination man will prevail.

76

Entering the High-Tech Age

Technology Advances and New Wars Erupt

People living in any age probably insist that their era is the most dramatic, exciting and challenging in the long story of mankind. The landing on the moon in July 1969 seemed to mark a new stage in human ingenuity and triumph. The 1960s had been, for the most part, a period of great optimism; the 1970s were not. In the 1970s and early 1980s, even our greatest scientific achievements seemed to be a mixed blessing. And some of the perpetual problems of the human condition have obstinately refused to disappear. The deterrence of nuclear war and the protection of our environment may be the greatest challenges mankind has ever faced.

There seems no limit to the astonishing advances that science has brought technologically advanced countries and people who can afford them. The space exploration programs of the United States and the Soviet Union have continued at great cost. Both powers sent spaceships far into our universe. In 1970, a dramatic rescue operation occurred far away in space when an explosion in an oxygen tank aboard the "Apollo 13" spaceship risked the lives of the astronauts. Several years later, an unmanned craft transmitted close photos of Saturn, revealing some of the secrets of its rings. These spaceships can travel as fast as fifty thousand miles

Race for Space

per hour. "Viking I" landed on Mars in 1976, sending back pictures for nightly television news. So many satellites circulate in outer space that those of us left back on earth may soon have to worry about "space junk" falling to our planet. Advances in the space programs of the United States and the Soviet Union may have been made with another purpose in mind: the waging of war, which could bring the popular "Star Wars" movie series and the computerized video games of amusement arcades into a terrifying reality.

Back on *terra firma*, the electronics revolution, the most recent stage of the Industrial Revolution, has made an incredible impact on our lives, from how we bank to how we cook our food. A computer that twenty years ago would virtually fill an entire room has been reduced to pocket size. The age of the "personal computer" is upon us. Knowledge of computers ("computer literacy") may very well become mandatory for students in college, high school, and even some grade schools. Computerized video games became the rage in the late 1970s. Airplanes now can practically fly themselves. Instant telecommunications and word processors have modernized business and education, leading to bitter economic struggles between the giant IBM corporation and its competitors, and between Japan and the United States. When people first learned about computers in the 1950s, there was talk that the era of the "push-button" might eventually cause our bodies to waste away from inactivity. Only our fingers might get exercise pushing buttons. Now, more than ever, computers have replaced manual labor in some fields. Computerized robots almost bring to life early science fiction novels as they take their place on the assembly lines of auto factories in Detroit and Japan. While few would disagree that computers have contributed greatly to making many aspects of our lives easier, there have been some costs to humans as well. The computer revolution has created a new level of white-collar personnel trained in computer skills. But the number of jobs in industries has been reduced because of the computer, contributing in some measure to the higher unemployment rates in certain industries. The computer has "dehumanized" business, reducing personal contact. While greatly increasing productivity in some industries, computers have contributed to increasing economic power in the hands of a few giant companies, as only the largest can afford to keep up with the rapid and expensive advances in computer technology. Those less able to compete fall behind. Advances in electronics technology are also apt to widen further the gap between rich and poor nations. And some people worry, with a degree of justification, about the use to which the government could put the computer—collecting information on citizens at the push of a button. It may be difficult to safeguard computerized information stored by governments, companies, universities and hospitals. What happens when a rival company or a foreign power is able to tap into someone else's computer? Can laws be rewritten to punish for stealing computerized information just as they do for breaking and entering a home or a store? The computer has been, so far, the friend of mankind, but it also could become its foe if citizens were arbitrarily subjected to what an expert has called the "quiet violence" of the computer.

The development of genetic science has made astonishing progress, allowing scientists to understand as never before the makeup of the human body. Some possibilities may be both reassuring and unsettling. As we come to understand human genes, it seems possible to predict which people may inherit certain diseases or be particularly susceptible to contracting them later on in life. At the same time, doctors can determine the genetic makeup of babies before they are born; learning the sex of the baby and the presence of certain

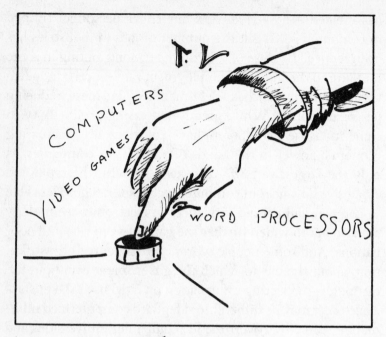

Push-Button Age

forms of mental retardation are only the first steps. Soon it may be possible to know if an infant will be susceptible later to diseases such as muscular dystrophy and hepatitis. Such prenatal "screening" for genetic defects becomes ever more sophisticated.

Yet as scientists push toward understanding more about the origins and genetic characteristics of the diseases that afflict mankind, certain ethical questions inevitably follow. Should doctors be able to alter some aspects of the nature of mankind? Could families be tempted to terminate the pregnancy of an unborn child whom doctors find might risk developing a disease forty years later? Could someone be turned down for a job because scientists had determined that his or her genetic makeup suggested the possibility of disease sometime in the future? The manipulation of genes has already developed an oversized mouse; what would be the implication of such alterations on mankind in the distant future?

Other major advances in science and technology have posed threats. In 1979 radioactive water leaked from a nuclear power plant at Three Mile Island in Pennsylvania, threatening the safety of the entire vicinity. For several days, specialists sought to cool the nuclear generator to prevent "meltdown," an overheating of the nuclear facility that would have spread radioactive materials over hundreds of miles of heavily populated areas. Residents of towns near the plant waited anxiously, ready to flee their homes in case of disaster. Luckily, experts were able to avert such a catastrophe. But the near-accident raised new questions about the safety and practically of atomic energy as a feasible alternative to oil. Several years later, policymakers began to wrestle with the problem of what would be done to dismantle nuclear plants when they were obsolete, something those who originally built them may never have considered.

The nuclear arms race remains an even greater danger to our planet, particularly as that race no longer involves just two powers, the United States and the Soviet Union. Great Britain, France and China certainly have the capacity to wage nuclear warfare. So probably do India, Pakistan (the two are bitter enemies), Israel, South Africa and perhaps Argentina. Every year the survivors of the atomic bombs in Hiroshima and Nagasaki in 1945 gather to remind the world of what incredible horrors might again take place. One can only hope that mankind has learned a lesson.

The environment in the United States and other countries as well did not fare well in the 1970s. The dumping of toxic chemicals and other hazardous waste materials in many cities was discovered to pose grave health risks, making it necessary to evacuate many people, even whole towns.

Recently the Environmental Protection Agency, originally established to protect the United States, permitted big companies to continue to pollute the environment. "Acid rain" became a diplomatic issue between Canada and the United States, as pollutants produced in the latter country were carried to Canada and fell as contaminated rain, killing fish and plants in distant lakes. Even supersonic air travel posed a similar dilemma between technological advance and human needs. In 1976, the first supersonic airliner, the Concorde, a joint venture of France and Great Britain, cut almost in half the time it takes to travel across the Atlantic. The Concorde links Paris and London with New York and Washington, and the flight takes little more than three hours. But many people were worried about the ecological consequences of supersonic transport. Furthermore, the cost of tickets on the Concorde was prohibitively expensive for almost everyone. For these reasons, the Congress of the United States refused to approve funds for an American supersonic transport.

The French were responsible for the most impressive improvement in rail travel. Japan had long since had a "bullet" train running between its largest cities when the French inaugurated their TGV ("train of great speed") in September 1981. The French train was even faster, able to travel safely at speeds of up to 220 miles per hour. The TGV has cut the travel time for the 275-mile trip from Paris to Lyons, France's second-largest city, to less than two hours, an average speed of almost 150 miles per hour. This train carries thousands of people each day, and its speed allows it to compete successfully with the airplane.

Acid rain, toxic waste and air and noise pollution are relatively new problems. During the 1970s, the world's oldest problem, hunger, remained as grave as ever. At the end of 1974, the world's reserves of grain reached a twenty-six-year low. It was then estimated that half a billion people through-

Acid Rain

out the world did not have enough to eat. About ten thousand people perished each week in Africa, Asia and Latin America. In West Bengal, experts estimated that fifteen million people were starving to death. The so-called Green Revolution had increased agriculture yields and brought more land under cultivation in many parts of the world. But even this good news was not enough to meet the world's food needs in the face of rapid population increases and shifts in the world's weather.

The population of our planet has continued to grow by about 200,000 people per day, or 7.5 million per year. In January 1984 there were approximately 4.7 billion people on earth. It was estimated that the same rate of population growth would double the world's population by the end of this century, no longer so far away. Cities such as Singapore, Mexico City, Calcutta and Rio, whose resources were already straining under enormous populations, were inundated with thousands of poor migrants from the countryside, many living in shanty towns propped up on the outskirts of the burgeoning metropolises. Despite some reduction in population growth over the past few years—for example, in China, India, Russia and some western countries—food resources are increasingly strained by an ever-expanding population. Compounding this terrible problem, the world's weather began to change in about 1970. Harsh winters and burning droughts became commonplace throughout much of the world. Some ocean currents changed, with disastrous results. For example, when the currents shifted off of the coast of Peru, the small anchovy fish was almost wiped out. The anchovy is a source of protein for animal feed. The result was a reduction in meat supply. For the first time in twenty years, the total production of food in the world fell, declining by an estimated thirty-three million tons.

Changes in weather, however minor they may seem on a chart, had a dramatic and disastrous impact on the growing season in some nations. Since the 1940s, for example, the average world temperature has fallen by one degree Fahrenheit. Such a drop in temperature reduced the growing season by as much as ten days in many of the countries lying in the middle latitudes of the earth, our most productive regions. Wheat and rice, those crops most associated with the Green Revolution, are particularly vulnerable to changes in weather. A drop in moisture reduces crop yields. An increase in the icy winds that whip around our planet from top to bottom prevented the moisture-laden equatorial winds that bring rain to many regions from forming. West Africa and India suffered terrible droughts. On the other hand, growing pollution of the atmosphere may be causing a "greenhouse" effect, heating up parts of the earth. If the giant polar ice field begins to melt, the level of the oceans could rise dangerously, perhaps submerging some of the world's coastal cities.

Population growth, changes in weather and limitations of the Green Revolution contributed to increase the gap between rich and poor nations. People began to speak of differences between "north and south" instead of just "east and west," contrasting the wealthier northern nations of the world to their less developed southern neighbors.

Hunger threatened to become a source of global conflict. People sometimes referred to those nations that were not industrial and capitalist or Communist as the Third World, although, as time has passed, many of these countries have chosen one camp or the other. Differences between countries in economic growth have led some economists to subdivide the Third World with its population of two billion people into three parts: the "third world," with enough raw material to attract foreign investments and technology (nations such as Zaire, Morocco and Brazil); the "fourth world," with some raw materials but without capital (such as Peru and the Dominican Republic), and the "fifth world," those nations without raw materials and unable even to grow enough food to allow their own people to survive. These countries, such as Chad and Ethiopia in Africa and Bangladesh in Asia, all suffered deadly droughts during much of the 1970s. The plight of these impoverished lands has been made even worse by internal wars.

As if this were not enough, the temporary refusal of the Arab nations to sell oil to the west, the oil embargo of October 1973, began a period when the price of energy skyrocketed in much of the world. During the next ten years, the price of gasoline quadrupled, rising in the United States from about 30 cents per gallon to a peak of more than $1.40, although still far less than the price in western Europe. The embargo had an immediate impact in the United States and led to long lines at gas stations. The speed limit was reduced from seventy to fifty-five miles per hour to save fuel. Americans took fewer trips in their cars and in airplanes, as the cost of airline tickets rose with the rapidly mounting price of

Gas Shortages

fuel. Many cities and companies started "carpool" programs to encourage riders to share energy use and costs. Americans who had always owned large cars now bought smaller and more fuel-efficient models, an increasing proportion of which were made in Japan. Over the next years, people adjusted to higher energy costs by keeping their houses and offices at cooler temperatures during winter. Some Americans reacted to these deprivations with bitterness, blaming the oil-producing nations, particularly the Arabs, for changing the American way of life. "We're like a castle," observed an expert on the energy crisis, "a brilliant medieval castle, defending itself against foreign attackers. Then we suddenly discover that the water supply was outside the castle." The British discovered oil in the North Sea; Mexico and Venezuela prospered as oil-producing countries, at least until oil prices slid back in the early 1980s. Average Americans and also Europeans had to accept some alterations in their life-styles. They envied the oil that lies under the sands of the Middle East. The question of oil and energy, which put the United States at a comparative disadvantage with the Soviet Union—which had access to more oil reserves—came to affect the diplomatic policies of American presidents and the domestic decisions of ordinary people confronted with the rising fuel costs and cold winters.

The Iranian Revolution of 1978–79 brought a second period of higher oil prices. The price of a barrel of oil rose to more than ten times what it had been before the first price rises and the original embargo. But consumption, too, fell, as Americans cut back their use of energy. The United States' share of the total consumption of oil in the world fell from thirty-one percent in 1970 to twenty-five percent in 1982. The average American home in 1983 used one-fifth less energy than at the time of the embargo. Government controls on the oil industry were ended, which increased production and gave the oil companies enormous "windfall profits." At the same time, weaker controls on pollution allowed the burn-ing of other fuels, notably coal, still a vast resource of the United States. In 1977, the $7.7 billion Alaska pipeline opened to bring oil from that large, mineral-rich state. At the same time, automobile companies proved they could develop cars that were more fuel efficient. Between 1973 and 1983, the average car's mileage per gallon doubled.

In 1983, a relative "glut," or oversupply, of oil occurred; oil prices stabilized and even temporarily fell; some oil-producing but relatively poor nations, such as Venezuela, Mexico and Nigeria, that had been given considerable credit found themselves unable to pay their national debts, caus-ing fear of an international financial crisis. But the economic costs of the oil shortage have stayed with us. The oil crisis and higher energy costs short-circuited progress in many underdeveloped countries lacking energy sources of their own. On the other hand, the oil-rich countries of the Middle East found themselves with more money—particularly American dollars—than they knew what to do with. Kuwait's oil supply has made it the richest country in the world of any size in per capita income. Large amounts of real estate in Europe and the United States were purchased by Arabs with U.S. dollars. For many Europeans and Americans, the world seemed to be stood on its head, as the western world became a "bargain basement" for the oil-rich nations. The energy crisis eroded the confidence of the United States, making Americans wonder if all things were still possible. The nation's position in the world economy also changed. The American steel industry and the automobile and electronic industries faltered against stiff competition from abroad, as Japanese- and German-made products, often technologically superior and produced less expensively, flooded the American market.

In foreign policy no other conflict has so burdened the soul of the American people as the war in Vietnam. Formal American involvement in that troubled land began during the 1950s. The Communist forces of Ho Chi Minh had defeated the French, who had colonized the country, at the battle of Dien Bien Phu in May 1954. At a conference in Geneva, Switzerland, Vietnam was divided into two parts, north and south, with Ho Chi Minh founding a Communist government in the north. Ngo Dinh Diem became the premier of South Vietnam, backed by the United States. In 1955, the possibility of reunification ended when the United States went along with Diem's decision to refuse to agree to elections that could have led to a united Vietnam. Guerrilla warfare in the south between supporters of the Communists and the government of South Vietnam became an increasingly familiar scene. Several American military advisers were killed in July of 1959.

Four years later, Diem's dictatorial government faced waves of protests. He was overthrown as Americans stepped aside, and then executed. Thirteen governments in nineteen months followed, as the Vietcong—the South Vietnamese Communists—grew in strength in the countryside and launched a full-fledged war against the government of South Vietnam.

The involvement of the United States in the Vietnam civil war "escalated"—one of those words that came to symbolize the 1960s. In 1964, President Lyndon Johnson asked Congress to pass a resolution calling on him to take "all necessary steps" in Southeast Asia. He alleged that North Vietnamese ships had attacked American destroyers in the Gulf of Tonkin. By 1965, American marines were sent to Vietnam. Another *coup d'état* in South Vietnam, this one by the South Vietnamese Army, left General Nguyen Van Thieu as head of state and Marshal Nguyen Cao Ky as premier. Some 150,000 American troops were brought to Vietnam by the end of 1965. Three years later, U.S. forces in Vietnam had risen in number to well over half a million.

The United States thus found itself fighting an undeclared war on the other side of the world that an increasingly large number of its citizens did not believe was necessary, moral or worth its enormous cost in lives and money. The first open discussions about and against the war ("teach-ins") took place on university campuses as early as the spring of 1965. Students burned their draft cards defiantly. As fighting spread to the demilitarized zone between the north and south in 1967, waves of American aircraft began to bomb the north. But neither bombs from the air nor troops on the ground could destroy the Vietcong, aided by troops from the north. On January 30, 1968, they launched the Tet offensive, attacking virtually all important cities in the south. Despite the eventual defeat of the Tet offensive, the Communist forces dealt a

Vietnam

major blow to South Vietnam. They proved that they could mount a major military campaign in the south as well as continue to strike in guerrilla fashion against the South Vietnamese and Americans. The Tet offensive also gave the world one of the most awful images in the war, a picture seen by millions of people on their television screens. The director of the South Vietnamese National Police was captured forever on film as he fired his pistol into the temple of a prisoner. An even more gripping image was a terrified peasant woman with a child hideously disfigured by a burning chemical solution called napalm dropped by American planes.

In America, President Johnson announced he would not run for a second term in 1968, and truce talks finally opened in Paris between representatives of the United States and North Vietnam. Senator Eugene McCarthy ran for the Democratic nomination as president, with opposition to the war his number one issue. Richard Nixon, who defeated Hubert

Humphrey, presidential candidate of the Democrats, emphasized secret negotiations in the Paris talks and sought "Vietnamization" of the fighting. But antiwar protests spread in the United States, particularly in the fall of 1969.

In April of 1970, President Nixon sent troops into Cambodia to attack areas where the Vietcong had been relatively secure across the border. Massive bombing killed thousands of villagers. In the United States, waves of protest, especially among college students, followed, one climaxing in the shooting of four unarmed students at Kent State University by the National Guard. In the spring of 1972, the Communists launched another major offensive. Nixon then ordered American ships to mine Haiphong Harbor and other major ports. But already secret talks were pointing toward an American withdrawal from combat. In June 1972, the same month that the Watergate break-in began to cast an enormous shadow over President Nixon and American political life, most American troops were withdrawn from Vietnam.

A peace agreement was signed in January 1973, but the war—for the Vietnamese—was far from over. Both sides violated the cease-fire. The South Vietnamese army, facing a cut-off of military funds from the United States and weakened by corruption and indifference, gradually abandoned the highlands. The Vietcong took over cities in the south one by one. In 1975, South Vietnam fell to Communist forces. Once again, television cameras caught the most memorable moments of that disastrous war, as Americans and South Vietnamese civilians desperately pushed their way into helicopters to get out as Saigon "fell," or "was liberated" (depending on one's point of view—once again history often seems to be a question of "whose ox has been gored"). By the end of 1976, Cambodia and Laos were Communist as well.

The United States' longest war was over. More than 56,000 Americans had died in Vietnam, far fewer than the approximately 1,250,000 Vietnamese who were killed. Vietnam left many marks on the America of the 1970s and early 1980s. For one thing, it had been brought by television into American living rooms. And the costs were enormous. Over $140 billion had been spent, a sum that fueled inflation at home. Other costs were large, as well. The war helped alienate many among those of college age in the late 1960s and early 1970s. Some students evaded the draft by going to Canada, registering as conscientious objectors, or even going to prison for their beliefs that the war, and war in general, was wrong. American campuses exploded in anger, rocked by protests and, sometimes, violence. Some hard-core protesters sought to "bring the war home." An explosion set by an antiwar activist killed a researcher in one American university in 1970. But the war touched the conscience of America. An American army lieutenant was convicted of mass murder for his actions in a massacre of civilians in My Lai, Vietnam, in 1968. The savage Christmas bombing of North Vietnam in 1972—just after Secretary of State Henry Kissinger had promised, before the election of that November, that peace was "at hand"—angered many Americans. What is more, the war caused great strains on America's relations with its allies. American embassies in almost every country in the world were scenes of demonstrations. Daniel Ellsberg, who revealed the contents of the "Pentagon Papers," telling of a secret American war in supposedly "neutral" Cambodia, forced the country to confront the morality of its own policies. Yet, despite the carnage, American citizens helped bring the war to a close. The Vietnam experience forced the United States to reexamine its role in the world.

Gravely shaken by the Vietnam War, American self-confidence was further weakened by what came to be called the Watergate scandal. Richard Nixon, Dwight Eisenhower's vice president from 1952 to 1960, had never succeeded in completely overcoming his reputation as "Tricky Dick," which went back to his early political life. Victor over Hubert Humphrey in the 1968 election, the Republican Nixon was elected by a landslide over George McGovern in 1972. Few people paid much attention earlier that year in June to the arrest of five men caught planting listening devices in the headquarters of the Democratic National Committee at the Watergate building in Washington, D.C. The fact that these five "burglars" were linked to the CIA and to Nixon's reelection committee had little influence on the election.

Yet the trial of these Watergate burglars revealed that they were "taking the rap" for highly placed people. As the Watergate scandal came to occupy public attention, the responsibility for the seedy affair moved closer to Nixon himself. His former counsel, John Dean, named the president as a conspirator in the cover-up of the Watergate affair. It became known that Nixon had taped conversations held in his Oval Office. The president tried to keep the tapes from scrutiny and asked Attorney General Elliot Richardson to fire the special prosecutor for the Watergate affair, Archibald Cox. Richardson refused and then resigned. Nixon's bold effort to subvert the judicial process, known as the Saturday Night Massacre, brought increasing demands for Nixon's resignation or impeachment. When the tapes were finally turned over to the Watergate prosecutor, one had a gap of over eighteen minutes long. It turned out that the Watergate burglary was merely the "tip of the iceberg," just one of a whole host of dirty tricks and illegal activities by Nixon administration officials, including accepting illegal campaign contributions from big business. The tapes themselves revealed a large dark side to Nixon's presidency. Some of the men who had surrounded him and been engaged in wrongdoing were convicted and went to jail, including the president's closest associates. Nixon himself, who had lied about the affair, resigned

in disgrace in August 1974, before he could be impeached by
the Senate. He was replaced by Gerald Ford, himself only
recently named vice president to replace Spiro Agnew, who
resigned after pleading no contest to charges of income tax
evasion. Gerald Ford offered a "full, free, and absolute pardon" to Nixon, who returned to his San Clemente, California,
estate to write his memoirs. The reputation of the American presidency was certainly tarnished, but the American
Constitution and the people of the United States had proved
themselves resilient. Gerald Ford in some way appeared to
be an unlikely person to become president of the United
States. One television commentator asked him if he could
"grow into the job." For many people, public confidence in
Mr. Ford was shaken when he granted Nixon a presidential
pardon, while some of the lesser culprits in the Watergate
mess went to prison. Although Ford restored some integrity
to the presidency, he was not able to defeat Georgia Governor Jimmy Carter in the election of 1976. Carter, elected
by a coalition representing the south, labor and minorities,
was something of a populist. But his reputation too quickly
faded, as he proved unable to deal with mounting domestic
economic problems and foreign policy crises. Public confidence in Carter as an experienced and decisive head of state
eroded. He was defeated in a landslide by Ronald Reagan in
the 1980 election, winning only two states and the District of
Columbia.

The newly elected president promised to reduce the role
of government and balance the federal budget while restor-
ing the country's powerful image in the world and leading
the country out of the economic morass. To some people,
though, Reagan also seemed an unlikely man for the most
crucial job in the world. A former actor, Reagan's election
suggested that powerful financial backing and a slick presentation were the most important assets for a would-be president in our age of television.

Whereas in the past incumbent American presidents had a tremendous advantage over challengers in an election, during the sixties and seventies the pattern changed with the defeats of both Mr. Ford and Mr. Carter. The performances of American presidents have become subject to close and almost instantaneous scrutiny by the media. Their speeches are quickly analyzed and graded with the same speed and intensity as the performance of baseball players in the American World Series, or soccer players during the World Cup. Yet the problems recent presidents have had in being reelected also point to diminished public confidence in them; they have lacked the ability to generate public faith that characterized Franklin Roosevelt, Dwight Eisenhower and John F. Kennedy.

The 1970s saw advances for the rights of women, particularly in the United States. In 1972, the Senate passed the Equal Rights Amendment to the Constitution to end discrimination based upon sex. Yet ten years later the amendment had not been ratified by a sufficient number of states to become law. But there were other changes that altered the legal position of women. In 1973, the Supreme Court legalized abortion during the early stages of pregnancy. More women entered the labor force, including the professions of law, medicine, business and university teaching, although women continued to be paid lower wages for the same work as men in many occupations. Women running for and winning political office were no longer unusual. In 1974, Ella Grasso of Connecticut became the first woman, who had not succeeded her husband as governor, to be elected governor of a state. Sandra Day O'Connor was appointed by President Reagan as the first woman on the Supreme Court. Women made great strides in athletics, as federal law guaranteed financial support for women's sports in high school and college. Tennis players Billie Jean King and Chris Evert Lloyd became national sports figures. Margaret Thatcher became the first female prime minister in England when her conservative party won the 1979 elections. In 1983, Sally Ride became the first American female astronaut to go into space. For millions of women, the gradual shift to being addressed as "Ms." instead of "Miss" or "Mrs."—as a parallel to the address of "Mr." for men—helped enhance their image as a complete person without reference to marital status. All of this was a good beginning. One must never forget the story of mankind is equally the story of women.

The civil rights movement had been one of the most significant occurrences of the 1960s. During the 1970s, blacks began to attain political office, particularly as mayors in a number of major American cities, such as Detroit, Los Angeles and Atlanta. On the twentieth anniversary of the great "march on Washington" of August 1963, when Martin Luther King gave his famous "I Have a Dream" speech, few could deny that American blacks had achieved more advances. But there was still much more to accomplish. Segregation continued in many school systems. The Supreme Court's ruling in the "reverse discrimination" case of Allan Bakke, a California student, set back court-ordered preference for minorities in education and business. The civil rights movement escaped another defeat when the Reagan administration's attempt to grant tax exemptions to schools that discriminate against blacks failed. The economic future of young blacks remained bleak, as they continued to suffer the highest unemployment rate in the United States, while the government reduced many of the welfare programs that had helped the poor subsist.

During the 1970s homosexuals began to assert their rights to fair treatment. Despite a conservative backlash, communities of "gays" flourished in many cities, particularly New York and San Francisco, and found far more acceptance than before, and some political representation.

Life in the 1970s and early 1980s reflected a combination of continuity with the past and of change. Symphony orchestras, opera and the trumpeted arrival of great artistic exhibitions brought from Europe found eager audiences in America's largest cities. But television, radio, recorded music and the best-seller book list—all aided by technological improvements—remained the heart of popular entertainment. Cable television brought many channels into more and more American homes. No longer does television reception depend on topography, weather or the size and location of an antenna. Some channels began to offer full-length feature movies twenty-four hours a day. One can push a button and find round-the-clock news and weather, or sports, brought from afar by satellite. The development of electronics has made it possible to record television programs for later viewing and to rent cassettes of popular movies for showing at any time in private homes, with popcorn readily available in the nearby kitchen. FM radio remained popular, particularly stations that emphasized either classical music, usually public radio, or rock and roll. In the late 1970s, the recording industry began to experience some difficulties, largely because of astonishing advances in tape-recording techniques, which seemed on the verge of making the record obsolete. Rock concerts, while less resembling the massive events of the late sixties and early seventies (such as the most famous, in Woodstock, New York, in 1969, attended by hundreds of thousands of people), still were eagerly awaited by the younger generation, their numbers swollen by the grudgingly aging generation of the 1960s who still fill a concert hall or sports stadium to hear groups such as the Rolling Stones and the Who. The fact that the star lead singer of the Stones, Mick Jagger, turned forty in 1983 did not seem to have slowed him or his legions of fans down. Fads like the "Disco-mania" (discotheque music) proved short lived, as nostalgia for the rock and roll music of twenty years earlier survived. One found the same nostalgia in the great success of movies like "American Graffiti," the story of high school students growing up in the mid-1960s, and "Animal House," the pranks and pitfalls of college students in the age of innocence before the war in Vietnam.

This nostalgia accompanied the emergence of a new generation of college students who seemed to have abandoned the social activism of the late 1960s. Getting good grades and worrying about careers in a highly competitive age became of paramount importance, this at a time when the quality of American education, particularly in the high schools, was apparently falling, or at least not progressing. Some expressed dismay at the end of idealism expressed by the slogan "Looking out for Number One." Others would argue that, in order to build a better world, one has to be practical.

Yet despite the inevitable aging of the generation of the sixties and the ever-increasing life-span of mankind, at least in the developed world, much of our culture continues to be centered on youthfulness and the young. Young actresses such as Brooke Shields and Jodie Foster symbolized the cult of youth in successful movies, but in a far more worldly and less innocent way than Shirley Temple had four decades earlier. Just as "think young" became a maxim for commercialized advertising, "staying young" emerged as common sense for life. Jogging became a national craze in the United States, and many people took the old saying "You are what you eat" seriously and tried to eat healthier foods. So-called natural foods, once associated with hippies who had dropped out from the American scene, now were found in the average household. Scientists made considerable progress in the search for the causes of cancer, that great killer of our century, warning us against the danger of smoking cigarettes and reminding us that certain foods that we had taken for granted for centuries, such as salt and red meat, were not necessarily good for us. Scientists made much less progress in the monumental struggle to find a cure for cancer, despite improvements in detection techniques and enhanced public awareness.

Some years ago, a Russian writer wrote a small book entitled *Will the Soviet Union Survive Until 1984?* So far, however, the U.S.S.R. has proved that it could weather economic problems, repress dissent and survive surges of nationalism in those countries dependent upon it and within its borders. The Soviet Union showed few signs of change during the years of the leadership of Leonid Brezhnev, who died in 1981. Life for dissidents remained grim. The most famous voice of opposition within the Soviet Union, the writer Aleksander Solzhenitsyn, emigrated to the United States as a refugee. The number of Jews leaving Russia for the United States and Israel increased. President Jimmy Carter offered dissidents encouragement in the name of human rights when he sent a letter to the physicist Andrei Sakharov in 1976 pledging to "seek the release of prisoners of conscience."

Although both President Carter and Russian Premier Leonid Brezhnev signed the second Strategic Arms Limitation Treaty (SALT) in 1979, the two superpowers remained bitter enemies. Since then, despite much talk, neither country has seemed serious about reducing its nuclear arsenals, with the Americans placing powerful Pershing missiles in Europe, despite strong antinuclear movements in both Europe and the United States. Certainly Soviet actions have not inspired confidence in the west even after Brezhnev's death. In 1979, the Red Army invaded its neighbor Afghanistan when the Soviet-backed faction faced unyielding opposition in that mountainous, poor country. The Soviets played a role in the repression of the Solidarity trade union in Poland and became involved in events in Africa, particularly Angola,

Mozambique and Ethiopia. When the Russians shot down a Korean airliner that strayed over the strategically critical Soviet island of Sakhalin north of Japan in September 1983, taking it for a spy plane, an international uproar followed. We appeared to be on the verge of the return of the Cold War, particularly as the Red Army began to assert a more forcefully political role in the Soviet Union and the question of leadership within the elite of the Soviet Politboro's elderly membership remained unsettled.

During the 1950s and 1960s, Americans, including those who carried out the foreign policy of the United States, tended to lump the Soviet Union and China together as Communist powers hostile to the interests of the free world. After the Vietnam War, in which both the Soviet Union and China aided North Vietnam and the Vietcong, the western world became more aware of the many historical, territorial and ideological issues that divided the two powers. By the 1970s, it sometimes seemed that these giant neighbors would be fighting each other rather than the United States.

While the United States and the U.S.S.R. were so heavily armed that they could destroy each other in much less than an hour, they found that the force of arms was not enough to enforce their wills or win friends throughout the world. The Soviets crushed the spark of liberty, the relative freedom of expression that characterized the "Prague Spring" in Czechoslovakia in 1968. Following their invasion of Afghanistan in 1979, they found themselves bogged down in a war against guerrillas determined to fight them to the death.

In 1980, a trade union movement arose in Poland called Solidarity. The support that the Polish people gave to the movement, which opposed the arbitrary decision making of the state in the name of freedom, indicated that other cracks in the eastern European bloc might occur. The threat of the Soviet army and the imposition of martial law by the Polish authorities could not stamp out the call for greater freedom. Lech Walesa, a worker from Gdańsk, the scene of antiregime riots in 1970, won the 1983 Nobel Peace Prize for his role in the events there as the leader of Solidarity.

Like the Soviet Union, the United States must take some responsibility for the problems democracy has had in some of the world. In September 1973, the Chilean army, aided and encouraged by the CIA, moved against the popularly elected president, Salvador Allende, a Marxist. The military government that followed inaugurated a reign of terror, torture and execution. Ten years later, the United States still backed the dictator General Pinochet in that unhappy country. It also supported other dictatorships in Latin America, such as those in Argentina (although America leaned toward the British during the brief war that England fought against Argentina over the Falkland Islands in 1982) and in Brazil. In Central America, the United States backed oppressive regimes in Guatemala and El Salvador. In Asia, the support of the United States helped lend legitimacy and power to the governments of the Philippines and South Korea, which many of those nations' people saw as repression. After a left-wing revolution ended the dictatorship in Nicaragua, the United States government blamed the Russians and Cubans for that and similar developments in Central America. Such a policy brought criticism from a number of American allies, such as France and our neighbor Mexico.

In October 1983, the United States invaded the tiny Caribbean island of Grenada (population of 110,000), near the coast of Venezuela. This invasion, although planned earlier, came in response to requests by neighboring islands that the United States remove from power a recently installed leftist faction. Claiming that the United States medical students on the island were in danger, President Reagan cited the presence of Cuban and Soviet advisers and arms on the island as justifying such an invasion. This action, which was widely supported in the United States, brought overwhelming criticism in the United Nations from over one hundred countries, including some of America's closest allies, who deplored the violation of international law. On a smaller and much less bloody scale, the United States intervention recalled for some the Soviet invasion of Afghanistan, showing that both superpowers were willing to ignore world opinion to accomplish their ends. At the same time, the United States worked openly to overthrow the government of Nicaragua in Central America, as the Soviets engaged in similar activity in Africa. Old Machiavelli, were he still living, might quote the proverb "The more things change, the more they remain the same."

In Iran, American support could not keep the shah in power in the face of overwhelming opposition that powerful and wealthy emperor faced. He was driven from power in 1979 and took refuge in the United States and then Egypt before his death. The Iranian Revolution brought to power the Ayatollah Khomeini, a religious leader intent on creating a state based on Islamic fundamentalism. Many ordinary Iranians, who hated the feared secret police of the shah, now had reason to fear the new regime, particularly if they were Communists or Bahais, a religious group.

The close association of the shah with the United States generated a tremendous hatred of America and Americans in Iran. On a Sunday morning in November 1979, an angry crowd stormed the American Embassy in Teheran and took 150 hostages. The Iranians kept the hostages in bleak conditions for over a year, while the world watched. The United States, despite its power, was unable to secure their release. An attempt to free them by force failed. Finally, they were released after over a year in captivity.

Although at the time it was still the undeclared enemy of

the United States in Vietnam, China received a visit from President Nixon in 1972. During the next decade, relations improved dramatically between the two powers. President Carter was the first American chief of state to recognize China officially. Inside China, the Cultural Revolution, begun in 1966, greatly set back the development of the economy. The young "Red Guards" stormed through China in an attempt to "purify" the supposed enemies of Mao and reeducate the intellectuals and other potential enemies by putting them to work in the fields. Mao himself, an increasingly feeble old man, was rarely seen. His wife, Jiang Quing, and the "Gang of Four" ruthlessly eliminated opposition. Lin Biao, commander of the army, plotted to kill Mao but himself died in a plane crash trying to escape the country after the plot was discovered. He may have been assassinated. A major earthquake in China seemed to augur the fall of the Communist "dynasty," as such natural disasters had during the traditional imperial dynasties signaled the end of God's approval (the mandate of Heaven) and the fall of the emperor. Chou En-lai, China's respected leader who had opened the way for better relations with the west, died in January 1976. Mao Tse-tung, chairman, one of the major figures of our century, passed away in September of the same year.

How long could the madness of the Cultural Revolution go on? Two generals, Ye Jianying and Li Xiannian, led a virtual palace coup, putting the "Gang of Four" under arrest. The old generals brought back into political leadership one victim of the Cultural Revolution, Deng Xiaoping. In 1981, the Chinese Communist party admitted that certain errors had been made. Mao remained a great hero, but one who was human and had made great mistakes. It was left to the new regime to undo much of the damage that had been done during the 1966-1976 period. In this they have succeeded remarkably well. China remains a poor country with four out of every five people working in agriculture. When peasants were given more control over the land they worked, production increased. The level of industrial production grew dramatically, with the city of Peking producing ten times more steel than all of China in the early 1940s. China's industrial centers began turning out more consumer goods, some of which could be traded to the west. Lately, commercial advertising has begun to be seen on Chinese television. The government continued to tackle the enormous problem of overpopulation, its population having more than doubled, to the astonishing figure of one billion since World War II. The current leadership of China wants to maintain good relations with the United States and, at the same time, to improve those with the Soviet Union. Three significant issues still stand in the way of better relations between the United States and China. The United States continues to support and to arm the government of Taiwan, that troubled island occupied by the defeated Nationalist troops who fled Mao's armies in 1949. The successor of Chiang Kai-shek, Mao's rival for power during the Chinese civil war, still claims to be the legitimate government of China. Furthermore, while the Chinese would like the United States to increase trade with their country, at the same time American manufacturers worry about being flooded with products produced in China at a much lower cost. Finally, the Chinese resent the fact the American government prevents the export to China of particularly sensitive technological equipment that could serve military ends. But, these problems aside, Chinese in major cities are no longer surprised to see American tourists gaping at the wonders of one of mankind's most fabulous civilizations, one with the potential to contribute as gloriously to our world as did its ancestors who so amazed pioneering European visitors such as Marco Polo and Matteo Ricci centuries ago.

The Middle East became the world's most dangerous hotspot in the 1970s, adding to tension between the Soviet Union and the United States. A permanent state of unrest between the Arab countries and Israel continued to engulf the entire region. In 1973, six years after the first Arab-Israeli war, Israel's Arab neighbors launched a sudden attack on the day of the Jewish religious holiday of Yom Kippur. After some initial success they were soundly defeated by the superior Israeli army and air force. The support the western powers, particularly the United States, gave Israel led to the Arab oil embargo, which, as we have already seen, had disastrous consequences for the world economy. Israel and Egypt finally began to discuss possibilities for mutual peace. In 1978, Egyptian President Anwar Sadat and Israeli Prime Minister Menachem Begin signed the Camp David accord. Sadat, who visited Israel in 1977, earned the undying enmity of some Arab states for his part in these difficult negotiations. He was assassinated in 1981. The Camp David accords, in which President Carter had played such a large part, led to the return to Egypt of the Sinai Peninsula by Israel.

But peace in the Middle East has yet to be obtained. The Arab states have refused to acknowledge the existence and legitimacy of the state of Israel, which had been carved out of lands that Jews and Arabs had occupied for several thousand years. The question of the Palestinian people remained unresolved. Some 3.2 million Palestinians remained a people without a land, pawns in the disagreements among the Arab states and second-class citizens in Israel. Several hundred thousand of them were living in terrible conditions in refugee camps on the West Bank and in Jordan. Out of this desperation and poverty emerged the Palestine Liberation Organization. The violent factions of the P.L.O. struck at Israel through terrorism, making Israelis everywhere vulnerable to their bloody attacks.

The tactics of the P.L.O. obscured the fact that something has to be done for the Palestinian people. Israeli expansion on the West Bank, seeking to create the biblical kingdom of Israel, has continued to dislocate them further. The hardline policies of Premier Begin, who resigned in September 1983, prevented any compromise. Begin, himself a terrorist during the struggle against the British after World War II, ordered an invasion of Lebanon, from whose territory the Palestinian guerrilla groups had been able to launch attacks on Israel. In the summer of 1982, the Israelis drove out much of the P.L.O., including its leader, Yassar Arafat. The Israeli presence permitted a shaky victory of the Christian forces over the Moslems in Lebanon, and the massacre of hundreds of Moslems in the Palestinian refugee camps of Sabra and Shatila in Beirut by the Christians. Sadly, while P.L.O. terrorists killed Jews and Israeli bombs rained down on civilians in Beirut, the Palestinian question moved no closer to being solved. At the same time, Lebanon's tragedy continues. That battered land remains sharply divided between Christians and Moslems. Even within these two major religious groups, bitter rivalries remain as small and heavily armed factions compete for power, despite the presence of international peace-keeping forces. In October 1983, enormous bombs shattered the early morning, killing over two hundred United States marines and half as many French troops sent to try to keep the peace. The loss of American life, the most devastating day of casualties suffered by an American military force since the Vietnam War, raised doubts about the role of the United States in the Middle East.

In Europe, the period after 1970 brought the left to power in the Mediterranean world, while the right did better in northern Europe. A revolution unseated Portuguese dictator Salazar. General Franco, who had ruled Spain with an iron fist since the end of the civil war in 1939, died in November 1975, long after his admired colleagues Adolf Hitler and Benito Mussolini. The personal prestige and determination of King Juan Carlos helped bring about a surprisingly peaceful transition to democracy in that long-troubled country, with the socialists coming to power in 1982. One would-be coup by army officers failed after they held the Spanish Parliament hostage. France, too, elected a socialist, François Mitterrand, president in May 1981; he succeeded Valéry Giscard d'Estaing and appeared to be even more anti-Soviet than his supposedly more rightist predecessor. The Gaullists, having lost their hero, de Gaulle, in November 1970 and his successor, Georges Pompidou, several years later, turned increasingly to Jacques Chirac, the mayor of Paris, who was elected president of France in 1995. In Italy, government succeeded government. Terrorism from the extreme left and the extreme right intensified that country's instability. In Greece, a military coup brought George Papadopoulos to power in 1967. In 1973, a student rising preceded another military coup, with an evolution toward a troubled socialist government, while the United States worried about the fate of its bases in that strategic country.

The Catholic church went through a period of change. The Vatican II council in 1962 had approved freedom of discussion within the church. In an effort to bring the faith to everyone, it ruled that the mass no longer had to be said in Latin, but could be in the language of every nation. In 1978, smoke from the traditional Vatican chimney announced astonishing news to the world's seven hundred million Catholics: the cardinals had chosen the first non-Italian Pope in 455 years, Karol Cardinal Wojtyla of Cracow, Poland. The new Pope won great popularity in much of the world, visiting more countries than any of his predecessors and surviving an assassination attempt in 1981. He followed events in his own country with particular energy and was a source of support for the men and women of the trade union Solidarity against the Communist government.

Africa remains a troubled continent, torn by poverty, hunger and civil war. Biafra's three-year war for independence from Nigeria ended in 1970, with two million Biafrans dead. A racist regime based upon white supremacy and segregation continues in South Africa. After a civil war, Rhodesia made a relatively peaceful transition from white minority rule to black majority rule and was renamed Zimbabwe. Libyan-backed forces fought a civil war in Chad against a regime backed by the United States and France, its former colonial power. In Uganda, madman dictator Idi Amin's murderous reign appalled the civilized world, and he was driven away by Tanzanian troops in 1979.

Not all political violence, of course, was directed at its citizens by dictatorships. Political assassination remained a sad sign of the times; terrorism became a way of life for many groups intent on achieving their goals against powerful states. The assassinations of President Kennedy in 1963, his brother Robert in 1968, and Martin Luther King, the great civil rights leader, that same year were followed by attempts on the lives of presidential candidate George Wallace in 1972 and two attempts to kill President Gerald Ford. Both the Pope and President Reagan survived the bullets of assassins in 1981. And much of the world mourned the murder of former Beatles singer John Lennon, who sang of peace, gunned down in New York City by a crazed man in 1980.

Terrorism emerged as a deadly weapon for violent groups. The Olympic Games, symbol of the possibilities of international cooperation and peaceful competition, were held in Munich, West Germany, in 1972. Eight heavily armed Palestinian terrorists took Israeli athletes as hostages, killing eleven of them as police stormed the building where they were held. The world, shocked by such bloodshed and

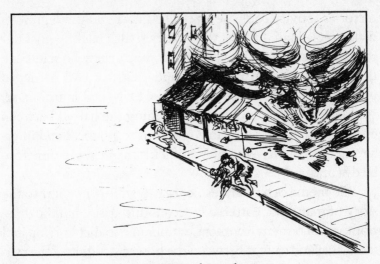

Terrorist Bomb Explosion

stunned by the cold-blooded resolve of men to kill innocent people and be killed, saw other such tragedies. In Northern Ireland, violence escalated, beginning in 1969, as the out-lawed Catholic Irish Republican Army struck savagely and often at their Protestant Irish and British enemies, demanding that Northern Ireland cease to be part of Great Britain. Protestant groups retaliated in kind. The 1970s witnessed a number of bloody attacks against Jews. Few could forget the horrible sight of bodies lying before a synagogue in Paris in 1980, or in the Jewish quarter in that same city. There were a number of attacks on officials and airlines by Armenians, who were protesting the massacres of their countrymen by Turks before World War I. In Italy the far-left Red Brigades launched a series of bloody attacks against the state. Right-wing terrorists blew up the railroad station in Bologna, kill-ing nearly one hundred people, and were responsible for a murderous explosion at the Munich Oktoberfest in 1980. Ter-rorists seemed to be able to strike almost everywhere, even near Buckingham Palace in London during a parade. Some terrorist activity could be traced to Libya and the regime of dictator Gaddafi. In 1976, the Israelis struck back against terrorism, as commandos rescued 104 hostages who had been flown to Entebbe airport in Uganda. One or two hardened people, willing to die for what they believe is a just cause, could create a mood of fear, sharpening the hatred between enemies, making reasonable solutions to political and international problems even more difficult than ever in our troubled world.

The theme of human resilience is certainly not new to the story of mankind. Battered by economic crises and the deterioration of our environment, vulnerable to dictatorship and terrorism and caught between the power struggle of the two superpowers, the people of our planet can take considerable consolation in knowing that mankind has outlasted previous dangers. We have seen the revival of several blighted American cities, such as Baltimore and Detroit, and the rebirth of some temporarily destroyed natural resources, such as the Thames River in England and Lake Erie in the United States. Perhaps the gigantic environmental challenges we face can be met by determined action. We should find hope in the massive anti-nuclear arms movement in Europe and in the ground swell of support for ecological movements in the United States concerned with protecting our environment. We also have in our world the example of many people whose courage, integrity and energetic commitment to mankind we can admire: people such as Jacobo Timerman, the intellectual who stood up to the persecution of Jews and democracy in Argentina; Anwar Sadat, who worked so hard to unite his country, Egypt, and to bring peace to the Middle East; Mother Teresa, the diminutive nun who worked anonymously for years among the desperately poor of Calcutta before winning the Nobel Prize for Peace and calling the world's attention to the hungry, the poor, and the forgotten in that vast subcontinent and elsewhere; Gabriel García Márquez, another writer who survived the authoritarian regime in Chile to win the Nobel Prize for Literature; playwright Athol Fugard, who emerged from the racially segregated world of South Africa to delight audiences with his plays, and Lech Walesa, who led the Solidarity trade union in Poland in its fight for freedom. These men and women have worked selflessly for a better world. The more difficult the challenges mankind must face in the future, the more we must work together.

77

A New Millennium

New Freedoms and Global Connections

The last two decades of the twentieth century have been marked by dramatic political changes, most notable for their peaceful character, that have brought freedom to many nations that previously had authoritarian governments. At the same time, intriguing and enriching technological changes have made the world seem smaller. To be sure, some of the same problems that seemed to have always afflicted humanity—hunger, disease, violence and war—continue to weigh heavily on the lives of millions of people. Yet, with the increasing interdependence of nations and the significant changes in communication, much of humanity has reason to be optimistic, indeed excited, about the future.

Without question, the major event in recent decades, and arguably since the end of World War II, has been the end of Communism in Europe. As representatives of the Soviet Union and the United States glared suspiciously across the table in the mid-1980s during talks on the reduction of nuclear weapons, few could have imagined that within a few years Communism in the Soviet Union and eastern Europe would collapse, and that the Soviet Union itself would disintegrate, as one after another of its satellites broke away. Of the factors that combined to bring down Communism, the most important was that, despite promises of bringing economic well-being, Communism had not worked. Furthermore, the absence of political freedom in the Soviet Union and its smaller satellite states had brought massive, sullen dissatisfaction among many people.

In 1985, Mikhail Gorbachev became general secretary of the Communist Party and thus head of the Soviet Union. Compared to his elderly predecessors, Gorbachev was young and dynamic. He realized that if Communism were to survive, which he hoped it would, essential economic and even political reforms would have to be implemented. He brought into government some relatively liberal people and ordered a relaxation in the tight censorship that had for so long strangled artistic and political expression. And, for the first time, a Soviet leader began to discuss openly the grim fact that the Soviet economy was incapable of growth unless workers and farmers had real economic incentives to work hard. Gorbachev announced the advent of *perestroika*, or restructuring of the Communist economy to make it more productive and to provide more consumer goods. Insisting that "we need a revolution of the mind," he called for an increase in private ownership in the Soviet Union, and he hoped to convince Western countries to invest in the Soviet Union. But in the meantime, the high cost of keeping up with the United States in the arms race and the flourishing "black market" whereby goods and services were exchanged illegally shackled the Soviet economy.

In the late 1980s, strong nationalist movements grew more influential in Lithuania, Latvia and Estonia—the "Baltic states" of the north—and in Ukraine, Georgia and Armenia in the vast southern expanse of the Soviet empire. Throughout much of the Soviet Union, the democratic opposition gained confidence, demanding further reform, joining forces in some places with nationalist groups. At the same time, the economic crisis within the Soviet Union accelerated as productivity slowed down almost to a halt in 1988. This convinced many reform-minded people in Russia and in the other states of the Soviet Union that reforms within the Communist system would not be enough, and that Communism, which had been in place since 1917, had to go.

In the meantime, Gorbachev made highly successful trips to Washington, London and Paris, where he was embraced as a friend. Gorbachev began to end Soviet involvement in a long and bloody civil war in Afghanistan. Above all, as nationalist movements in eastern Europe swelled among wrenching economic discontent, Gorbachev made it clear that the Soviet Union would no longer send tanks and soldiers to back up the Communist leaders of Poland, East Germany and other states as they repressed their own citizens. Shouts of "Gorbi, Gorbi, Gorbi!" from protesters made clear that a remarkable transformation was occurring: whereas in the past, the Soviet leadership stood as a powerful threat to movements for change within its sphere of influence, now a Soviet leader was becoming a symbol of hope for reform. During the summer of 1989, Gorbachev boldly announced, "Any interference in domestic affairs and any attempts to restrict the sovereignty of states, both friends and allies or any others, are inadmissible."

Freed from the threat of Soviet interference, the states of Eastern Europe one by one rejected Communism. In Hungary, where opposition groups were well-organized, and in Poland, where they were closely tied to the influential Catholic church, the Communist leadership sought compromise. In Hungary, reform-minded leaders had already come to power in 1988. Now, the government simply abandoned Communism and in May 1989, it took away the barbed wire that defined the border with Austria. In Poland, the government had already begun a year earlier to negotiate with Solidarity, the political opposition group that had emerged out of the strikes and movement for reform that began in 1980 in the shipyards of a port city, Gdasnk. In 1989, the first free elections since before World War II were held in Poland. Candidates supported by Solidarity did very well, forcing the government to share power. A year later, the long Communist era in Poland came to an end when the Polish Communist Party changed its name and began to function like any other political party.

Winds of change came quickly to East Germany and Czechoslovakia, two of the most repressive Communist states. In spired by changes in the Soviet Union, Hungary and Poland, ordinary East Germans began to demand freedom. Thousands voted with their feet, escaping to West Germany in record numbers; the efforts of the East German police to stop them became increasingly half-hearted, even though the East German leader Erich Honecker refused any accommodation with reform. A visit by Gorbachev in October 1989 brought more demonstrators into the street, shouting his name. Honecker was forced from power, replaced by a leader who announced that henceforth East Germans would have the right to travel to the west, and that the Berlin Wall, since 1961 a symbol of the division between east and west, would be torn down. Enthusiastic crowds thronged to the wall, and guards were helpless or unwilling to stop them from pouring through or over it to embrace people on the other side. Within a matter of days, three million East Germans had crossed into the German Federal Republic, most for the first time. An East German poet commented, "I must weep for joy that it happened so quickly and simply. And I must weep for wrath that it took so abysmally long." In the first free elections held in East Germany, conservatives who favored unification with the German Federal Republic won easily. East and West Germany became the unified state of Germany in December 1990.

In Czechoslovakia, news of the fall of the Berlin Wall led

The Berlin Wall Comes Down

to a mass mobilization of ordinary people and the end of the Communist regime within ten days. Enormous, excited crowds gathered in the center of Prague, the capital, to demand reform and protest the beating of demonstrators by police. Lacking the support of the Soviet Army, the Communist leadership was forced to negotiate with those demanding free elections. In December 1989, the Communist–dominated Federal Assembly voted to end the Communist Party's domination of political life. Václav Havel, a young playwright whose works had been banned by the government and who had suffered in prison for his political activities, was elected president. What Havel called a "Velvet Revolution" had brought freedom to Czechoslovakia virtually without bloodshed. Nonetheless, rivalries between Czechs and Slovaks subsequently led to the creation of two separate countries, the Czech Republic and Slovakia, in 1993.

The Communist regimes in Bulgaria, Romania and Albania also collapsed late in 1989 amid economic crisis and popular aspirations for a better life. In Bulgaria, some Com-

munist Party officials and army officers decided that change
was inevitable, and tossed aside the ruthless leader who had
sought to curry popular support by attempting to turn the
ethnic Bulgarian population against the Turkish minority.
In Romania, the corrupt Nicolae Ceausescu and his wife
used force in an attempt to retain power as discontent and
demonstrations spread. When protesters shouted him down
as he began a speech, Romanian security forces fired on
the crowds. The Ceausescus tried to flee by helicopter, but
they were captured, tried by a quickly constituted tribunal,
sentenced to death, and shot, their frozen bodies left on the
ground to be filmed by television cameras. Finally, Communism fell even in Europe's most backward and isolated
country, Albania; food shortages led to strikes, riots, and
the resignation of the Communist government in June 1991.
Here, too, the speed with which Communism collapsed was
astonishing.

The sudden, dramatic collapse of Communist governments in eastern Europe increased pressures for swift change
within the Soviet Union itself. Early in 1990, non-Communist
parties were permitted to form, and restrictions on religious
worship were ended. Gorbachev was elected by the Congress of People's Deputies to serve as president, a position of
authority no longer automatically linked to the Communist
Party. Russia and several other states affirmed that they could
pass laws invalidating those laws that were implemented by
the Soviet Union. Lithuania was the first republic to declare
its independence from the Soviet Union.

Still, Gorbachev believed that Communism could be saved
by further reform. Within Russia, Boris Yeltsin, a tough-
talking, hard-drinking, and increasingly popular reformer,
began to challenge Gorbachev's authority, especially when
Gorbachev seemed to move away from the course of reform
in early 1991, as he drew criticism from hard-line Commu-

nists who wanted little or no change. Further enraging hard-liners, Gorbachev reversed himself again in April, when he accepted the idea that the Soviet republics should be auton-omous, which would effectively end the existence of the Soviet Union. In August, influential figures within the army, the Communist Party, and the K.G.B. (the Soviet Secret Ser-vice) placed Gorbachev under house arrest in his Crimean summer house. In Moscow, Yeltsin encouraged resistance to the coup, and the army remained loyal to the constituted government. The failed coup accelerated the collapse of the Soviet Union. Gorbachev returned to Moscow a hero. Yeltsin, president of the Russian Parliament, suspended the Commu-nist Party. Gorbachev brought in more reform-minded min-isters, and the Soviet government recognized the autonomy of the republics that had constituted, increasingly against their will, the Soviet Union. By the end of 1991, thirteen of the fifteen republics of the old Soviet Union had declared their independence. On Christmas Day 1991, the exhausted Gor-bachev resigned, after six extraordinary years in power. The Soviet Union no longer existed.

The collapse of Communism brought an end to the Cold War and suddenly freed the world from the threat of nuclear war between the United States and the Soviet Union. Nonethe-less, the road to economic and political stability was not easy for either the states that had made up the Soviet Union nor for the formerly Communist states of eastern Europe. Most of these states lacked traditions of parliamentary govern-ment. Furthermore, the transformation of state-controlled Communist economies into free-market economies proved to be extraordinarily difficult. Free-market economies could not be implemented without bringing immediate turmoil and continued price increases. Thus, prices soared dramat-ically everywhere, rude shocks that western economists considered necessary in order to increase production and

bring more consumer goods into stores. But galloping inflation brought great hardship to ordinary people. By the time
Yeltsin announced the end of price controls in Russia in January 1992, the cost of many essential consumer items had
tripled. Furthermore, a decline in state authority, however
oppressive it had been, encouraged a wave of criminality
and violence, as underworld gangs took advantage of chaos.
Freedom had its price.

The end of Communism also brought a rapid increase in
bitter—and sometimes extremely violent—rivalries between
different peoples who had been forced to live in relative harmony during the Soviet period. Nowhere was this more true
than in Yugoslavia, where Serbs, Croats and Bosnian Muslims comprised the three largest ethnic groups, each with
its own religion—Russian Orthodox, Catholic, and Muslim. Yugoslavia broke up into belligerent ethnic groups, and
first Croatia and then Bosnia declared their independence
from Serb-dominated Yugoslavia. Civil war soon followed
in Bosnia, with evidence of "ethnic cleansing" and geno-
cide. "Europe is dying in Sarajevo," warned a wall poster in
Germany about the Bosnian capital, which was being sys-
tematically shelled by Serbs. The fighting in Bosnia may
have killed as many as 150,000 people, with about 2.8 million people becoming refugees. Finally, in 1995, the U.S.
government encouraged the Serbs, Croats, and Muslims to
sign the Dayton Peace Agreement, which was to be enforced
by the presence of about 60,000 blue-helmeted U.N. troops,
a third of whom would be American. The troops were supposed to protect ethnic minorities, but in many cases, they
stood helplessly by as cease-fire after cease-fire failed to hold.
Long-standing ethnic rivalries elsewhere could not easily be
swept away either. This was particularly true in states with
significant ethnic minorities, such as Russia, Romania and
Latvia. Aggressive nationalism remained a threat in eastern

Europe. The substantial nuclear military installations left over from the Soviet period remained in Ukraine, Belarus and Kasakhstan and continued to pose a potential threat to world peace.

With the demise of the Soviet Union, the eyes of the world turned increasingly toward the remaining Communist states, above all, to China. The Thirteenth Congress of the Chinese Communist Party in 1987 had marked a compromise between moderate economic reform—away from state control and toward capitalist enterprises—and continued opposition to any kind of political reform. It was presided over by Deng Xiaoping, the aged Chinese leader whose encour-

Democracy Movement in China

agement had brought significant economic reforms beginning in 1979. However, early in 1989, a popular movement on behalf of democratic reforms grew up in China, particularly in Beijing; in May, more than a million people demonstrated. Following the imposition of martial law in China on June 4, 1989, Chinese troops moved in to Tiananmen Square in Beijing, crushing the pro-democracy movement. For one dramatic moment, a single protester stood in the way of a Chinese army tank, as millions of television viewers worldwide held their breath. But the ouster of the reform-minded Zhao Ziyang and his replacement by Jiang Zemin reflected the ascendancy of hard-liners within the Chinese Communist leadership. In the repression that followed, hundreds of activists were killed and thousands imprisoned, further setting back Chinese relations with the west.

Western leaders subsequently looked in vain for signs of meaningful political change in the country of 1.3 billion people, almost a fourth of the world's population. Trading with the west made consumer goods available in China, at least in the largest cities, but the economy was plagued by high inflation and both unemployment and underemployment. More Chinese felt alienated from the authoritarian Communist regime. Despite Deng's cheery message that "to get rich is glorious," China remained for the most part an extremely poor country. The countryside in particular remained impoverished and occasionally on the verge of instability; and as a result, as many as 100 million people crowded into the large coastal cities of the country during the 1990s. In addition, China added considerably to its population when Hong Kong, the prosperous, teeming port territory of six million people that the British government had held as a territory since the nineteenth century, passed by prior agreement to Chinese rule in 1997. The Chinese Communist government promised to maintain capitalism and democracy in Hong Kong for a period of fifty years.

With the collapse of the Soviet Union, Cuba remained the only Communist outpost outside of Asia. Cuban leader Fidel Castro remained as ruler despite a U.S. economic embargo intended to limit trade with the Caribbean island and bring hardship to the Cuban people, in the hope that they would overthrow Castro. The sudden withdrawal in 1991 of millions

of dollars that the Soviet Union had provided each year worsened the economic situation in Cuba, for which not even the
arrival of considerable foreign currency brought by tourists
could compensate.

Economic sanctions did have a vital effect in another
part of the world. In South Africa, apartheid (the legal separation and forced inequality of blacks) finally ended, the
result of heroic efforts by reformers inside the country and
mounting international diplomatic and economic pressure
on the all-white government. Bishop Desmond Tutu, who
won the Nobel Peace Prize in 1984, had promised his people
that "We shall be free." As violence swept through much of
South Africa, the government declared martial law in 1985
and orchestrated bloody reprisals against some black leaders. International economic sanctions were imposed on the
South African government, and ultimately many corporations sold their South African operations. In June 1991, laws
that had segregated South Africans by race were repealed.
Two years later, South Africa's white government accepted
a power-sharing arrangement with a multi-party transition
committee, making it possible for blacks to have a role in
government for the first time. The end of international economic sanctions followed. In 1994, in South Africa's first free
universal elections, Nelson Mandela, who had been a political prisoner for twenty-seven years, became South Africa's
first black president. South Africa is slowly trying to overcome decades of inequality, as well as age-old tribal rivalries
that have erupted in violence.

In much of the rest of Africa, war and nature conspired
against the people, most of whom lived in poverty. Famine
and hunger stalked drought-ravaged Ethiopia, Chad, Niger,
Sudan and other African nations in the 1980s, as well as in
wartorn Somalia, Rwanda and Zaire in the 1990s. Civil war
in Angola ended in 1991, while another in Mozambique raged

Refugees

on. Red Cross contributions and gifts from more prosperous countries helped ease some of the horrific suffering.

In 1992, the United States sent 20,000 troops to Somalia at the tip of East Africa at the request of the United Nations. The goal of "Operation Restore Hope" was to restore order. Civil war between warlord armies raged following the overthrow of its longtime dictator, preventing the distribution of food arriving from abroad in a country where a leader of one armed faction said, "If you have a gun, you are a man; if you don't, you are nobody." The peacekeeping force sent by the United Nations accomplished very little, while several of the peacekeepers were killed.

Central Africa became a focal point of the 1990s. In

Rwanda, the government was threatened by economic collapse, ethnic strife between the Hutus and Tutsis, and the
formation of rival political parties. As the Hutu government
struggled to hold onto power, over half a million people
were killed and about two million people fled to the neighboring countries of Zaire, Tansania and Burundi. Thousands
died when cholera broke out in wretched refugee camps,
and many others were eventually driven back into Rwanda
by troops in Zaire. The new Tutsi government in Rwanda
then arrested thousands of Hutu whom it accused of partic-
ipating in massacres, and the U.N. established a tribunal to
try a number of those accused of crimes against humanity.
The massive flow of refugees from Rwanda also contributed
to instability in Zaire and Burundi, which had their own
change of regimes.

Yet, all was happily not as bleak in other parts of Africa.
In some states, such as Zambia, the early 1990s brought more
political freedom, the gradual weakening of authoritarian
rule, and the emergence of party politics. In Zaire, the longtime dictator Mobutu Sese Seko, who had accumulated a
vast fortune at the expense of his country, was driven from
power, as Zaire became known as Congo.

In South America, a marked trend toward democratic
rule could also be seen, as one by one authoritarian governments were replaced by elected governments. In Argentina,
where thousands of ordinary people had been tortured and
killed during the years of right-wing military rule in the
1970s, a moderate conservative became president in 1984. In
Brazil, a mass mobilization of ordinary people helped bring
democratic rule to that country in 1985, after twenty years of
military rule. In Uruguay, too, moderates came to power, as
another military dictatorship passed into the night. In Chile,
voters in 1988 turned down a bill that would have extended
the term of the country's military ruler, General Augusto

Pinochet. In Paraguay, dictator Alfredo Stroessner, who had made his small Latin American nation a paradise for some Nazi war criminals, was driven from power by a military coup in 1990.

In Nicaragua, right-wing rebels—the "Contras"—waged civil war against the Marxist "Sandinista" government. Beginning in 1985, the Contras were financed in part through the profits from the illegal sale of U.S. arms to Iran. Besides attempting to overthrow the government of Nicaragua, the other goal of the operation was to gain Iranian support for the freeing of hostages being held by Muslim factions in Lebanon (they were released at the time of the Gulf War). When details of the "arms for hostages" deal became known in 1986, the White House denied all knowledge of the affair. However, lengthy congressional hearings the following year revealed that the president's top officials were involved. The congressional report asserted that President Reagan had "created or at least tolerated an environment" conducive to such illegal acts. The scandal put into the light of public scrutiny a president who was increasingly detached from his own presidency. Several of the president's top advisers, including his national security adviser, were forced to resign because of the "Iran-Contra" affair and were convicted on criminal charges.

In 1987, the presidents of Costa Rica, El Salvador, Honduras, Nicaragua and Guatemala signed an agreement intended to put an end to the bloody civil wars in Central America. The agreement called for cease-fires, free elections, and the end of outside support for rebels. In 1990, the presidents of the Central American states signed another agreement that declared that the Contra forces in Nicaragua should disband. Power in Nicaragua was transferred peacefully to a non-Marxist government in 1990, when Violeta Barrios de Chamorro defeated the former Marxist president, Daniel Ortega, in an election.

In Panama, where strongman Manuel Antonio Noriega was linked to the lucrative drug trade with the United States, American troops invaded the country in 1990, arresting the Panamanian leader and bringing him to the United States, and installing a government more to its liking. Noriega was convicted by a jury in Florida on drug-trafficking charges and sentenced to a lengthy prison term. The long civil war ended in El Salvador in 1991, when leftist rebels and the government reached an accord, although sporadic violence continued. In Guatemala, the civil war that had lasted thirty-six years ended with a peace agreement signed in 1996.

Elsewhere in the world, dramatic political changes also brought democratic rule to countries whose citizens had long lived under oppressive governments. In the Philippines, Ferdinand Marcos, who had originally been elected president in 1965, was barred from a third term of office in 1972. Yet, enjoying the unqualified support of the United States because of the strategic importance of the islands for the U.S. navy and air force, Marcos declared martial law and then oversaw the passage of new laws allowing him to be elected again in 1981. Yet, pressure for reform mounted from inside and outside his country, and left-wing guerillas battled government troops. Opposition leader Benigno Aquino was murdered in August 1983, shortly after stepping off a plane as he returned to Manila after many years in exile. The assassination was planned at the highest levels of the Marcos regime. In 1986, Marcos's opponent in a presidential election was Corazon Aquino, widow of the assassinated opposition leader. Following allegations of widespread voting fraud, Marcos fled the Philippines, which he and his family had virtually looted for decades. The Philippines became a viable democracy.

Other countries were experiencing similar dramatic upheavals with less resolution. In Cambodia, literally millions of people had been exterminated in the "killing fields" of the brutal dictator Pol Pot and his Communist Khmer Rouge supporters in the late 1970s. Hope that peace and governmental stability could come to that war-ravaged nation still appeared slim even after the Vietnamese army withdrew from Cambodia in 1990 after more than a decade of occupation. In 1991, Prince Norodom Sihanouk returned to his former capital of Phnom Penh as president following a peace agreement. In the meantime, amid continued political instability and Sihanouk's forced exile again, millions of land mines remained buried close to the surface, thousands of them killing and maiming people, principally children, unlucky enough to step on them.

The Middle East remains probably the most volatile region in the world. In 1980, Iraq and Iran began a war that lasted until a cease-fire was finally signed in 1988. During the 1980s, U.S. relations with Iran, whose fundamentalist leader the Ayatollah Khomeini had called for the defeat of the United States, which he called the "great Satan," deteriorated. In 1985, a U.S. warship in the Gulf shot down an Iranian airliner, mistaking the jumbo jet for an Iranian fighter plane; 259 people perished. Following the death of the Ayatollah Khomeini in 1989, however, relations between the United States and Iran gradually improved, as those between the United States and Iran's rival, Iraq, worsened.

Whereas the war between Iran and Iraq had dragged on for years, the Gulf War of 1991 was over very quickly. In August 1990, Iraqi dictator Saddam Hussein ordered the invasion of the smaller neighboring state of Kuwait. The lengthy war against Iran had brought Iraq to the verge of economic disaster. It owed large unpaid loans to Kuwait and other Arab states. Saddam claimed that Kuwaiti overproduction was forcing down oil prices on the world market. His smaller neighbor's vast oil reserves proved an irresistible temptation to the dictator.

Gulf War

Iraq's invasion of Kuwait broke apart Arab unity, as the Arab League condemned the invasion. In November 1990, the United Nation's Security Council authorized military measures against Iraq if its forces did not withdraw from Kuwait by mid-January. Iraqi troops stretched across their country's border with Saudi Arabia, an ally of the United States, and along the coast of Kuwait, digging themselves in behind fortifications and vast fields of mines, as rumors spread that Iraq was preparing for chemical warfare. Following a buildup of more than half a million troops, the U.N. forces, largely consisting of U.S. troops and warplanes ordered to the Persian Gulf by President George Bush, began air strikes against Iraq and its installations in Kuwait on January 17, 1991. The allies quickly gained control of the skies, and Iraqi forces crumbled on the ground before superior planning and equipment. The skies were filled with the black smoke from hundreds of oil wells set ablaze by Iraqi forces as they retreated. On February 24, the ground attack against Iraqi forces in Kuwait and into southern Iraq began. "Operation Desert Storm" quickly drove back Iraqi forces, whose numbers and quality of arms had been overestimated by military analysts. Television brought the war home in large parts of the world, as if it were some kind of video game, as reporters from the major networks broadcast dramatic accounts of incoming Iraqi Soviet-built "Scud" rockets fired from the ground toward U.S. bases and into Israel. Whereas the allied forces lost 340 combatants, at least 110,000 Iraqis, including civilians killed in air raids, died during the Gulf War. In mid-March, the Kuwati princes returned to their palaces. The Gulf War ended with a cease-fire agreement. Iraq agreed to inspections of its military installations by the United Nations, which suspected that Saddam had hidden chemical and biological weapons.

The Gulf War, however, did not end Saddam's power. He continued to provoke the United Nations, and particularly the United States. When Saddam refused to allow inspection of suspected sites of chemical weapon production and storage in 1997 and 1998, the United States threatened air strikes. In the meantime, a U.N.-imposed embargo on trade with Iraq brought great hardship to ordinary Iraqis, who continued to pay the price for their leader's megalomania.

Elsewhere in the Middle East, the Palestinian question had long poisoned relations between Israel and its Arab neighbors. In 1988, hope glimmered for a lasting resolution to the Palestinian question when the Palestinian Liberation Organization (P.L.O.) agreed to renounce terrorism as a tool and to recognize the right of the state of Israel to exist. That year, Jordan's King Hussein gave up Jordanian claims to the West Bank and Gaza Strip, both occupied by Israel. In 1992, Yitzhak Rabin became prime minister of Israel when a left-center coalition came to power. At Rabin's instigation, the Israeli cabinet announced a halt to the construction of controversial new Jewish settlements in the occupied territories, an impediment to any lasting peace. That year, the Israeli cabinet granted Palestinians limited self-rule in the Gaza Strip and the West Bank. An accord formally providing for Palestinian self-rule was signed in May 1994 and sealed in

July of that year in Washington by a handshake on the lawn of the White House between Israeli Prime Minister Yitzhak Rabin and Palestinian leader Yasir Arafat.

A multitude of problems remained as Arafat and Rabin tried to implement the peace. Arafat faced great pressure from militants who continued to demand a Palestinian state. Terrorist attacks against Israelis escalated, bringing a harsh Israeli response and hardening the opposition of right-wing Israelis to any compromise. Then, in November 1994, as he was leaving a peace rally, Prime Minister Rabin was shot and killed by a young Israeli extremist. In 1996, conservative Benjamin Netanyahu was elected prime minister by a narrow majority, leaving the possibility of a lasting peace very much up in the air.

Despite the easing of tensions between former enemies in the world, the easy availability of guns, bombs and poison gas, and the difficulty of preventing acts of violence have contributed to a continuing feeling of unease in the world as terrorists have waged campaigns leading to the wounding and death of many innocent victims. Much of the political terrorism of the 1980s and 1990s has been linked in some ways to the unstable situation in the Middle East. Israelis and Jews have been particularly vulnerable to terrorist attacks. The most murderous act of terrorism came in 1988, when a bomb planted by terrorists from the Middle East blew apart a Pan Am 747 airliner high above Lockerbie, Scotland, killing all 259 people aboard. Terrorists from the Middle East also set off a bomb in the basement of the World Trade Center in New York City in 1993, killing six people and injuring a good many more.

Extremists throughout the world have continued to use violence to try to achieve their aims. Thus, Islamic fundamentalists were responsible for terrorist attacks in Arab states where they wanted to impose a strict religious government. Fundamentalists groups undertook bloody attacks against foreign tourists in Egypt in the mid-1990s; in Algeria, fundamentalists slaughtered thousands of men, women and children to show their opposition to the secularized Algerian government that had canceled elections when it appeared that the fundamentalists might sweep into power and impose a strict religious state. In the United States, despite a fall in the overall crime rate in the 1990s, right-wing anti-government militant groups carried out several awful attacks. One bomb detonated in 1995 outside a government building in Oklahoma City killed 168 people, including children playing in a nursery school in the building. Another attack took place in a park in Atlanta during the 1996 Summer Olympics, killing two people. Extremists who were opposed to abortion bombed health clinics in which doctors were performing abortions and harassed and even shot at some of these doctors at the clinics. In Northern Ireland, extremists continued to carry out terrorist attacks in an effort to wreck the peace talks between Protestants and Catholics. Thus, violence continued intermittently, despite the cease-fires that went into effect in 1994 and again in 1997, and despite the efforts of Tony Blair, head of the "New" Labour Party, to effect a settlement.

The economic hardship, civil war, and political chaos that have often resulted from changes in governments have swelled the numbers of refugees pouring across borders in search of a better life in more prosperous economies and freer societies. Thousands of Haitians took to the seas in flimsy boats, sailing across sometimes stormy and always shark-infested Caribbean waters in an attempt to reach the United States. Kurds fled repression in Iraq and Turkey. Albanians packed themselves into anything that would float as they attempted to cross the Adriatic Sea to reach Italy. The comment of an Albanian journalist about his country spoke for refugees in many other parts of the world: "There is no bread in the bakeries, no milk. There is a shortage of salt. . . . All are disillusioned. There is no money and no hope." Hundreds of thousands of North Africans reached France and other western European countries via Spain, dodging police while working odd jobs. In 1995, almost three million people were living illegally in the countries of western Europe.

During the economic recession of the early 1990s, immigrants in relatively prosperous states sometimes became scapegoats for economic problems, such as unemployment, and were blamed for working clandestinely for very low wages. Xenophobia (hatred of foreigners) and racism became more apparent in western Europe than at any time since before World War II, swelling the number of voters for candidates of the extreme right in France, Austria and Germany, where far-right "skin-heads" and extremists perpetrated several deadly attacks on immigrant hostels. In the United States, fears that illegal immigrants were swamping the country and straining medical and educational resources were reflected in attempts to limit welfare benefits to immigrants, to oppose multicultural education, and to insist on English as the only official language.

Yet, these were, for the most part, booming years for the American economy. In the United States, from 1982, when the stock market began a sharp rise, five years of "easy money" made many Americans wealthier. "Yuppies" (young urban professionals), the butt of many jokes, laughed all the way to the bank as jobs in high finance brought huge financial rewards that many spent lavishly.

Often frenzied merger and acquisition activity led large corporations to gobble up smaller firms. High-risk "junk bonds" proliferated. A number of prominent Wall Street traders were imprisoned for illegal "insider trading," using privileged information on developments in various companies to invest and make large sums of money. Deregulation was another hallmark of the 1980s. The new era of increased competition in the United States even rocked the American Telephone and Telegraph Company, where the venerable "Ma Bell" lost the monopoly it had enjoyed for decades, bringing lower prices to consumers.

Due mainly to big increases in defense spending during the early years of the Reagan presidency, the U.S. federal debt tripled and the foreign trade deficit grew each quarter. Wall Street stocks became vastly overvalued and suddenly crashed on "Black Monday," October 19, 1987. The Dow Jones average plunged 500 points, or 23 percent, and many investors feared another Great Depression. The chairman of the New York Stock Exchange commented grimly, "This is the nearest thing to a financial meltdown that I ever want to see." However, the economy weathered the storm, with stock prices soon turning up again.

Growth in the U.S. economy in the 1990s was fueled by companies rapidly enhancing their products and productivity with information technology, much of it born and bred in California's Silicon Valley. The economic boom created many jobs in the United States, where nearly 60 percent of all adult women now worked, as opposed to only about 35 percent thirty years earlier. Women's wages moved closer to those of men, and women's sports made rapid progress at the college and professional level. Yet, a "glass ceiling" remained in some occupations, notably in some businesses, preventing qualified women from doing even better. Likewise, the wages of African Americans rose, although unemployment among young blacks and other minority groups such as Hispanics remained disproportionately high.

The U.S. economy played a decisive role in American politics. In 1992, Bill Clinton, a former governor of Arkansas, defeated President George Bush, whose campaign was hurt by the economic recession and rising unemployment. Clinton assumed the presidency with high hopes of effecting meaningful change; however, his attempts to create a national health insurance plan soon ran up against the opposition of the American Medical Association and many ordinary Americans who feared the cost and restrictions of such a program. In 1994, sweeping Republican victories in congressional elections gave the Republicans control over both the Senate and the House of Representatives for the first time in fifty years. Nonetheless, aided by a surging economy, Clinton was reelected in 1996, although he continued to be dogged by financial and sexual scandals. Clinton's success, in part, stemmed from the fact that he had moved toward the political center, sometimes echoing Republican positions in calling for a reduced role for government. In 1996, he signed a bill designed to, in his words, "end welfare as we know it." In 1998, President Clinton submitted the first balanced budget in thirty years.

The United State's economy did not exist in a vacuum. The economies of the world became increasingly dependent on one another. The Treaty of Maastricht was signed in that Dutch city in 1992 by the twelve members of the European Community (EC), as well as by most of the nations of the European Free Trade Association. In 1994, Austria, Norway, Sweden and Finland were formally invited to join the European Union, although Norwegian citizens in 1994 rejected membership. The treaty anticipated the creation of a European Economic Area, which would eliminate national trade barriers, as well as, in principle, border-crossing checkpoints. The European Community took a greater (but not uncontroversial) role in economic planning and coordination between states, and prepared to implement a common currency—to be called the "euro"—scheduled for introduction at the beginning of 1999, leading to a period of transition and anticipated full implementation in 2003. In the meantime, however, considerable opposition to increased European economic and political integration came from several directions, notably from conservative British "Euro-skeptics," who feared that the consolidation of more authority in Brussels would undercut Britain's sovereignty. At the same time, while most of Britain drew nearer to the Continent in spirit, it also did so in reality. In 1994, the "Chunnel," a thirty-mile tunnel linking Britain and France by train, began service, putting London just a few hours away from Paris and Brussels.

Faced with competition from the EC, the U.S. Congress passed the North American Free Trade Agreement (NAFTA) in 1992. With NAFTA, trade restrictions were gradually lifted among the United States, Canada, and Mexico.

When Asian markets and currencies fell late in 1997, particularly in Seoul, South Korea, and Singapore, their impact was felt on stock markets around the world. These international financial repercussions reflected the fact that regional economies were increasingly interconnected. The globalization of the international economy necessitated huge bailouts of troubled economies whose collapse could have had a serious impact on the world economy. A U.S. loan of fifty billion dollars in 1995 aided the floundering economy of Mexico, whose currency, the peso, had plunged in value, raising the risk of political instability. In Europe, by contrast with the United States unemployment rates remained extremely high, nearly 20 percent in Spain, 13 percent in France, with that of Germany not far behind. Unemployment particularly affected the young, who, facing what seemed to be uncertain futures, manifested higher rates of crime and drug use.

During the last two decades of the twentieth century, the problem of illegal drug use in both the United States and Europe leapt beyond the capacity of authorities to prevent the arrival of drugs from Southeast Asia and Latin America, particularly from Colombia. Following its introduction into the United States in 1985 by drug-dealers, "crack" cocaine addiction increased both among the middle class and among the poor of urban centers, who turned to drugs to escape the feelings of hopelessness engendered by unemployment and poverty. Various national crusades in the United States against illegal drugs, increases in federal financing of airport and border surveillance, and education programs fell far short of their goals. For an increasing number of young people, it proved harder and harder to "just say no" to illegal drugs.

In addition to the problems deliberately created by people—war, crime, drugs and terrorism—mankind also remained vulnerable to catastrophic accidents and natural catastrophes. Murderous earthquakes killed at least 30,000 people in Armenia in 1988, 10,000 in India in 1993, and more than 5,000 in Kobe, Japan, in 1995. In Colombia, a volcanic eruption unleashed murderous mud slides that buried more than 25,000 people in 1985.

In addition to natural disasters, catastrophic accidents also plagued the world. In December 1984, the worst industrial accident in history killed more than 2,500 people when poison gas was released from the Union Carbide insecticide plant in Bhopal, India. In April 1986, the worst nuclear accident in history occurred at the Chernobyl power station in Ukraine. A nuclear reactor ruptured, spewing out radioactive debris and dust that winds carried across parts of Europe and Asia. "Please tell the world to help us," implored a ham radio operator. A massive evacuation of people living near the reactor could not prevent many deaths, serious illnesses, and subsequent birth defects, as well as the contamination of some agricultural products and water supplies.

Oil spills caused less lethal but still considerable damage to the environment, endangering wildlife and fish in waters and beaches. In March 1990, the oil tanker *Exxon Valdez* ran aground in Prince William Sound in Alaska, dumping 250,000 barrels of oil into the water, one of the greatest ecological disasters in history. Other major spills spoiled the environment in Puerto Rico and the south coast of England.

Pollutants have seriously damaged our atmosphere. Photographs taken by satellites circling the earth have revealed the depletion of the ozone layer that protects the earth from some of the harmful effects of the sun's direct rays. Environmental damage literally poured from the sky as well. "Acid rain," which has its origins in industrial chemical pollution on earth, increasingly concerned environmentalists and scientists. It began to destroy forests in western Germany, the United States and Canada, as well as in eastern Germany and the Czech Republic which, under Communism, had had

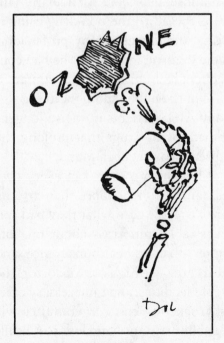

Ozone Pollution

virtually no restrictions against pollution. Growing concerns about damage being done to the environment led to
the "Earth Summit" held in Rio de Janeiro in Brazil in 1982,
which was attended by delegates from 178 countries.

Even as advances in science and medicine continued to
reduce or even eliminate the threat of many diseases in most
of the world, deadly strains of old disease, as well as some
new ones, took their toll. In central Africa, an epidemic of the
deadly Ebola virus took thousands of lives in 1995, reminding
scientists that certain diseases still remained beyond the ability of medicine to find cures. The AIDS virus, which causes
a fatal, slow-developing disease that destroys the human
immune system, was first observed in the early 1980s and
was isolated by scientists in 1984. AIDS ravaged the Central
African Republic and Zaire, but spared virtually no country.
In the west, homosexuals were particularly vulnerable; but
the disease also spread to the non-drug-using heterosexual
population. The announcement by professional basketball
superstar Magic Johnson in 1991 that he had contracted HIV
and his subsequent retirement had the salutary effect of putting the disease in the public spotlight in the western world.
Although many AIDS patients now live longer than before
due to combinations of drugs that prolong their lives, no
cure for the disease has yet been found.

The cost of health care soared in every country. In the
United States, families spent more than $730 billion a year
for health care in 1990, twice what they had spent a decade
before; yet, a sizable minority—about one of every nine
working families—had no health insurance, and no regular
access to health care. The high cost of doctors, hospitals, and
other health-care facilities, and unnecessary care helped generate these skyrocketing costs. In countries with extensive
programs of public assistance and low-cost health care, such
as France, Great Britain and Sweden, medical costs threatened to outstrip the ability of governments to pay for them.

Cloning Dolly

Remarkable advances in science and medicine have also posed some ethical problems. Nowhere was this clearer than in the rapidly changing field of genetic medicine, in which scientists have identified genes that are linked to disease. While such research could be used to identify and alter defective genes that lead to such inherited diseases as muscular dystrophy or sickle cell anemia, it might also be misused by prospective parents (aborting a fetus who has a predisposition for cancer) or employers (not hiring someone who has the genetic likelihood of early onset Alzheimer's disease). Moral quagmires as well as legal ones are likely to result. Other ethical issues have been raised by the cloning of a sheep in Britain in 1997. People feared the possibility that humans could also be cloned, leading to furious debate.

Compared to the drama of the first spaceship landing on the moon in 1969, space exploration seemed almost routine in the 1980s and 1990s. A year after two U.S. astronauts became the first men to walk in space without being attached to their spaceship, tragedy struck the space program. In 1986, the spacecraft *Challenger* exploded in space seventy-three seconds after takeoff. The crew of seven were killed when the spaceship's capsule crashed into the ocean before horrified onlookers at Cape Canaveral and a live television audience. Among those who perished was a New Hampshire schoolteacher and mother, Christa McAuliffe, who had been taken along for the ride as a publicity gesture by the space program.

It took more than two years before another manned American space shuttle lifted into space. In the meantime, as the space program gradually revived, the United States encouraged the development of rockets for commercial use. It sent out unmanned rockets to gather information about the stars and planets. *Voyager* 2 flew past the planet Uranus in 1986, and four years later drew to within 3,000 miles of Neptune. In 1991, the space shuttle *Columbia* successfully completed a scientific mission of eleven days in orbit, sending out a communications satellite. In 1997, the Hubble Space Telescope, originally launched by the space shuttle *Discovery*, sent back to earth dramatic new views of the distant reaches of the universe and beyond, including photos of hundreds of galaxies that had previously been unknown. In the meantime, symbolizing the end of the Cold War, in 1995, the *Atlantic* Space Shuttle and the Russian *Mir* space station linked up in space. And, in 1997, an unmanned spaceship landed on Mars.

To several generations almost habituated to dramatic explorations in space, the communications revolution of the 1980s and 1990s on earth seemed even more remarkable. Television brought the world closer together, with the rapid expansion of cable and then satellite television, first in the United States and progressively in much of the rest of the world. When the 1998 Winter Olympics began in Japan with the singing of Beethoven's "Ode to Joy," the conductor stood before the orchestra in Nagano, and five choruses were heard from South Africa, Australia, and three other continents, their voices transmitted instantaneously by satellite.

As television helped shrink the distance between continents and countries, the U.S. basketball star Michael Jordan became one of the most well-known figures in the world.

Professional sports sweatshirts, caps and expensive trade-mark shoes (often produced by destitute people in Asia for pitiful wages) were worn by many young people, both in the west and in distant corners of the world.

Beginning in the mid-1980s, the personal computer transformed the way we generate, discover and communicate information. Advances in personal computers and computer programs came so rapidly that it took an ever-larger army of high-tech wizards to keep track of them. With astonishing improvements in computer chips raising exponentially the memory capacity of computers, they became smaller and, at the same time, more reliable. "E-mail" (electronic mail) made communication virtually instantaneous among people owning computers anywhere in the world, facilitating, for example, collaborations among research scientists living far apart. The "Internet" opened a world of informative "web-sites" to anyone sitting at a computer. Students began to "surf the net" in order to find information for their papers; universities and colleges put their best foot forward on their websites; parents banked and made airline and hotel reservations, ordered books and even clothes, and followed their favorite sports teams and read foreign newspapers available via the Internet. In the mid-1990s, as well, mobile "cellular" phones became commonplace on street corners, in banks, buses, restaurants and cafés (often to the annoyance of other dinners), and in automobiles.

Yet, the computer revolution raised questions of ethics and thorny legal issues such as the right to free speech (does one have the right to put pornography on the Internet) and privacy. At the same time, worries mounted that the technological innovations and global interconnections through the Internet have made programs vulnerable to "viruses" and pose a threat to privacy by allowing unscrupulous computer "hackers" to collect information, for example about finances

World Wide Web

or aspects of private life, about virtually anyone using a personal computer.

When the twentieth century began, it took weeks to
travel around the world by ship, the only way that such a voyage was then possible. The world seemed very large indeed,
and most of the peoples of the world seemed like an after-
thought to the West. Now, jet planes take us quickly to the
far reaches of the world, and information on the movement
of the Japanese economy and on possible political changes in
China, India, Southeast Asia, the Middle East and anywhere
else in the world is instantly available and is important to us
all. In like fashion, people who might once have mattered
only in their own nations have taken on universal signifi-

cance. Thus, much of the world craved news of Princess Diana of Great Britain—from her marriage to Prince Charles to the births of her sons to her bulimia and the disintegration of her marriage. And all mourned her untimely death in a high-speed car accident in 1997, as hundreds of millions of people watched the somber funeral procession carried worldwide by live television.

The remarkable revolution in transportation transformed humanity's horizons, as first travel by car and then by plane surpassed in importance that by ship and even that by nineteenth-century invention, the railroad. The revolution in communications has arguably been even more dramatic, as the invention of the telephone was followed by the invention of the radio, the television and then the computer. The average person living in many parts of the world at the end of the twentieth century has a world of information at his or her fingertips via travel, the news and the personal computer. The globe has truly become smaller.

In the meantime, the conditions of life for most people have improved dramatically over the past hundred years. In the last decades of the century, the percentage of the world's population without enough to eat has declined to about 25 percent, although great misery remains in Africa and Asia, as well as in other places, and there is still much to be accomplished. But as the horrors of fascism and the failed experiment of Communism fade into the past in most of the world, we have every reason to hope and to be optimistic that the first century of the new millennium will bring, not only further progress in science and technology, but a better life for an even greater percentage of the world's population.

78

A Line

How a Line That We Thought We Saw at
the Very Beginning of a New Millennium
Turned Out to Be a Kind of Distraction

When we look to the past, we tend to define history in lines or points—those precise moments in which things were different before and after. And while, yes, there are days that matter more than others to us on a personal basis (for example, your birthday, just to name one), we also know that picking one day, week or month in time as a turning point is risky, like taking one drop of water out of a changing tide and saying, "This is it. This is the one. It was this drop with which the tide changed." Thus, while things might be very different for you, dear reader, on the day *after* you were born, in comparison to the way things were the day *before*, it is the case that for the great majority of the billions of other people on the planet, daily life nonetheless goes on without a blink. And yet, having said all that, we can say a line seemed at least temporarily visible at the beginning of the twenty-first century.

But before we discuss that line, let's look very quickly at another, a line that was identified, proclaimed and eventually forgotten, because the second millennium A.D., or C.E.—as

the years of the Common Era are now frequently termed—
began with a moment of panic that would eventually pass
into trivia. They began with an abbreviation that became a
phenomenon, a line since erased called "Y2K."

Y2K was not an actual line, like the tail of a comet, or
a military line, like the famous Maginot Line, the chain of
fortifications that France ran across its border with Germany
prior to World War II. It was a line of calculation—the separation between 1999 and 2000—on digital clocks and watches
and in digital computing systems. And it was that switch,
from the digits 99 to 00, that governments around the world
feared might cause catastrophe. Maybe it is difficult for you
to believe now, but government officials imagined difficulties with power grids and municipal services. So, governments did what governments throughout time have done
when faced with a potential crisis in the future: they studied
it. Questions surrounding the problem filled newspapers in
capital cities around the world, at a time when people still
read newspapers, given that online news outlets and blogs
were not yet commonplace. Commentators suggested that
because airplanes run on potentially confused computer systems, they might fall from the sky. There were concerns that
city water systems would shut down, that hospitals would
fail, that electrical grids would shut power down everywhere. (In some places in the United States, people hoarded
food and supplies.) Though, when midnight approached, and
we moved in time from the decade known as the 1990s into
the first seconds of the new decade, which we would sometimes call the "oughts," or more frequently call by no name
at all, the problems were minimal. As it happened, it was like
any other day of computer glitches, and Y2K turned out to
be a distraction from other problems we might have noticed
had we not been watching our digital wristwatches.

Still, the beginning to the oughts, and to the second millennium in the Common Era, can be looked at as a nice example of how we tend to go about things in our modern day and age. In retrospect, the Y2K crisis, or the crisis that wasn't, is an analogy for the way many governments and news outlets viewed the world at the dawn of the twenty-first century, especially in the United States and in Europe: we were focused on the revolutionary advances in computing and all the information technologies that went along with the development of the Internet. But we also let that fascination with the future get in the way of what we could see at that particular moment in time. By worrying about the switch from 99 to 00, we didn't notice that some of the age-old complications were still with us, such as poverty and war and the lingering resentments associated with those things, all of which could act as kindling to raging intolerances based on religious beliefs.

The 1990s was a decade during which a lot of the very issues that we had not been worried about—the aforementioned extreme poverty and political instability—ended up bringing much of the world to a halt. Unfortunately, many of the new connections that linked nations in terms of communication and cheap travel could also be used, it turned out, to share stock prices or pop songs or to transmit anger as well as fear.

79

Close Call

The Election That Almost Wasn't:
George Bush vs. Al Gore and the Saga
of the Crazy-Sounding Hanging Chad

Considering all the attention that had been paid to the possibility of a disastrous computer error in the previous year, Americans were shocked to watch as the election of 2000 became bogged down for weeks in a dispute that centred over the counting of ballots—not by an extremely complicated computer, but by hand.

It was a close race, and a strangely uninteresting one, with neither candidate coming off on TV or on the radio as sounding terribly convinced that he was either the best candidate or really *that* interested in getting the job. All through the fall of 2000, the race was close, though George W. Bush, the governor of Texas and the son of former president George H. W. Bush, seemed to be gaining as things wound down. Bush was running against Al Gore, a former senator from Tennessee who was serving as vice president under Bill Clinton, a popular Democrat who managed to stay afloat in the political game despite all that the Republicans threw at him. In 1998, Clinton's party lost its majority in the House to Republicans during the midterm election, and then his own

accidentally-made-public personal indiscretions resulted in
the House of Representatives nearly forcing him to resign, in
a process known as "impeachment." And yet, amidst all this
personal scandal and tumult he somehow managed to stay
in office and preside over what many people considered to be
a fruitful final four years, in terms of jobs and investments.

But back to the race between Bush and Gore, in 2000.
On the evening of Election Day, the closeness of the race
caught people by surprise. After the ballots came pouring in,
newspapers called the race in Governor Bush's favour, then
reversed themselves. The *St. Louis Post-Dispatch*'s early headline said, "Bush Wins a Thriller." The subsequent headline
cautioned, "The Nation Waits." Eventually reporters and—
weirdly—people in the streets and at home began talking
about something called a "hanging chad." (We didn't need to
set that phrase in quotes but it deserves it, we feel.)

Though it sounds like something you get with a bad cold,
or a plumbing problem, a chad is the little dot-sized piece of
paper that a person punches through a ballot when casting
a vote. Voting machines did not count the votes if the chads
were not completely punched out, or were hanging. Was a
hanging chad a vote or not a vote? And weren't these sorts
of problems supposed to happen in nations that were new at
elections and not a place with more than two hundred years
of experience with electing presidents? At one point during
the debates over votes and chads, the entire election came
down to a few votes in the dog leg–shaped state of Florida—
just under 1,700 votes in a nation of 281 million people, which,
when you count the number of people who actually voted,
ends up to be less than one-half of one percent of all the votes
that were cast.

For not just days but weeks, the nation waited. For more
than a month, people who did not normally think at all about

the functions of government were discussing the balance of power between the Congress and the Supreme Court, wondering who would control the Executive Branch. People who normally watched baseball or basketball were looking at Florida and saying, *This is crazy!*

The election was eventually decided, not by the voting public, a chad expert or a coin toss, but by the Supreme Court, in a case called *"Bush v. Gore."* To explain precisely how it went would take several books, but a short version goes like this: The court stepped in to stop a recount of votes in Florida. The court said the election could not be legally continued as far as the Constitution is concerned. Of course, this was a majority of the court, five justices, saying this. Four justices disagreed with their colleagues, making the court's decision even more interesting (and controversial).

Though Vice President Gore had won the greater number of votes, the election was decided in favour of Governor Bush, who, when the Florida votes were counted in his favour, won the majority in the Electoral College, a complicated system that ultimately decides presidential elections.

To review (because it was confusing even to political scientists), the Supreme Court, in a decision that four of the nine justices were not happy about, ruled that the guy who got fewer votes should win the election. Would voters be upset? Would the system fail? Was this the Y2K of American politics, and now our political system was like a broken computer, useless? What did it mean that teams of legal attorneys, a Republican team and a Democratic team, were down in Florida and then at the Supreme Court presenting their cases?

It was a nail-biting time, when people didn't know how things would move forward and when every little ceremonial ritual was scrutinized. On a grey and rainy January day in 2001, when Vice President Gore faced the newly inaugurated

President George Walker Bush on the west steps of the U.S. Capitol—seconds after Bush was sworn in as the first American president of the new millennium—the terse handshake seemed to show that somehow, even when it is confused, and possibly corrupted and certainly ugly, the American political experiment had managed to press ahead, for the moment.

80

A Sad Day

A Small Group of Terrorists Attack New York City
and Change the World

The sky was clear and blue on the morning of September 11, 2001, crisp and clear in a way that, if you saw it and think back on it, would seem to mean something, though of course it was only a sky, taking only whatever meaning you would have given it at the time. The New York Yankees were headed to the playoffs, though a game against their historic rivals, the Boston Red Sox, had been called off due to the previous night's heavy rain. Into that morning sky, two planes had taken off from Boston. But, instead of continuing on to their final destinations, they were quickly hijacked by terrorists, who turned both aircraft into weapons aimed at the World Trade Center towers—the iconic 110-story Twin Towers in Lower Manhattan.

The first tower was hit at 8:46, the second 17 minutes later. Fire made worse by fuel from the planes eventually destroyed both buildings. People in neighbourhoods surrounding Manhattan, and in villages and towns miles away, stood on hills and overlooks and peered toward New York Harbor. There, clouds of smoke and ash blanketed Lower Manhattan and blew into other neighbourhoods, a giant black plume leaning sadly off into that crisp sky.

Thousands of rescue workers—police and firemen and emergency personnel of all kinds, some from blocks away, many eventually from neighbouring states—raced to the scene, many of them losing their lives as they ascended the towers in the moments before both skyscrapers tragically collapsed. Not long after, another hijacked plane hit the Pentagon, the headquarters of the U.S. Defense Department, and one crashed in a field in Pennsylvania after passengers managed to overpower their captors. Had they not, it is thought that the terrorists might have attempted to strike the White House or the Capitol. Almost three thousand people died in the World Trade Center attack itself, the deadliest in U.S. history, and later on, rescue workers would continue to perish as a result of illnesses brought on by the hazardous conditions at the disaster sites.

At first, it was unclear who caused the attack, and it was very difficult—as it always is—to imagine why anyone would want to kill innocent people who were just going about their own business. The identities of the hijackers slowly became known, and they turned out to be members of a terrorist group that called itself "al-Qaeda," a name meaning "the base." Its leader, Osama bin Laden, had declared war on the United States.

Only a few years earlier, the United States had supported bin Laden. In the 1980s, he fought the Soviet Union's occupation of Afghanistan, a war that the Soviet Union eventually lost. (Remember: during the Cold War, the United States was friendly with groups simply because those groups were not friendly with the Soviet Union—always a risky endeavour.) At that point, the Soviet Union was only the last in a series of nations and empires to fall in the vast and harsh terrain of Afghanistan. Because the country had an ancient route that once connected

Europe to Asia, it had been fought over for a long time by people like Alexander the Great and Genghis Khan.

Bin Laden practiced an extremist and puritanical version of what he called Islam, an interpretation so extreme that followers of Islam everywhere rejected it. He saw the world in terms of a holy war, and he believed that Christians and Jews in the western world were out to destroy Islam. His army was not a traditional army, but one that used suicide bombers to attack civilians. They were not connected to any particular government.

As a result of these beliefs, bin Laden, as noted, declared war on the United States, as well as its allies. Previously, al-Qaeda members had managed smaller deadly attacks against the United States. In 1998, they set off bombs at American embassies in Kenya and Tanzania, Africa, and in 1993, they attacked an American warship visiting Yemen. In that same year, a terrorist affiliated with al-Qaeda set off a bomb in the bottom of the World Trade Center, killing six people and damaging (though not destroying) one of the Twin Towers.

For years—and possibly even now, as you read this—the events leading up to the 2001 attacks were debated. The U.S. government reportedly had information that some kind of attack was about to happen, so why did it not do something to stop it? What would that something have been? And in response to the questions, people came up with answers that made sense—and some that made much less sense, or no sense at all, such as the group that claims the Twin Towers are still there, hidden by giant skyscraper-sized mirrors.

After the attacks of what we now call "9/11," Ground Zero—the site where the 110-story towers used to stand—became a destination for pilgrimage, a place where people could express sadness and remember what had happened. People began to visit the site not long after the towers fell, though in the very first few weeks the streets in Lower

Manhattan were shut down. Businesses were shuttered, and homes were covered with the deadly dust. For days, no airplanes were permitted to take off from U.S. airports, and police inspected trucks and cars coming into and leaving the city. All around the nation, public safety officials went on alert for terrorist activity. As opposed to a few months before, where people were relieved that Y2K was not the end of the world, September 11 seemed to change things. The date was a line, after which the world was different for a while.

81

Striking Back

Remember that last American presidential election, the one we were talking about only a few pages ago? The one in which the candidate who won—George W. Bush—had not won by the popular vote but by a vote of the Electoral College, the college that is not really a college, but a college of people elected to represent the states of the Union? Remember how we were saying that things were a little shaky in the United States after that? Remember when we mentioned that people took a big gulp when the winner of the popular vote, Vice President Al Gore, said, OK, fine, you can be president, and did not say, No way! Well, let's just say that when that election was over, President George Bush did not seem to have much of a mandate.

What's a mandate? It comes from a Latin term, "*mandatum*," meaning "command." The president did not have much of an order, in other words, from the American voting public. Nor did he have a lot of support. But then, after the attacks of 9/11, he suddenly had both of those things. If you have read this book with some care, you will have little difficulty imagining a moment when a group of people, feeling attacked, have rallied around their leader. Since long before

the Greeks attacked the Trojans, people have naturally rallied around their leaders after an attack. After September
11, Americans—feeling the pinch of a recession and the lingering dread of that surprise attack by hijacked jets—rallied
around George Bush. Indeed, President Bush suddenly had
a mandate, or seemed to anyway. It was, first, to make certain that there were not going to be anymore attacks, if that
was possible.

The president stood among firemen and rescue workers
on the edge of the burning pile of rubble—the site known as
"Ground Zero"—and with a bullhorn, he said, "I can hear
you. The rest of the world hears you and the people who
knocked these buildings down will hear all of us soon."

The rescue workers cheered, but this was the kind of
statement that made people who were not Americans anxious. It was as if the biggest guy in the neighbourhood had
been knocked down and he was going to start swinging his
fists and asking questions later. For weeks after September 11,
a lot of people around the world were holding their breath.
What would the United States, the country with the largest
military in the world, do?

For its part, the world offered sympathy. Many governments expressed support for the United States. The French
newspaper *Le Monde* ran as a headline, *"Nous sommes tous
Américains,"* which can be translated as, "We are all Americans," a reference in part to President John F. Kennedy's
famous speech in Berlin at the height of the Cold War, when
Berlin was cut off from Europe by the Soviet Union. (Kennedy said, *"Ich bin ein Berliner,"* which means "I am a Berliner.") Islamic leaders and theologians denounced the attacks
by al-Qaeda. In the streets of Tehran, the capital of Iran, people held candlelight vigils.

About a month later, President Bush, with the authoriza-
tion of the U.S. Congress, announced that he would bomb

Afghanistan. The targets were al-Qaeda camps. Several governments around the world supported his decision, but many also feared that the Americans would use the issue to strike out in other ways—in the Middle East, for example, to protect their access to oil, which the American economy, like many economies, is always hungry for. To strike al-Qaeda, the U.S. military also targeted the Taliban, the Islamic regime that ruled much of the Afghan territory that al-Qaeda inhabited.

We already mentioned that Afghanistan is a point in the world that various empires have attempted to control over time, a junction between continents, rugged country on an ancient route, the Silk Road, from Europe to Asia. Another thing that bears repeating is that in Afghanistan, friends and enemies have switched sides. At one point the United States was friendly with anyone who wanted the Soviet Union out of Afghanistan, groups of farmers and rural leaders, usually, who tended to have orthodox religious beliefs. That was during the Cold War. After the Soviets left, and their empire collapsed, these groups ruled Afghanistan and set up a militant Islamic state where, for instance, women have few rights. Now, the United States was after the Taliban, arguing that the militant regime was sheltering Osama bin Laden, the man responsible for masterminding the attacks of 9/11.

A part of the story of humankind that seems to become more true as time marches on has to do with the very earth that humankind lives on: history and geography—old roads and mountain passes, strategic rivers and waterways—affect what happens in the world as they always have, and as a result, the same battles are fought over and over, using the same advantages, the same defences. You can cover the land with satellites and computers, but the land is still the same.

And so with this in mind, we can say that in the nineteenth century the British attempted to rule Afghanistan and failed. Then the Soviet Union tried and failed. (And part of that fail-

ure, by the way, meant that the Soviet Union, an authoritarian empire, lost control of countries it had conquered in the
twentieth century so that it went back to being a smaller, but
still tough Russia.) By 2002, the U.S. military finally removed
the Taliban from power in Afghanistan, even though Osama
bin Laden somehow slipped away. Thousands of U.S troops
were in the position that Soviet troops, and before that British
troops, had been in—they were stuck, fighting local farmers
who knew the land better than they did and who had fought
repeatedly over generations against outside forces trying to
control them. It was a difficult position for the American
troops to be in. Thousands of Americans and Afghanis died,
stirring up the history of Europe and Asia. Again, the world's
only remaining superpower was entangled in ancient rivalries and geographies, and it was, let's not forget, a chain of
events that began with smoke from two buildings, two tall
towers, the image of their destruction repeated over and
over on TV and increasingly on the Internet.

82

A New Coin

Let's Just Look for a Second at What a New Coin
Can Mean, the Past Achievements It Represents
and the Future Difficulties

While dark clouds were moving over Afghanistan and
the Middle East, Europe celebrated a bright, joyous New
Year's night in 2002. In the first minutes of the new January, a
million people got together in Berlin to celebrate the arrival
not of a political leader or a rap star or a celebrity, but of a
new kind of money. It was a bill that replaced the German
mark, as well as the French franc and the Spanish peseta. It
was a new currency, the euro!

The world's economy was beginning to show signs of what
would be a major crash—which we shall discuss shortly—
but the day the euro debuted as a world currency, its value
rose, and it was off to a good start. It was a European currency accepted in all (or at least, most of) the countries that
are part of the European Union, or EU. That January, it was
very quickly used to buy everything from champagne to cof-
fee. The very first time anyone used a euro was in Réunion,
a French department in the Indian Ocean. (A "department"
is a territory ruled by France.) In the town of St. Denis, the

administrative capital, the mayor spent seventy-six euro cents at a fruit stand. He bought a kilogram of litchis.

But the euro was *not* small change. It was a big deal, even if it is—let's face it—really boring, the very stuff you keep in your pocket to use for buying soda or chips. At that New Year's moment, the euro represented a triumph of a movement begun in Europe after World War II. Around that time, a French minister, Robert Schuman, called for "a European federation for the preservation of peace." Shuman grew up in a region on the border of France and Germany—an area the two countries regularly fought over. He was born a German citizen, but when France annexed his hometown after World War I, he became French. When he became prime minister of France, he proposed a European assembly of some kind, a union, a way to stay together rather than repeat another world war–igniting fight. You only have to look back through these pages to notice that the nations of Europe have fought with each other a lot.

The thinking was this: if Europe could be linked more deeply—through trade, through currency, through a political assembly and a constitution and, at some point, through their militaries—then European nations might be less likely to go to war against each other. Usually, two or three nations would team up to protect themselves from another one, or in certain cases, to attack other nations. This is what Hitler was thinking when he aligned with Stalin in World War II.

Looking back, we see that Schuman, being a French minister, was probably also thinking a European union might protect him from another battle with an aggressive Germany. The union began with the establishment of the European Coal and Steel Community, by France, West Germany, Italy, the Netherlands, Luxembourg and Belgium. England would have nothing of the union; Shakespeare's homeland thought of itself as more closely linked with the United States than with its European neighbours. England stuck with the pound and skipped the euro. Same for Norway, which has voted several times not to use the euro.

But eventually more and more European nations signed on, forming, first, the European Community, which in the 1990s changed its name to the "European Union." Combining armies and navies is more complicated, naturally, especially since West Germany, after World War II, ended up being a giant again, economically. That's why the currency that stands behind the euro is the German mark. Which means that Germany has a kind of power over the other nations' economies, which, yes, makes the other nations nervous.

That's what the EU is all about, really—tying Germans' interest to everyone else's interest. Does it always work out? No. The euro would have its troubles, as we shall see, and even though the EU would eventually be awarded the Nobel Peace Prize, it would face many challenges in the near future. The euro, though, comes from the impulse to connect Europe, even if it has from time to time pulled it apart.

83

War in the Middle East, Again

How the United States Decided to Go to War to
Prevent a War and Ended Up Starting One Anyway

Power is dangerous. Power can be an enemy in itself. It's
not difficult to understand why a leader might want more
power, even when not at war. And while more power is usually very difficult to obtain, all President Bush had to do was
ask for it, and he was given more power.

In October of 2012, the U.S. Congress passed something
called the "USA Patriot Act." The name of the act was an
acronym, which stood for "Uniting and Strengthening America by Providing Appropriate Tools Required to Intercept
and Obstruct Terrorism." The act gave the president more
authority to fight terrorism. Nobody is saying that fighting
terrorism is easy. Consider why they are called "terrorists."
Causing terror has to do with frightening people, and what is
more terrible than a dread buried in our daily lives, waiting
to strike when we least expect it. In fighting terrorists, it is
easy to lose track of the target, especially since the terrorists are hiding among us. Our everyday lives—with all the
freedoms that we enjoy—can be injured while we are attacking terrorists. The idea of fighting for freedom and attacking
freedom quickly became tangled. Am I giving up my free-

dom *for* my freedom? Am I protecting liberty by stripping others of their liberties? At what point does the battle to save freedom destroy it?

These were the questions that the United States was dealing with after September 11, and many of the powers the government asked for turned out to be secret, kept from the public. We learn of them only when reporters find out. But we know that President Bush managed to expand the government's ability to collect information by means of the Internet and in telephone communications. The U.S. government also rounded up thousands of immigrants and detained them in camps. In some cases, these prisoners were sent, along with Taliban fighters from Afghanistan, to a prison in Cuba, on a U.S. naval base along Guantánamo Bay. There, U.S. officials did not follow the rules of interrogation accepted by international treaties, such as the Geneva Convention. At Guantánamo Bay and elsewhere—covertly, the United States utilized the overseas bases of numerous countries—terrorists were tortured, as were individuals who did not turn out to be terrorists.

If the contested election of 2000 was a test to the American democracy—would there be a peaceful transition even if it was not clear who won the vote—then the uses of torture and the elimination of civil rights was for many people a failure of American democracy.

BUT MAYBE THE largest expansion that President Bush called for (and got) was an expansion of what war is for. President Bush argued that to defend the United States, it was necessary to attack another country ahead of time, in what's called a "pre-emptive war." The Middle East has been fraught with boundary disputes since the times covered in the early chapters of this book. There is the struggle between the Israelis and the Palestinians, and since industrial countries became

addicted to oil, the area has been watched carefully and
fought over by outsiders. The country that President Bush
decided he wanted to attack in a pre-emptive strike was Iraq,
a middle eastern nation that was a little more than twice the
size of the state of Idaho, and the home of one of the world's
earliest civilizations.

At the outset of 2002, the president defined Iraq, Iran
and North Korea as an "axis of evil." This is something that
the United States has often done in its history—describe an
enemy as "evil"—and it has often made it difficult for the
United States to deal with that country later on, when everyone wants the war to end, for instance. It happened in Vietnam, for instance. But that's what President Bush did. He also
began to build his case for a pre-emptive war against Iraq,
where, President Bush said, Saddam Hussein, the brutal dictator of Iraq, had developed horrible weapons, presumably
powerful and poisonous bombs. President Bush and his vice
president, Dick Cheney, referred to the weapons as "weapons of mass destruction," or "WMDs." Though international
inspectors could not find the WMDs, the United States
claimed to have special intelligence. Even though many people were sceptical, a *New York Times* reporter went to Iraq and
claimed to confirm the existence of the WMDs.

The Americans insisted—in presidential press conferences, even in a dramatic presentation to the United
Nations—not only that there were WMDs but also that
Saddam Hussein was working with al-Qaeda, the group that
attacked the World Trade Center. The United States attacked
Iraq and captured Saddam Hussein, who would later be
killed, and thousands of Americans and Iraqis died, but there
never were any WMDs. The Central Intelligence Agency,
under President Bush, would say they never existed. Likewise, links between Saddam Hussein and al-Qaeda turned
out not to be true. In 2013, on the tenth anniversary of the

invasion, the *Times* would write an editorial that said this: "The Iraq war was unnecessary, costly and damaging on every level. It was based on faulty intelligence manipulated for ideological reasons. The terrible human and economic costs over the past 10 years show why that must never happen again."

But days before invading Iraq, President Bush delivered a new ultimatum on TV, demanding that Saddam Hussein and his advisers leave Iraq within forty-eight hours. Three days later, on March 20, 2003, the United States and a few allies invaded Iraq, pre-emptively. It soon became clear that the United States had not planned on a large enough army to hold Iraq, to govern the state, to make it secure enough so that people could get food and water and live safely, no matter how hard the American soldiers who were there fought. And yet, on May 2, 2003, with Saddam Hussein still at large, President Bush landed on the deck of the aircraft carrier USS *Abraham Lincoln* in a flight suit and, then wearing business attire and standing beneath a banner that said, "Mission Accomplished," gave a speech. "In the Battle of Iraq, the United States and our allies have prevailed," he said. A civil war followed in Iraq, and the American combat mission did not end until 2010, up to fifty thousand troops remaining as what the next president would describe as "a transitional force," troops that would stay there until something else happened. (All U.S. forces were eventually withdrawn by 2011.)

Think of the world as a busy and dangerous intersection, where there are only a few laws. Crossing the street becomes more dangerous if people decide you are an especially dangerous vehicle. They will ignore the few laws there are in order to protect their own safety. Even if you were a careful and safe and respectful driver, the rest of the people on the street would begin to worry about you and then fear you, and then perhaps decide that you are making things worse for everyone, that you are a menace and ought to be restrained in some way, ought to be dealt with.

Your own safety—in your own life, and as a nation on the world stage—has a lot to do with how other people understand you. It is for that reason that a low moment in the Iraq War came in 2004, when a group of photos from an American prison in Iraq, called Abu Ghraib, were published and spread around the Internet, and then in newspapers and on TV programs being broadcast all over the world. The photos showed the prisoners being tortured and mishandled and possibly killed in ways that the world—even conscientious American soldiers—found disgusting.

They were offensive to everyone in every country, in fact, but aspects of them were particularly offensive to Muslim religious practices. And so, some people who might have felt badly for the United States after September 11, the people who did not like the terrorists attacking innocent people in the name of Islam, began to not feel so badly for the United States. Since the end of the Cold War, between the United States and the Soviet Union, there had been only one superpower, the United States, and now people feared that that superpower might proclaim war pre-emptively whenever it wanted to and that it would act whatever way it wanted to.

84

A New Look at Big Cities

Cities Flooded with People, and We Realized That
They Were a Natural Place for People to Be,
Which Means We Have a Lot of Work to Do

The twenty-first century, as it began, was looking like a very good century if you were a creature growing in the mud. Why? It takes a few pages to explain, which we shall do by looking at cities, where people had been moving to for a long time. People migrated to cities during the twentieth century for jobs, mostly, or because it was becoming more difficult to live off the land. Often people moved from the countryside when it was stripped of job- and food-related resources, like trees, or when water was ruined, polluted by factories or by farming with too many chemicals. Over the past century, farms went from being small-family and community operations around the world to being run by large companies, which often pay less money to a fewer amount of people. But the point is that, by the beginning of the twenty-first century, half of the world's population had moved to cities, which in developing nations around the world were gaining five million residents a month. That's right, five million people a month. Imagine the population of Singapore moving into your city in August! Imagine twenty times the number

of people in Toledo, Ohio, showing up in your town every
few weeks!

It is not good to arrive in a city without much money, but
people are drawn there for the possibility of survival. There
are different kinds of economies in cities, some of them
operating outside of the laws of the rest of the economy. But
in many large cities there are now vast, too-crowded areas
called "slums." People in urban slums face many problems
with security and with getting clean water, though, on a
hopeful note, the United Nations reported that the sanitation
and water in cities improved between 1990 and 2008. Still,
the fast growth of slums means that positive improvements
in them will be under strain. It is expected that halfway
through the twenty-first century, there will be two billion
people living in urban slums, two times the number of people living there now.

But let's look at why people live in cities, which will
require a few more questions to be answered.

Why do people live in cities?

Part of the reason is that cities are where people are
already. People like to live near people. Among people,
people feel they have a chance to work things out, through
various kinds of transactions or deals, through good deals
though often very bad deals. But mostly people settle near
each other. You might want a place to wander off alone, and
you need quiet and rest, but as a creature, you like to settle
in groups.

How did we end up with big cities being where they are now?

People set up shelter where they will be safe from the
wind and storms and high seas, places where the elements—
rivers, bays, oceans—will provide food for them. Sometimes
the very same reason why humans settled the city is a reason
why they are hurt by the place. Port-au-Prince is a city in
Haiti that was settled because the high mountains around

the city protected ships in the bay and offered its visitors
wood for building and cooking fuel. The same is true for San
Francisco, in California. Indeed, both cities have their high
mountains, but both are susceptible to earthquakes, the very
same earth forces that produced the protective mountains—
we're talking geology here, where we read the earth itself
like a history book.

Places that seem safe to us in the short term can, on occasion, be dangerous. If you walked through the streets of Port-
au-Prince in the beginning of the twentieth century, after it
was hit by a devastating earthquake, you saw a city with little
water, with no safety for men, women or children—a dangerous urban slum. At night, there were fires in the streets,
no power, little safety—it was a kind of war zone without
any armies.

*What started the change in how we think about the ecology of
our cities?*

As more people started to live in giant cities, and as giant
cities in many western nations began to take better care of
the waters that ran in and around the cities—in 1972, for
instance, Republican President Richard Nixon signed the
Clean Water Act in the United States—the idea of what was
natural for us began to expand. We started to look at our
cities as being more of a natural place—a place that could
benefit a large number of us if it was kept clean and envi-
ronmentally friendly. And remember: when we are talking
about the *us* that lives in cities, we are talking about most
of us.

*How are ecology and economics related? And how does that
relate to cities?*

Like economics, ecology has its root in a Greek word,
"oikos," meaning "house," and the ecologist is looking at
what exactly an animal or insect or bird calls home, and how
it lives there. It is probably no coincidence that around the

same time that people began to move from the countryside
to cities in the world, ecologists began to think about the
nature of cities. In the 1970s, when clean water laws were first
put into place and industrialized nations began to do something about their disgusting rivers—in Cleveland, Ohio, a
river was so polluted it caught fire—a ball started rolling,
so that now, in the first years of the twenty-first century,
communities have begun to take dams down in the United
States, releasing the waters to allow the free flow of fish. But
the point I'd like to make here is that cities are a natural settlement for humans. Cities, with all their ecological and economic activities, are our homes.

*How is the number of fish in an area related to the number of
humans?*

Surely people have long thought likewise, but in the first
decade of the twenty-first century it became popular—and
it even made economic sense—to worry about the ecology
of a city. In the 1950s, a large number of people in American cities, such as New York City, got sick when clouds of
pollution hung over them. Now, it was cheaper to take care
of people if they weren't sick, if their air was not polluted,
and a lot of people were protected if the air in a city was
clean. And not just the air of the people who could afford to
live in nice places. Early in the twentieth century, it became
clear that people work better when they are healthy, work
smarter when they are educated, feel better when they can
read a book at a public library or hear music in a park for free!
Access to the economic diversity of a city—when facilitated
through good public transit—helps people rise out of poverty as well.

It also became even clearer that large cities throughout
the world have many things in common. You might say their
ecologies are similar. As we discussed, cities tend to come
into existence near good food supplies, often on the water,

often where rivers empty into or are about to empty into the sea. The landscape of a city is protective in some sense—as ports for ships, for example. And, as noted, they are built near abundant food supplies, food supplies that might start, if one were to look back into the history of the city, with fish. It's no coincidence that places where huge numbers of fish live and breed are the same places that became very large cities. Of the three-dozen largest cities in the world, almost 70 percent of them are on estuaries.

What's an estuary?

The word "estuary" comes from the Latin word for "tide," and an estuary is a place where rivers meet oceans. Estuaries are the most productive ecologies in the world, given all the nutrients and myriad creatures that thrive in and around them. For example, the tiniest creatures growing in the Pearl River estuary of Hong Kong can be found in the stomachs of white dolphins and finless porpoises along the coast of China. Herring from the rivers of Massachusetts can end up in the stomachs of Canadian seals, and flood control in the Chao Phraya River basin in Thailand matters for flood control in the city of Bangkok, as well as for farms' production of Bangkok's food.

In the 1990s, scientists around the world began to document the importance of urban estuaries and their startling resilience. Even though they had been beaten up, slammed with pollution and toxins, incredibly, when scientists went back to look for them, they were still around. And now, with cleaner waters in some places, it was a good time to be a creature in the mud, the bottom of our food chain.

What is the future for creatures in the mud?

Hard to say. Given that the number of fish in the ocean has been declining, we'd better hope the future for creatures in the mud improves. Scientists were beginning to understand that the mud of tired and stressed old marshes can be replanted. On the other hand, because of global warming, scientists were also aware that the levels of the oceans have been rising, quickly. Today's marsh on the edge of a harbour looked as if it might be tomorrow's harbour. Should we make the old downtown tomorrow's marsh? These were the kind of tough questions we found ourselves having to deal with quickly, always by considering people and cities as part of the natural cycles, as creatures too.

The United Nations' World Meteorological Organization determined the years between 2000 and 2010 to be the warmest recorded since record keeping began in the 1850s, with especially warm temperature readings in Africa and in parts of Asia and Antarctica, though maybe when you are reading this book, you will be aware of a warmer year since then. In 2010, there were extreme summer monsoons in Asia, extreme summer temperatures in Russia and unusually heavy rains and flooding in Indonesia, Australia, Africa, Europe and South America. The Amazon River saw drought, and the famed Northwest Passage across the Arctic Circle from Europe to Asia, a dangerous and impossible route through the Arctic ice that explorers died searching for in the nineteenth century, was nearly iceless in the summer, a breeze to get through in comparison to earlier days.

If there were questions in the previous century about global warming, they were answered in the twenty-first. The atmosphere was warming up for certain, and it was clear that the emissions of human industry created the conditions for warming. By burning coal and fossil fuels, we filled the atmosphere with gases that created a kind of greenhouse, the gases holding temperatures in.

How fast will the temperatures rise?

The answer to this question is not exactly clear. Don't be confused by people who have said that the temperature increases the world has been experiencing are a hoax, these people pointing to a big snow storm as evidence that the world is not warming. They are confused themselves, perhaps by the difference between "climate" and "weather." The difference has to do with time. Weather is when it snows on a Wednesday in February; climate is the chance that it will typically be cold enough to snow over the course of many Wednesdays in many Februarys. But as we said, climate and weather are often confused. Yes, it might still snow on a Wednesday in March in New England, but by the year 2010, we could look back on recent numbers of Wednesdays and see that it was less likely to snow in a place where it formerly did snow, a lot.

We also began to see that the weather that did come was more and more extreme, more severe than people were used to. Hurricane Sandy hit the states of New York and New Jersey in 2012 harder than any hurricane had in a century, causing billions of dollars of damage to the region and its economic vitality.

But what about the creatures in the mud?

By seeing the city as a natural setting for humans, and by seeing it as naturally linked with the region in which it exists—with its nearby river and hills, and suburbs and train routes and highways—governments took paths to blow off less pollution from their cities, to build better mass transit, to take better care of the forests, for the sake of the water supplies and for the sake of the health of their citizens. Cities began rethinking themselves as natural in a sense, as places where humans might naturally live, and where they depended on the well-being of those little creatures in the mud, to feed the fish, to feed the insects that feed the birds, to nourish the grasses that make the marshes that absorb the water when the big storms come.

The idea that a city is in some ways natural is itself a hopeful notion; it affords us with more and more tools to stop global warming, for instance. The countries with the largest economies—the United States, for example—were reluctant to sign treaties to address global warming, even though scientists urged them to do so, in an attempt to pull back on the greenhouse effect. Young people were also pushing hard to convince them to do so. In 2012, college students began to ask their colleges and universities and towns and cities to take their investment money out of companies that contributed to the increase in global warming. In 1992, a ten-year-old girl addressed the United Nations, and said this:

Hello, I'm Severn Suzuki speaking for E.C.O.—The Environmental Children's Organization. We are a group of twelve- and thirteen-year-olds from Canada trying to make a difference: Vanessa Suttie, Morgan Geisler, Michelle Quigg and me. We raised all the money ourselves to come six thousand miles to tell you adults you must change your ways. Coming here today, I have no hidden agenda. I am fighting for my future. Losing my future is not like losing an election or a few points on the stock market. I am here to speak for all generations to come. I am here to speak on behalf of the starving children around the world whose cries go unheard. I am here to speak for the countless animals dying across this planet because they have nowhere left to go. We cannot afford to be not heard. . . . All this is happening before our eyes and yet we act as if we have all the time we want and all the solutions. . . . Are we even on your list of priorities? My father always says, "You are what you do, not what you say." Well, what you do makes me cry at night. You grownups say you love us. I challenge you, please make your actions reflect your words. Thank you for listening.

85

A Black Man Becomes
the American President

A Century and a Half after the American Civil
War, Barack Obama, a Senator from Illinois,
Wins a Historic Election

You might recall that earlier in this book, we discussed the election of a lawyer from Illinois to the American presidency in the mid-1800s. We noted that upon that president's subsequent "Emancipation Proclamation," issued in 1863, slavery, in van Loon's words, "had come to an end in every part of the civilised world." (The exception at the time was Cuba, which, under Spanish rule, maintained the institution of slavery.)

While this statement was true insofar as it related to governments that openly condoned slavery, slavery persisted in ways beyond those that the American government talked about openly. Even at the outset of the twenty-first century, up to twenty-seven million people in the world could still be called "slaves." How do we define slaves? People who are forced to work for no payment beyond the food they need to stay alive, who are held through fraud and with the threat of violence. (Governments argue that the number of slaves is half that, but organizations outside of governments that carefully follow governments as they deal with human rights estimate the number to be double what the governments say it is.) The high modern number of slaves is partly due to the sheer number of people on the globe—nearly seven billion people live on the planet as this sentence is being typed. But at the same time, it also has to do with just how cruel humans can be, especially humans who are dealing with issues surrounding money and greed.

The United States has always confused the world. On the one hand, it declared itself a nation based on self-evident truths—one being "that *all men are created equal*"—when it declared independence from Great Britain. Meanwhile, President George Washington kept a plantation of slaves, as did President Thomas Jefferson, the author of the Declaration of Independence, while Jefferson's and Washington's friends from France and even the departing British generals told the Americans to let their slaves go. Even after President Lincoln, a former senator from Illinois, freed the slaves by presidential proclamation, less open versions of slavery continued to exist, on top of age-old prejudices.

"And yet words on a parchment would not be enough to deliver slaves from bondage, or provide men and women of every color and creed their full rights and obligations as citizens of the United States." This was said by another senator from Illinois, Barack Obama, in 2007. "What would be needed were Americans in successive generations who were willing to do their part—through protests and struggles, on the streets and in the courts, through a civil war and civil disobedience, and always at great risk—to narrow that gap between the promise of our ideals and the reality of their time."

Obama was running for president when he spoke these words. He was giving a speech in Philadelphia specifically about race, black and white relations, long a vexation to Americans. Obama told the audience that he was running for office because he believed, as he put it, "that we may not look the same and we may not have come from the same place, but we all want to move in the same direction—toward a better future for our children and our grandchildren.

"This belief comes from my unyielding faith in the decency and generosity of the American people. But it also comes from my own story."

Obama had written a best-selling memoir as a young senator, and already he was known as an excellent orator. He spoke of being the son of a black man from Kenya and a white woman from Kansas. He told of being raised in part by a white grandfather, who survived the Great Depression and fought in World War II, and a white grandmother, who worked in a factory building bombers while her husband was overseas. He went to Harvard University, one of the wealthiest schools in the world, and lived in Indonesia, one of the world's poorest nations. "I am married to a black American who carries within her the blood of slaves and slaveowners—an inheritance we pass on to our two precious daughters," he said in his speech. "I have brothers, sisters, nieces, nephews, uncles and cousins of every race and every hue, scattered across three continents, and for as long as I live, I will never forget that in no other country on Earth is my story even possible."

One hundred and forty-five years after the Emancipation Proclamation was issued, an African-American became president of the United States. He received almost seventy million votes, which at that point was the most ever received in a presidential election. Things did not go easily for him, and he quickly went from a moment of high symbolism to crashing politics-as-usual—most of his first term was spent working through a political deadlock with Republicans, who nearly caused the shutdown of the federal government on several occasions, due to differences in how to deal with the government's budget. He did manage to pass major health care legislation.

Obama was re-elected in 2012, after numerous voter-identification laws had popped up around the country, laws designed to make it difficult to vote. A report showed that if a person were to comply with the new laws, it could cost each one about eleven dollars, a figure that is higher than the poll taxes that black voters had to pay and that Civil Rights legislation banned in the 1960s. And as his second term began, exactly a century and a half after Lincoln issued his proclamation to free slaves, African-American voters, it turned out, had voted at a higher rate than did the general population.

In 2007, Obama had campaigned to close Guantánamo, the American prison camp in Cuba, but he did not. Under his command, U.S. Special Forces captured and killed Osama bin Laden in Pakistan. Note that Obama did not give up many of the new presidential powers offered by the Patriot Act—power, as we mentioned, is a difficult thing to give up. And he increased the American military's reliance on unmanned remote-controlled aircraft, or drones, which were capable of not only striking military targets but also killing civilians. But much of his presidency focused on the tremendous economic downfall that struck the world as he was elected.

86

Apologizing

A Very Brief Note on Something That Was
Happening More and More Around the World, as
Governments Looked Closer at Their Own Histories

As we step away from the subject of the Obama presidency, I would like to briefly take up the subject of apologies. This is a very serious subject, even though it is often treated lightly, or with derision when it is discussed in the news. I mention apologies because of an incident that occurred during the first year President Obama was in office. He gave a speech in Cairo that sought a reconciliation with Muslims around the world. This speech was frequently referred to as an "apology." It was not. The speech was asking that the west and Islam examine their relationship. That's a lot to ask.

"The relationship between Islam and the West includes centuries of co-existence and cooperation, but also conflict and religious wars," Obama noted. The speech was warmly accepted in the Middle East. "So long as our relationship is defined by our differences, we will empower those who sow hatred rather than peace, and who promote conflict rather than the cooperation that can help all of our people achieve justice and prosperity. This cycle of suspicion and discord must end."

If you think about it, the American space program depended on the algebra formulated by Muslim mathematicians—there is a relationship between our cultures. Or, as George Washington said in a speech defending a Jewish community in Rhode Island, "We are all sons of Abraham." Here's how the forty-fourth president of the United States put it: "I have come here to seek a new beginning between the United States and Muslims around the world; one based upon mutual interest and mutual respect; and one based upon the truth that America and Islam are not exclusive, and need not be in competition," Obama said. "Instead, they overlap, and share common principles—principles of justice and progress; tolerance and the dignity of all human beings."

I bring up Obama's speech here for two reasons. First, it is an instance of one set of people, or in this case the leader of one set, the United States, looking more closely at their relationship with another set. It is looking at the history of the relationships between those groups. The second reason I bring it up is because nations suddenly seemed more likely to do this kind of thing in the oughts, or even a few years before. Nations were attempting to look back at events that had happened, to understand them as a group of people. In England in 2010, the government apologised for "Bloody Sunday," a day when British soldiers killed more than a dozen Irish Catholic citizens in Northern Ireland. In 2013, the Irish state apologised to ten thousand women and girls incarcerated, and treated as slaves, in Catholic church–run laundries. In 1988, the United States apologised for interning American citizens of Japanese descent in prison camps during World War II. When Obama ran for a second term, his opponents described his speech in Cairo precisely as an apology, though it was not. Another government did, however, apologise, very explicitly, at about the same time.

In 2008, a crowd outside the Australian parliament wept

as they listened to the then prime minister, Kevin Rudd, apologise to the aboriginal people of Australia, people who had been taken off their lands, which other Australians then populated. He apologised in particular to a group called the "Stolen Generations," the tens of thousands of children who had been removed from their families and forced to assimilate with non-aboriginal people, up until the 1970s. "For the pain, suffering and hurt of these Stolen Generations, their descendants and for their families left behind, we say sorry," Rudd said. "To the mothers and the fathers, the brothers and the sisters, for the breaking up of families and communities, we say sorry. And for the indignity and degradation thus inflicted on a proud people and a proud culture, we say sorry."

87

Downturn

In Which We Look at a Time When
a Lot of People Lost Their Jobs Around the World
All at Once, and Think about Why That Happens
and What It Says about Us

What is a recession, anyway? It sounds clinical, like something you hope your cold is doing, and it is, in the sense that a recession has to do with not expanding. We tend to hear it discussed in the news, as something we are entering or coming out of, and it can apply to an industry and an illness, as well as a country. There was a recession in the long-playing record industry—people called them "LPs" for decades—when compact discs, or "CDs," became the popular way of playing music, in the early 1990s, and the CD industry began to recede as more and more music was purchased and listened to on digital files in handheld computers. A nation is considered to be in a recession when the gross domestic product of all its industries decreases for two three-month periods in a row. That is the technical—that is, boring—description of a recession.

Another way to think about a recession is in terms of

connections. When the LP industry went out of business, the owners of LP factories likely ended up making fewer LPs, and may have fired people working in their factories, who then would not be able to buy, say, ice cream for dessert every night at their local ice cream store. The ice cream store would then lay off people or even close, which would make for more people having more difficulty to initially pay for what you might call extras in their life, things like desserts. And soon they would have trouble paying not just for extras but for essentials, like bread. When this happens on a national scale, millions of people end up losing their jobs, often through no fault of their own—it is as if they are caught in a current or a tide, as an economist will tell you. We might hear people saying we are in a recession—a reporter on TV news, for example, or a presidential candidate who might blame another presidential candidate for causing one, or not doing enough to stop one, even though there is often very little that one leader can do—in some sense recessions are almost like a natural phenomenon, as markets adjust. On several occasions over the course of the twentieth century, there have been global recessions, meaning nations around the globe have seen their economies simultaneously shrink, causing people around the globe to lose their jobs and income.

The most famous example in recent history was a recession so deep it was called a "depression"—the Great Depression, which we discussed earlier in relationship to Hitler's rise to power in Germany. The Great Depression began in the United States in 1929 and went on into the early 1940s. The Great Depression also reached into Europe, where, still financially unsettled after World War I, economies staggered. As noted, Hitler was aided in his rise by the financial havoc caused by the global effects of the Great Depression.

When people have nothing, no food, no housing, they get desperate.

GLOBAL RECESSIONS OCCURRED on several occasions in the 1990s and again in 2001, but the global recession that began in 2008 is worth examining for what it reveals about the links between countries.

First of all, notice that when international bankers were talking about the future in the first decade of the twenty-first century, when they were thinking about where they were going to invest their money to get more money, they weren't looking hard at the so-called "developed nations," like France, Spain and the United States. Bankers were thinking that these countries would be places where their money will grow slowly. The countries they refer to as developing—Brazil, India, China and many places in Africa—were the countries the bankers were watching closely. But in 2008, the U.S. economy mattered a lot, as did the economy of the other developed nations.

So let's examine the global economy in 2008, when the things that people study when they are deciding how an economy is doing (for example, the stock market, the number of people employed) were looking pretty good, or seemed to be at least. No one can say exactly what is happening in a world economy at any given moment. Trying to would be like attempting to say something about all the fishes in all the world's seas. But we can say that the U.S. economy is a big fish, or the biggest—the total monetary value of everything produced, from jet planes to loaves of bread, in the United States is bigger than any other nation's total (though not as big as the European economy if you look at all the nations in the European Union). Therefore, what happens to the big fish matters.

But if we had to choose two things that in hindsight

turned out to be tiny ripples that eventually had giant wave-like effects, we might look first at the repeal of the Glass–Steagall Act, a banking regulation that was passed during the Great Depression, part of Franklin Delano Roosevelt's historic New Deal. What the act was designed to do was prevent banks that were supposed to take care of your money from taking your money and basically gambling with it through investments in risky places. Without a little separation between a savings bank and an investment firm, you might end up in a situation that was like asking a shark to watch your goldfish while you go to work, only in real life your goldfish is your life's savings.

Not all investment houses are sharks, but after the stock market crash of 1929, which led to the Great Depression, a lot of people felt the sharks had eaten their goldfish, and the Glass–Steagall Act was put in place to prevent that from happening again. In 1999, the act was repealed by the Republican majority in the House of Representatives with the support of a Democratic president, Bill Clinton. Investment banks and brokerage firms began to buy commercial banks. The sharks, it seemed, were minding the goldfish.

The other thing to notice about the global recession of 2008 was that a creeping problem in the American economy suddenly became the world's problem. After all, we all swim in the same financial sea these days, certainly more so than when we were all working out of caves, although let's not forget that while touring the North American continent in 1804, the Lewis and Clark expedition visited the Mandan nation and noted trading objects from China and other places on the Pacific Rim.

But getting back to the United States, we see that at the beginning of the twenty-first century, there was a mortgage crisis. The phrase "mortgage crisis" doesn't sound that bad until you realize that "mortgage" means "death pledge" in

Latin. A mortgage is what a bank gives homeowners when the bank helps them buy a house, and people can spend a good part of their life paying off a mortgage. The crisis happened because lenders offered mortgages to borrowers who normally would not qualify for a loan. These new mortgages were called "subprime," meaning "not the best." Large numbers of these subprime mortgages were bought and sold among institutions, a process that went along fine for a while. Then those loans were bundled up into larger deals and investments, investments made first by sharks but then by goldfish, by businesses and families and governments, by everyone who makes investments.

Everyone's investments were rolling along making lots of money, and no one realized that there was a problem at the bottom of it all. And then, all of this buying and selling of not-so-great mortgages was made worse by the prices of houses going sky high in 2007, so that everyone was looking to make even *more* money than usual. A lot more people than usual were feeling like sharks.

Eventually, given the economic downturn, people started to not be able to pay their mortgages. The deals and investments began to unravel. And so it went for the economy, first the American economy—especially when the financial institutions began taking away millions of people's homes. What happened next for the world was an intensified version of what happened in the United States. Banks around the globe looked into their holdings and realized that they had bought a lot of shoddy packages of investments over the previous ten years or so. It was like looking in your kitchen and seeing that it contained only snacks, no meals.

One by one, countries saw their economies suffer—people lost jobs, governments had to fire workers and offer fewer services. Banks and lending institutions became nervous about handing out money. Around the globe, money stopped changing hands. There were protests around the world. The government of Iceland, which found itself bankrupt, stepped down, as people lined the streets in protest. There was a general strike in Greece, and protests in China, where factories that made goods for people outside of China began laying people off.

Naturally, with things going so badly for so many people, there were a lot of fingers pointed—at the banks that seemed to have forgotten about safely holding people's money and had become more interested in gambling with it; at governments that had allowed this to happen; at people everywhere who seemed interested not just in making more money than usual on their bets but an amount of money that, in the clear view of hindsight, seemed greedy.

Around the world, fingers were pointed at many of the same people they were pointed at after the Great Depression, and it seemed to some people that governments were too quick to help the banks and the investment firms that had raced into the mess, and not quick enough to help the people whose homes had been taken away. More protests began. In the United States, a group called "Occupy Wall Street" protested near the New York Stock Exchange, a global money capital. They were saying that the cause of what was called the "Great Recession" was similar to what caused the Great Depression: a vast difference between the wealth of the small number of wealthiest people and the wealth of the vast majority of regular people. Occupy protests set up around the world. A slogan on a placard said, "Wall Street Talks— Too Much!"

If you were a president, or a government minister, or an elected official or anyone who is making policies (which doesn't sound like much but it is), taking care of an economy means keeping it in shape on a daily basis, preparing for whatever cold or flu may strike. It's important to watch the sharks and take care of the goldfish. And a goal for people in government and for business leaders who are paying attention to the long-term interests of citizens and consumers and investors is to keep their patients healthy, so that a cold doesn't kill them.

88

China Is Back

Not That It Ever Went Away

As far as any consideration of China goes with regards to the history of the world, it is not difficult to imagine that the book you are reading might be very different had it been written by someone born in China in 1882, someone other than, say, Hendrik van Loon. Rather than Shakespeare at the court of Queen Elizabeth in 1599, he might have focused on the court of the Qing dynasty and the dramatist Kong Shangren, who, around 1699, wrote "The Peach Blossom Fan," a play concerning the last days of the Ming dynasty. From the point of view of the Chinese, the age of European exploration—when Spanish, French, Portuguese and British explorers sought easy access to China—might be called the age when people often got lost and distracted while trying to find us. In 1405, a Chinese military commander sailed a military fleet, with sixty-two vessels with twenty-eight thousand men, to explore the world, making port in the Persian Gulf, in Africa and maybe in Australia.

To say that China burst onto the world stage in 2008 is foolish. And yet, China could seem somewhat reticent from the point of view of foreign relations for decades at a time. After dealing with European aggression around the turn of the nineteenth century, and after dealing with its own civil war, China could be said to have focused on itself for many years. Sometimes the Chinese were dangerously quiet. Chairman Mao led a brutal march to modernization, killing perhaps forty-five million people in the process, between 1958 and 1962.

Deng Xiaoping, who ruled China in the 1980s, pushed for economic reforms, allowing free markets and introducing business models from the rest of the world, and the Chinese economy began to grow at a rapid pace. Needing natural resources, China started to become a big investor in the African continent, at a time when people were talking about Africa's entering into an era of peace if not greater prosperity. (In 2012, the global coal industry used 10 percent of China's fresh water.) More recently, the Chinese government spent heavily on infrastructure, so that by the time the world economy was not feeling so great, in 2008 (see page 724), China just happened to be feeling outgoing. At the lowest moment of the global recession, China held large amounts of U.S. currency, and when the European economy was feeling the weaknesses of the euro, China was only just beginning to see its economy slow down.

AND SO THERE was China in 2008, hosting the Olympics. Ai Weiwei, a world-renowned Chinese artist, designed the glorious bird nest–like National Stadium, and when people watched the opening games on TV around the world, you could hear chins hitting floors in awe. It was spectacular, and even though, as we just noted, it was *not* a party for China's taking a big step onto the world stage—since it had been on the world stage from before the world stage was invented—it felt like one.

But there were many contradictions. In the Chinese government's push for economic growth, it had opened up markets but had not necessarily opened up other freedoms in society. A short time later, in the spring of 2011, the Chinese government arrested Ai Weiwei, the same artist who designed the stadium for the Olympics, and held him without trial for several months. He had been critical of the government. In one art piece, he decorated the side of a building with schoolchildren's backpacks, to remind people of a government scandal that allowed a shoddy school to be constructed in an earthquake zone, where, when the school collapsed, thousands of children died. (The actual number of dead is not known as the Chinese government has not released it.)

When Ai Weiwei was imprisoned, other nations and human rights groups complained. If you hear one particular nation take another nation to task for human rights violations, you can be sure that the nation doing the accusing will have some violations of its own that it would prefer not to mention. But an important distinction between China and the countries complaining about China is that China does not have a free press that would reveal violations, although at the beginning of the twenty-first century there were signs that maybe, possibly, the Chinese press was becoming a little bit more free.

Which brings us to a question that arose at the start of the second millennium. Is future economic growth more likely for a country with a political system in which the state has a high amount of centralized control over its society and the economy, like China, or Brazil, in South America? Is Russia likely to grow more given that the government limits individuals' rights and freedoms, such as freedom of the press?

89

Spring

Revolutions in the Middle East and
the Rights of People Everywhere

In December of 2010, a man was selling fruit in Tunisia, an ancient place settled by the Phoenicians, around 1100 B.C. The man selling fruit in Tunisia was, more precisely, in Tunis, the capital. He sold fruit on the street to support his family. He was a small business, the smallest kind: one man. One day, a government inspector took his fruit, argued with him, slapped him and, by the best accounts, in slapping him in public humiliated him. (The inspector was a woman, which complicated the situation.) The man protested to the government, but nothing came from his complaint. A few days later—with no business, with nothing to pay for food for his family—he set himself on fire, in horrible protest.

It does not need to be said that this was an extreme act. It was an act of desperation, not only personal desperation but also desperation as a citizen, a citizen who had no say in his government, which seemed to him not just badly run but corrupt, uncaring and humiliatingly so. By the time the fruit seller died a few days later, Tunisians all over the city had taken to the streets, to protest for his cause, but mostly to protest what they saw as corruption in all levels of their government, from the business inspectors to the highest leaders.

Incredibly, the protest kept building. The situation felt like a wildfire, a wildfire that keeps spreading, one that changes the landscape completely. Before they knew it, the corrupt and autocratic ruler of Tunisia had been kicked out, and Tunisians were preparing to put a new government in place. And the protest continued, even after it had transformed Tunisia. It raged out into the Arab world, and in a few weeks there were protests in Egypt, where again people took to the streets, clashing with police, protesting what they saw as a government that did not fairly represent them. Eventually, the dictator of Egypt was unseated, and slowly a representative government was put in place.

In Cairo, people shouted a chant: "the people want to bring down the regime." Various versions of the chant were shouted in Bahrain, in Tunisia, in Syria, in a season that was soon called the "Arab Spring," and commentators noted that young people fuelled the political fire by using their cell phones and computers to send out messages behind the rulers' backs. Crowds of people filled squares, singing, lighting candles, hearing speeches. There were also many women at the protests. This was significant owing to the fact that in the Middle East, women have had limited legal rights. Soon, protests in Libya caused the fall of Muammar Gaddafi, the dictator of Libya. After protests in Jordan and Lebanon, both countries had new governments, and in Saudi Arabia, after protests by women, the king suddenly granted women the right to vote.

Imagine the difference between one day in Tunisia and the next, between one year in the Middle East and the following one. Imagine that your neighbours are out in the street, chanting in a square, and then imagine that your government steps down. This seemed to be happening all over. It could be exciting, and it could be terrifying because, as it always does, when today turns to yesterday, it causes us to wonder about tomorrow. History makes for questions: What would happen in the Middle East after this wildfire was put out? What other governments would it consume, and by the way, where had it come from? It is one thing to imagine a revolution in France, or protests in the United States in 1765, but here were people shouting to take control of their governments across a huge swath of the globe, all together, one spring—and people around the world could watch it happen on TV or on a computer.

You could see some patterns to the protests, or so it seemed. The governments that were being overturned used corruption, military might and a strong police presence to stay in power, and suddenly that power was being overturned by a citizenry that was younger and more educated than previous generations. For decades, westerners had claimed that Arab citizens could not manage democracy, that elections were somehow beyond them—westerners speaking as westerners often do, with an inherent racism, as if they were able to handle things that other regions were not. But in 2011, democracy seemed to no longer be a question or a theory for the Middle East: the Arab people were quickly taking control of their governments.

Some revolutions failed, or they were long and never ending. And many of the elections that followed produced results—governments that gave power to Islamic parties— that concerned the western world. Islamic political power, with parties in Egypt and elsewhere, had not been as extensive since before Napoleon invaded Egypt. Again, more questions: What would happen? Which states would team up with which states? Would Israel, a Jewish state created in the region in a century when the Nazis attempted to destroy the Jewish people, see its security at greater risk, in light of radical Islamic fundamentalists' animosity toward Israel and in its complicated dealings with the Palestinians who are living in Israeli-controlled lands?

Would democracy mean that religious fundamentalists would win elections and then take control of governments, not allowing women to vote, for instance, or taking away further rights from women? Women's rights were described as "the unfinished business of the twenty-first century" in a speech by U.S. Secretary of State Hillary Clinton in 2012, and women with the right to free speech were asking if it was a coincidence that countries that threatened the security of the world were also places where women and girls had less dignity and opportunity?

"It is no coincidence," Clinton continued, "that so many of the countries where the rule of law and democracy are struggling to take root are the same places where women and girls cannot participate as full and equal citizens. Like in Egypt, where women stood on the front lines of the revolution but are now being denied their seats at the table and face a rising tide of sexual violence. It is no coincidence that so many of the countries making the leap from poverty to prosperity are places now grappling with how to empower women. I think it is one of the unanswered questions of the rest of this century to whether countries, like China and India, can sustain their growth and emerge as true global economic powers. Much of that depends on what happens to women and girls."

IT'S NO COINCIDENCE either that women's rights are easily connected to the land, to the earth or, to put it another way, to the daily collection of the resources that keep life going, the food and water that, for instance, feed children. Anyone who sat and studied the Arab Spring as it happened, or even looked at the protests around the world in that year, would have noticed that they were often related to issues connected to the land, to water, to food and to clean air. In Syria, droughts had cost herders their livestock and affected the food supply of more than a million people. And the Middle East region itself—where wells were already at risk of running dry—was not able to recharge its underground water supplies without rain: the giant underground ponds, called "aquifers," were dangerously low at the start of the twenty-first century. Saudi Arabia used oil-drilling technology to dig to a giant underground water source, and spent decades growing wheat for itself, but by the time the Arab Spring came, that water was drying up. Yemen was the country that scientists, at the beginning of the warmest century on record, predicted would be the first to completely run out of water. Meanwhile, the population of the region was increasing, with more and more young people looking for work, with more and more people needing clean water and food.

While industrial countries like the United States lost jobs and industries, the countries with growing economies—and fewer rights for citizens—were the places where protests against the misuse of the earth became more likely. In China, the number of people petitioning the government against industrial pollution grew wildly, as did protests. On several occasions at the beginning of the new millennium, Beijing had to shut itself down because of industrial air pollution—the smog was killing people.

This could seem scary, or it could seem hopeful. Wasn't it good that people were protesting to protect their land? Perhaps people's rights are becoming more and more tied to their land as the world goes on. Perhaps our safety is more and more tied to how well we treat each other rather than how savagely we fight a war. In 2001, Wangari Maathai died. She was a Kenyan woman who began a movement to reforest Kenya. She paid poor women a small amount of money to plant trees. The trees stopped the loss of soil that prevented farming. The trees could also be used as firewood for poor families. When she protested the Kenyan government's plan to build a skyscraper in Nairobi's central park, the police beat her unconscious. This did not stop her. A United Nations official called her "a force of nature." She was the first African woman to win the Nobel Peace Prize.

The calendar is a human invention, dates on paper or on a screen. It's just an account of days that have passed and days that are to come. But when you arrive at the end or the beginning of a century, you might feel as if you are standing in a doorway, a threshold, leaving one time and heading into another. What did we see behind us on the threshold? Wars in Europe, huge world wars, with over sixty million people killed in World War II alone, nearly 2 percent of the earth's population. We saw the planet ravaged, stripped of resources, some that will come back, some that will not. We saw people attempt to build organisations that would prevent world wars, organisations attempting to control nation-states that acted aggressively against other states, by which I am referring to Europe's work in relation to Germany, and even the United States' building of close economic and political ties with Japan, after World War II. We saw people try to reign in the tendency to destroy the planet. We saw young people stepping up. And we understood that, more and more, the battle for basic human rights was a battle that helped everyone, that lifted the human boat, the kept us high and dry on always rough seas.

90

Friends

ıllıllıllıllıllıllıllıllıllıllıllıllıllıllıllıllıllıllıllıllıllıllıllıllıllıllıllıllıllıllıllıllıllıllıll

The Ways in Which We Changed How We
Communicate with Each Other

Often, when we look back at the various technologies
that we have used to communicate with each other in the
past, we snicker. Cave paintings! How primitive! That's what
the Egyptians might have said when they were writing notes
to each other on papyrus. Changes in the way we communicate often alter the way we think about distances too. The
ocean was once a method of communication in itself—for
Phoenician rafts in 700 B.C., and even for transportation of
letters until the first cross-ocean cables were laid for commu-
nicating by telegraph, in the mid-1800s. When the telegraph
came along—with the dots and dashes of Morse code—and
later when telephone cables were laid on ocean floors, the
world seemed to get a little smaller.

The world changed again at the beginning of the twenty-
first century; it was a moment of sudden upheaval in terms of
how we communicated with each other. Who knows what
you, the reader, think of the communication changes that
were so forward-seeming in 2004, when a company called
Facebook began? But the kind of interaction that Facebook represents—people meeting while connected by com-

puter terminals, or phones with computer terminal–like capabilities—was once unheard of. Facebook began as a platform for social networking, for organising and collecting contacts, which the company termed "friends." Millions and then more than a billion people "connected" with each other by Facebook, though in a page or so we will pause to consider what exactly it means to be connected.

Facebook became a way for people to show each other via a computer what they were doing and thinking about—it was a way to share photographs. People joined "groups," organised by common interests. It became a kind of obsession, people everywhere signing up and linking to other people. People began using the word "friend" as a verb—I friended him on Facebook. Other different but similar social networks popped up around this time—Tumblr and Twitter—brand names that may or may not fade with time. Twitter was used as a way of writing short lines, what might be called "headlines," and, again, connecting to and following people who shared interests. Like Facebook, Twitter became a way for groups to communicate outside of traditional news media. For instance, around the world, groups protesting governments used Twitter accounts, or even Facebook pages, to communicate their goals. Protests in Egypt, Tunisia and Moldova, in and around 2010, were aided to some extent by Twitter. (They were aided less than originally reported, though Twitter was still a factor.) As a result, some governments tried to shut down Twitter accounts.

Sometimes people used social networks to confuse or harm others. In 2012, a Twitter account for a major news agency was taken over by an unauthorised user—it was hacked, in other words. After it reported false news about the U.S. government, the stock market suddenly plunged, since companies that were buying and selling stocks had programmed their computers to follow various Twitter accounts. Likewise, governments began to use Internet interactions as a kind of weaponry—one government's secret hacking team fighting another government's secret hacking team, circling each other, like nuclear submarines during the Cold War.

Much has been written and much said about the influence of all the rising forms of twenty-first-century social media, and while it certainly changed human relations, twenty-first-century social media still posed the same question that previous upheavals in communications had posed. One can argue, in other words, that Twitter and a handheld Internet device offer the same challenges to a human being in 2012 as a telegraph offered in antebellum America. Henry David Thoreau, the nineteenth-century American philosopher and poet, saw the challenge in the arrival of new inventions as a matter of personal composure. "We are eager to tunnel under the Atlantic and bring the Old World some weeks nearer to the New," he wrote in *Walden* in 1854, "but perchance the first news that will leak through into the broad, flapping American ear will be that the Princess Adelaide has the whooping cough."

His point? That everyone is in a race to be connected, to get the news, but there really isn't that much news. Thoreau, who was a big fan of technology, despite what you might have read or heard—he ran his father's pencil-making business, designing the best pencils in the United States at the time—called inventions like the telegraph "appliances." He enjoyed appliances. And of appliances he had but one test: Am I using the appliance to improve my own condition, rather than allowing the appliance to use me?

Apply the question to any invention, to whatever communication device or program or account you are using today, to whatever you are interacting with. Ask yourself questions along these lines: Am I really connecting? Am I linking or actually understanding? Is my life interactive, or am

I merely pushing buttons and clicking? How can I actually connect with ideas and people in my physical world? What is a true friend?

Like most good, clear thinking, Thoreau's test seems as if it were designed yesterday. The world, too, seems as fresh and new, despite all we've done to muck it up, as when he set up a wilderness exploration not in a faraway place, but in his very hometown. He might wonder why we are using GPS to figure out where we are when we might do better by looking up and looking around.

An Animated Chronology

500,000 B.C.–A.D. 2000

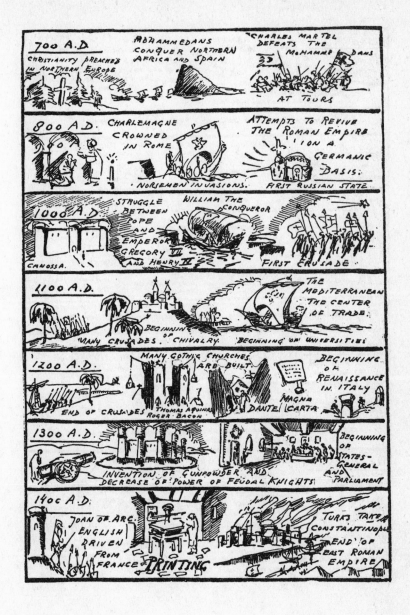

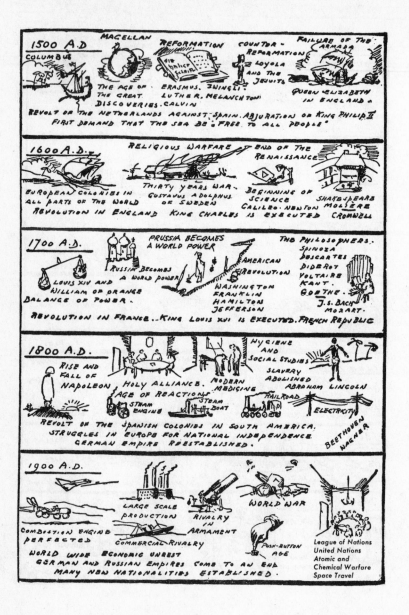

Index